D0498401

RUSSIA

in

1913

RUSSIA

in

1913

WAYNE DOWLER

NORTHERN

ILLINOIS

UNIVERSITY

PRESS

DeKalb

© 2010 by Northern Illinois University Press

Published by the Northern Illinois University Press, DeKalb, Illinois   60115

Manufactured in the United States using postconsumer-recycled, acid-free paper.

All Rights Reserved

Design by Julia Fauci

Illustration Credits—

Figures 1 through 5 are courtesy of the Slavic and Baltic Division, The New York

Public Library, Astor, Lenox and Tilden Foundations.

Figures 6 through 9 are courtesy of the Hoover Institution Archives.

Library of Congress Cataloging-in-Publication Data

Dowler, Wayne, 1945–

Russia in 1913 / Wayne Dowler.

    p.   cm.

Includes bibliographical references and index.

ISBN 978-0-87580-427-9 (clothbound : alk. paper)

1. Russia—History—1904–1914. 2. Russia—Politics and government—1904–1914.

3. Russia—Social conditions—1801–1914. 4. Civil society—Russia—History—

20th century. 5. Russia—Economic conditions—1861–1914. I. Title.

DK263.D69 2010

947.08'3—dc22

2010014126

Contents

Preface   *vii*

Introduction   *3*

1—Population and Economy   *18*

2—Estates and Classes   *51*

3—Social Integration and Civil Society   *90*

4—Expanding Civil Society   *141*

5—State and Society   *190*

6—Discourses   *233*

Conclusion   *272*

Glossary   *281*

Notes   *285*

Bibliography   *319*

Index   *337*

Preface

Most historians would agree that the principal concern of their discipline is the study of change over time. The question arises, change toward what? The obvious answer is change toward what happened next. The answer is obvious but misleading. Unlike the historian, history has no notion about where it is going and is indifferent to outcomes. History piles detail upon detail, circumstance upon circumstance, relationship upon relationship, complexity upon complexity. The main goal of this work is to record what history had piled up in the Russian empire by the end of 1913. By that time the Russian polity had reached levels of cultural, economic, political, and social maturity and sophistication that historians are just beginning to appreciate. The preoccupation, until recently, in the historiography with broadly Marxist concerns as well as generalizations about an indeterminate period labeled "late Imperial Russia" has concealed the degree of complexity that life in Russia had attained just before World War I.

Any time and place is full of possibility. A secondary objective of this book is to uncover the possibilities for development that existed in Russia in 1913 as well as the obstacles to their realization. A detailed study of a society in a single year not only reveals its complexity, but also the potential that complexity contained. The Russian empire was by no means stable in 1913; its future was uncertain in the minds of its leaders and citizens. The challenges posed by the need to modernize for survival and the balance between forces for continuity and change were, nevertheless, conducive to compromise and incremental development. The domestic and international environments of 1913 still favored the evolutionary processes that since the revolution of 1905 were slowly altering the cultural, economic, political, and social landscape. The coming of the war in July 1914 and the economic and psychological toll that it increasingly exacted on the population dramatically altered the environment and began to promote forces very different from those favored in 1913 and the first half of 1914. Socialist revolution was, of course, a possibility inherent in the Russia of 1913. It was not, however, very probable. Other, more likely, possibilities were also present. Only with the significant environmental change that the war inflicted on the empire did their fortunes fade.

This portrait of Russia in 1913 is built, in some measure, on work in primary, especially printed, sources. In addition to consulting writings, speeches, memoirs, literary works, and other materials from and about 1913, I decided to read two daily newspapers from beginning to end rather than to read selectively from a number of papers. Instead of searching out in the press what preoccupied me about 1913, I opted to open my mind to the changing preoccupations of Russians as the days slipped by. My goal was to immerse myself in the density and intensity of life in the empire and to experience, however vicariously, the rhythms and dislocations of the daily news as Russians experienced them. I chose *Russkie vedomosti* and *Moskovskie vedomosti*. Both newspapers were published in Moscow and so were partly shielded from the preoccupation with the concerns of the capital characteristic of the St. Petersburg press. The former was a progressive newspaper with loose ties to the liberal Constitutional Democratic Party (Kadets). It had a readership in the upper mid-range of major Russian dailies and drew on a broad network of correspondents in the capital and the provinces for its stories. It maintained high standards of reporting. The latter was a highly conservative, but thoughtful, newspaper with a more modest number of subscribers than *Russkie vedomosti*. It was edited in 1913 by Lev Tikhomirov, a former revolutionary populist turned ultraconservative. His was an eloquent and intelligent voice for the conservative cause, and his newspaper set an instructive counterpoint to the liberal *Russkie vedomosti*.

Above all, however, this is a work of synthesis. It draws on the writings by many scores of scholars from several countries about the last years of the Russian empire. Whatever originality this book can claim lies in its attempt to create a relatively comprehensive picture of life in the empire in 1913 by bringing together research across the divides of cultural, economic, political, and social history and by searching for the common threads among them. The literature is extensive and my indebtedness is large. While attempting not to overburden the text with references, I have tried to represent the arguments of scholars fairly and to acknowledge my debts as fully as possible. I have, however, at times used evidence adduced by some researchers to support conclusions rather different from their own. Inevitably, I will have missed important studies that would have cast further light on 1913. Regrettable as that may be, at some point the research must stop and the work must take its final form.

I am deeply grateful to the staffs of the Bakhmeteff Archive at Columbia University, the Hoover Institution library and archives at Stanford University, and the Slavic Division of the New York Public Library, who pointed me to a daunting quantity of valuable material. My special thanks go to my close colleagues Professors William Dick and Robert Johnson of the University of Toronto and Professors Ronald Suny of the universities of Michigan and Chicago and Rex Wade of George Mason University. All four commented in detail on an earlier draft of this book. Thanks to their suggestions the work in its present form is greatly improved. The suggestions of two anonymous readers also helped to shape the final version. Any remaining defects are of my own doing. I thank as well the editorial and production staff of Northern Illinois University Press for their professionalism and good cheer.

For nonspecialists in the Russian field, I have provided a glossary of Russian words and terms. Except for names well known to readers of English in established transliterations, I have used the Library of Congress transliteration system. All dates are given according to the Julian calendar, which in 1913 was thirteen days behind the Gregorian calendar used in the West.

RUSSIA

in

1913

Introduction

On a chilly night in late January 1913, Professor N.S. Kogan of St. Petersburg University spoke at the Polytechnical Museum in Moscow. His subject was "From Death to Life in Contemporary Literature." Learned public lectures were popular, and a large audience attended. Early in his talk, the professor referred to restrictions on freedom of speech and assembly in contemporary Russia. On cue, the police monitor, who was a fixture at most public events, intervened and ordered the speaker to stick to his pre-approved text. Kogan resumed his lecture. When he raised the name of Friedrich Nietzsche, the monitor again interrupted him. The professor explained that he spoke about Nietzsche only to oppose his views. Unconvinced, the policeman declared the lecture closed. A brief negotiation did not change his mind, and he ordered the audience to disperse. When spectators angrily demanded to know on what grounds, an anonymous voice replied, "On the grounds that we are living in Russia in 1913." Police reinforcements arrived and sent the listeners home.[1]

In May 1913 V.K. Smirnova founded the Society for the Development of Women's Artisan Work in Tambov. Under her presidency the society put on exhibitions of the work of local female artisans and opened cooperatives to purchase raw materials and shops to sell the finished products. The society also offered free courses in hand production techniques.[2] To the north, in Dvinsk, the district *zemstvo* decided to establish a telephone exchange. The thrifty zemstvo executives set up the exchange in a local elementary school, which the zemstvo also funded, and ordered the teacher to serve as the telephone operator for an extra 15 roubles a year. She objected that the frequent ringing distracted her pupils and interrupted the lessons. She asked the zemstvo officials to release her from her duties as operator and remove the exchange from the school. They refused. The teacher appealed to an influential relative who was a member of the district school board. At his prompting, the school superintendent intervened and the exchange went elsewhere. The zemstvo withheld the two-and-a-half months' pay owed to the teacher for her services as an operator.[3]

The peasants of the village of Beloomut in the Zaraisk district of Riazan' province were descendants of serfs freed in 1846, fifteen years before the general emancipation, by Nikolai Ogarev, poet and friend of Alexander Herzen. Ogarev was still revered in the village and honored with portraits in the school and many peasant cottages. To celebrate the centenary of his birth in 1813, the villagers established a special commission to recommend a suitable memorial to their benefactor. In December they announced the establishment of a fund to build a residence for the old and the disabled of the area in Ogarev's name.[4] Social conscience among the peasantry was matched by peasant entrepreneurship. The blacksmith in the peasant village of Ekaterinsk in Perm province, after years of repairing imported machinery, undertook to build a reaper designed for local conditions. The machine weighed 2.5 *poods*, was easily transportable by one man, and could cut three-quarters of a *dessiatina* in a day. It cost sixty roubles.[5]

In a village near Barnaul the peasant parents of an eleven-year-old son and seven-year-old daughter went out visiting, leaving their children in the cottage. Later, a knock came at the door and a voice demanded that they open up. When they refused the voice claimed to be their uncle. The children opened the door and were confronted by a dark figure, who announced that he was the devil. He promised to eat them unless they told him where the family cash was hidden. They pointed to the hole under the floor, into which the devil descended. The boy whispered to his sister that no devil would eat him and asked for the family gun. When the devil emerged the boy shot and killed him. The children ran for help. The neighbors searched for the village elder to investigate, but he was nowhere to be found. They summoned the hundredman (a village official), who ran to the cottage and found the body of the village elder slumped in the floor hole.[6]

On 8 January an organized fistfight took place between the residents of the town of Orekhov and the villagers of Preobrazhensk. Several hundred combatants and spectators gathered on the ice on the river between the two settlements. The ice broke and some two hundred people fell into the water. One drowned, many were hurt, and four later died of their injuries.[7]

In the Far East the stock exchange committee of Vladivostok petitioned the Ministry of Trade and Industry in spring 1913 to lift restrictions on the hiring of Chinese labor in the region, rescind a crippling passport tax on Chinese merchants, and reestablish a free trade zone with China. Many industries in the region were facing bankruptcy because of the restrictions, the committee complained, and the local Chinese community was starving and restless. The Moscow Society of Factory and Mill Owners strongly supported the petition. The Chinese, they argued, carried on trade worth 13 million roubles annually with Moscow businesses. The editors of the conservative *Moskovskie vedomosti* grumbled that for a mere 13 million roubles in the pockets of a handful of greedy Russian merchants, the government was expected to turn the Amur region over to Chinese merchants and deprive the whole Russian people of the bounty of the East.[8]

Late in the year in the southern port city of Odessa an old and respected Jewish doctor was giving a report to the Odessa Medical Society. Two students burst in. They were members of a student offshoot of the reactionary and anti-Semitic Union of the Russian People. One of the boys brandished a pistol and shouted, "It's time for this Jewish meeting to end" and "We'll shoot the lot of you." When challenged, one of the boys retorted, "I'm not afraid of being expelled—I'm a governor's son."[9]

At the Chebsara station near the northern city of Arkhangel'sk a mysterious notice appeared on 31 March. It announced that a man with two heads would be traveling on the train the next day. At each stop on the route, the notice promised, the man would get off the train and mingle with the crowd. Some three hundred people from villages as far away as ten *versts* came to greet the man. When he did not appear as promised, many of the spectators waited patiently for the next train.[10] Readers can decide whether the fools were the people who came to see the spectacle, the editors of *Moskovskie vedomosti*, or its subscribers.

Anecdotes like these provide a few glimpses into the rich and complex life of the tsar's subjects in 1913—public engagement and police repression, the roles of women, peasant initiative and ingenuity as well as crime and retribution in the village, economic ties and ethnic divisions, even humor. The dominant news story in the first half of the year was the celebration of the three hundredth anniversary of the establishment of the Romanov dynasty. It also reveals much about political and social relations in the empire immediately before World War I. The extended gala highlighted both the complexity of the Russian state and society and the tensions that complexity fostered. The festivities unfolded in two phases. The first took place in St.

Petersburg late in February. The ceremonies and receptions in the capital founded by Russia's first emperor, Peter the Great, on one hand, stressed the extent and diversity of the Russian Empire, sources of pride and identity for Russians by 1913. On the other hand, the centrality at each event of the emperor and his family and the almost constant presence at their side of the highest Russian and foreign hierarchs of the Orthodox Church symbolized the unity and sacred mission of the empire under crown and cross.

The celebration opened on 22 February with a twenty-one–gun salute at 8:00 a.m. at the Peter and Paul fortress in the capital. At 10:30 religious processions with icons aloft and choirs in full voice set out from the opposite directions of the Peter and Paul church and the Aleksander Nevskii monastery and other points to converge on the Kazan' Cathedral on the Nevskii Prospekt, the main avenue of the capital. Vladimir, the metropolitan of St. Petersburg, met the processions on the steps of the cathedral and led them into the building where the patriarch of Antioch awaited at the altar. At 11:00 the liturgy began in the presence of some four thousand guests, including royals from various principalities and the diplomatic corps. In addition to the metropolitan and the patriarch of Antioch, Orthodox hierarchs from Russia, Serbia, Galicia, and Tripoli officiated.

Beneath the soaring vaults of one of the greatest symbols of Russian Orthodoxy the vast and diverse array of representatives of the imperial state and society assembled. At the center were the ladies-in-waiting of the court and the court officials. Near them were the members of the Council of Ministers, headed by Prime Minister Vladimir Kokovtsov. Next to the ministers were the members of the two houses of the legislative branch of government, the State Council and the State Duma. Across from them were the members of the Senate, who, among other roles, headed the imperial judiciary. Behind them were the governors of Russia's provinces and governors-general of various cities and territories in the empire. Under the columns of the vast cathedral, stretching along its entire length, stood the *volost' starosty*. Symbolically backing them were the marshals of nobility, who since the time of Catherine the Great had played an important part in provincial and district administration. Mayors and leaders of the district zemstvos were also present. And "in the depths of the cathedral," as the reporter for *Moskovskie vedomosti* put it, "stood the representatives of Finland and the non-Russian (*inorodcheskoe*) population" of the empire. In the background as well stood the merchants and foreign entrepreneurs, just behind the noble ladies of St. Petersburg.[11]

At noon, after a damp and chilly ride in an open carriage from the Winter Palace, the emperor and empress along with the heir to the throne, Alexei, and his sisters entered the Kazan' Cathedral to ringing bells and shouts of greeting. A royal manifesto and the prayers of the patriarch of Antioch proclaimed the unity of the emperor's assembled subjects in devotion to his person and to his faith. The royal family left the cathedral to shouts of "Hurrah" from the thousands of troops on hand and the waving of flags by residents of the city. The sun shone brightly on their majesties' return to the palace. The day concluded with an evening display of fireworks.

Several days of lavish receptions followed the service at the cathedral. The royal couple received at the Winter Palace all of the groups in attendance at the religious ceremony, either at a massive event on 23 February or at less grand occasions. Dignitaries of the Orthodox Church were highly prominent at these worldly parties. Also occupying a place of honor at the main events were delegates of the leading nationalist-monarchist groups. The emperor made his preference for these ultraconservative or reactionary organizations clear. One observer noted that at the grand reception at the Winter Palace, "The representatives of the Russian Assembly, the Union of the Russian People, the Society of the Archangel Mikhail and the Moscow Monarchist League and its sections ranged along the whole length of the Central Hall alphabetically by province."[12]

The volost' peasant elders were excluded from the main reception but were treated to a lunch presided over by the prime minister, the minister of the interior, and the head of the Main Administration for Land Reorganization and Agriculture, which was overseeing a massive reform of peasant land tenure in European Russia. The emperor briefly appeared and toasted his peasant subjects. His words stressed the primacy of throne over nation: "I am glad to see all of you, the representatives of Great Mother Russia. Our Russia has grown and become strong through faith in God, the love of your Tsars for the people and the devotion of the Russian people to the Tsarist Throne. And so it will be forever! Health and prosperity to Our ardently loved Mother Russia, and to your health!"[13]

The major motif of the tercentenary celebrations was the embodiment in the person of the emperor of the needs and wishes of all of his subjects. But the special ties between the emperor and the peasants as the bulwark of the national idea were heavily emphasized. During the February phase of the celebration, an emotional command performance of Mikhail Glinka's *A*

Life for the Tsar solemnized the bond between tsar and people. Russia's first popular native opera sanctified Ivan Susanin, a peasant on the Romanov estate in Kostroma. According to the story, Susanin sacrificed his own life in 1613 to save young Mikhail Romanov, the founder of the dynasty, from Polish assassins. The myth of Susanin was widely promoted before, during, and after the tercentenary year as a model for the tsar's subjects.

The second phase of the celebration took the form of a pilgrimage in May into the heart of old Russia by the royal family. It began in Kostroma on the Volga River, where envoys of the *zemskii sobor* had in 1613 invited Mikhail Romanov to accept the throne of the Muscovite state. Once more the emphasis was on the unity of tsar and church, symbolized by the solemn ceremonies conducted at the Ipat'ev monastery where Mikhail had taken refuge from the armies of Poland. Leaving Kostroma, the pilgrims steamed up the Volga in the wake of Mikhail, stopping at the old Russian cities along the route for more prayers and gala receptions. The procession culminated in Moscow, where Mikhail had been crowned three hundred years earlier. The second phase of the tercentenary celebration underscored the deep historical roots of the modern empire in the old Russian heartland and the preeminent place of the Great Russians and their culture in the imperial polity. The journey also provided the emperor with a stage to dramatize the reciprocal devotion of tsar and people. Along the way he took part in several traditional bread and salt ceremonies of welcome by the peasants of the Volga region.

At first glance, the tercentenary celebration was a huge success, especially from the point of view of the dynasty. The pomp and circumstance and the celebrity of the royal family drew thousands to their public appearances, particularly during their progress up the Volga. Many Russians of all social estates were genuinely and deeply moved by the personal appeal of the emperor to their loyalty and by the patriotic and religious overtones of the celebration. The tercentenary, with its single-minded message about the monarch as the sole focus of political life in Russia, briefly encouraged, though in the end failed to unite, the political right. The impresarios at the court who staged the celebrations inundated the empire with images of the Romanovs and hammered home the emperor's simple message that he alone cared and spoke for all of his subjects. They astutely exploited the full range of available media to get the message out, even the fledgling Russian film industry. Major newspapers reported extensively on the events of the celebration as they unfolded.

A closer look, however, reveals that behind the scenes the Romanov tercentenary highlighted the stresses and strains within both the state and the society that rapid economic and social change was generating. A number of ministers of the crown, especially Prime Minister Kokovtsov, were shocked by the apparent contempt in which they were held by the man who had appointed them. Ministers trailed after the royal party during the celebrations at their own expense, in spite of having official roles to play at various events. The emperor left little doubt that he regarded the ministers and the government apparatus they represented as a barrier between him and the people and an impediment to the unlimited exercise of the royal will. In his memoirs Kokovtsov made it clear that by 1913 most ministers and leading bureaucrats and the elected members of the State Duma had already rejected the emperor's ideal of autocracy and were seeking control of the executive power.[14]

The members of the State Duma also felt the lash of contempt from the imperial court. At the central and most highly symbolic event of the tercentenary celebrations, the service in the Kazan' Cathedral, Duma members arrived to find that the master of ceremonies had seated them far away from the central place accorded members of the Senate and State Council. The president of the Duma, M.V. Rodzianko, complained and made his case. The senators were moved back and replaced by the Duma representatives. When Rodzianko discovered Grigorii Rasputin, the emperor and empress's scandalous confidant, seated in the Duma section, he ordered him out. On the next day Rodzianko had to fight once more, this time in order to be seated equally with the president of the State Council at the royal reception.[15] Order of precedence had social as well as political implications. The placement of the merchants toward the back of the Kazan' Cathedral in February was no accident. At the May celebration in Moscow the merchant estate lobbied, and finally succeeded in getting treatment by the planners equal to that given to the Moscow nobility. The slight signaled the court's disdain, if not for commerce and industry, then for those who engaged in it.

The tercentenary raised other concerns. Interested citizens noted that the many decorations conferred by the emperor to mark the occasion were most often awarded to known reactionaries, further underlining the prominent place the political right held at the royal receptions.[16] Observers noted the vitality of the Dowager Empress Maria Fedorova that contrasted painfully with the demeanor of the pale, unsmiling, and clearly bored Empress

Alexandra. At the grand reception she lounged in her chair, departed early, and on the following day did not attend the reception for ladies that she was meant to host.[17] Others remarked on the cold, formal ceremonial nature of the receptions. Guests could neither speak to the emperor nor even see him properly as they made their bows, so surrounded was he by courtiers and state and church dignitaries.[18]

The imperial procession along the Volga in May exposed more problems. The emperor's daughters made a strong and favorable impression on spectators, but the empress's chronic fatigue and absence from most events stirred comment. More serious was the sight of the faithful sailor guardian of the ailing heir to the throne, the Tsarevich Alexei, carrying the boy in his arms at several events. The spectacle stirred both the pity and concern of loyal subjects, especially those from outside the capital, who had not until then known the extent of the heir's infirmity.[19] The ceremonies in Moscow were marred not only by the initial slight of the merchants but by the exclusion from the principal reception of Moscow's representatives in the State Duma as well.

The large and enthusiastic crowds that turned out to greet the royal family, especially in the Volga region, convinced the emperor that his vision of a holy union of tsar and people was shared by ordinary Russians, especially the peasants. In Kostroma, a large welcoming crowd, many on their knees, fervently sang "God Save the Tsar." The emperor was delighted and concluded that the people were "to the right of the Duma."[20] The sight also impressed foreign observers, but the emperor's uncle could only sigh and remark that it could not be good for modern Russia that people were behaving as if they were living in the seventeenth century.[21] Not everyone believed that the peasants who took part in bread and salt ceremonies were acting out of spontaneous devotion. The peasant delegation of Shuisk volost' that greeted the emperor in Kostroma, for example, was led by the district land captain.[22] The land captains were officials who since 1889 were appointed, usually from the local landowning nobility, to supervise closely the conduct of peasant affairs.

The events in honor of the tercentenary pointed to the isolation of the imperial family from most of the citizens of Russia, the rift between the emperor and his ministers, the hostility of the ruler and court officials to representative government, and the illusions that the emperor dangerously harbored about the mood of the country. The celebration had served to expose the monarchy and its relations with state and public to critical scrutiny.

By 1913, the Russian empire was too economically and socially complex and culturally and politically sophisticated for Nicholas's simplistic vision to resonate either in state or public spheres.

Research into Russia in the years before World War I conducted during the past fifteen to twenty years has uncovered at least some of the complexity and sophistication that the country had attained by the time of the tercentenary celebrations. New areas of study, such as the growth of civil society or the travails of the non-Russian nationalities, have provided fresh insights into the dynamics of social and political life in the empire. Yet many of the new findings stand in an uneasy and largely unresolved tension with the main postulates that underlie the broad historical narrative about the Russian empire in the years immediately preceding the outbreak of war in 1914. Although sometimes far richer in detail than earlier accounts, general surveys of the period have perpetuated an analytical framework that was established, for the most part, in the 1960s.[23] Textbooks rarely reflect the new findings or, when they do, tend to marginalize their significance.[24] The same framework often informs the broad assumptions about the empire into which writers of monographs fit their particular subjects of study. The findings in many of those studies, however, have directly or indirectly challenged essential aspects of that framework and exposed its reductionism. No comprehensive and broadly based revisitation of the established general narrative in light of the large body of new research exists, however.

This work will draw on a wide range of secondary studies and primary source materials to test the established narrative and its main pillars in light of the evidence available for 1913 about the state of the empire. It will document the following case in successive chapters. At the heart of the story is the state of the Russian economy in the prewar years. The more recent findings of economic historians have been poorly integrated into the historiography. The fact that Russia trailed significantly behind its major Western neighbors by most leading economic indicators remains unchallenged. But the centrality of "backwardness" and responses to it that Alexander Gerschenkron and others posited has tended to obscure the rate and trajectory of structural change in the imperial economy during the last years of the empire. The role of the state in the development of the economy has been exaggerated and the contribution of the market understated. In spite of periods of setback, the overall rate of economic growth in Russia was unprecedented. It was, however, partially offset by the equally impressive rate of population increase.

By 1913 the economic infrastructure was highly advanced. Private banking predominated in the economy. Though far from adequate, petty credit was increasingly available, largely through the burgeoning cooperative movement. Russian companies were taking on modern corporate forms, and Russian corporate law was comparable to corporate law elsewhere in Europe. By 1913 overall Russian investment had far outstripped foreign investment, although the latter still prevailed in some modern sectors of the economy. The restructuring of the national debt by 1913 had shifted a majority of the liabilities from foreign to domestic holders. The land reform associated with the name of P.A. Stolypin, the prime minister of Russia who was assassinated in 1911, was extending the principle of private immovable property in the countryside. The market forces that were by 1913 driving the commercial and industrial economy were also becoming predominant in agriculture.

Although it has been challenged recently,[25] the idea of an irreparable gulf that separated state and society and of a competition between state and social actors to seize the public agenda is deeply embedded in the historiography. The October Manifesto that in 1905 promised a constitutional order in Russia and rights to its citizens and the Fundamental Laws of April 1906 that embodied the constitution and detailed the rights of Russians transformed the Russian polity and the nature of imperial politics. The transformation made the period from 1906 to 1917 unique. The interaction of state officials with the legislative branch that the constitution mandated and the greater (though not guaranteed) freedom of speech and of the press provided by the new order bared the many differences over policies and direction that existed among the ministries. In the process the myth of a monolithic state, which in any case had never existed, in confrontation with a uniformly hostile public was destroyed. That there was competition among groups to influence change in the country is undeniable. Competitive agendas within the government and within the public, however, made policy alliances across the state-public divide likely if not inevitable. The new publicity of the post-1905 period fueled public debate, and ministers actively enlisted and tried to shape public opinion to advance their goals through the press. The idea of a barrier between the state and the public has concealed the extent of cooperation between the two sectors, the amount of movement between state and private employment, and the level of participation of state employees in institutions of civil society in their capacity as private citizens.

Merely coping with the pace of change in the early twentieth century forced a measure of cooperation between the state and the public. Modernization proceeded unevenly, but its dislocations and disorientations were widely felt. Many welcomed change. Even opponents of change had to acknowledge it and accommodate to the new circumstances and opportunities that it offered. In many ways the dynamism that had been building since the emancipation reforms of the early 1860s, augmented by the external pressures of international competition and opinion abroad, set the agenda for state and social actors. Pressing needs that could not be ignored pushed the state and the public in similar directions and demanded collaboration, however reluctant. Tensions arose less over what to do than over how to do it and who ultimately should manage the process. Complexity required new techniques and institutional sophistication. The past had poorly prepared state administrators and the institutions they manipulated for the challenges of modernity. The complications of modern life also frustrated social activists, who were hampered by lack of practical experience and burdened by ideologies too simplistic for the tasks they faced. The absence of effective leadership at the center only made a difficult transition all the harder and deeply frustrated concerned people in both state and society.

Belief in the polarization of state and society has limited historians' understanding of the nature of Russian society before the war. In the tradition of the postrevolutionary intelligentsia, the focus in the historical literature has been on *obshchestvo*. Obshchestvo, which is translated as "society," was made up of educated people; it was broadly defined by its opposition to the bureaucratic state and its public-mindedness, particularly its desire to serve the *narod*. Obshchestvo included members of the professional and creative intelligentsia. After 1905 many people among educated society grew increasingly wary of the small revolutionary intelligentsia that continued to support violent solutions to the empire's problems. For all its sympathy for the masses, obshchestvo was said to be deeply alienated from them, especially from the working class.[26] This neat tripartite division of state, society, and people and the tensions said to divide them underpin the interpretation of the social dynamic of Russia in the prerevolutionary period in much—but no longer all—of the historiography.[27]

Matters in the empire were far more complex by 1913. Interaction between the state and social groups was increasingly common. Obshchestvo was only a part of a much larger educated and semi-educated public. In urban areas an array of intermediate groups filled the social spaces between the educated elites and the working classes. Rural society, too, was diversifying. Social dislocation not only dissolved the old but created new social formations and alliances as well. In particular, the prominence of obshchestvo in the historical discourse and the persistence into 1917 of the legal structure of social estates have obscured the rise of a relatively large functional middle class in urban Russia by 1913. Changes at the end of the nineteenth century in the right to engage in business opened wholesale commerce, the retail sector, and industry to all social estates and transformed the business class. A complex middle class drew for its membership from all social estates. Its members were defined by professional affiliation, relationship to the market, and salaried public or private service employment. They included great industrialists and bankers, professionals in private or public employment, and a host of white collar workers from managers to telephone operators and commercial employees. The values of the Russian middle class were increasingly aligned with the values of bourgeoisies in other European nations. Urban trained professionals and semiprofessionals who worked in rural settings were transmission lines for the transfer of middle-class values to the countryside.

A large body of excellent work on various aspects of civil society in Russia has come into existence in recent years.[28] The growth of the press, the spread of voluntary associations, the rise of leisure industries, professionalism, and other topics have received extensive treatment. These studies have raised awareness of the enormous diversity of social interests and activities in Russia before World War I. Prominent in the literature as well have been the many restrictions that the state placed on the functioning of civil society. Numerous anecdotes about the closing of lectures, the jailing of newspaper editors, or the revocation of the charters of whole societies have tended to obscure the extent and functioning of the institutions of civil society by 1913.[29] The number, diversity, and social significance of mutual aid societies and social clubs, for example, have been underestimated.

The growth of civil society in Russia speaks to the issue of social cohesiveness. Claims about the fragmentation of society caused by divisions both within social groups and among them constitute a powerful element of the historical narrative. By 1913, however, there is evidence that a discourse of social difference and antagonism was beginning to give way to the pluralist ideals of civil society and social cooperation. Some worker groups were reaching out to participate in the wider life of civil society, and employers' organizations were advancing broad social objectives ahead of narrow economic interests. The advances made by women in education, access to the professions, and legal status, though modest, pointed toward their greater incorporation into the public sphere in the future. In the countryside, several forces, both from outside and within peasant society, were preparing conditions for the further growth of civil society. External pressures included urban influences transported by peasant-workers and traders and by intelligentsia workers in the zemstvos, cooperatives, and institutions of petty credit. The Stolypin land reform, by mandating new forms of peasant land tenure, was promoting a new social diversification in rural areas that is one of the hallmarks of civil society. Internal forces included the deepening of market relations in the village, the internal negotiation among villagers of the Stolypin reforms, and the rising importance of law in peasant justice. In one area, however, the growth of civil society was already by 1913 producing conflict. The progress of civil society was a source of identity and social cohesion by 1913 not only for Russians but for non-Russians as well. The close historical link between the nation-state and the rise of civil society potentially posed a major challenge to the imperial project.

The most striking feature on the Russian cultural scene in 1913 was the rapid rise and wide dissemination of a market-driven mass culture comprising books, magazines and newspapers, film, music, theater, and leisure and recreational activities and industries. The growth of mass popular culture was accompanied in Russia, as elsewhere, by the market segmentation of cultural production. Popular culture posed a powerful challenge to a formerly dominant high culture. One matter on which the government and the guardians of high culture passionately agreed was their opposition to the spread of the new commercial popular culture at the expense of both high and folk culture. Public and private energy and money flowed into the production of elevating literature for the masses, the construction of People's Houses as alternative sites of entertainment to taverns and music halls, the mounting of the classics of drama through urban and rural theater companies that reached out to new audiences, and the promotion and preservation of folk song and dance.

Although their output was segmented to appeal to both lowbrow and middlebrow audiences, the producers of popular culture not only entertained but disseminated the values of individualism and self-reliance, along with consumerism, that were closely associated with the middle class elsewhere in Europe. The consumers of popular culture in Russia embraced a broad spectrum of urban working people from factory workers through shop assistants and their managers and employers to civil servants. More and more literate peasants, too, were drawn into the ambit of mass culture, which provided a framework of common cultural reference for all who consumed it. Some educated workers scorned the taste of fellow workers for popular pieces. But by 1913, even some elite artists were taking up the themes of popular culture or embracing it in its newest forms like film. Others retreated into the esoteric. Individual and team sports competition at the local level could reinforce class identities and rivalries. Inter-city, inter-regional, and international sporting events, however, fostered broad identities across social divides among spectators. Football (soccer) was by 1913 becoming a national obsession with teams and leagues at all levels of skill. Ice hockey was well established in urban centers in 1913 and even reached out to challenge foreign teams. Traditional peasant recreations were showing signs of giving way to the new sports and other leisure activities of city dwellers.

The successful functioning of civil society rests on the mutual recognition of and respect by citizens for difference. Civil society recognizes pluralism within a framework of rules. Although the institutions and relations of civil society were growing rapidly in the Russian Empire by 1913, the discourse of civil society was weakly developed. Only a few liberals spoke its language. There were a number of powerful discourses competing in Russia in 1913, but many of them had in common several dominant themes. These themes ran counter to what was actually happening on the ground in the imperial economy and society. Running across the political spectrum was a strong strain of anticapitalism. Closely allied to it was distrust of the bourgeoisie and refusal to acknowledge its extent in Russia. Behind these two themes lay a deeply embedded notion of Russian exceptionalism. In this view, the capitalist, bourgeois, rights-based, pluralist, liberal parliamentary order of Western Europe was alien to Russia or at best a temporary stop on the path to a different and superior future. Instead, the Russian ideal was the integral, not the pluralistic, society. The integralist ideal was fundamentally hostile to the workings of civil society. Its supporters interpreted the development and relations of civil society not as signs of social health constitutive of civil and political liberty but as proof of social disintegration and national and moral decline; in its place they demanded renovation along integralist lines. Their discourse of social dislocation and disintegration and Russian essentialism has left a powerful legacy in the historiography.

The year 1913 provides a convenient vantage point from which to assess the condition and potential of Russian cultural, economic, political, and social life immediately prior to World War I. It was the last full year of relative peace before the catastrophe of war and revolution. The goal of this work is not to demonstrate that Russia was on the eve of a liberal-democratic transformation in 1913. It was not. The abruptness of the unraveling of the Soviet Union in 1991, which almost no one anticipated, suggests, however, that the seeds of dramatic change can accumulate, perhaps not unnoticed but certainly not understood by contemporaries, and mature and blossom suddenly and unexpectedly. Many of the processes at work in 1913 had been in train for a century or more. The emancipation reforms of the 1860s put yet other forces into play, as did the economic reforms of the 1880s and 1890s. Nevertheless, the period from 1906 to 1914 had distinctive features that set it apart from what is often called "late Imperial Russia."[30] For a monograph tracing change in a particular institution or set of relationships over a specified time, the designation "late Imperial Russia" can be meaningful. But the rapid pace of economic, social, and even political change after 1881 or 1890 renders generalizations about the economy, society, or politics in late imperial Russia largely meaningless. What was so in 1895 may no longer have held in 1913. The years from 1906 to 1914 have greater coherence than those from 1890 to 1917. In many ways, 1913 was the culmination of that brief period before war imposed new constraints and a new dynamic on the empire. A major objective of this work is to document as concretely as possible the state of the empire and the forces at work that were changing it from within in that year. A detailed study of Russia in 1913 will allow readers themselves to judge whether the evidence that has accumulated in recent years supports the old plot of the prewar narrative or whether some substantial re-plotting is in order.

The work is structured with a view to examining social groups and their relations under a number of different lenses: their place in the economy; relations within social groups; relations among social groups; relations within the state and between state and society; and competing political and social discourses.

POPULATION AND ECONOMY *I*

Early in June 1913 representatives of Russian banks gathered to assess the financial position of the empire relative to the major countries of Western Europe. The threat of war in the Balkans had driven down stock prices in the financial centers of the West and credit had tightened. In Russia, the bankers noted, the solid fundamentals of the economy had so far shielded the price of stocks. They anticipated a further credit squeeze and higher interest rates in the West. They were confident, however, that Russia had more than enough domestic credit available to support the needs of both industry and agriculture and stave off an economic and financial crisis in spite of the necessity of raising interest rates in the empire over the coming months.[1]

The meeting highlighted several aspects of the Russian economy. The bankers were well aware of the extent of the integration of the Russian economy with the world economy. Both the price of Russian commodities in world markets and the cost of goods in the domestic market moved in broad conformity to prices abroad. Their cautious optimism that Russia was in a position to weather a financial storm pointed to the striking successes of the economic recovery that had begun in 1909 and to the vitality of the economy by 1913. Their confidence that Russian financial institutions could meet the demand for credit from agriculture and industry spoke to the strides that the country had made in building the economic infrastructure and developing the private business and financial sectors. In particular, the availability of domestic credit marked a sharp reduction in the dependency of the empire on foreign capital for development.

The most striking feature of the Russian economy since at least 1890 was the speed with which it was changing. The peak rates of growth of the main economic indicators in Russia matched or exceeded the historical peak growth rates of nearly all other countries at similar stages of economic development. National averaging concealed sharp regional variations. Some areas achieved spectacular rates of change while others lagged behind. The greatest changes were in the commercial and industrial sectors of the economy, which together by 1913 generated nearly 40 percent of the national wealth.[2] Agriculture was still experiencing the dislocations of the Stolypin land reform that began in 1906. Nevertheless, greater investments in the agricultural sector, the rural infrastructure, and agronomic education, along with the changes in land tenure that the reform brought, were beginning to transform the rural economy as well.

Rapid growth in the economy was matched by an increase in population. In per capita terms, therefore, the imperial economy had on average achieved by 1913 only modest gains over the 1860s. National averages, however, often conceal the dynamics of differential change within the economy. The population was not only larger in 1913 than in 1860 but different in its composition and characteristics. The government had recognized the links between modern economic development and education well before 1913. A widely supported push toward universal primary education was well under way by 1913. The need for expertise drove the expansion of tertiary education, especially of professional and semiprofessional training. The challenges that demography posed to the economic advance of the empire were much on the mind of the public in 1913.

THE POPULATION

The main driver of economic change in the empire was population growth. Demographic change largely accounted both for the striking successes of the Russian economy in the last decades of the empire and for its chronic weaknesses. The exact size of the population in 1913 was unknown. The 1897 census, the first in the empire, had been marred by a variety of errors and provided an uncertain basis on which to estimate the size and composition of the population in 1913. The problem of calculating the growth rates of the population since 1897 and the complexities that resulted from extensive internal migration since the beginning of the century added to the difficulties.[3] Rumors circulated in the press early in September 1913 that the government was preparing to undertake a fresh census of the population. That was welcome news. Editors, however, questioned not only the ability of officials to frame the questions effectively but also their integrity in interpreting the data objectively.[4]

The Central Statistical Bureau estimated the population of the Russian empire, excluding Finland, to have reached 175,137,800 by the end of 1913. The estimated increase in the total population since 1897 was roughly 30 percent.[5] A trend toward later marriage that began around the end of the nineteenth century meant that by 1913 the growth in the birth rate was slowing.[6] The population of the provinces of European Russia on 1 January 1914 was believed to be 128,864,300. The 1897 census probably underestimated the number of non-Russians in the empire but still revealed that Great Russians were in a minority. Counting Poles, Belorussians, and Ukrainians along with Great Russians, Slavs constituted 73 percent of the peoples of the empire. Nationalist movements in Poland and Ukraine, however, dampened any comfort Russians might have taken from that figure. On the contrary, ethnic politics in the empire stoked a more strident Russian nationalism that increased tensions as World War I neared. In the east, southeast, and far east a variety of Turkic, Finnic, and Mongol peoples added to the ethnic and linguistic diversity of the empire, as did several non-Russian groups of the north. In all, more than one hundred languages and dialects coexisted in the Russian empire. In 1913 the presses rolled out books in forty-eight of them, in addition to Russian.[7]

In 1913 the Russian empire had three times the population of Germany, the second largest European nation, and twice the population of the United States. Only the latter matched the empire's pace of urban population growth. The population of imperial cities more than doubled between 1897 and 1917, from 12,490,000 to 25,840,000. It was in fact even larger than official figures indicate. Many areas of urban density and especially areas with factory and mill concentrations lacked official urban status. Irkutsk and Azov, for example, had nearly thirty thousand inhabitants each and Sergeev Posad another twenty-five thousand in 1913. There were around one hundred such urban agglomerations without official urban status in that year.[8] In 1913 there were 35 cities in the empire with populations greater than one hundred thousand. The largest were St. Petersburg, which in 1914 had 2,200,000 inhabitants, and Moscow with 1,700,000 residents. Poland was the most urbanized part of the empire, with 24 percent of its population living in cities, and Siberia the least urbanized at 11.9 percent. European Russia stood at 14.4 percent.[9] In many major cities of the empire Russians made up less than half the population. Of the empire's nineteen largest cities, only nine had Russian majorities.[10] It is noteworthy that in 1910 the roughly 23 million urban dwellers of European Russia far outnumbered the 17 million Frenchmen and 9 million Italians who at the same time were experiencing urbanization and all that it entailed.

Urban growth in the empire was largely the product of in-migration as peasants came to cities in search of work. Migrants significantly outnumbered those who were born in cities, although the gap was narrowing by 1913. The challenge of accommodating such numbers was considerable. Among migrants, males significantly outnumbered females. As a result Moscow in 1912 had only 839 females for every 1,000 males. At the same time, Berlin had ratios of 1,083 females per 1,000 males and New York 1,015 females per 1,000 males. In elite residential areas of Russian cities, however, women outnumbered men as a result of a sharp gender imbalance among servants.[11] By 1913 the gender gap in Russian cities was narrowing as more single women migrated from the villages to cities and more males brought wives to live permanently in town. The influx of migrants into many Russian cities, about two-thirds of whom were peasants in search of temporary employment, resulted in a highly unstable urban population. The median length of residency of migrants in Moscow was about seven years.[12] Although some other cities had lower rates of turnover, many urban residents had little commitment to life in the city.

Death rates in Russia not only pointed to the country's relative backwardness, but also suggested that Russia was following a path already traveled by Western nations. The infant mortality rate in the Russian empire remained high compared to that in most European countries. In 1850 infant mortality in Russia had been roughly the same as in Germany, Italy, and Austria-Hungary. Since then Russia had failed to keep pace with gains by its neighbors. From 1907 to 1911 the average infant mortality ratio to age one in European Russia was 245 deaths per 1,000 births, compared to 174 per 1,000 in Germany and 128 per 1,000 in France in the same period. The high rate of death among newborns was believed to result from the peasant traditional practices of giving infants cloths wrapped around partly chewed food as soothers and the early introduction of solid foods into babies' diets. Health professionals targeted these practices. By 1913 the infant mortality rate was falling at a pace comparable to earlier declines achieved in Western Europe. The improvement was perhaps due to medical workers' efforts but more likely was the result of a better diet that improved the health of mothers and the resistance of their infants. Russians in 1913 on average enjoyed an adequate diet, measured in calories and protein, by international standards.[13] Health authorities made some small progress in the battle against infectious diseases, but the death rate from epidemics remained far higher in Russia than in Western Europe. The overall death rate was also high by Western standards.[14] On average death and birth rates were lower in the cities than in the countryside, largely because of the excess of young males in urban populations. As was the case with the birth rate, the death rate in the years before World War I was declining at a pace similar to declines earlier achieved by West Europeans.[15]

Trade, commerce, and crafts contributed as much to the growth of cities in the empire as large-scale industry. The extent of Russian capitalism before World War I cannot be measured adequately by the number of big industries in the country and the size of their workforces. Middle- and small-scale production in nonfactory environments for a growing consumer market were equally important in the development of capitalist attitudes and practices among Russians. The number of artisans in St. Petersburg was roughly the same as the number of factory and mill workers, but in Moscow the former surpassed the latter by half again. In Moscow, workers in commercial enterprises also significantly exceeded industrial workers. In Riga and St. Petersburg, as many residents earned a living in commerce as made their way in industry. In Kiev, nearly 40 percent of the population was inscribed in the *meshchanstvo*.[16] In St. Petersburg in 1912, some twenty thousand retail shops were in operation, and the value of small trade outstripped the value of industrial production.[17] White collar workers also made up a significant and growing segment of the urban population. There were more of them in Kiev and Warsaw, for example, than there were industrial workers. A government survey of heads of households in 57 cities in European Russia conducted in 1913 revealed that petty property owners made up the largest portion of urban populations.[18]

EDUCATION

Firm data on literacy among the empire's population in 1913 are scarce. The census of 1897 counted 29.3 percent of males and 13.1 percent of females as literate. The average figure concealed significant regional differences. In a number of central provinces, such as Kaluga, Orlov, Pskov, and

Voronezh, where Russians made up the vast majority, less than 20 percent of the populace was literate. The three Baltic provinces had the highest rates of literacy, which ranged from 70 to 80 percent. St. Petersburg and Moscow provinces reached 55 percent and 40 percent respectively.[19] Age made a significant difference. While forty-to-fifty-year-olds in 1897 had a literacy rate of 22.9 percent, twenty-to-thirty-year-olds reached a rate of 31.9 percent.[20] The growth of the elementary school network since 1897 had significantly advanced literacy among youth by 1913. In autumn 1914, 46.4 percent of urban and 28.3 percent of rural children between the ages of eight and eleven years attended school.[21] The army had been schooling its recruits since the 1870s. In 1912, of 1,260,159 men in the bottom ranks of the army, nearly half were deemed by the army to be literate, another quarter minimally literate, and the remainder illiterate.[22] Progress toward literacy was slow even in urban areas. The urban survey mentioned above revealed that about one-quarter of urban tax payers were illiterate and two-thirds had only an elementary education.[23]

Schooling the population was a high priority by 1913. Legislators had set the goal of achieving universal primary education throughout the empire by 1922. The literacy drive had begun in earnest in the 1880s and by 1913 was transforming the cultural, economic, and social landscapes. The Russian Empire was endowed with a wide variety of educational institutions that operated under various and sometimes competing jurisdictions. Late in 1914 there were nearly 124,000 elementary schools in the empire.[24] The level of teaching was basic at best. In the countryside several different types of schools provided as few as two and as many as five years of elementary schooling. Religion, church singing, Russian language, the four functions of arithmetic, and penmanship comprised the basic curriculum. Pupils who went through four or five years of schooling took history, geography, basic science, and drawing as well. Where they were available the upper levels of elementary schooling were still thinly attended. A long-standing tendency of peasants to remove their children from school after two years of study was still prevalent but declining by 1913, as the practical uses of literacy and numeracy became more apparent to them.

In cities by 1913, most elementary students received six years of schooling. They studied reading and writing, religion, singing, Russian language, arithmetic, and geometry as well as drawing, drafting, Russian history, geography, science, and Church Slavonic. In 1912 the government added another educational layer by transforming some existing urban schools into higher elementary schools with four years of study. Subjects included algebra, geometry, physics, drafting, singing, drawing, and gymnastics. The school system hindered progression from level to level. Only a small proportion of elementary school pupils moved on to secondary schools. On 1 January 1914, of the 8,902,621 elementary and secondary students in the empire, 82 percent were in elementary schools of various types, while only about 9 percent attended general or specialist secondary schools of all types.[25]

Qualified teachers were in short supply. In 1913 the minimum annual salary for a teacher was set at 360 roubles, apparently not enough to attract the numbers needed to take up a difficult calling. In that year around 14,500 students were preparing to be teachers in teachers' institutes or seminaries.[26] The shortage of teachers put the target of universal primary education by 1922 in doubt. A contemporary estimated that to achieve the goal about thirty thousand new teachers had to be certified every year merely to maintain a class size of fifty pupils. Current rates of graduation fell far below that number.[27] In July 1913 a new measure provided teachers with salary supplements at the end of five, ten, fifteen, and twenty years of service. Lack of funds, however, made a long phase-in period of these benefits necessary.[28]

Advanced education was also beginning to blossom. In 1914 only about 136,000 of the emperor's subjects had tertiary degrees. But in that same year around 125,000 individuals were studying in institutions of higher education.[29] Table 1.1 details attendance at all institutions of higher education in the empire in 1913–1914. The social base of the educated sector significantly broadened in these years as well. Whereas in 1900 more than one-half of students in universities and one-third in technical institutes came from noble, bureaucratic, or officer families, in 1914 these higher-ranking students made up only about one-third of the student population at universities and one-quarter of the students at technical institutes.In that year, one-half of university students and nearly three-quarters of students in technical schools came from middle- and lower-class backgrounds.[30]

Spending on education at all levels rose significantly from 1900 to 1913. For example, the budget of the Ministry of Education increased by 475 percent during that time, to 14.6 percent of the total imperial budget.[31] No other ministry received even remotely comparable increases. Other ministries were also active in education. The Ministry of Trade and Industry ran a variety of schools and courses linked to economic development. In 1913

Table 1.1—Attendance in All Institutions of Higher Education
in the Academic Year 1913–1914

Institution	State	Civil and Private
Universities*	35,695	
Higher Women's Courses**		23,534
Coeducational Universities		7,659
Law	1,036	
Oriental Studies	270	
Medicine	2,592	
Women's Medical Institutes		1,254
Pedagogy	894	1,237
Military Academies***	1,796	
Religion	1,185	
Industrial Engineering	23,329	642
Agriculture	3,307	2,274
Veterinary Sciences	1,729	
Fine Arts	260	7,189
Commerce		8,364
Total	72,093	52,153

Source: Adapted from A.P. Korelin, ed. *Rossiia 1913 god. Statistiko-dokumental'nyi spravochnik* (St. Petersburg, 1995), 297 and 346–47.
*State universities were restricted to males.
**The Higher Courses for Women provided university equivalent education for women.
***Including students in the Military-Medical Academy.

more than thirty thousand men and five thousand women studied in public commercial schools sponsored by the ministry. Another 14,500 men and women attended the ministry's trade schools. The ministry also operated schools for industrial arts, technology, artisan production, and mining. The Main Administration for Land Reorganization and Agriculture on 1 January 1913 had almost fifteen thousand students studying in more than three hundred primary and secondary institutions under its auspices.[32]

Zemstvos were also increasing spending on public education. By 1913, 40 of the 50 provinces of European Russia had signed agreements on joint educational development with the Ministry of Education. In that year they spent more than 90 million roubles of their own revenues on elementary education. Cities also were allying with the Ministry of Education to advance the goal of universal primary education through coordinated spending on schooling.[33] The outlay of the city of Moscow on education increased nearly four times between 1905 and 1913, and its student population more than doubled.[34] Higher literacy nurtured a reading public for the new merchants of popular literature. The advances in literacy were reflected in the holdings, circulation, and number of users of public libraries, all of which rose rapidly in cities. The number of users and total circulation in St. Petersburg public libraries, for example, nearly doubled between 1903 and 1912.[35]

THE RUSSIAN ECONOMY IN HISTORICAL PERSPECTIVE

Deep structural changes in the economy of the Russian Empire stoked the urgency officials and the public felt about improving education in the years before World War I. Historians have written extensively about the nature of the Russian economy in the decades before the war began. The questions are many. What role did the state play in industrial development? Was the economy market-driven? Did agriculture pay a heavy price to support rapid industrialization and high military expenditures? Had Russia created the legal structures and financial institutions necessary for Western-style capitalist development? The most recent answers to these questions have been poorly integrated into the narrative of Russian history in the years immediately preceding World War I. Rapid economic advances from 1907 to 1914 make broad generalizations about the Russian economy in the "late imperial" period inappropriate. The years before the war bore distinctive features that clearly distinguished them from the earlier years of the empire's economic transformation.

Technically, at least, the state budget in 1913 was in surplus and had been for several years. Total budget expenditures and revenues had almost doubled since 1900. Direct taxes accounted for only 8 percent of revenues. Indirect taxes and duties and income from state properties and investments made up more than two-thirds of the remainder. Controversial in Russia in 1913 was the 26 percent of state revenues derived from a state monopoly on spirits and wine distribution and sales.[36] Many complained that, whatever its original intentions in establishing the alcohol monopoly, the state was promoting drunkenness in exchange for revenue. Although many in 1913 also grumbled about the militarization of the state budget, the budget increase for education since 1900 was in percentage terms almost three times greater than the increase of the much larger budget of the Ministry of War and nearly one and a half times larger than the increase in the navy budget. The share of state expenditures allocated to the Ministries of War and the Navy together totaled 26.7 percent in 1913, up only slightly from 26.1 percent in 1900 in spite of a military rebuilding program following the devastating losses of the Russo-Japanese War.[37] Russia was the world's largest debtor in 1913, and servicing the debt was costly.[38] In the years before World War I, however, the state began not only to pay down the debt but also to reduce its foreign component and shift it to domestic sources, largely through state-guaranteed securities. By 1 January 1914, Russians held considerably more than half of the state debt.[39] The larger municipalities also borrowed heavily abroad to advance public works projects.

The Russian Empire ranked among the world's largest economic powers in 1913. By most indicators it was fourth or fifth in the world in absolute terms and sixth or seventh in per capita terms.[40] Its national output doubled Austria-Hungary's, exceeded that of France, roughly equaled Great Britain's, and was about 80 percent of Germany's. The salient feature of the Russian economy from around 1875 was that it performed as well as or better than those of most countries in the West at similar stages of economic development. Paul Gregory has pointed out that the growth rates of the tsarist economy in the last 30 years of the empire both in output and productivity were "comparable or superior to those of the West." Structural changes in the Russian economy in those years were also similar to the changes that took place in other countries during their early years of modern economic growth. In Gregory's view, economic growth in Russia made inevitable additional deep social structural changes that would have lowered obstacles to further economic growth and sustained or even accelerated rates of growth in the economy in the 50 years after 1913.[41]

The population explosion that Russia experienced in the second half of the nineteenth century largely accounted for the empire's rapid growth rate in total economic output. From 1861 the empire's average rate of growth in national output was greater than that of all of its major rivals except the United States.[42] The rate was particularly impressive in the 1890s.[43] The disruptions of the revolution of 1905 significantly lowered the average for the first 14 years of the twentieth century, but the average conceals the rapid recovery that the economy staged beginning in 1909–1910. The increase in the population also contributed significantly to the high rate of growth in total national income. Only Sweden and Germany achieved income growth greater than Russia's in this period.

So great was the increase of the imperial population, however, that the gap in per capita output and income between Russia and most other European states had narrowed only slightly since the 1860s. Annual per capita output by 1913 was still less than 40 percent of the output of France and Germany and around half that of Austria-Hungary. The increase in the rate of growth of per capita output achieved in Russia in the 40 years before World War I was, however, respectable by European standards.[44] Although in 1913 per capita income in Russia was still lower than in all major countries except Japan, the five years before World War I witnessed an accelerating increase in the rate of its growth. Per capita income also varied widely from one part of the empire to the next.[45] Uneven though its development was in the last 40 years of the empire, overall the Russian economy kept pace with or out-performed Western economies at similar stages of development and passed through comparable structural changes.

The balance of trade of the Russian Empire was favorable, with surpluses of exports over imports in every year from 1901 to 1913. The empire was eighth in the world in volume of external trade in 1913, with a modest 4.2 percent share of world exports and 3.5 percent of imports.[46] In per capita terms, Russian trade lagged behind that in much smaller economies such as those of Turkey, Persia, Bulgaria, and Greece. In 1913 about 30 percent of Russian exports went to Germany, 18 percent to Great Britain, 12 percent to Holland, and 6.5 percent to France. Despite state efforts to diversify trade, especially by looking for markets in China, Russian exports to its four lead-ing trading partners had increased by more than 2 percent by 1913 over the turn of the century.[47]

Goods from Germany accounted for slightly less than half of Russian imports in 1913. Great Britain trailed far behind at around 12.5 percent of imports. China at 6 percent of the total was the empire's third largest source of imports. The German share in Russian imports had grown substantially since 1900, when it was 35 percent. The percentage of Russian trade with nearly every nation other than Germany was down or stable in 1913 com-pared to 1900.[48] Russian exports were heavily weighted to grain, meat, dairy, animal products (especially leather), iron ore, petroleum, lamp and lubricating oil, and forest products. Imports included coal (especially in 1913 in response to a fuel shortage), a wide range of minerals including nickel and zinc, fertilizer, raw cotton, industrial machines and machine parts, agricultural machinery, and chemical products.[49]

Russia was the dominant agricultural producer in Europe. At the beginning of the empire's push toward economic modernization, the share of agriculture in the economy was relatively high and that of industry low compared to those in other modernizing states. In 1913 roughly 85 percent of the population of European Russia still lived in rural areas, and about three-quarters earned a living in agriculture, animal husbandry, or forestry.[50] Agriculture still accounted for approximately 54 percent of the national income, but the gap with commerce and industry was narrowing quickly.[51] In the years from 1885 to 1913 the amount of change that occurred in the relative shares of agriculture and industry in the economy was comparable to that of other nations in the early stages of industrialization. Again to quote Gregory, "Russian agriculture was progressing at normal or even above normal rates (as judged by the experience of western Europe) in its last thirty years."[52] By these several measures in both the industrial and agricultural spheres, Russian economic backwardness was a function of the country's late start toward modernization and not of the quality or quantity of its modernizing performance.

A widely held view in the early twentieth century was that Russian agriculture was in crisis and that a dual economy, comprising a dynamic industrial sector and a backward peasant agricultural sector, was coming into existence. The strong overall performance of the empire's economy measured in real growth of per capita output and income casts doubt on this belief. With nearly three-quarters of all employment in agriculture in 1913, a decline in per capita income of any significant proportion of the empire's predominantly rural population would have severely depressed the country's total average per capita income. Beginning in the 1880s both factory production and agricultural production grew faster than the population. Improved outputs in large estate cultivation cannot account for the overall rise of agricultural production. Just before the outbreak of World War I about 90 percent of all sown land was in peasant tenure.[53] In addition, many estate owners by 1913 leased land to peasants. Before the revolution of 1905, peasants were both producing more grain per capita and also effectively resisting coercive tax policies by allowing tax arrears to accumulate.

Voluntary sales of grain by peasants grew substantially. In addition, between 1885 and 1901 the value of grain retained by peasants for consumption exceeded population growth in the villages by three times. Overall, urban and rural consumption rates showed no striking differences.[54]

The revolutionary disturbances of 1905–1907 interrupted but did not end the pre-1905 growth pattern. The substantial growth in per capita output in agriculture quickly resumed. It is true that the weather in the years from 1909 to 1913 was particularly favorable in large parts of the country and crop yields were high. But the long-term trends indicate that, while future setbacks due to climate were inevitable, the near steady improvement in rural per capita income was by no means weather-dependent. Other factors were at work. The redemption payments that compensated landlords for land alienated to the peasants, which had been imposed on peasants as part of the emancipation land settlement in the 1860s, were halved during the revolution of 1905 and abolished at the beginning of 1907. In 1912 changes in direct taxation resulted in a further reduction of the peasants' tax burden. Between 1901 and 1912 the share of their gross income from agriculture that peasants paid in taxes and rents fell by nearly one-half, to less than 10 percent. Peasant savings were on the rise. On 1 January 1913 fully one-quarter of the 1,639,000,000 roubles in savings banks belonged to peasant depositors.[55] All relevant indicators suggest no decline in the average rural standard of living before World War I; instead they point to a significant improvement in the overall quality of peasant life.

There were exceptions. Every year one or another part of the vast territory of the empire suffered unfavorable weather, diminished food resources, and hunger and disease. 1913 was no exception. In that year Astrakhan province in the southeast was particularly stressed. Such chronic regional crises kept the problems of agriculture in the forefront of contemporaries' concerns. Many attributed peasant hardship in the Central Industrial and Central Black Earth regions to land shortages due to rapid population growth since the emancipation. This perception appears to have arisen from peasant petitions, especially during the upheaval of 1905. One study has shown, however, that in Vladimir province, at least, peasants, who during the revolution petitioned the authorities for more land, significantly overstated the number of peasants who had a claim on allotment (communally owned) land in their villages. They also made no mention of land privately owned by peasants either as individuals or groups.[56] These distortions in the petitions created a perception of peasant land impoverishment in central regions that has left a mark on the historiography. Closer examination through more precise measurements of actual peasant holdings in the various regions of the empire is needed in order to test this perception.

There were other reasons for the relative impoverishment of central regions. Opportunities for exports or the creation of new markets through innovation were fewer there than in some other regions. Moreover, in spite of the decreases in taxes affecting all peasants, peasants in the central agricultural provinces paid on average 1.6 times more in taxes than did the peasants in the provinces of northwest Russia. The reason was that the heavy concentration of troops in the northwestern and western provinces brought with it subsidies, which reduced the tax burden on the local inhabitants in those areas. In the central provinces, where these subsidies were not available, the peasants' lot was comparatively worse.[57] Although other traditional grain-growing areas also fared worse than the average, in much of agricultural Russia living standards rose at a pace comparable to that in urban areas. No dual economy of poor agricultural and wealthy industrial sectors existed, and peasant living standards were not sacrificed on the altar of industrialization.[58]

The great majority of peasants in the Russian Empire had traditionally lived in villages rather than on individual homesteads. The peasant commune, made up of heads of households who farmed communal allotments, administered the land that the village held in use. The main economic function of the *obshchina* was to allocate arable land to families, usually according to their labor capacity to work it. As family sizes changed over time, the commune periodically redistributed the lands. Cultivation of the land was carried out individually by families and not collectively by communal members. Herding of animals, however, was often a collective responsibility. The members of the commune also used common meadows, water resources, and sometimes woodlands.

The commune allocated arable land in small, nonadjacent strips that took into account the quality and crop capability of the land as well as distance from the village and other relevant factors. Periodic land reallocation was motivated more by considerations of collective survival than by sentiments of economic equality among members. Most peasants farmed their strips by the three-field system, a crop rotation that left one of the three fields fallow each year. Fallow land was most often used for grazing from spring to early or even mid-summer. In most cases the three fields were in fact separated into multiple plots widely scattered and usually far distant from one another. The distance from plot to plot forced peasants to invest hours of valuable labor time in travel. Ditches or narrow strips of wasteland, which served as access paths, separated the plots. Both encouraged the growth of weeds and restricted the turning of teams at plowing time. The small size of the plots also limited machine use. Adjacent villages often held overlapping land with the plots of members from different villages interspersed.

In addition to their communal (or allotment) lands, villagers bought lands either jointly or as individuals, usually from local noble landlords through the Peasant Land Bank, or leased land from them on a long-term basis. Between 1862 and 1905 noble land holdings were reduced from 42,660,000 dessiatinas to 25,663,000 dessiatinas. Private peasant holdings at the same time grew from 3,276,000 dessiatinas to 13,375,000. Village societies or peasant partnerships made the majority of purchases in those years.[59] Peasant individuals who purchased lands sometimes separated fully or in part from the commune. Withdrawals from the commune and the establishment of individually owned farms were widespread in the northwestern and western provinces before 1905.

By 1913 the commune was no longer the dominant institution it had once been in peasant life. The emancipation of the 1860s brought with it the reform of village administration. The village society, with its assembly, took over the fiscal and social responsibilities formerly assigned to the commune. The village assembly assumed the authority to take decisions arising from collective ownership of the land and to accept or reject new members. It also elected a number of officials: the village elder, the scribe, and the hundredmen. The village society also had representation in the volost' assembly that had a number of functions, including peasant justice. Village societies were often not the same unit as the communes they replaced. Communes had frequently incorporated more than one village, or peasants from different communes lived in the same village.[60] In other cases the old obshchina and new village assembly were tightly linked or even identical. Whereas landless peasants and nonpeasant village residents were excluded from the commune, they belonged to the village assembly. Senate rulings in 1884 and 1889, however, permitted village assemblies to exclude from their membership villagers who did not conduct agriculture or have an allotment or household plot.[61] Village societies were also charged with the welfare of all who had a claim to membership regardless of whether they had village land in use.

The number of communes practicing full repartition declined sharply after the emancipation reform. Since 1861, communal populations had on average more than doubled by 1913. Household sizes shrank from 8.4 members in the 1850s to 6.1 in 1900 as children left parental homes.[62] A consequence of these changes was a growing reluctance by the members of the commune to subdivide the land further. In 1910 more than 58 percent of all communes in European Russia had long ceased to repartition allotment land.[63] In regions with predominantly Great Russian populations the figure was higher. In half of the Great Russian provinces fully two-thirds of communes had stopped repartitions.[64] A majority of peasant families, therefore, effectively had household tenure of the allotment land they worked. Partial repartitions continued when, for example, a family emigrated or died out. These, however, were minor adjustments that could not serve either the principle of equity or the dictates of survival that marked the old repartitional commune.

The collective responsibilities originally assigned to the village assembly had mostly withered away by 1913. The redemption payments were abolished, collective responsibility for taxes and dues had ended, and universal military conscription had replaced the responsibility of village societies to provide peasant recruits. Following the revolution of 1905 the restrictions that the assembly could impose on the mobility of members were also abolished. The village assembly did continue to perform important welfare and other social duties. Also, a significant minority of assemblies continued to carry out periodic land repartitions. Between 1906 and 1911 assemblies also held the right to prevent individuals from separating their holdings from the commune.

The growth of individual farming at the expense of the commune, especially in the northwest and west, the widespread decline of the practice of repartition, and the diminished usefulness of the village assembly as an instrument of collective fiscal responsibility persuaded many agricultural experts and government officials that in conformity to a growing culture of individualism, communal tenure in the empire was destined to disappear. Some also agreed that the process ought to be accelerated. They maintained that the land use practices of the peasant commune and the conservative attitudes to innovation that they were believed to sustain posed an obstacle to agricultural modernization. Well before the revolution of 1905, the government had evolved plans to break the hold of the commune on land distribution and use. In 1906 the new prime minister, Petr Stolypin, began to implement them. On 9 November 1906 Stolypin issued a regulation that later was ratified by the State Duma and State Council into law. The decree enabled individual peasants, with the consent of the assembly, to take the strips of communal land that were presently in their use into ownership by the household head. They could also negotiate with communal members to consolidate their strips into a single block of land. Such individual peasant consolidations could take the form of a *khutor*, a homestead separate from the village, or an *otrub*, in which the owner of the consolidated block continued to live in the village rather than on his new property.

As the process unfolded, the government supplemented the 1906 regulation with others that it hoped would hasten the transition to individual farming. A law of 14 June 1910 provided that any commune that had not undergone land redistribution since 1887 was dissolved and its members given hereditary tenure of their plots. In many such instances, however, the villagers affected by this law continued to act as they had before it was passed. In May 1911 a law on land reorganization conferred property rights on any male household head who consolidated his plots and withdrew from the commune without prior petition for a change of tenure. It also enabled peasants to merge privately owned and former allotment land into a single unit.[65]

Initially, reformers hoped to achieve reorganization by means of individual separations, which over time would eradicate communal land tenure. Officials and agricultural experts were well aware, however, of the problems raised by multiple plots, interspersion of the holdings of different villages, and distance from one plot to another. They recognized the role that group land reorganization could play in improving peasant agriculture, whatever the form of tenure, by reducing or eliminating such obstacles to more efficient farming. Group land reorganization engaged whole communes in the rationalization of peasant holdings; the settlement could end in either individual or communal ownership. The law of 1911 greatly facilitated group land reorganization and enabled partial consolidations with the retention of some features of communal village life. From that year the focus of the land reform tacitly shifted from title change to group land reorganization.

The overall response to the reform was enormous. Under all of the provisions of the laws of 1906, 1910, and 1911, nearly 6,200,000 or two-thirds of peasant households in European Russia had made requests for some form of land reorganization. Village assemblies refused or forced applicants to withdraw about one million of those requests. They most often refused peasant separators who wanted to set up khutors or otrubs but had far fewer objections to group land reorganization. For all that, in European Russia 3,373,000 or 36.5 percent of households had requested to leave the commune by 1916. The volume of requests overwhelmed the land reorganization commissions that formed to oversee and register land conversions. By the end of 1915, 2,376,000 reorganized households had received full documentation, but in reality many more consolidations and departures had occurred that remained officially undocumented.[66] Roughly two hundred thousand registered khutors existed in Russia by 1914, although about half of them were in the western provinces and predated the reform. Households had registered another 1,300,000 otrubs. As well 1,700,000 peasant households in communes had, officially at least, foregone the right to repartition the land under the law of 1910. In all about a third of communal allotment lands in 1906 were converted to private tenure by 1915. Moreover, 20,200,000 dessiatinas of land had been reorganized by 1915, of which 59.4 percent passed into individual tenure and 40.6 percent into group tenure. In addition, peasants had purchased 260,000 consolidated plots of land from land made available through the Peasant Land Bank.[67]

It is seldom remarked that the land reform included changes to a different practice of land tenure in the western provinces of Bessarabia, Grodno, Kovno, Minsk, Vil'na, and Vitebsk, and in the Ukrainian provinces of Chernigov, Kiev, Podol'ia, Poltava, and Volynia. In those provinces much land was not communal but was instead held in household tenure (*podvornoe vladenie*). Before the reforms the whole family, in theory including all of the heirs no matter how distant they were from the actual operation of the land, had had to agree to any change in ownership, even by inheritance. Such a complex process had produced family conflict and at times prevented the most efficient use of the land. The land reform enabled peasants, on proof that they worked the land directly, to take personal ownership and assume full rights to sell, divide, and bequeath the property without the consent of distant heirs. There were 2,749,000 heads of households that attained individual ownership of 20,626,000 dessiatinas of land under this provision of the land reform.[68]

The Stolypin land reform accelerated the transfer of land into the hands of peasants. The post-emancipation pattern of land purchases intensified after 1905. The principal sellers were large estate owners, many of them nobles. By 1915 properties larger than 50 dessiatinas accounted for only 10.9 percent of the sown area of the Russian Empire.[69] The main buyers were peasants. Many of the sales and purchases passed through the Peasant Land Bank, which in addition to land it purchased from private individuals also sold lands belonging to the state. Moreover, large amounts of land passed from peasant to peasant in these years. The peasant buyers included whole villages that bought land together and put meadows, ponds, and woodlands into common use. Some arable land purchased by villages became communal but just as often it became the private property of individuals. Other peasant buyers formed partnerships or companies to buy land parcels. When purchased, this land went into individual ownership and seldom was held communally by the partners. A third category of buyers among the peasantry was individual peasants.[70]

The changing pattern of purchases reflected the growth of peasant individualism. When the Peasant Land Bank began to operate in the 1880s, only 1.3 percent of sales were to individual peasants and the rest were to collective buyers; in 1913, 87.5 percent of sales were to peasant individuals.[71] The role of private banks in financing peasant land purchases grew significantly as well, as the Peasant Land Bank scaled back its own land purchases from 1908 onward.[72] If before 1905 peasants wanted to seize land, in the postrevolutionary period they were prepared to buy it and by 1913 were doing so, overwhelmingly as purchases for individual ownership or use.

The land reform also stimulated the growth of the cooperative movement in the empire. The movement had begun in the last quarter of the nineteenth century. It had two main sources. In part it arose as a result of the increase in numbers of small-scale producers who discovered in cooperation an instrument to enter the market economy and compete more effectively with large-scale producers, and in part from politically or socially motivated members of the intelligentsia who looked to cooperation, if not as the road to socialism, then at least as an alternative to individual capitalist production and consumption.[73] By 1913 the majority of cooperatives took the form of credit and savings and loan societies. Credit societies made loans available to small landowners, artisans, and cottage industrial producers as well as to their organizations such as artels and peasant partnerships. Loans of up to three hundred roubles could be made without collateral and up to one thousand roubles with it. By 1913 institutions of petty credit had 6,610,000 participants, involving 31.6 percent of all peasant households, up from 17.4 percent in 1910. Local cooperatives were also increasingly combining into regional unions.[74]

Consumer and producer marketing cooperatives were forming as well. Consumer cooperatives engaged in a broad range of activities such as bulk purchases on behalf of members. The most successful producer marketing cooperatives were the dairy and butter cooperatives of western Siberia, which by 1913 even owned their own ships for export abroad. A flax marketing cooperative shipped 15 million tons of linen abroad in 1912–1913. Tar and tobacco producers also formed marketing cooperatives.[75] The consumer and marketing cooperative movement was older and more entrenched in the Baltic provinces, Vil'na, the north, and Siberia, but by 1913 more than three-quarters of all consumer cooperatives in the empire were located in European Russia.[76] Though large in numbers, members of cooperatives were short on administrative experience, but for all their failings the cooperatives were having an economic impact. They were particularly active in facilitating the purchase and use of agricultural machinery. The value of machinery in Russian agriculture, which in 1908 was 61,300,000 roubles, had reached 109,100,000 roubles by 1913.[77] A majority of machine purchases were made through the cooperatives.

A major element of the land reorganization program was resettlement. Resettlement had started well before the reform but became better organized and supported when the reform got under way. Between 1897 and 1914, more than four million people resettled in Siberia or the recently acquired central Asian territories. Resettlement was arduous. Many returned to their old places of residence after a brief try at relocation. In 1913, for example, while 234,877 peasants moved to Siberia, 42,956 settlers left it for their former villages in European Russia.[78] Programs that enabled potential settlers to send advanced scouts to report on conditions and likely locales for resettlement did not prevent the disappointment of many on arrival, nor did it check the return flow.

Cottage (*kustar'*) industry continued to play a significant role in the rural economy in 1913. From the 1880s mechanization of factory manufacture and the rising costs of cottage production led to a decline of cottage industry but by no means to its demise. Writing in *Russkie vedomosti* in March 1913, A. Rybnikov estimated that in 40 provinces of European Russia around 1.5 million cottage producers supported fully or in part some 6–7 million dependents.[79] The line between factory and cottage production was porous. Cottage producers frequently used materials produced in factories or supplied factories with semifinished goods.[80] State and zemstvo agricultural assistance work included support for cottage and rural artisan production. Central and local authorities jointly encouraged the creation of marketing artels and cooperatives for cottage producers and facilitated access to credit for small-scale production.

By 1913 Russian agriculture was experiencing dramatic changes. On average, economic conditions in the countryside were improving at a pace comparable to improvements in urban life. The individualism that had traditionally characterized peasant land use under communal tenure was finding new expression in the form of personal, hereditary landownership. The small to middle-size producer was increasingly dominating production in the countryside, not only for family consumption but for the market as well. Market opportunities for peasants were still limited but growing in a number of regions. Institutions of petty credit, though still in formation, were by 1913 sufficiently capitalized to support further significant change in agriculture. New forms of land tenure and the growth of the market, while disruptive, enabled peasants to seize new opportunities on their own terms.

Russian industry in 1913, like agriculture, was in the middle of a period of rapid growth and structural transformation. In that year, Russia stood fifth in the world in industrial output at 5.3 percent, up from 3.4 percent since 1881–1885, when Russian industrialization took off.[81] Large-scale industrial output in 1913 was eleven times greater in Russia than it had been in 1860.[82] In 1913 roughly 21 percent of the empire's net income derived from industry. Large-scale industry accounted for 15 percent of the total and for 4 percent of all employment. Such impressive growth since the 1860s had enabled Russia to close the gap in industrial output with France and Austria-Hungary, but the empire still lagged well behind the other leading states. Only in the production of textiles was Russia competitive with other European industrial powers.

Though diminishing, Russia's dependency on the West for technology remained significant. The high price of iron in Russia compared to its cost in much of Western Europe drove up domestic construction and machine-building costs.[83] Consequently, about half of the machinery used in Russia was imported. There were other signs of lingering backwardness in Russian industry. As late as 1913, product specialization in Russian factories was weakly developed. A factory that made agricultural machinery might bid on a contract to make street cars. Such practices were an obstacle to standardization of machine tools, agricultural equipment, and rolling stock.[84] The need for greater efficiency was recognized, however. Russian engineers and technical personnel strongly advocated the introduction of scientific management along the lines of Taylorism into Russian factories. By 1913 experiments with Taylorist techniques in large enterprises were common. Owners often hired university students to carry out time-motion and other studies.

Per capita industrial output was low in Russia, 10 percent of French output and 7 percent of that in Great Britain and the United States. The disparity was in large part due to rapid population growth in the empire. Per capita labor productivity also lagged. Russian workers' productivity was 50–60 percent of British workers' and only 20–25 percent of American workers'.[85] By 1913 the mechanization of large-scale Russian industry was well advanced. Even the long-established textile manufacturers of the central industrial region, especially in Moscow province, were importing modern machinery. Such improvements in technology during the boom years enhanced factory productivity.[86] Nevertheless, the continued use of unskilled workers to perform auxiliary tasks at both ends of the manufacturing process in most Russian industries held down productivity per worker. For all that, from 1908 to 1913 industrial productivity per enterprise increased dramatically. Worker productivity also rose substantially, though more modestly, as new, untrained workers learned their jobs. The most impressive improvement was in the oil industry, where productivity per enterprise rose by 85 percent and per worker by 65 percent. The metallurgy and cement industries also saw substantial increases in productivity in those years.[87]

Of growing concern to critics of Russian industrial practices was the role that syndicates played in industry by 1913. The largest were in coal and metals and to a lesser extent in oil. Russian companies could not compete with foreign rivals in most export markets. A lack of markets abroad encouraged the growth of syndicates at home. Member companies doled out contracts among themselves and sought to restrict competition in the domestic market. A high degree of vertical integration also characterized heavy industry in Russia prior to World War I. Metallurgical factories, for example, often owned or leased coal and iron mines. In 1913 twelve metallurgical companies controlled 80 percent of Ukrainian iron ore supplies. They also established close ties with manufacturers that used metals in their finished products.[88] Rising demand for fuel and metal shortages triggered a highly contentious energy crisis in 1913. The press accused the syndicates of producing below capacity in order to keep prices high and of price fixing. The syndicates denied the charges and blamed rapidly rising demand and government land-use restrictions on mineral exploration for the shortages. The government responded late in 1913 by permitting, to the dismay of the syndicates, the importation of cheaper coal and oil from abroad.

Rising domestic demand from 1910 through 1913 strongly stimulated consumer industry, and competition in the consumer sector forced efficiencies on producers. Profits in consumer industry were generally higher than in heavy industry. As a result per capita investment in consumer industry doubled in 1909–1913 over 1894–1898.[89] Investment in heavy industry rose more slowly in the same period, and agriculture's share of investment declined, especially in livestock. Investment in agricultural machinery, however, rose significantly. Investment in Russia also remained attractive to foreigners in 1913. The heady days of 9 percent returns in the 1890s were gone, but a solid 7 percent for ordinary investors and higher returns for privileged insiders still attracted outside finances.[90] In 1913 about 40 percent of all investment in industry was foreign. Domestic savings, therefore, were making a majority contribution to industrial investment.[91] In the years before World War I foreign investment increasingly took the form of portfolio investment rather than entrepreneurship and direct participation. By that year much foreign investment went into Russian banks, which then reinvested in the Russian economy as well as abroad. At the end of 1913, 44 percent of the capital in Russian banks was owned by foreigners.[92]

An increase in the proportion of Russian companies that invested in national industries accompanied the shift away from direct and toward portfolio investment from abroad. Between 1911 and the beginning of 1914 the capital of Russian joint stock companies rose from 2,175,132,300 roubles to 3,376,780,300 roubles. In the same period the capital of foreign-owned joint stock companies in the empire increased from 410,348,250 roubles to 587,346,600 roubles.[93] The growth of Russian participation in some sectors was especially rapid. From 1911 to 1914 the number of Russian chemical companies grew by around 20 percent, but their capitalization skyrocketed from 10 million to nearly 150 million roubles.[94] The capitalization of Russian companies in processing minerals other than iron more than doubled between 1911 and 1914.[95]

Russians were just beginning to invest heavily in the more modern sectors of the economy. The nascent electro-industrial and electro-transportation sectors were particularly attractive to foreign investors. In 1913 Belgian groups operated 20 of Russia's 41 tram services. In May 1913 German and Swiss banks underwrote a company to build a peat-fired electrical station 70 miles from Moscow. It began to produce power in 1915. A few months earlier a French company bought out the Society for Electricity in Russia.[96] Although the Russian share in those critical modern sectors was only around 14 percent in 1914, it was increasing rapidly. Between 1909 and 1914 the share of Russian companies in the electro-technical industry nearly doubled. Russian investment in electro-transportation industries grew by 176 percent between 1910 and 1914, compared to an increase of 63 percent in foreign investment in the sector.[97]

Some contemporaries feared that heavy investment from abroad and the large foreign debt could compromise the autonomy of the Russian state, the economy, and its financial institutions. There is little evidence to support their case. By 1913 the Russian government had learned not only to value foreign investment but also to manage it. Foreigners tried unsuccessfully to change Russian tariff policies and also failed to block an unpopular progressive tax on corporate profits.[98] Their heavy investment in Russian banking also gave foreigners little leverage in shaping economic or political outcomes. Like banks elsewhere in the world by 1913, Russian banks were enmeshed in an international monetary and financial complex with its own imperatives. This state of things precluded both control by any single group of investors and significant manipulation by the state.[99] The independence of Russia was further assured by the fact that the total capitalization of Russian companies greatly exceeded that of foreign-owned enterprises.

The capacity of Russian banks to provide credit for a growing economy grew quickly in the prewar years. Between 1900 and 1912 private Russian banks witnessed an increase in their capital of nearly 200 percent. In the same period the capital of the State Bank grew by a comparatively modest 42 percent. At the beginning of 1914 there were 50 private banks in Russia with 778 branches. More than one thousand cooperative credit societies and some three hundred urban society banks operated by municipal bodies were also functioning at that time.[100] By 1913 most towns had at least one savings bank, but in rural areas only a quarter of settlements of over one thousand inhabitants had a bank.[101] However, cooperative institutions of petty credit were beginning to take up the slack in the countryside. Their numbers doubled from 1911 to 1913, as did their membership.[102] Since they paid higher interest on deposits than savings banks, their holdings increased at the expense of the banks. Demand for credit expanded rapidly in rural areas. Wherever the Stolypin land reforms had a major impact, institutions of petty credit made strong inroads.

Russian banking was highly concentrated. In 1913 twelve St. Petersburg and seven Moscow banks along with the Moscow Merchants' Society controlled fully 90 percent of Russian financing. Six commercial banks accounted for 55 percent of all bank liabilities.[103] Russian banking and industry were highly integrated as well. The largest banks held extensive direct interests in industries rather than simply providing credit for their operations. The power of the private banks in the economy as a whole, however, should not be overstated. Capital for many Russian industries and businesses often came from relatives or close groups of partners rather than from the banks.[104] The State Bank also invested in Russian industry through loans and subsidies and the purchase of shares in industries of state interest. The State Bank was also active in providing credit, often through private credit institutions. In 1913, for example, 75 percent of State Bank credits went to private banks, enabling them to increase their capital for short term credit significantly.[105]

By 1913 Russian banks were in a position to end German monopolies in various industries but saw little advantage in doing so. At times they fought foreign monopolies vigorously but also cooperated extensively with German and French companies. The earlier hostility of Russian industrialists and businessmen to foreign competitors within the borders of the empire faded in the prewar years. The lessons of competition had honed the skills of Russian entrepreneurs and their confidence had grown. The economic spurt beginning in 1909 was for the most part Russian-led. It served as proof that Russians were capable of managing the development of their own economy.[106] Profits, not nationalism, increasingly determined their relationship with foreign investors.

Foreign corporations were recognizing Russian management skills as well. By 1913 many had "russified" their operations. Fewer foreigners now managed enterprises in Russia. Instead, effective management of foreign companies more and more entailed the placing of Russian personnel in

charge of commercial and administrative matters while a few foreign directors oversaw the whole business from behind the scenes. Foreign engineers
and technicians still provided much of the practical expertise, however. This
blend of foreign and domestic management was widespread among foreign-
owned companies by 1913.[107] The decline of direct investment and growth
of portfolio investment by foreigners through the banks further distanced
foreigners from Russian-based foreign companies.

The Russian-owned company was changing as well. The old family-owned
and -operated company was in decline, although still significant, especially
in Moscow. Even there by 1913 family combines were lowering share prices
in order to enable outsiders to invest in their enterprises. In 1913, 44 percent
of new companies offered shares worth 100 roubles or less.[108] The public
joint stock company was coming into its own in the empire. Shares in the
Russian stock exchange were not sold at public subscription but were purchased by a number of institutional buyers, especially banks. More than
2,000 Russian and 260 foreign stock corporations operated in Russia in 1914.
Between 1910 and 1913 Russian-based entrepreneurs established 774 joint
stock companies. By contrast, in Germany only 220 new companies came
into existence from 1907 to 1913. Companies in the empire were also geo-
graphically dispersed.[109] Existing Russian companies increased their capital
significantly in these years as well. New investment reflected the shift from
foreign to domestic sources of capital. Around 30 percent of the capital for
these new companies was formed abroad, and the rest derived from domestic sources.[110] In addition to the 383 Russian-based companies that traded
on the domestic stock exchanges,[111] 66 Russian-based companies were listed
on the Paris Exchange in 1914, 66 more on the Brussels Exchange, and 74
on the London Exchange.[112]

There were other signs that Russian business was reaching out to the
larger world. Russian corporate law had made great strides by 1913. In most
respects, it was equivalent to corporate law in the leading West European
countries. Unlike in Western Europe, corporations in Russia still required
state approval to form. The approval process was not notably corrupt, however. Approval rested more on the financial viability of the proposed corporation than on political influence or considerations.[113] Even this restriction
was on its way out. The Ministry of Trade and Industry in 1913 opened a
debate about withdrawing the need to apply to the state for permission to
incorporate a business.[114]

In the period before World War I Russia displayed many of the characteristics later associated with developing societies. An important feature of such development has been dependency on foreign capital and technology to support economic transformation.[115] The evidence is strong that in the years immediately preceding the war Russia was beginning to escape from dependency. Although still reliant on the importation of Western technology, Russia was approaching or had reached entrepreneurial self-sufficiency by 1914. Foreign companies continued to play a leading role in some sectors of the economy, but the Russian share even in them was increasing by 1913. The role of direct foreign investment in economic development was declining, and foreign portfolio investment was beginning to support new Russian-owned corporate enterprise. Although for tax reasons companies tended to overstate their assets, the total capitalization of Russian corporations, after allowances, still swamped that of foreign corporations. Although about 44 percent of the capital of Russian banks was foreign, it was divided among the French, Germans, and British in a way that prevented any one of them from attaining a position of dominance. In the prewar years Russian banks led a major upsurge of Russian entrepreneurial activity. Private Russian, not foreign, banks were the main institutional partners of Russian industry, and their role by 1913 far surpassed that of the State Bank. Increasingly, foreign capital was desirable in a growing economy but no longer urgently required to sustain it.

State and Economy

It is a commonplace in general accounts of the "late Russian Empire" that the state played a decisive role in advancing Russian industrialization. Writing in the mid-1980s one commentator observed that "a broad consensus of scholarly public opinion" existed that state intervention was decisive in the industrial boom of the 1890s.[116] Alexander Gerschenkron notably argued that in the near absence of an entrepreneurial middle class and sufficient domestic capital as well as a deficit of skilled labor, Sergei Witte, the minister of finance in the 1890s, substituted for them state-led economic measures, especially railway construction, high tariffs, and the importation of high-technology, capital-intensive machinery. The policy further included large-scale grain exports in order to gain a favorable trade balance in support of the rouble; tax and pricing policies that transferred income from peasant agriculture to industry; state investment in railways and defense industries; and a tariff policy designed to attract foreign investors to set up industries behind Russian tariff walls and to protect key Russian industries from the competition of foreign imports, while goading them into greater productivity through competition with internal foreign industrial concerns. Gerschenkron himself maintained that while the state led industrial development before the revolution of 1905, from 1908 the market drove the advance of industry. Broad generalizations in the historiography about "late Imperial Russia," however, have often obscured that crucial point.[117] Others have argued that in the boom years beginning in 1909–1910 the role of state defense purchases was almost as decisive in leading the economy as was state railway construction in the 1890s.[118]

Witte's own testimony indicates that his intentions as minister of finance were more or less as Gerschenkron described them. But as was often the case in Russian history the avowed intentions of the state were a poor reflection of its policies or their outcomes. As seen earlier in this chapter, the evidence does not support the contention that the Russian peasantry paid a punitive price for industrialization. Instead, rural dwellers shared roughly equally with city folk in an improving standard of living. Urban and rural consumption patterns diverged minimally during the period of industrialization.

Economic historians have cast doubt as well on the real impact of other components of the state's avowed industrialization strategy. Agricultural exports combined with the placing of the rouble on the gold standard did help to stabilize the rouble against foreign currencies as the policy intended. Tariff policy, however, was primarily designed to generate state revenue and not to favor specific industries or to attract foreign industrialists to set up enterprises behind tariff walls. Contemporaries chronically complained about the failure of government tariff policy to distinguish between fiscal needs, on the one hand, and the stimulation of Russian industry, on the other. The state imposed few discretionary tariffs to protect struggling Russian industries. Indeed, their absence severely undercut the growth of the critical Russian machine industry. High tariffs on imported goods required for Russian production were common and frequently hindered rather than promoted the development of domestic industry.[119] Tax policy did not generally encourage industrial investment either.[120] Bureaucratic obstacles and corruption were barriers to foreign investment and undercut state publicity about favorable investment opportunities in the empire. High overall returns on investments compared to those available in other European countries played a far greater role in attracting foreign investment than did state promotional policies.[121] The great majority of foreign investors had traditionally opted to enter the private sphere of the Russian economy in preference to areas of state significance. Profits, not inducements of the state, generally governed their choices.[122]

The contention that state spending played a disproportionate role in Russian industrial development compared to other European countries is equally contestable. State support for railways in the 1890s did have a significant impact on growth, but the state's role in railway construction in Russia was little greater than in other European countries in their early industrialization periods. Only Great Britain built a railway network without massive state aid.[123] The German state heavily financed the construction of its railway network, which for the most part it owned by 1900. During the Second Empire in France the state put massive investment into the infrastructure of the country. Private entrepreneurs in Russia loudly expressed their resentment of state industries, but they were in fact few in numbers. Railways, posts and telegraphs, some munitions plants, and the large, monopolized production and sale of vodka were among the few state-owned enterprises.[124]

An overwhelming proportion of Russian industry was in private hands. After 1905 state spending focused on defense and played little role in other sectors of industry. Defense spending was, however, dwarfed within the larger economy. In 1913 all direct and indirect state expenditures attributable to defense needs totaled 965 million roubles.[125] That represented 1.4 percent of the estimated total national wealth of the empire in that year and about 7.2 percent of the contribution of heavy industry and the transport and communications industries, both sectors into which flowed the government's indirect defense spending, to the total.[126] In the same year defense expenditure in Germany was 865 million roubles, in Great Britain 705 million roubles, and in France 552 million roubles.[127] It is not clear what proportion of those expenditures went to industry; but the sums in each case were significant. Military contracts were no doubt as important to German, British, and French arms manufacturers as were the slightly larger military expenditures of the Russian state to some Russian industries. As well, since the total industrial economy in Russia was much smaller than in the larger European economies, defense spending potentially had a proportionately larger effect in the empire.

In reality, few private Russian industries received defense contracts. Many defense orders were filled by government-owned factories, although some trickle-down through their purchases of materials entered the private sector. Foreign firms also won orders that Russian plants lacked the capacity or skill to handle. In February 1913 the Russian government tendered for thirty-six 14-inch guns, thirty 8-inch guns, and one hundred 131-mm guns for naval artillery. Armstrong, Vickers, and le Creuset bid on the contract. It went to Vickers, much to the irritation of the French government and press. The contract empowered Vickers to build a factory at Tsaritsyn to make the needed weapons.[128]

Government contracts of any kind were likely crucial for certain industries, especially in St. Petersburg. High-ranking bureaucrats sat on the boards of key industries to ensure their compliance with state needs. The State Bank also gave loans and subsidies to industries of state significance, although most often in hard times only and to a tiny minority of enterprises. But state contracts, subsidies, and loans were miniscule in relation to the total economy. The great majority of industries received no direct benefit from state purchases. Defense spending did not divert scarce capital from the rest of industry. By 1913 private capital and credit, as has been seen, were not in short supply.[129] Although significant for certain companies, therefore, defense spending did not lead the industrial economy by 1913 or even make a large contribution to it. The private sector dominated overwhelmingly.

Before the war, Russian industrialists faced a dilemma familiar in developing economies. Their short-term interest dictated the priority of production over consumption. Their long-term interest, however, was tied to the cultivation of demand by a mass market of consumers. They also faced a government and parliament more committed to agrarian, free trade interests than to a tariff policy that consistently advanced industrial growth. The shortages of fuel and metals created by the industrial boom alarmed some members of the government. In December 1912 Prime Minister Count Vladimir Kokovtsov lamented the incapacity of Russian industry to meet rising demand and promised to remove barriers to industrial development, encourage healthy competition, and foster individual initiative.[130] Little was done, however, and far from improving the climate for industry, the state instituted in 1913 a variety of measures harmful to industrial interests. Kokovtsov was removed from office in January 1914.

His dismissal convinced many businessmen that the government was now an obstacle to the modern economic development of the country.

Some advances toward the economic and financial integration of the empire had been made by 1913. An underdeveloped system of transportation and communications still hindered the growth of an imperial market. In 1913 there were 46,284 versts of state and 22,085 versts of privately owned railway lines in the empire, excluding Finland. The Russian railway network was the longest in Europe, but on a per capita basis it fell well short of that in almost all other European nations.[131] Maintained roads were few and for much of the year in a deplorable state. The development of the telegraph service speeded up business communications and expedited the advancing of credit. Though growing rapidly, telephone services were still weakly developed. In 1910, there was one telephone per thousand inhabitants in Russia compared to five per thousand in France, thirteen in England, fifteen in Germany, and seventy-six in the United States. Urban telephone systems served areas in which 12,500,000 lived, and another 18,100,000 lived in areas served by the rural zemstvos. Most networks were local; interurban services were few.[132] In late summer 1913 the Ministry of the Interior announced a plan, to begin in 1914, for a major expansion of the internal telephone network to provide extensive intercity communications.[133]

For all its inadequacies, the growing railway network facilitated the forging of some interregional economic links. By 1914 central Asian small farmers met half of Russia's demand for raw cotton. Not only Russian but Polish textile manufacturers depended on Turkestan for raw materials.[134] The Trans-Siberian railway also assisted a lively trade, fiercely defended by the Moscow Society of Factory and Mill Owners, between the Moscow region and the Far East. Witte had established a single tariff regime that excluded only Finland. The approach of the government to economic and financial policy was, however, unsystematic and seemingly indifferent to harmonizing the parts into an efficient whole. The Russian Empire had neither a ruling conception of the financial system as a whole nor laws and institutions to deal with the economic lives of the regions. As Ekaterina Pravilova concluded in her study of imperial finances, "The organization of financial administration in the regions, the conduct of tax reform and the creation of the credit system were extraordinarily labor intensive and wasteful measures."[135] The government would assist the development of regional infrastructures but also turned the regions into economic colonies that served the needs of the state and of industry in the center. The frequent result was unsustainable development in the regions and diversion from more intensive development in the Great Russian heartland.[136]

CONCLUSION

As World War I neared, the challenges to sustained Russian economic development were many. The great size of the country and the distribution of its natural resources, which required long-distance transportation, were chief among them. High transportation costs raised the price of fuel, raw materials, and finished products. The domestic market, though rapidly expanding, still generated only limited demand for all but essentials, and the weak distribution system placed limits on its growth. Capital was no longer hard to generate but skilled labor remained in short supply. The industrial spurt, as will be seen, put pressure on cities, especially St. Petersburg, to accommodate and to assimilate to urban ways a workforce continually replenished from the peasantry. Far from implementing a systematic industrialization strategy, the government, in search of revenues, maintained a hodgepodge of fiscal and monetary policies and practices that sapped energy and confidence from industry and commerce and hampered regional development. Late starters pay a high price for their tardiness. Even record growth rates do little to close the gap with competitors who began earlier and refuse to stand still. The world economy before World War I witnessed an intensification of global integration. International trade and markets abroad were essential to maintaining the vigor of domestic industry. As newcomers, Russian industrialists found it hard to penetrate or to compete in long-established global markets.[137] Grain and mining products made up the great majority of Russian exports. A significant drop in the prices of grain and minerals would have severely stressed the new Russian economy.[138]

In spite of the many challenges it still faced, Russia was by 1913 unmistakably on the path to a market economy. Demographic dynamism fueled economic change. It was lateness and not the direction or the pace of Russian development that separated it from its major competitors. Peter Gatrell noted the coexistence of advanced and backward forms in the Russian economy by 1913. He concluded, however, that "...the tendency, nevertheless, was for capitalist forms to grow and supplant pre-capitalist forms."[139] The role of the state in Russia's economic development from 1890 to 1914 has been overstated. The state placed few major obstructions in the way of market functions, although it lacked a coherent industrial policy. State-run enterprises were not numerous, but the fuel crisis encouraged talk by 1913 about creating more of them in critical sectors. State subsidies to industry were few and taxes and tariffs generally served revenue needs and not industrial policy. The state did not engage in systematic or effective economic planning; it was the market that set prices and drove production decisions. The Russian economy was integrated into the world economy and its commodity prices were set by world markets. Prices in Russia over time adjusted to conform to world prices.[140]

By 1913 the market economy was firmly in place in the empire and private industry was flourishing. Foreign investors sought, largely through portfolio investment, to take advantage of the strong returns that were still available in the growing Russian economy. The stocks of many Russian corporations traded on domestic and foreign exchanges. Contemporaries had no doubts about the integration of the Russian economy with European economies. They understood the importance of the international money market for the development of Russia's manufacturing sector.[141] Nevertheless, Russia's dependency on foreign capital for further development was rapidly declining. Domestic investment far outstripped foreign by 1913. A whole host of new Russian companies in a broad range of economic sectors had formed. Even Russian technology in some sectors was making giant strides, and Russian management was well established not only in domestically owned but also in foreign enterprises. The market was on its way to driving much of agriculture production, and state policy worked for the most part to encourage rather than dampen the growth of the agricultural market. Gregory concludes that in the Russian Empire before World War I, "The major test of a market economy—prices being set by market forces free of government intervention—was being met."[142] Perhaps of even more importance was the advanced division of labor that economic growth fostered and the mobility and individual risk-taking that it stimulated. These were not only indicators of a maturing economy but also the fundamental ingredients of an emerging civil society.

ESTATES AND CLASSES

2

Growing specialization in the economy and the complexity of a society experiencing the differentiation that economic modernization imposed exerted ever greater pressures on the traditional social arrangements of Imperial Russia. The population in 1913 was still legally divided into social estates (*sosloviia*).[1] Individuals attained legal standing primarily through estate membership or designated religious, ethnic, or regional status. Estates had a semi-functional character: membership in a particular estate carried both privileges and obligations, which varied considerably from one estate to the next. The rights of individuals derived in part from their estate standing, but the Fundamental Laws of 1906 also provided common rights to all citizens. The corporate standing of social estates was expressed in institutions as well as in the rights and duties particular to each. The origins of the estates and, in part, their persistence reflected the inability of the state to administer a huge territory through bureaucratic means alone.

Table 2.1 shows the numbers in each estate or station and their share in the total population as recorded in the census of 1897. No comparable information is readily available for 1913. With the great reforms of the 1860s, a new social structure began to superimpose itself on the traditional estate structure that had shaped social relations in Russia since at least the early eighteenth century. Once serving as useful instruments of administration, the estates by 1913 were becoming obstacles to the good governance of the empire. The incorporation of new groups into the old social structure strained the boundaries that separated the estates. The original functional purposes of estate distinctions were disappearing. Duties originally assigned to each estate had in some cases become outmoded

Table 2.1—Population in 1897 by Estate or Station

Estate	European Russia		Empire	
	Nos.	%	Nos.	%
Hereditary Nobility and Families*	885,754	0.95	1,221,939	0.97
Personal Nobility and Families	486,963	0.52	631,245	0.50
Christian Clergy and Families	501,483	0.54	589,023	0.47
Honorary Citizens and Families	307,597	0.34	343,111	0.25
Merchants and Families	239,563	0.26	281,271	0.22
Petty Merchants and Urban Artisans	9,945,971	10.64	13,391,701	10.66
Peasants**	78,641,432	84.16	96,923,181	77.12
Cossacks	1,439,750	1.54	2,929,313	2.33
Non-Russians (Inorodtsy)***	423,075	0.45	8,297,965	6.60
Finnish-born	35,140	0.03	35,934	0.04
Foreign Citizens	256,015	0.27	605,683	0.48
Others	280,121	0.30	425,748	0.34
Total	**93,442,864**	**100.00**	**125,676,114**	**100.00**

Source: Adapted from A.P. Korelin, ed., *Rossiia 1913 god. Statistiko-dokumental'nyi spravochnik* (St. Petersburg, 1995), 219.

* Of the 1,221,939 in the empire, 135,055 were Polish and 170,967 were Caucasian nobility.

**There was no separate estate for industrial and mining workers, who were mostly counted among the peasantry. According to the 1897 census 5,200,000 workers and their 7,100,000 dependents earned a living in large- and small-scale industrial production.

***In 1897 *inorodtsy* officially referred to non-Russians living in the northeastern, eastern, and southeastern parts of the empire.

or in others had grown too burdensome for their members to support. In cities especially, estate obligations were by 1913 significantly weakened. In the smaller cities the urban estates were still charged with providing various public services, but as city populations grew that function most often passed into the purview of elected city councils.[2] The complexity of urban populations stretched the estate structure to the breaking point. In 1913 the legal classification of 75 percent of the citizens of Moscow and St. Petersburg was peasant when, in fact, they were workers, artisans, shopkeepers, service providers, servants, waiters, white collar workers, and persons engaged in a number of other pursuits.[3]

As estate identities became less distinct, class and occupational identities strengthened. An estate mentality did not entirely disappear. Social status and influence continued to flow from estate membership until the end of the empire. Changing one's estate remained an avenue to social advancement, and many citizens still set as their goal the improvement of their place in the hierarchy of social estates.[4] Class, or position in the economy, mattered more and more, however. Privileges attached to membership in a particular estate were increasingly difficult to justify as the balance of economic power shifted. Flexible as the estate structure was in absorbing new social groups, the unequal privileges traditionally afforded by the estate system, which advantaged noble birth over new money or expertise, no longer satisfied many members of the new and growing capitalist and professional elites. Out of the social turmoil, a complex middle class was being constituted from individuals increasingly detached from the old estates. Not only were new social groupings developing but they were also evolving new forms of organization that enabled them to project their concerns and interests into the public sphere. The transition from traditional social identities to the complexities of modern social life was disruptive and even traumatic for many.

THE NOBLE ESTATE IN FLUX

The smallest but most advantaged of the estates was the nobility.[5] By 1913 it in no way constituted a cohesive social group. An ever shrinking minority still retained rural landed estates, but many noble families had sold their country properties within the last two or three generations. Access to title had, since the reign of Peter the Great, rested on position in the Table of Ranks. The Table of Ranks equated social status with rank in state service. There were fourteen ranks, each with an equivalent across the three service branches, civil, military and court. The lower six ranks conferred nonhereditary nobility, and the top eight, hereditary nobility on servitors of the state. Those in military service attained hereditary nobility at the sixth rank. Later the government raised the bar to entry into the hereditary nobility to promotion to rank four. A large portion of noble families had acquired hereditary nobility by dint of an ancestor's or their own state service. Many military or state servitors had never been large property owners; they had slight or no connections at all to the countryside. Those on the lower rungs of the Table of Ranks, the nonhereditary nobility with their families, made up just more than one-third of all nobles in European Russia. Another one-fifth of nobles in the empire were Germans, Poles, or natives of the Caucasus. The hereditary and nonhereditary nobility of all ethnicities made up just less than 1.5 percent of the population of the empire.[6]

Many of the privileges and most of the duties of the nobility as an estate were linked to landownership and residency in rural districts. The decline of landowning among the nobility had been relentless since the emancipation in 1861 and a cause for concern by 1913. Even the conservative press, however, was surprised by the tone of the congress of the United Nobility that took place in early March 1913. The United Nobility had formed after the revolution of 1905 with the goal of defending the estate structure that underlay the nobles' dominance in rural life.[7] Observers at the congress detected a note of panic in the debates about the decline of the estate and erosion of its privileged role in state and society. The congress delegates angrily condemned the development of industry, which, they believed, the government promoted at the expense of agriculture. In the face of the resources being expended by the state on peasant land reorganization, which encouraged small-scale farming, the nobility felt the need to remind the state that large estate agriculture also deserved the state's attention. Delegates demanded cheaper loans from the State Bank to prop them up and free them from the high interest rates of private banks. They railed against the influence of Jews in industry and trade and supported motions calling for a stifling press law.[8]

The United Nobility had reason to panic. The sharp decline in noble landholding since the 1860s meant that the division of the electorate into three curiae for purposes of district zemstvo elections was no longer viable. Since the establishment of the zemstvos in the 1860s the nobility, as big landowners, had dominated the first electoral curia. As we have seen, by 1913, however, holdings of over fifty dessiatinas made up about 11 per cent of arable land in European Russia. The nobility's share of even that shrinking percentage was in decline as non-nobles purchased large properties. In many districts by 1913, the number of noble electors barely exceeded the number of representatives in the zemstvo assembly to which the first curia was entitled, and in a few the entitlement exceeded the number of electors. Sixteen eligible voters in one district were required to elect twenty representatives from their own numbers to the zemstvo and nine voters in another had to elect twelve zemstvo representatives.[9] Even those nobles who owned land often rented it out to peasants, lived in cities, and took no interest in rural elections or responsibilities. In Iaroslavl' district, three of the nobles elected to the district zemstvo lived in the district capital and also held seats on the city duma.[10] Elections to the State Duma were also based on the curial system. In 1913 around thirty-one thousand noble families met the qualification for direct voting in the landowning curia established by the electoral law of June 1907. That constituted only 20 percent of all noble landowners and 12 percent of hereditary landed nobles.[11] Those who fell below the qualification pooled their votes.

The Ministry of the Interior intended to reform the local electoral law in order to conduct elections to the district zemstvos on the basis of a single, relatively high, property qualification. The ministry and the Duma had also agreed on a plan to create a smaller unit of local self-administration by transforming the peasant volost' into local zemstvos elected by all local residents equally. The proposed creation of an all-class zemstvo at the township level was intended to undermine the remnants of the legal system of social estates in rural self-government. For that reason, the United Nobility roundly condemned the plan at its March congress. Zemstvo activists supported the proposed legislation but lobbied for a more democratic franchise than the government was proposing.

Depending on the property qualification adopted, the electoral reform plan would bring small private property owners, including many peasants who left the commune, fully into local political life. The reform included the abolition of the noble land captains, who had since 1889 supervised peasant affairs. It envisaged relieving the marshals of the nobility from the onerous task of chairing a wide range of district or provincial zemstvo committees and replaced the marshals with appointed officials. Zemstvo activists opposed the appointment of committee chairs and lobbied for their election from among elected members of the zemstvo assembly. The reform was long overdue. A government survey of the time revealed that the nobility in many districts grossly neglected their local administrative responsibilities. Fewer than half of the marshals of the nobility, for example, carried out half of the duties attached to their office, and a third performed no duties at all.[12] Finally, the ministry aimed to abolish the estate-based peasant volost' court and bring the peasants fully under the jurisdiction of the circuit courts.

In spite of their shrinking numbers in the countryside, the rural nobility strongly resisted calls for the abandonment of the curial system of voting in zemstvo elections or for other measures designed to abolish the estate structure of imperial society. The rural nobles' near monopoly on local offices not only profited them but justified their existence as a separate estate. The pleas of the United Nobility did not go unanswered. Legislation to reform the zemstvo electoral franchise was slow to pass in the Duma, thanks to obstruction by rightist deputies. When the bill reached the State Council in 1913 it was effectively blocked by the nobles' allies.[13] The State Council also rejected a bill that proposed to abolish the peasant volost' courts, which conservative councilors dismissed as an assault on the estate system. Pressure from the landed nobility gradually cooled the enthusiasm for reform of the estate principle among government ministers as well. By the end of 1913 the Council of Ministers had quietly backed away from plans to weaken or abolish estate distinctions in the countryside. The council also shelved plans to extend the zemstvo structure to Siberia, the Russian north, and the Caucasus, in spite of pleas from local governors who desperately needed a legal mechanism to receive advice from the public on resource allocations in their jurisdictions. In those regions peasants dominated; large estates and a landed nobility barely existed there. Conservatives feared the setting of a precedent that allowed peasants independently to elect and manage institutions of local self-administration.

Declining landownership among the nobility did not necessarily signal the economic decline of nobles who left the land.[14] Many who sold their estates invested the profits in urban properties or shares in industrial or commercial enterprises. Although the proportion of hereditary nobles in the state bureaucracy had decreased, their long tradition of state service and family ties assured their continued predominance at the upper levels of state administration. The high proportion of nobles in the memberships of the State Duma and State Council was in part the product of a curial electoral structure that overwhelmingly favored them; but it also reflected the persistence of their traditional monopoly on public life.[15] As in state service, the ratio of nobles to other social groups in higher education was in sharp decline. Nevertheless, they remained proportionately by far the best educated social group in the empire and so played a significant part not only in the state but in the military, professions, the sciences, and the arts as well.

Politically, the nobles did not speak with one voice. The official organs of the nobility such as the United Nobility were conservative or even reactionary in outlook. Many nobles, especially those with land, voted for the parties of the right in the Duma. But those parties did not represent the full range of political opinion within the estate as a whole. In 1913 among the center-left and center-right parties in the State Duma, 24 of 59 Constitutional Democrats (Kadets) were from the hereditary nobility as were 69 of 100 Octobrists and 19 of 45 Progressives. On the right, although 50 of 89 Nationalists came from the hereditary nobility, only 25 of 64 on the extreme right did so.[16]

Even among the staunchest noble supporters of the old order there were disagreements and rivalries. As the centenary of the battle of Borodino and the tercentenary of the Romanov dynasty approached, the council of the United Nobility tried to take over the organization of the celebrations. Since the United Nobility did not represent noble societies in a number of provinces and excluded the Baltic and Caucasian nobility from membership altogether, many nobles objected to giving them control of the planning. A compromise resulted in the subordination of the United Nobility to the marshals of the nobility.[17]

The personal identity of nobles was also complex. For many nobles membership in the noble estate was only one marker of social identity and often not the most important. There were national differences. Though predominantly Russian, the nobility of the empire was ethnically diverse. They also had various family experiences. The gentry's long tradition of state service had blurred the line between bureaucracy and nobility. But a bureaucratic family that had earned hereditary noble status through state service likely had little in common with a family with generations of estate ownership behind it. A rapidly diversifying economy and a growing demand for social services created new career opportunities for nobles and non-nobles alike. Professionals from the noble estate were as likely to identify with other members of their profession or with professionals in general as with a noble entrepreneur or landowner. A noble urban rentier or business investor had more in common with capitalists from other social groups than with the rural nobility. Multiple identities, therefore, further undermined coherence in an already divided social estate.

RISE OF A COMPLEX MIDDLE CLASS

The erosion of the estate structure was most pronounced among the urban estates. Nobles who lived in cities and earned their living through rents and investment income or as salaried employees or professionals were functionally part of a growing urban middle class. The nobility had been free since the eighteenth century to engage in industry and commerce in competition with merchants. In 1898 the state freed anyone else who wished to take part in industrial or commercial enterprise from the need to register in the merchant estate. Peasants and urban petty artisans and traders flooded into business as a result. Since merchant status carried higher prestige and better chances of mobility than some other estate designations, some of the newcomers were willing to pay the merchant guild dues in order to acquire merchant status. But many merchants, while continuing to trade, stopped paying annual guild fees. Some old merchant families went on paying the guild fees for social reasons but ceased to engage in commerce. The result was that the merchant estate lost its traditional commercial-industrial significance. By 1913 estate membership had markedly shrunk. In the city of Riazan', for example, there were 130 families in the first and second merchant guilds in 1895. In 1913 there were only 76 despite the fact that the number of businesses operating in the city had grown dramatically.[18]

In spite of declining estate membership, merchant societies continued to be an important voice of business. The Moscow Merchants' Society celebrated its fiftieth anniversary in December 1913. Observers detected a tone of condescension in the speech that the minister of trade and industry delivered on the occasion.[19] As the importance of industry and commerce in the economy grew, however, so did the boldness of the merchant society representatives in demanding respect and a voice in national decision-making. During the tercentenary celebrations, as we saw, the merchants of Moscow had clashed with court planners over issues of precedence. Their protests met with some success. Such squabbles were little more than cases of wounded amour-propre and of minor political significance. The speech in August 1913 by A.S. Salazkin on behalf of the merchants of the empire at the Nizhnii Novgorod fair in the presence of Prime Minister Kokovtsov was another matter.

Salazkin, who was the mayor of the city of Kazimov, consulted widely with merchant societies throughout Russia about what to say in his welcoming remarks to the prime minister. According to him, all agreed that above all he should ask for the full implementation of the October Manifesto of 1905, that is, the creation in Russia of a fully constitutional political order. Salazkin chose his words carefully. He clearly understood that he no longer spoke for a narrow, traditional merchant estate but for a heterogeneous business class. He pointed out that the commercial-industrial class mingled within it all of the social estates and nationalities of the empire. He was, he said, speaking on behalf of his estate first as citizens and only then as merchants and industrialists. As citizens they deserved to "participate closely in social self-governance and state building."[20] The merchants also petitioned Kokovtsov at the fair for reform of the zemstvo electoral process.[21] Stock exchange committees and city dumas around the country greeted Salazkin's speech with telegrams of support. Calls for the realization of the promise of the October Manifesto were common in the summer of 1913 and not unique to the merchants. But as observers commented, Salazkin's speech was a far cry from the old days when merchants at the fair greeted a visiting minister with the words, "You are our father and we your children."[22]

Children of merchant families frequently aspired to lives very different from those of their fathers. In Riazan' the sons of merchants studied in gymnasia and universities or trained in commercial high schools. They choose careers in the bureaucracy, professions, and academia. Merchants' daughters increasingly entered high school, and some went on to studies in the higher women's courses. Like their brothers they too entered a variety of occupations. The successful merchant family in the nineteenth century emulated the noble life style and sought to attain noble rank. By 1913 few aspired to nobility; instead, their mode of life and mentality resembled those of the broader educated society of professionals with whom they were closely affiliated.[23] The pattern in Riazan' was repeated throughout the country in larger centers. In the years before World War I, in most dynamic cities the distinction between bourgeoisie, in the sense of the commercial classes, and educated society was blurring. It was not, however, the case in the majority of small cities, where most of the commercial middle class still had little formal learning.[24]

The same transformation the merchants of Riazan' and other major provincial cities underwent could be witnessed among the merchants of Moscow. There a number of young men from merchant backgrounds successfully combined careers in business with a life in politics. As Princess Lidiia Vasilchikova recalled in her memoirs, the younger generation of the Moscow Merchants' Society was highly educated, often in West European universities, well traveled, modern, and socially sophisticated. It was, she said, the Moscow nobility that clung to tradition and lived in the past.[25] Her opinion is not widely shared. At the beginning of the 1860s, the literary critic N.A. Dobroliubov dubbed the merchant world the "dark kingdom."[26]

It was a powerful image and a difficult one to overcome. Bernard Pares recognized "significant change" in the Moscow business world that was dividing merchants along traditional and modern lines. Nevertheless, he reached the astonishing conclusion that in 1913 the Moscow merchant estate was the "most conservative element in Russia."[27]

Later historians of the merchants only grudgingly acknowledge the transformation the merchants were experiencing in the prewar years. Irina V. Potkina granted that commercial culture in Moscow was rapidly acquiring "a European face" but believed that merchant Moscow maintained "its innately Russian character" as reflected in its "correspondence to the life style and mentality of the Russians of that day."[28] It is not clear what the "European face" of commercial culture looked like or how it would be possible to conduct business effectively without sharing the mentality of one's customers. Anyone who has done business in Paris, Lisbon, or London even today will have experienced cultural differences and mentalities that conform to national conditions and practices. Thomas Owen rightly concludes that "an enlightened, self-confident and politically liberal bourgeoisie did emerge among the Moscow merchants" but adds that it did so "only at a very late date and in such small numbers as to undermine the notion of universal progress common to both Marxist-Leninist and liberal historiography."[29] The lateness of the Russian bourgeoisie was relative; it was in 1913 much more mature than the bourgeoisies of many countries in Asia, Africa, and South America, and even in Southern and Eastern Europe. As Owen notes, the Russian bourgeoisie was too late to fulfill the role in the early twentieth century that Marxism erroneously assigned to it. Its appropriate historical role, however, as one of the pillars of civil society was already well advanced. By 1913 significant segments of the Russian bourgeoisie were already the bearers of the attitudes and values that are the hallmarks of a liberal civil society.

As Salazkin made clear in his speech at the Nizhnii-Novgorod fair, the commercial-industrial class in 1913 embraced elements from well beyond the merchant estate. The merchant societies had been transformed into advocates for that vastly expanded group. Almost all of the traditional estates—noble, peasant, and meshchanstvo—contributed members. It was ethnically diverse as well. Armenians, Baltic Germans, Jews, Poles, and Tatars among others joined Russians in the world of business. Foreigners also played a significant part in the exploitation of Russian resources. The level and type of industrial and commercial development differed from region to region. Heavy industry concentrated around St. Petersburg, the textile industry focused on the Moscow region, and extraction industries predominated in the southern and eastern parts of European Russia. Each of these regions hosted, however, a variety of industrial enterprises, both in type and size. There was a mining and smelting industry in Siberia as well as food processing, especially of dairy products. The Volga River and Caspian Sea littoral also had a growing food and fish processing industry. There was a viticulture and wine industry along the Black Sea and in the Crimea, and a large sugar beet industry in Ukraine. In the north the lumber and fur industries predominated.

Russian industry, therefore, incorporated a wide variety of interests. Industries that were attached to the government economy generally enjoyed greater stability of markets; industries that produced goods for the domestic consumer had to cope with less reliable markets. Those who produced goods for export had yet another set of concerns. Profits in consumer industries such as textiles, foodstuffs, and their distribution were high in the years before the war. Profitability in heavy industry was generally lower. As a result consumer industry experienced heavy investment in the boom years of the Russian economy from 1910 to 1913.[30] In light of such diversity among commercial and industrial interests it is not surprising that agreement on the particulars of economic policy was hard to achieve among them.

Disagreement over details did not, however, preclude broader accord on the nature and direction of the imperial economy. A number of multinational and multicultural combines of entrepreneurs were functioning effectively and investing in Russian economic development by 1913.[31] Most industrial and commercial branches had their own representative trade-specific associations.[32] The most inclusive organization of commerce and industry was the Association of Industry and Trade. It limited its membership to large-scale enterprises, but a majority of trade-specific associations was represented in it. Although the association maintained its headquarters in St. Petersburg, its membership broadly reflected both the branch and geographical diversity of the empire's trade and industry. Through its congresses and press organs the association publicized the growing contribution that industry and trade made to the economy and pressed the government to advance the pace of industrialization. It tied the security and independence of Russia in the international arena to the strength of its industry and advocated tariff protection for all products that could be produced in the empire. Rising demand from 1910 to 1913 had led to a large increase in imports that altered the balance of trade. The relatively poor harvest of 1912 had slowed exports, worsening the trade balance in 1913. The answer, the association argued, was to increase domestic industrial production as rapidly as possible. In particular, its spokesmen contended that an expanding industry could absorb the surplus of agricultural labor as well as make greater use of agricultural products in manufacture. They also underlined the role of industry and trade in the cultural development of the population and the growth of civil society.

The Association of Industry and Trade defended syndicates and monopolies as a necessary aspect of early industrialization and a buffer against foreign competition. It argued that until industrial development was well advanced the needs of production should take precedence over the needs of consumption. It encouraged government economic policies designed to create more favorable conditions for industrial growth and better terms of trade. The association particularly pressured the government to improve transport and communications. The capacity of the physical infrastructure, it argued, no longer met the needs of a booming economy. Otherwise, it deplored government interference in business. It was especially critical of government-owned industries, with whose subsidized costs the associations' members could not compete for orders, and the tendering of government contracts abroad.

Ambivalence about the role of government in industrial development in the positioning of the association arose from conditions of the day. Public opinion in Russia was not generally sympathetic to the capitalist development of the country. A lengthy intellectual discourse of anticapitalism that was often tied to antiwesternism had turned influential setters of public opinion against the merchants and their aspirations. In the face of such reluctance, industrialists found themselves reliant on the support of government to establish the conditions necessary for free enterprise. In spite of growing nationalism before the war and public fears about foreign investment, the association stoutly defended the need for foreign capital investment as necessary at the present stage of the empire's economic development.[33]

The association also rejected government interference in management-labor relations. It argued that labor unrest was the product of the economic boom. Members favored the formation of trade unions to organize and voice the interests of workers.[34] Its position on labor put it at odds with the St. Petersburg Society of Factory and Mill Owners. The society was dominated by about a dozen owners, many of whom were non-Russians. Although a minority of society members advocated some concessions to labor, the majority opposed any form of worker organization, including unions. They sought to coordinate wages, hours, and working conditions from factory to factory and circulated blacklists to exclude militant workers from employment.[35] These efforts at coordination met only limited success.[36] Such antilabor views were more the exception than the rule among Russian employers. The Moscow district branch of the Society of Factory and Mill Owners, for example, adopted a conciliatory attitude to labor relations, supporting the formation of labor unions. During the strikes in the oil fields around Baku in the summer of 1913, employers were prepared to meet with "workers' commissions" to negotiate terms. The local state administration, however, banned the establishment of worker negotiating teams.[37]

An influential member of the Association of Industry and Trade was the Association of Southern Coal and Steel Producers. It brought together entrepreneurs of various social origins with engineers and other specialists. Like the Association of Industry and Trade, the Southern Association saw in industry the key to economic prosperity and the cultural advancement of the population. It promoted education and championed rational organization and the primacy of work and merit over social status. Geographical and branch differences did not prevent the Association of Industry and Trade from supporting major causes dear to the Southern Association: the reform of property law, removal of restrictions on passports, improved technical education, lower transportation costs, the defense of foreign capital, the expansion of domestic markets, and improvements in tariff policy.[38]

Businessmen across Russia also found common ground in the defense of business investment without discriminatory restrictions. In May 1913 the Council of Ministers forbade stock companies that had a majority of Jewish or foreign shareholders from purchasing rural land in 15 provinces of the empire. The Association of Industry and Trade, with the strong approval of the Association of Southern Coal and Steel Producers, petitioned against all such restrictions. They argued that Jewish and foreign capital infusion was essential for Russian industrial growth. In August the minister of industry and trade, S.I. Timashev, supported the association's petition in the Council of Ministers. The matter dragged on, but in January 1914 a majority in the Council of Ministers upheld the exclusion of Jews from the exploitation of land. The association fought on, however, and in the spring was rewarded with the removal of most restrictions on Jewish participation in land purchases.[39]

The campaign on behalf of Jewish investors indicates that for many Russian businessmen class interest trumped ethnicity. In fact, the defense of the rights of Jews was not restricted to the Association of Industry and Trade. In January 1913 the All-Russian Congress of Stock Market Committees petitioned the state to permit all qualified students to study in commercial schools without restriction. In particular, the petition asked that Jewish students presently enrolled in the Kiev Commercial Institute be permitted to complete their studies despite a law of July 1912 that excluded them from residency in Kiev.[40] Many Russian businessmen opposed the forced resettlement of Jews to the Pale (see chapter 4) that the government ordered to begin in 1913. In February 1913 the stock market committee of Kursk sent a note to the Council of Ministers pointing out the importance of Jews to the local economy and recommending the cancellation of the Jewish resettlement program.[41]

Commercial and industrial associations had largely avoided the adoption of overt political stances. That position was becoming untenable by 1913, as the campaign for Jewish rights demonstrated. The quiet lobbying of bureaucrats that businessmen preferred had not been effective, and more public efforts were required. The image perpetuated in the historiography of the Russian commercial and industrial bourgeoisie as narrow-minded, provincial, and backward, generally apolitical but monarchist if pressed, and of their associations and clubs as "loyally subservient to the government yet still more radical than their constituency,"[42] no longer held by 1913 (if indeed it had ever been accurate). By then, business leaders had accepted that the present regime was an obstacle to real improvement in the position of trade and industry. In June 1913 A.I. Konovalov, a leading industrialist and a Duma representative, denounced government economic and labor policies. He called for the "rapid renovation of our state and public life."[43]

The great majority of members of the State Duma, with their bases in rural Russia, had little sympathy with urban-based commercial interests. The same was true of the majorities in zemstvos around the country. Traditionally, Russian industrialists had provided housing, health facilities, and schools for their employees and their families. Although the second electoral curia, in which many small industrialists and merchants voted, was by far the fastest growing electoral group, they were weakly represented in the zemstvos compared to the agricultural interests. The zemstvos were happy to extract a large portion of their tax resources from commercial interests but reluctant to allow the employees of factories to use the educational and health facilities the taxes supported.[44] The Association of Southern Coal and Steel Producers believed that industry should take greater responsibility for social welfare than in the past but wanted to partner with their employees and government bodies in the creation of universal social services. They advocated the creation of a society of taxpayers, assessed on their incomes, that would provide social services to all citizens. They therefore joined in the chorus calling for zemstvo reform in 1913.[45]

Conflict between the government and business associations became particularly acute in 1913. Not only did the government restrict Jewish investors but it also introduced laws aimed to weaken the syndicates and to enforce higher standards for air and water pollution.[46] The fuel crisis of 1913 witnessed bitter exchanges between government and business interests. The rapid rise in production from 1910 to 1913 increased demand for fuel beyond domestic supplies. By 1913 there was a fuel shortage, which society and some in the government blamed on the coal and oil syndicates. They also blamed growing metal shortages on monopolies. Although there is little concrete evidence that the syndicates were limiting production in order to keep prices high, the government, as previously noted, permitted the importation of duty free coal and oil from abroad in the second half of 1913. The extraction industries opposed that measure. They also stepped up their attacks on the government for policies that they believed inhibited foreign investment. They sharpened their opposition to "state socialism," that is, government ownership of industries; and they attacked state industries as inefficiently run.[47] At the same time the government was discussing plans to augment the number of state-operated industries so as to secure the state against the growing power of private industry.[48] At the Eighth Congress of the Association of Industry and Trade in May 1914 a speaker, to wide acclaim, blamed the current political conditions in Russia for hindering the economic development of the country.[49] The discourse of laissez-faire in the domestic economy was widespread in industrial circles by 1913. Industry spokesmen argued that the government could create nothing of lasting value in the economy: "The government can only create favorable conditions for the release of industrial and commercial energies," one wrote in

Russkie vedomosti, "and the populace itself, through its own powers, will generate the country's wealth under these conditions."[50]

The relative prosperity of the prewar years also increased competition within industrial and commercial groups. Disagreements over protective tariffs for costly or scarce goods inevitably arose. Even the syndicates showed signs of fracturing, as a few companies broke ranks to pursue their own interests. Such tensions did not, however, mean that divisive matters were greater than common interests among Russian commercial concerns. One member of the executive of the Association of Southern Coal and Steel Producers argued in defense of its membership in the Association of Industry and Trade that it was entirely possible to compromise with Moscow industrialists on most issues through patient negotiation.[51] As Susan McCaffray, the historian of the Southern Association, aptly points out, the failure of Russian industrialists to form permanent alliances is not "evidence of a chronically fragmented or politically immature society."[52] Shifting business alliances and negotiated compromises are a feature of business life everywhere and reveal little about social cohesion. The Russian industrial-commercial bourgeoisie by 1913 had achieved a remarkable level of agreement about fundamental economic needs and, as dissatisfaction with the central government and local bodies of self-government grew, about political needs as well. They were moving toward a liberal political stance that also contained a strong element of shared social responsibility. Unlike many other groups in Russia, they had the means, through congresses and their publications, to disseminate their views at a national level.

Spokesmen for commerce and industry in Russia increasingly addressed issues beyond narrow business concerns. The new civic awareness of the business class found its clearest expression in the publications and activities of the Association of Industry and Trade in the years immediately preceding World War I. The association urged its members to transcend the narrow life of business and assume a larger role in national life. In promoting the importance of their class to the future of Russia, they won both critics and supporters in the Russian press. Newspapers with broad readerships such as *Russkoe slovo* and *Russkie vedomosti* noted the new self-consciousness of businessmen and praised industrialists who, unlike the nobility, addressed interests beyond the narrow concerns of their group.[53]

Like the merchant estate, the other urban estate of artisans and shopkeepers, the *meshchane*, was also experiencing significant change. Although the estate retained legally mandated institutions and functions, the opening of urban trade and production to all in 1898 effectively negated the role and protections they had formerly enjoyed. People who engaged in artisan production and retail trade were merging into a single petty commercial class in the prewar years. The old estate organization, however, was still used effectively as a lobby for reforms to further the interests of the petty commercial class as a group, much in the same way that the merchant societies had evolved as spokesmen for the business class. The Moscow Meshchane Society was busy in autumn 1913 organizing an All-Russian Congress of the Representatives of Meshchane Societies for May 1914. Among the goals set for the congress was the establishment of a Meshchane Bank to provide credit for small businesses, to organize financial aid for the middle and higher education of the children of meshchane, to increase the role of the petty commercial class in state, city, and zemstvo governance, and to lower the qualifications for the vote in state and urban elections.[54]

Mutual aid societies were a more common form of organization among people of similar occupations. They were not unions but groupings of people with a common occupation or activity that provided services such as funding for funerals or aid to sick or injured members. Many nonindustrial workers were members of mutual aid societies. Often their occupations were intermediate between industrial working-class and middle-class designations. They included artisans, typographers, shop assistants, and many others in small production or service industries. Mutual aid societies were self-organized and self-managed. In addition to their local functions, some mutual aid societies organized regional or national events. In March 1913, for example, the Moscow Artisans' Mutual Aid Society met to plan an All-Russian Artisans' Exhibition in the summer of 1914.[55] In May the annual general meeting of the Mutual Aid Society of Moscow Typographers declared a membership of 862 members who paid total fees of 32,280 roubles in 1912. The society had a capital fund of 160,000 roubles and owned property valued at 148,000 roubles.[56] These societies provided members with valuable lessons in participation, democratic organization and decision-making, and self-help. Their members were stewards of themselves and not the wards of intelligentsia mentors. The growth of mutual aid societies was not confined to Moscow. In 1913 the Volga city of Saratov saw the establishment of several mutual aid organizations. They included one for Old Believers, another for Muslims, and a third for apartment renters.[57] Other cities experienced similar growth of mutual aid groups.

Consumer cooperatives taught similar lessons to urban dwellers. Cooperatives were common in cities and their environs. The Moscow District Union of Consumer Societies celebrated its fifteenth anniversary in November 1913. It started with thirty-seven member societies with a budget of thirty-one thousand roubles. In 1913 it had 1,083 member societies and a budget of 8 million roubles.[58] At the end of the year the union opened a fund to build a sanatorium to be named after Lev Tolstoi.[59]

Urban service employees were also organizing. Commercial employees, who worked in private businesses, were particularly active. One estimate in 1913 placed their number in Russia at about four hundred thousand, about a quarter of whom were in Moscow.[60] About twenty societies of commercial employees existed with a membership of around ten thousand in the city. The largest was the Moscow Mutual Aid Society for Merchant Employees, founded in the 1880s, with a membership in 1913 of roughly three thousand. An initiation fee of 25 roubles and an annual fee of 15 roubles largely excluded lower-level clerks from the membership. The society supported one commercial school for boys and another for girls. Many of the students were children of society members. The society also provided stipends for study in universities, technical schools, and the academy of commercial sciences. In 1913 it was in the process of building two seven-class commercial schools for 1,200 students. The society maintained a library with fifteen thousand volumes and its own clinic with several doctors on staff. It also provided an employment service for members. Widows of deceased members could be housed in free apartments maintained by the society. It also ran the Aleksandrovskii home for the aged.[61] From May 1912 to May 1913 the society found work for 2,776 members and supported 4,139 needy members and their families with a total of 225,504 roubles.[62] In Kharkov in 1913 the commercial employees' mutual aid society joined forces with the Society of Professional Shop Assistants and the Society of Office Workers and Accountants to raise funds to establish a clinic for members. They had by summer 1913 raised 40,000 of the needed 130–150,000 roubles.[63] In Iaroslavl' the Society for the Empowerment of Private Clerks resolved in October to organize a regional congress of commercial and industrial white collar employees.[64]

In July 1913 the Fourth All-Russian Congress of Commercial Office Workers met in Moscow. The congress discussed issues relating to hours of work, vacations, health and safety, and health insurance. Most of the issues were the same as those discussed at the third congress seven years earlier. A new item, however, was a request to the government to extend existing health insurance fund legislation for factory workers to workers in commerce.[65] The Ministry of Trade and Industry had introduced to the third Duma a law to regulate the hiring of commercial employees, but the Duma commission examining it had amended the act to exclude several kinds of businesses from the legislation. When delegates to the office workers' congress expressed dissatisfaction with the exclusions, the Ministry of the Interior ordered the closing of the congress and the arrest of three of its delegates.[66]

Not all white collar workers had formal organizations, but some still found means to defend their interests. In Kiev, postal and telegraph workers in the employ of the state-owned Kiev telegraph and telephone company faced a bizarre and contradictory set of regulations. They were informed that telephone workers could only marry workers in the same office or risk dismissal. In one office there was only one male worker and he was already married. In the Kiev telegraph office, on the contrary, a worker was forbidden to marry a fellow worker in the same office on the grounds that if one of the couple fell ill the other would miss work to care for the ailing spouse. The workers petitioned the State Duma for redress. The organizer of the petition was fired.[67]

In Siberia the sales staff in the Irkutsk store of the Vtorov chain of stores struck in the spring of 1913 to protest violations to an employment agreement of 1905. The management argued that salaries had to be lowered in order to keep prices down. The management used six strike breakers to keep the store open. The public organized a boycott of the store and flooded local newspapers with letters of support for the workers. The workers created a strike fund. Informed of the strike in Irkutsk, the sales staffs in all of the Vtorov stores struck in sympathy. By mid-May eleven stores in Siberia and one in Ekaterinburg in the Urals were closed and 1,200 workers were on strike.[68] The employees of rival stores supported the Vtorov workers by contributing 5 percent of their wages to the Vtorov strike fund.[69] Siberian newspapers that reported on the strike were heavily fined.[70]

Workers in nonfactory manufacture were also effectively organizing. In March 1913 the Union of Workers in Tailoring held their annual general meeting. Earlier the union had requested that the owners of tailoring shops cooperate with the union in setting up an arbitration board to resolve a number of long-standing disputes in the trade. By March the owners had agreed and the general meeting elected five delegates to represent the workers on the new board.[71] Arrangements such as these outside of the factory context were common but are seldom remarked on in the literature, which has focused almost exclusively on factory workers.

If the Russian commercial classes had changed, an even greater transformation had overtaken the intelligentsia. By 1913 "intelligentsia" as a descriptor had lost much of its original meaning. Since the 1860s the intelligentsia had emerged as a group of educated individuals drawn from several social estates devoted to opposition to the existing order and to reform in the interests of the common people. What had emerged out of it by 1913 was a diverse group of educated people occupying multiple and multiplying places in a complex economy. The expansion of higher and technical education in the last quarter of the nineteenth century, the beginning of the industrial spurt from the late 1880s, and accompanying urbanization greatly expanded the intelligentsia and altered its nature and attitude to work on behalf of the people. Even before the revolution of 1905 the scope for constructive legal work to meet popular needs expanded rapidly. From the middle of the 1880s the zemstvos greatly extended their educational and agricultural aid programs and began to provide a growing list of other social services. The number of the intelligentsia hired by the zemstvos for rural development significantly increased. The industrial, commercial, and professional sectors of the economy also provided new outlets for the energies of the intelligentsia. After 1905, for all its fears about public initiative and spasmodic repressions, the state proved willing to work toward some of the goals of the intelligentsia, to hire them in pursuit of those goals, or to collaborate with them in zemstvo and city administrations. By 1913 the Russian intelligentsia was both better prepared for constructive legal work to advance the nation as a whole and, to a considerable degree, allowed to do so. In those conditions, the abstract and ideologically heated attitudes of the old intelligentsia to the people gave way increasingly to pragmatic work toward limited objectives rather than toward the wholesale transformation of society and politics of which a minority of more ideologically inclined radical intelligentsia still dreamed.

Russian professionals exemplified the changes in the intelligentsia. The revolutionary violence of 1905 and the savageness of government repression that followed it dampened the enthusiasm of many professionals for direct confrontation with the state. While some withdrew into personal and career issues, others showed greater willingness to cooperate with the state where common goals could be identified. Cooperation was facilitated by a greater readiness on the part of some government ministries to ally with professionals in pursuit of a modernizing agenda. Rapid change during transitional periods fosters a new pragmatism among the elites that works toward a realignment of old politcal and economic alliances to assure mutual survival.. In Russia the differences among the elites were no sharper than in other countries going through precipitous economic and social evolution. In spite of enduring tensions, the Russian elites by 1913 had created a wide area of agreement around the need to raise the cultural and economic level of the Russian populace through the improvement of educational and medical facilities and housing.[72] Both the state and professionals recognized their mutual dependency and the potential for mutual empowerment. Many professionals sought partnerships with the state rather than complete independence from it.[73] Accommodation was further facilitated by the fact that a large number of professionals worked in state service as experts for all or part of their careers; movement between the public and private sectors was not uncommon for professionals.

Accommodation was neither easy nor complete. Professional groups were themselves divided along ideological lines. Although few supported the tsarist state, many adopted an apolitical stance and were prepared to work for whatever reforms the state was prepared to permit and to press for more. Among professional engineers, for example, the ethos of positivism prevailed after 1905. They placed their hopes on science and technology rather than on social revolution as forces of liberation. In their view, experts alone had the skills needed to address socioeconomic problems effectively. In many ways their approach recapitulated the experience of engineers in the Second French Empire who transformed the urban and industrial landscapes of France under Napoleon III. Like their French counterparts, many of whom had drawn on the positivism of Saint-Simon, Russian engineers were prepared to work within the constraints of public and private institutions to achieve a more rational and productive economic order. Most professionals preferred cooperation to another revolutionary outburst despite their frustration over the glacial movement of reform. Kendall Bailes concluded that as a result of their new pragmatism the cohesiveness of the professional intelligentsia as a revolutionary force was by 1913 highly questionable.[74]

By 1913 most professionals were organized in local and regional societies; many had also won government approval for national congresses. During 1913 apothecaries, dentists, electro-technical engineers, gynecologists and midwives, optometrists, surveyors, teachers of various subjects and elementary school teachers, and veterinarians and veterinary *fel'dshers* (assistants), among others, held national or large regional congresses. The government, however, refused to sanction a broadly based congress of engineers in that year, perhaps for fear of encouraging technical professionals to articulate jointly their wide common interests. Russia and Russian professionals in 1913 were also very much part of the international community of professionals and scholars. Their representatives participated in a range of international congresses. A decision of the government to permit Jews from abroad to attend international congresses held in Russia cleared the way for Russian professionals to host international meetings as well. In late December the Fifth International Congress on the Treatment of the Mentally Ill gathered in Moscow. Despite the government's declaration on Jewish participation, local state authorities only reluctantly granted Jewish delegates permission to stay in Moscow for the duration of the conference.

Russian approaches to social policy attracted considerable interest from abroad. A French delegation arrived in the summer of 1913 to study how Russians dealt with poverty and homelessness. Led by the mayor of Paris, the delegation visited St. Petersburg and Moscow. Escorted by the police, they made a midnight visit to a Russian shelter for the homeless.[75] An American delegation that was visiting Europe to study European agriculture and the cooperative movement included Russia in its tour. In Moscow, they visited the Shaniavskii People's University, a people's university that was privately funded and run. The Americans were particularly interested in courses on cooperative organization taught at the university with the aim of preparing activists for the cooperative movement.[76]

The zemstvos employed large numbers of professionals. Experienced observers noted clear differences between the mentalities of state bureaucrats at the local level and zemstvo hired personnel. In state service, political intrigue was a necessary concomitant of career ambition. In the zemstvo, personnel felt free and even obligated to express their opinions in commissions and meetings.[77] Distrust between the two factions compelled to work side by side in overlapping competencies was endemic. But each side still needed the other. Shared initiatives, like the delivery of agricultural aid or schooling, brought state and zemstvo personnel together on a regular basis.

The Working Class and Its Goals

The heterogeneity of the blue collar working class in Russia in 1913 largely precludes generalizations about workers' conditions or states of mind. For all their hardships factory workers, who came under factory legislation and inspections and had recently acquired the benefits of new health insurance funds, had little in common with workers in small enterprises, which were largely unregulated. Workers in larger enterprises have been intensively studied. Although their way of life has attracted some attention from historians, most studies focus on the question of the relative militancy of various kinds of workers and their potential as revolutionaries. Were workers who retained ties with the village more likely to engage in disturbances in factories than workers who had long severed rural links? If so, what forms did the disturbances take? What sort of labor organization did various workers prefer, if any? What type of worker took an interest in socialist ideas or joined socialist movements? Tim McDaniel, who has examined capital and labor in Russia extensively, concludes that before the war the Russian labor movement was sufficiently united in goals and identity to be called a social movement. But he rightly warns against exaggerating the common culture and shared aims of workers.[78]

The number of industrial strikes rose sharply in Russia beginning in 1912. The massacre of workers in the Lena goldfields in early 1912 was one of the causes of a spike in strikes with political objectives. In 1910 economic strikes made up 96.4 percent of all strikes in the country. After the Lena goldfield killings in early 1912 the percentage of political strikes leapt to 64.1 percent of the total and then subsided in 1913 to 43 percent of all strikes.[79] The economic upturn of these years was, however, also a major contributing factor to the increase in labor activism as workers, aware of growing industrial profits, sought to secure higher wages. Moreover, in an international context the escalation of the strike movement in Russia in 1913 and 1914 was not exceptional. In the years preceding World War I industrial unrest was common across Europe. Britain, France, and Germany, in particular, witnessed massive strikes.

In Russia St. Petersburg was at the heart of the prewar strike movement. In the three years before World War I, St. Petersburg never hosted less than 40 percent of all strikes in the country. According to the Central Statistical Bureau of the new Soviet regime in 1921, the city of St. Petersburg experienced 755 strikes in 1913 with 353,662 strikers. The province outside the city contributed an additional 315 strikes with 73,182 participants. By comparison, Moscow had 268 strikes with 94,442 strikers and Baku 190 strikes with 25,852 activists. The total number of strikers in the empire in 1913 was 887,096.[80] Since many striking workers participated in multiple strikes during the year, the number of activists in the strike movement represented a relatively small part of the factory workforce.

The main locus of the strikes was metalworking and machine shops. In 1913, 64 percent of strikers were metalworkers compared to only 28 percent in 1905–1906. As well St. Petersburg contributed 95 percent of all political strikes in the empire in 1913.[81] Again metal and machine workers led the way. In 1912–1913 they made up 40 percent of political strikers whereas in 1913 textile workers supplied only 8 percent of those engaged in political strikes.[82] Most political strikes lasted for a day or less and carried symbolic value.[83] They commemorated anniversaries of events like Bloody Sunday or the Lena massacre or international labor days such as 1 May. In 1913, for example, 27 percent of the 1,025 political strikes in 1913 occurred on 1 May.[84] Few strikes had significant, direct leadership from the socialist parties, at least in part because of the heavy campaign of harassment and arrests conducted by the police against socialist leaders in 1913.[85] In the repressive conditions of Imperial Russia, which severely inhibited the growth of trade unionism, the strike was one of the few effective means of political expression available to workers.

Strikes were aimed at tsarism but not necessarily at capitalism. Workers were concerned about their roles and remuneration within capitalist modes of production and not about the abolition of the capitalist system. They did not reject the factory system in their strike demands but focused on specific conditions of work.[86] Changes in production techniques since the turn of the century, including a measure of mechanization in many factories, diminished the need for highly skilled workers and made work more routine. The introduction of Taylorist methods of management into some factories, such as the use of time clocks, disrupted old routines and provoked some resistance from workers.[87] Workers, however, were generally not opposed to modernization measures but sought instead to minimize their effects by fixing wages and limiting the replacement of male workers with women and teens. The strikes of the spring and summer of 1913 focused on matters of factory order, issues of control over the way workers spent their time in the factory, and solidarity with other workers seeking similar goals.

Demand for increased wages motivated more than a third of economic strikes in 1913.[88] Wages did rise for some during this period. In all of industry in European Russia the average wage rose from 243 roubles in 1910 to around 264 roubles in 1913. The greatest wage gains were in metalworking, mineral and food processing, and oil extraction. Most textile workers, among whom militancy was low, earned less in 1913 than they had in 1910. Only linen, hemp, and jute workers saw their low salaries of 169 roubles in 1910 rise to a modest 192 roubles in 1913.[89] The length of the working day provoked 23 percent of strikes in 1913. Although a little less than 50 percent of strikes in St. Petersburg in 1913 arose over authority at work, the figure nationally was only 15 percent.[90] Prominent among workers' demands were issues surrounding the dignity of the individual. Bullying by foremen, dismissal of coworkers, and sympathy for workers in other factories frequently caused strikes. Workers asked for polite address from managers, soap and towels and hot water in wash-up rooms, privacy in the lavatory, and respectful treatment by health personnel. They also wanted to standardize the length of apprenticeships and to end compulsory medical checks at hiring.[91] Specific grievances unfolded against a background of urban overcrowding and dislocation. Living conditions in the major Russian cities did contribute significantly to worker discontent. Housing was a particularly difficult issue for Russian cities with their burgeoning populations.

The Council of Ministers in autumn 1913 discussed the causes of labor unrest. Ministers broadly agreed that the growing strike movement among factory workers was motivated primarily by the failure, in workers' eyes, of employers to meet their legitimate economic needs; only secondarily did some strikes take on a political nature. In particular, the ministers identified the main targets of the strike movement as those enterprises where the conditions of work were inferior to conditions in other similar enterprises. The council also found that the deeper cause of the strike movement was the prosperity generated by the economic boom that industry was experiencing, the benefits of which workers sought a larger share. The minister of the interior surmised that strikes were often caused not by the immoderate economic demands of workers but by actions of employers. Employers frequently pro-voked workers into strike action in order to create conditions that enabled them to tear up old agreements with workers and impose new conditions more favorable to the owners. In plants fulfilling government contracts, em-ployers who realized that they were about to default on delivery dates often provoked workers into strikes to avoid contractual penalties. In most cases, however, strikes occurred over misunderstandings about economic terms of employment affecting a relatively small number of workers. Often peaceful resolution through negotiation was a realistic outcome. But the instruments for mediation were weak. Poor communication frequently led to further misunderstandings. Other workers in the name of worker unity joined the strike. Demands escalated. Socialist agitation contributed to an atmosphere of mutual antagonism between the two sides and incubated contentiousness. A minor dispute could mushroom into a major clash involving thousands of workers in a region. The ministers perceived what appeared to them to be the organized nature of these escalations as a threat to the existing state and social order.[92]

The contribution of state action to nurturing the strike movement was largely missing from the ministers' discussion. The anticapitalist bias of some ministers, which underlay much of state policy toward capital and labor, was evident in their rush to blame employers. Ministers raised the weakness of bodies of mediation but not the fact that the state was the main obstacle to the creation of effective, independent bargaining units. They did not mention the role of the police in suppressing the labor press, hindering or altogether blocking the legal functioning of unions, and harassing labor leaders. The paralysis in urban administration, particularly in St. Petersburg, which arose from state interference in housing, popular education, and the delivery of a range of social services, passed without comment.

A number of factors combined with crowded and squalid housing to make St. Petersburg the heartland of labor militancy. The St. Petersburg Society of Factory and Mill Owners, whose members included many of the large and middle-sized industrial enterprises of the city, were determined to restore the patriarchal factory discipline of the pre-1905 period. They stoutly resisted unionization, blacklisted militants, and resisted labor legislation and factory inspection. Socialists concentrated their efforts on St. Peters-burg, with its concentrations of workers in large factories. As a consequence, so did the police. Surveillance of workers in the capital was pervasive and intense. Workers resisted through organized action, and younger workers sometimes struck back more spontaneously, through hooliganism. Hooligans attacked police on their beats and taunted respectable citizens in public spaces. Much worker violence, however, was directed against other workers in the form of gang conflicts or organized mass brawls.[93] In such conditions it is not the militancy of some workers that is surprising but the moderation of the majority.

A growing preference for legal organization and activity was apparent among workers in 1913.[94] Around the turn of the century a group of worker activists emerged who became known as *praktiki*. The praktiki spearheaded the drive to win for workers a better deal within the emerging capitalist system of production and exchange. They came largely from legal worker organizations, such as unions, worker clubs, and cooperatives and distanced themselves from the ideological disputes of socialist intellectuals. In the prewar years, Russian workers had developed a broad labor movement across a network of autonomous worker institutions. The primary goal of the movement was economic gains.[95] Many of the praktiki had party affiliations but worked across the ideological divides to foster a unity movement among workers and to engage in legal work. The goals of the praktiki were widely supported by workers in spite of the fierce opposition of V.I. Lenin, the leader of the Bolshevik faction of the Russian Social Democratic Party, to the "liquidators," as he named them, and their allies. Many of the elite workers abandoned revolutionary social democracy and joined legal activities in the cooperative movement, mutual aid societies, and cultural societies, or entered parties like the Socialist Revolutionaries that deemphasized class struggle. In 1913 and 1914 there was also a strong revival of the trade union movement throughout the country.[96]

Lenin dismissed the older generation of the worker intelligentsia as a labor aristocracy, trapped in the trade union consciousness he so despised, and placed his hopes on younger workers.[97] The rapid expansion of industry from 1910 to 1914 required a steady flow of new workers from the countryside into the urban factory environment. The young peasant-workers, who filled the jobs, experienced cultural displacement, poor living conditions, and hazing by urban worker sophisticates for their country manners. They had not experienced the upheaval of 1905 and the repression that followed as adults or as workers. Their experience in the city fostered in them a spirit of labor activism, particularly among metalworkers in St. Petersburg.

Mensheviks among the Social Democrats called it *buntarstvo* and condemned it for its lack of clear purpose. Lenin chose to call it class consciousness.[98] St. Petersburg metalworkers, especially the rebellious youth among them, were not, however, typical of workers throughout the country. Lenin's hopes that younger workers were better exemplars of proletarian class consciousness than the labor elites were largely misplaced. Diane Koenker notes that in Moscow education through night classes drew young workers into larger social networks.[99] The same was true among many youthful workers in the capital and in other industrial centers. Calls from leading Social Democrats like Aleksandr Bogdanov for the creation of a unique proletarian culture that imbued art, philosophy, and science with proletarian class values went unheeded. Workers preferred to assimilate the culture of the educated and shape it to their own perceptions or more often to join with other social groups in consuming the new commercial culture.[100]

The extent of the influence that the Bolsheviks exercised over workers before the war remains contested in the historiography. Robert McKean, for example, argued that Bolshevik propaganda played little role in the radicalization of workers in St. Petersburg. "The trade unions, the social insurance institutions (*kassy*), the legal press, the educational societies and representation in the State Duma," he contended, "all proved incapable of providing Bolsheviks with a secure, permanent, mass base among the city's working population." Heather Hogan, on the contrary, maintained that though the Bolsheviks were fractious and organizationally weak, their way of seeing society made sense and metalworkers in particular were drawn to them.[101] It is true that the Bolshevik endorsement of illegal activities appealed to many young metalworkers in St. Petersburg, where a frustrating atmosphere of severe police repression restricted legal outlets for worker activities. In 1913 Lenin demonstrated his tactical skill by associating Bolshevism with the unity movement that was popular with workers. The tactic weakened support for the Mensheviks among workers committed to the socialist cause and gave rise to some gains by the Bolsheviks in worker organizations.

In the empire as a whole, however, and even in the capital, support for legal labor organs was on the rise and not declining by 1913. St. Petersburg had by far the highest level of labor activism. Living and working conditions in the capital and especially severe police repression fostered active resistance to the tsarist order. Even in St. Petersburg, however, the primary goal of such activism was to put an end to the tsarist-police regime. To the disgust of socialist intellectuals, the better-off and better-educated workers tended to move away from illegal and radical approaches to change and worked instead to advance their individual and group interests through legal worker-controlled organizations. Far from seeking to dispense with capitalism, most workers sought to defend their interests within it and to improve wages, working conditions, and social security provisions.

PEASANTS BETWEEN THE OLD AND THE NEW

If workers were diverse in conditions, interests, and opportunities, peasants were even more heterogeneous. Conditions for farming, land use practices, and types of tenure varied widely across the empire. Russia had at least twelve agricultural regions distinguished by climate, soil conditions, and the availability of water.[102] Before the emancipation in 1861–1863, landlord estate agriculture had prevailed in western, central, and southern regions of the country. Serfdom for peasants in those areas was an experience of private and, at times, personal exploitation. Elsewhere the state was the landlord, and the conditions of the serfs had quite different dimensions and effects. A small number of peasants had lived on crown lands, that is, land owned by the royal family, where conditions for the serfs were different from those on landlord or state lands. The various historical experiences of the peasants shaped attitudes toward the land and authority that differed from region to region. These attitudes were still operative in 1913.

In addition to ethnic and regional differences, there were divisions within villages themselves. The repartitional commune was intended over the years to match the labor capacity of families to the amount of land the family held in use. Such a system allowed for significant disparities in income among families, especially if repartitions rarely or never took place. The ability of individual peasants to buy land in addition to their communal holdings could further widen the gap between the richest and the poorest peasants in the village. The labor capacity of a family was only a partial check on land acquisition, since labor for hire was available in most villages. Although the law required villages to provide for landless members or those unable to care for themselves, many lived in abject poverty. Women who were or became single were often particularly disadvantaged. Peasants who derived regular nonagricultural income from cottage production or trade could also separate themselves from other villagers in terms of purchasing power.

Remittances from family members employed outside the village also supported income disparities within the villages. The abolition in 1903 of
collective responsibility for payment of taxes and other dues deprived the
commune of a tool to level incomes among village members.

The Stolypin reform, initially at least, underlined differences and increased tensions among peasants. Peasants responded variously according
to their conditions and needs. Some were reluctant to change; others seized
upon the opportunity. Few peasants were passive, and most took an active part in achieving acceptable outcomes. Coercion played only a minor
role in achieving the goals of the reform.[103] The government recognized
the diversity of conditions among the peasants from region to region and
ruled out a single, unified process. Land transformation was intended to be
gradual, voluntary, and alterable as experience dictated. Officials believed
that peasants would themselves seek change if they had examples before
them of what was possible. Peasants disagreed among themselves, however.
Until 1911 any peasant wishing to separate required the prior consent of the
commune. Many sought to leave but consent was often withheld.[104]

The government initially charged the gentry land captains with inform-
ing peasants about the reforms. Many of them at first did little or nothing
to implement the reform, and the government had to urge them to get
out and acquaint the peasants with the terms of the reform. Reproaches
for inaction on the part of local authorities sometimes led to overzealous-
ness on the part of some land captains. Threats to give the best land to
separators were the most common form of coercion when it occurred.
Wherever coercion was used, the incidence of failed farms was highest.[105]
In 1913 A.V. Krivoshein, who headed the Main Administration for Land
Reorganization and Agriculture, forbade the land captains to use police to
enforce compliance and set out a mediation process to facilitate peaceful
change.[106] The role of the land captains in land reorganization projects was
significantly reduced over time. In 1913 land captains directed only 12
percent of all projects whereas land commission members handled 45 percent and surveyors in the employment of the land commissions dealt with
the remaining 43 percent.[107] Peasants gradually began to respond more
favorably to the permanent members of the land settlement commissions,
whom they learned to distinguish from state officials. The commissioners
were prepared to meet with peasants and possessed the skills required to
deal with the practical problems of land settlements.[108]

Peasants had a number of reasons to take part in consolidation of their plots, depending on their particular circumstances. Where markets existed for their produce, peasants often responded to the opportunities available to them. In the northwest and west, agricultural production for the market was well advanced. Hence St. Petersburg, Pskov, Smolensk, Kovno, Novgorod, Vilno, Vitebsk, and Mogilev provinces, for which farming practices in the Baltic provinces provided models, witnessed high rates of participation in the reform. Ukraine and the southwest provinces, where the examples of Polish and Czech farming encouraged innovation, and the provinces of New Russia, Ekaterino-slav, Kharkov, Kherson, Samara, Saratov, Stavropol, and Tauride in the south, with access to the Western grain market through Black Sea ports, also achieved above average consolidations or group land settlements.[109] In these regions, the great majority of consolidations were achieved by village consent. The response was weaker elsewhere, especially in the north, the central industrial region, and the black earth area. Ready markets did not in every case guarantee consolidations. Central Russia and especially the Moscow region had favorable economic conditions but a low percentage of enclosures. In this region few separations were by village consensus; rather they were by individuals. In an area with strong communal traditions, examples of successful enclosures were few and communal solidarity persisted.

Within these regional variations, the responses of peasants to the opportunities provided by the reform depended heavily on the particular situation in which the family found itself. Peasants who had long ago left the land for urban pursuits but had retained a claim on communal land often hastened to assert their claim in order to sell the land. Peasants with small allotments or those who faced reductions in their allotments at the next repartition often took the land in hereditary tenure, some to sell it and leave agriculture and others to preserve what they had. Some peasants chafed under the restraints of communal tenure and wanted to escape it. Land-poor peasants welcomed the opportunity to intensify production on consolidated plots, which communal membership had inhibited.[110] Any family thwarted by communal decisions in its ambition to use a disproportionate share of the communal land found leverage in the reform to get what it wanted. Petitions by individual members to consolidate and withdraw their lands from the commune affected everyone in the village. Many villagers defended themselves against individual withdrawals by undertaking group settlements that involved the whole village, but did not in all cases entail plot consolidations.[111]

Defensiveness was one reason for the participation of villagers in the reform. The numerous positive benefits, however, were even greater incentives. Many who had long wished to sell their land were now able to do so to the benefit of others in the village. About one million peasants sold their allotment shares to about eight million households. A government survey of the sale of consolidated plots in five provinces showed that of 30,200 plots sold wholly or in part, 37 percent of their sellers did not engage in agriculture but worked in cities, 14 percent resettled in Siberia, 5.6 percent used the proceeds to buy land from the Peasant Bank, less than 1 percent found work elsewhere in the economy, and the remainder entered the landless labor force. Many of those who sold a portion of their land had holdings of 15 dessiatinas or more. They used the proceeds to buy cattle, renovate their houses, buy equipment, or build granaries on the remaining land.[112]

In 1913 the average communal holding in 47 provinces of European Russia was 7.1 dessiatinas, whereas the average consolidated holding was 9.8 dessiatinas. In those provinces the use of hired labor increased as did the number of new tools per household. In addition the Peasant Bank facilitated the sale of about 10 million dessiatinas of private or state lands to peasants. Landless peasants and peasants with six dessiatinas of land or fewer purchased almost 70 percent of all lands sold by the bank. Only a small proportion of purchased land went to wealthy peasant buyers.[113] Rich peasants not only bought little land but were less likely to separate from the commune than small and middle peasants.[114] On larger farms there was greater demand on their available labor in the spring through fall months, and such farms preferred to graze their cattle on communal land using common labor. Open fields assured access to grazing. It was to the advantage of many peasants with large holdings to preserve the grazing practices that the communal structure provided. Small to middle-scale farmers who had a high ratio of labor to unit of land had more to gain from consolidation and new land use practices. The decline in the number of livestock on their lands suggests that many of these farmers solved their grazing and fodder problems by reducing their livestock and turning to cash crops.

Agricultural innovation did not necessarily follow from land consolidation. In the northwestern and western provinces, the three-field system of crop rotation had begun to give way to clover and grass seeding well before the land reform was implemented. A majority of peasants in the region used clover in rotation with the main crop of flax by 1913. Improved crop rotations were, therefore, widespread in that area. In other regions, however, new individual farmers often continued the rotations they had learned in the commune. In the steppe region only a small minority of separators established new rotation regimens. In areas where market gardening and viticulture were possible, as in the Crimea, the pull of the export grain market actually slowed crop differentiation and innovation.[115] An obstacle to innovation for individual farmers was lack of funds. The start-up costs of an enclosed farm were considerable. By 1915 only 16 percent of such farms had loans and another 4 percent held grants.[116] Separators faced other challenges. Peasants who lost access to communal pastures usually had insufficient land to graze cattle and insufficient resources to stall-feed them year round. The result was a reduction in the number of cattle on enclosed lands.[117]

Land reform sought, among other things, to reduce multistripping, the interspersion of village holdings, and the distance to fields that peasants had to travel. The results of land reorganization were impressive. Before the reform 5.9 percent of peasant households in European Russia held between 60 and 100 separate strips of land and 7 percent had from 40 to 60 strips. Another 28.6 percent farmed between 21 and 39 strips and only 9.8 percent had the luxury of working from one to three strips. After land reorganization 26.4 percent of households had a single plot and the remainder held from two to three plots. As a result the 7 percent of land formerly devoted to borders between strips was significantly reduced. Much of the work of the land reorganization commissions went to disentangling the overlapping holdings of various villages. Plot consolidation greatly reduced that problem. Land reorganization also vastly reduced distances to fields. Before the reform only 22.1 percent of households had fields within a verst of their cottage. After land reorganization 49.9 percent of households lived within a verst of their fields. The percentage of those with fields greater than five versts from home fell from 36.7 percent to 17 percent.[118] The resettlement program also produced significant results. In spite of the hardships suffered by many settlers and the highly negative impact of settlement on indigenous nomadic peoples, the government could point to the migration of around 4 million settlers and the expansion of the crop areas of central Siberia and northern Kazakhstan from 11.5 million acres to 24 million acres between 1905 and 1914.[119]

In spite of the benefits that it brought, some peasants initially resisted the land reform. Peasants objected less to the goals of the reform than to the way authorities tried to implement it in its early stages. They especially resented the incentives offered by the state to commune members who were willing to leave the commune and establish khutors. As separations occurred, disputes over land reallocation and transfer grew. The reform disrupted traditional norms of peasant land transfer but failed to provide a clearly defined legal alternative. Another problem in the early years of the reform was its emphasis on the creation of individual homesteads of the otrub or khutor types and the allocation of agricultural improvement funds solely to them. The zemstvos successfully resisted the restriction of agricultural assistance and education to separators. From 1910 a compromise was reached in which greater emphasis was placed on group land conversions with partial consolidation, and agricultural education funds were extended to peasants who continued in communal land tenure. The shift toward group solutions to agricultural reform made the process more palatable to peasants.

Most resistance arose over the details of land settlements rather than over the principle of reform. Some peasants engaged in legal petitions and complaints to the land commissions about features of the settlement. Others took illegal actions such as chasing surveyors off the land or obstructing their work by moving surveyor stakes. Women often played leading roles in resistance. Separators could be harassed in various ways. Protestors pulled down their fences, pastured cattle on enclosed land, smashed their windows, and sometimes burned their buildings.[120] There were, however, only five recorded cases of arson involving khutors or otrubs in 1913.[121] George Yaney points out how few violent incidents the reform sparked: 50–60 events in 1911 with a sharp decline in 1912 and 1913.[122]

The reform marked a period of great instability in the villages. Many peasants were selling their land and leaving the village for the city or for resettlement in Siberia. Villagers had either to purchase the land of those departing or risk having it pass into the hands of outsiders.[123] Returnees posed another threat. Village societies were charged with the welfare of all of their members. Many peasants had long left the villages but had preserved some loose claim to allotment land. Quite a few of them now showed up to claim their share. The decoupling of membership in the village society from communal land use made it hard for peasants to resist these claims. Resist they did, however. Since there were no longer mechanisms internal to the village to resolve such disputes, many cases went to the volost' courts for settlement or were passed on to land settlement boards.[124]

The need to resolve disputes over land outside of traditional village practice, often in the courts, contributed to reinforcing peasant legal consciousness. Legal recourse to settle disagreements between peasants was already well developed in peasant culture by 1913. Peasants had differences, knew how to use the legal system, and went to court to get redress. The peasant volost' courts provided justice according to local customary law but were also linked to the higher courts of the land. Peasants respected the verdicts of the courts and paid their fines or went to jail as the judges ordered. In a time of rapid change peasants willingly accepted the law as final arbiter.[125] The volost' courts provided a venue in which to challenge patriarchy or other forms of village arbitrariness. The courts also supported the market economy by enforcing contracts and the integrity of business relationships.[126]

Peasants, at least in some regions, used the courts extensively. In 1913 the volost' courts in Moscow province handled 84,403 cases. That was 78 percent more than they had processed in 1905. In 1910 the crime of personal insult made up 54 percent of cases, an indicator of the peasants' growing sense of self. Fifty-six percent of all misdemeanors involved attacks on personal dignity.[127] The case loads of the volost' courts, which grew larger every year, testify to the courts' wide acceptance by the peasants. *Samosud*, peasant vigilante justice, did not entirely disappear before the war; it was, however, exceptional and reveals almost nothing about the attitudes or values of the great majority of peasants.[128] Arson also sharply declined as a means of peasant justice. In 1907 there were 106 reported cases of arson in the countryside. The number fell to 50 in 1908, 25 in 1912, 21 in 1913, and only two in the first seven months of 1914.[129] It would be inappropriate to generalize on the basis of regional studies, but by 1913 legal consciousness, that is, "an accepted resort to law" was taking hold among segments of the peasantry to a striking degree and conditions were right for its continued spread.[130]

The complex response of the peasants to the Stolypin land reform illustrates the impossibility of standardizing or universalizing peasant experience or attitudes in Russia. The regional differentiation of the peasants and their widely varying historical experiences were reflected in the outcomes of the reform in specific places and contexts.[131] Individual families responded to the reform according to their particular circumstances. The aim of those who stayed was to maximize their own access to village resources. Others took the opportunity to sell their village assets and take on different economic roles. The reality of the peasantry was one in which individuals made their own choices about their interactions with the rest of the world. In her study of the volost' courts Jane Burbank warns against collectivizing the people.[132] Peasants appeared in the courts as individuals. Men and women went to court in order to settle their disputes over money and resources and to determine social responsibility. The result was the incremental transformation of authority relationships in families and villages, which undermined rural tradition even more effectively than did urban influences.

Conscription, Taxes, and the Individual

Other forces were at work to undermine estate identity and noble privilege and to strengthen self-identity. The military reform of 1874, which introduced universal military service, formally ended the old estate structure in the army and created conditions that gradually weakened the monopoly of the nobility in the officer corps.[133] Universal conscription signified civic equality. The reform enabled the gradual growth of professionalism in the army, which was still proceeding in 1913. It also began to alter the attitude of the military toward society. Changes in warfare demanded a new kind of soldier. The firepower of modern weapons precluded the traditional massing of soldiers and neutralized centralized command. A soldier often needed to make his own decisions on the field of battle and summon his inner moral forces to check his fear. The military recognized that training alone could not produce the qualities and skills needed to perform well in service. Society had to internalize the values and motivation that the military expected of its soldiers and instill them into every citizen. Good citizenship and effective military service required a morally independent individual, yet one whose individualism was tempered by loyalty to the greater good of the nation. The civic nature of recruitment also shifted the focus of military service from the dynasty to the nation. Civic equality and the individualism it nurtured were ultimately inimical to the estate structure of society.[134]

A counterpoint to the trend toward greater inclusion in army recruitment and an object lesson in the ambiguities plaguing the modernization process in the empire was an attempt mounted in the wake of the revolution of 1905 to preserve the essence of the old officer corps. Especially difficult was the role of non-Russian nationalities. Religion had been the principal grounds for exclusion from a career in the army, and in practice those exclusions remained. Concerned, however, that Russian and Orthodox predominance might be eroded in the new era of greater civic equality and religious toleration, the Ministry of War in 1905 proposed a system of national quotas in the officer corps proportional to the percentage of each national group in the population but with Russians constituting at least 75 percent of officers. The plan suffered from problems concerning the definition of nationality and was never properly implemented. Instead, in 1913 the army reinstated the old exclusions on religious grounds and prevented non-Orthodox officers and various nationalities from serving in the more critical branches of the military.[135] Such an approach was far from the inclusion that an integrated civic society demanded and that universal conscription in the ranks mandated.

Tax reform, too, was shifting the focus of the state from the group to the individual and undermining estate identities. From the 1860s the person rather than the collective was the subject of taxation in the Russian Empire. The establishment of legal individual accountability for taxes brought the individual face-to-face with the state in a way not previously seen. It underscored the civic duty of individuals and recognized their participation in the business of governance. When the peasant redemption payments ended in 1906, the last vestige of collective responsibility for taxation was gone. Property taxes, business taxes, and apartment taxes were now levied on individuals. The nobility retained some tax exemptions as an estate, but they, too, were subject to apartment taxes. Proposals for the introduction of a tax on individual income won wide support in state circles and among the public. The right believed that income taxes linked the individual to the state; liberals took comfort in the recognition of the individual by the state that the tax implied. Vested industrial and landed interests opposed an income tax and sought exemptions. But both the Ministry of Finance and the State Duma stayed the course and resisted exceptions. Women who earned incomes were taxed as individuals, a major step toward the recognition of women as full legal persons.[136]

Like military service, the direction of tax reform advanced the idea of citizenship in Russia, a goal still far from full realization by 1913. The gulf between officers and men in the army remained immense, and the habits and attitudes of the old feudal army persisted, especially in the officer corps. The discussion of the income tax law dragged on; the tax was not introduced until 1916, when revenues to support the war were desperately needed. In the initial planning, the relatively high level of income needed to enter the income tax–paying class excluded most workers and peasants, who continued to bear a huge burden of indirect taxation. Officials doubted that civic consciousness was high enough among Russians to guarantee accurate voluntary reporting by individuals of their income. By 1916 the decline in the value of the rouble, the loss of revenues from the vodka monopoly as a result of prohibition, rising prices for agricultural goods, and a government decision to draw more of the population into active citizenship saw the income threshold drop from 1,000 to 850 roubles. As a result, when the tax came into effect a majority of the population qualified as income tax payers, although the mechanisms to assess and collect the tax were not in place. Taxation policy recognized the participation of citizens in the state but still provided no link between the paying of taxes and political representation.[137]

Conclusion

The estate structure conferred collective rights and a measure of identity on the social groups of the empire. It did not, however, unduly restrict Russians either in their ambitions or their ability to realize them. There was little loyalty of members to their estate. In response to new avenues of social mobility, able and ambitious peasants sought to leave agriculture. Some shed their peasant estate status and entered the petty commercial class. Others officially joined the organized meshchane, where they enjoyed a set of rights that better suited their aims. Peasants were not sharply set apart from the rest of society but moved into new roles and status. As Burbank argues, there was no collective peasant mentality of antielitism.[138] Nor did the existence of separate courts that based their decisions on customary law inhibit the growth of a legal consciousness among the peasantry. On the contrary, the volost' courts reinforced the peasants' sense of individual rights and dignity as well as their understanding of property and the nature of contractual relationships. As modernizing forces assailed the traditional arrangements of the villages, the courts served to facilitate the peaceful negotiation of new relationships, rights, and authority structures. The courts promoted greater awareness of legality among the peasants and were sites for the emergence of notions of citizenship.

The opening of commerce and business to all in 1898 removed the last formal restrictions on the growth of a commercial middle class. Nobles had long had entry to it in any case. Now able people from other estates could freely enter the world of business. In that world the estate structure posed no formal obstacle to social mobility. The children of merchants regularly entered professional occupations and merged their identity with professionals and intelligentsia. Collectively the commercial, professional, and intelligentsia segments of society were merging into a complex middle class. Workers' identity was also in flux. Self-help was strong among articulate workers, who increasingly took part in the pleasures of an emerging commercial culture that appealed across class lines to bourgeois and worker alike and shaped their values. New forms of organization increasingly gave a public voice to the aspirations and needs of social groups. The panic expressed at the congress of the United Nobility that estate distinctions were losing their force was well founded. Estate lines that had never been impermeable were increasingly porous. By 1913 the negotiation of new relationships among social groups was well advanced, and the shape of a broad civil society had clearly emerged.

SOCIAL INTEGRATION AND CIVIL SOCIETY

The emergence of a complex class society that coexisted with the old social estate structure was well advanced in Russia by 1913. The social estates had themselves significantly changed by then. Economic pressures and the opportunities they created had reshaped them from within. Old estate-based institutions were taking on new functions dictated by changing economic and political realities. Differentiation among classes was matched by growing differentiation within classes. Economic and social pluralism, the hallmark of modernity, was by 1913 a feature of Russian society. What many contemporaries saw as social disintegration was in reality an early stage in the constitution of a new social order in the context of an emerging market economy. A number of forces were at work that were integrating the amorphous middle levels of urban Russian society and drawing some workers into the middle-class ambit. Growing individualism was accompanied by the formation of a whole range of civil associations and activities that organized individuals around common endeavors, often across class divides. A new commercial popular culture drew individuals of various classes into a broadly shared framework of cultural reference that blurred traditional cultural and social boundaries. These developments enabled the formation of the multiple individual identities and attachments that constituted the foundations of civil society and strengthened the public sphere.

THE RUSSIAN EMPIRE AND CIVIL SOCIETY

This chapter deals with relations among social groups in the context of an emerging civil society. Civil society has proven to be an elusive concept. Most recently, its more extreme proponents have positioned it as the cornerstone of liberty, which staves off the tyranny of the state, on the one hand, and of private wealth, on the other. In this view, civil society breaks down the existing order and seeks to establish a new order rooted in moral choices. It is civil society that undermines bureaucracy and overcomes barriers that exclude citizens from participating in social benefits. Such a view posits a fundamental antagonism between state and society. Although more moderate proponents seek to create a balance among civil society, politics, and economics rather than privileging civil society, they also preserve them as opposing spheres.[1] Others have recognized areas of cooperation between state and civil society in the past. They point out that historically some European monarchies actively encouraged the formation of civic groups in the public sphere to advance scientific, charitable, and cultural goals. Such a view posits a basic harmony between the state and civil society, but one in which the state keeps a wary eye on its partners in the public sphere.[2]

The meaning of society in pre–World War I Russia is problematical and complicates the discussion of Russian civil society. Obshchestvo refers to society in the broad sociological sense but in the literature more often means something much narrower. During the second half of the nineteenth century obshchestvo came to denote a group of self-selected and self-designated educated individuals who were knowledgeable about the arts and sciences, had a grasp of social relations, believed in progress, and were critical of the autocratic state and its supporters.[3] Obshchestvo and intelligentsia were closely associated social phenomena. Their adherents shared an ethos of criticism of the regime and service to the narod. By 1913 the remnant of the militant intelligentsia distinguished itself from the rest of obshchestvo by the rigor of its beliefs, its pride in refusing to collaborate with the state or to assist in the advancement of Russian capitalism and, in some cases, its determination to end the old order through revolution.[4]

Closely associated with obshchestvo is *obshchestvennost'* (public-mindedness), which some students of Russian history equate with civil society.[5] Like obshchestvo, obshchestvennost' is a construct of the second half of the nineteenth century. It was the embodiment of the principled opposition of obshchestvo to the autocratic state as well as of civic-mindedness in the interest of the great mass of the population. The original moral connotations of obshchestvennost' as principled opposition to the autocratic state continue to influence historians' interpretation of civil society in pre–World War I Russia. Such a reading has transferred into the historiography the perception of members of obshchestvo as the self-appointed leaders of social and cultural progress in Russia and tutors to the masses. It works to restrict the scope of civil society and the public sphere and to perpetuate notions about deep divisions between social groups. In some cases it even assumes an implacable opposition between "society" and state. In recent historiography, civil society in Russia has been defined more broadly as "a mass of educated individuals, voluntary associations, journalistic media, professional societies, universities, patronage networks, cultural organizations, and other structures that establish intermediate identities between family and state."[6] Although more comprehensive than earlier enumerations, this definition still holds out education as a principal criterion of membership in civil society. In light of pre-twentieth-century notions of civil society even this remains a restrictive list.

In the eighteenth century, civil society theorists linked civil society to property ownership. Civil society was generalized private property and was located between individual property and the state. It was a bracing social sphere that expanded human needs and capacities, produced material wealth and culture, and was the foundation of freedom. It was also a sphere of inequality, conflict, and market anarchy and one from which many were excluded.[7] For the Scottish theorists Adam Smith and Adam Ferguson, civil society was not only a sphere of market exchange but an ethical sphere as well in which the interests and passions of individuals were not only realized but constituted through mutual recognition. It was the sphere in which people sought the respect, approval, and praise of others as the social affirmation of selfhood. In the Scottish philosophers' view, however, it remained a sphere of inequality and partial exclusion.[8]

In the nineteenth century G.W.F. von Hegel agreed with Ferguson that consciousness of self is rooted in the mutual exchange of property. Civil society is a realm of ethics constructed by reciprocal recognition. Hegel understood civil society to be a historical phenomenon rather than a metaphysical entity. For Hegel freedom could not be realized fully in civil society. In civil society individuals find recognition and the satisfaction of wants and needs in corporate groups and freely constituted associations that give affect to the public sphere. Corporations and associations provide security and teach members a sense of belonging. They advance the interests of their members within the larger society. Some individuals, however, are excluded from corporate life. Only the state, Hegel argued, can reconcile the conflicting particular interests of corporate groups and include all the members of society. Only the state makes the ethical realm of civil society concrete.[9]

Karl Marx shared many of Hegel's views about civil society. Both wanted to bring private morality into the public sphere and both understood civil society to be historically rooted. Marx, however, believed that far from resolving the conflict of particular wills in society, the state only justified them. Marx believed that community and citizenship in the political realm gave a public character to the individual. With the breakdown of feudal corporate society under capitalism, however, civil society was reduced to an arena of individual conflict. When the individual solely pursued his self-interest at the expense of other individuals, civil society was deprived of its communal and public features and was reduced to a sphere of conflicting personal interests, lacking communal mutuality. In a state of competing egos communal mutuality existed only in the political sphere. The goal for Marx was to return communality to the civil sphere by overcoming the clash of egos that bourgeois-capitalist society nurtured and reuniting civil and political society.[10]

The classical description of civil society as a robust sphere of social interaction within a developing market economy is applicable to the history of Russia in the prewar years. Market relations were growing rapidly and the exchange of property and commodities was engaging wider and wider segments of the population. The public sphere consisted of old and new corporate entities and associations that pursued their interests within the new economy. Despite the limitations placed on them by the state, freely constituted and maintained associations grew and even flourished. They taught members the habits of belonging and the practice of democratic organization.[11] Russian civil society was a sphere of inequality, conflict, and exclusion but also one increasingly constitutive of individual selfhood. Demands for respect and dignity and for individual and group acceptance were the leitmotifs of social relations in the prewar years. Russian civil society was a sphere of material and cultural production increasingly based on market forms. A new commercial culture functioned to draw parts of the public closer to one another, to form and refine tastes, and to shape new values. A modernist elite culture challenged the cultural norms of the past. Just as obshchestvo was a part of civil society but not the whole of civil society, obshchestvennost' was part of a broader process of the self-realization of individuals in an evolving economic and social environment.[12]

Following the Scottish and Hegelian tradition, Ernest Gellner has argued that liberty is impossible without pluralism, which rests on the division of labor and economic decentralization. Economic pluralism imposes limits on central political authority by restricting it to defined roles. Liberty also depends on the existence of a multiplicity of autonomous associations and institutions. Freedom of individual conscience requires the existence of an autonomous sphere, where rights reside, that is clearly distinct from other spheres, whether political or religious. Civil society both permits individualism without loss of political effectiveness and enables citizens' participation in a variety of associations that do not stifle the individual. In civil society citizens can enter associations and institutions without total surrender to them and leave them without the stigma of treason. The fundamental feature of civil society is that no ideology or institution enjoys a monopoly. No single doctrine rises above others and uniquely defines the social order.[13]

By 1913 Russia was rapidly attaining the economic and social pluralism, multiple identities, and variety of social institutions that support civil society. The impediments to the full development of civil society in Russia were, however, still both numerous and large. The division of the population into legal estates, however unstable they had become, preserved in the empire the remnants of what Gellner calls a segmentary society, in which the individual is seen as an integral part of a social unit.[14] Such a society precludes civil society, and its partial persistence in Russia slowed the transition to a new civic consciousness. The bureaucratic state had deeply entrenched interests that long preceded the emergence of civil society and also hindered its realization.[15] Although its hold on the state was weakening, the landed nobility, unlike the more socially conscious commercial-industrial class, used the considerable influence that remained to it within state circles to advance its corporate interests, which it raised above the interests of the nation. In a multinational empire, traditional ethnic, religious, and other group identities often remained paramount and slowed the development of the multiple legal, economic, and moral individual identities on which civil society is built.[16]

During the nineteenth century in much of Western Europe the withholding of social and political rights from lower social groups fostered class organization and the demand to expand civil society and citizenship beyond the upper and middle classes. At the heart of European socialism was the demand for social inclusion and political participation expressed in popular suffrage. Wherever civil society and citizenship were extended to the lower classes, radicalism faded. Wherever social exclusion and the denial of full economic and political participation persisted, radicalism grew.[17] By 1913 the example of successful civil societies elsewhere in Europe only fueled popular frustration at its slow advance in Russia. It was, however, advancing as it had elsewhere. Attitudes about inclusion were changing, even within the government. Most of the elements of civil society were in place in the Russian Empire in 1913, but impediments to its proper functioning persisted.

The Making of a Middle Class

The link between civil society and the growth of a middle class is tenuous. On the one hand, civil society arises from the development of the market economy, which promotes the growth of a commercial middle class. On the other, as the market develops it engages people from various classes in the public sphere, who can also advocate the values of civil society. Much has been made of Russia's "missing" middle class and the effects of its absence on the prospects for civil society.[18] By 1913 the middle class was far from absent: The great size of the population of the Russian Empire compared to other European nations meant that in absolute numbers the middle groups of Russian society were comparatively large by 1913. They were also growing. Industry, banking, cooperatives, trade, insurance, and local government among others employed larger and larger numbers, education engaged many more, the production and dissemination of print materials occupied an expanding group, and the service industry, from small retailers and their employees to hairdressers and telephone operators, rapidly grew. As a proportion of the whole population, however, the middle groups of Russian society remained small compared to those in most other European societies.

The historiography broadly identifies two factors that help to account for the weakness of civil society in Russia before the war and its limited potential for growth. The first proposes that the effectiveness of the Russian middle class was hindered not only by its small size but by its fragmentation or its failure to coalesce into an effective, united force, as well as by its near exclusion from political power. Some historians see the lack of cohesion within the middle class as a major factor contributing to the revolutionary outcome in Russia. At work in this interpretation is a fundamental misunderstanding of the nature of what has been called bourgeois society in the nineteenth and early twentieth centuries. In her study of French society in the hundred years from 1750 to 1850, Sarah Mirza undermines what she calls the myth of the bourgeoisie, that is, "the myth constructed by modern historians of a hegemonic, self-conscious, and more or less unified bourgeoisie."[19] Peter Gay, the leading authority on the European bourgeoisies in the pre–World War I period, notes that to understand them the historian has to deal with "pervasive conflicts" among them as well as qualities that aligned them. Conflict arose on a wide front, from the location of a railway to differences over tariffs, religious beliefs, ideological convictions, or the proper place of women in society. They were also divided by accomplishment and status. Bourgeois society was hierarchical but also dynamic. Social mobility was a fact for some in the bourgeoisie and an aspiration, often frustrated, for many. Disdain for those below, jealousy of those above—such were the markers of middle class existence.

The great majority of the bourgeoisie of Europe struggled to make ends meet and lived in fear of falling back into the working class. The precariousness of their position caused them to cling all the harder to the bourgeois manners and morals that distinguished them from those below and which the ambitious from below sought to acquire. For all their diversity, the bourgeoisie shared certain values, particularly the belief in individual autonomy and dignity. The bourgeois ideal was to live as free, but self-disciplined, individuals within the context of family and stable political and social institutions.

Gay points out as well that the supposed political dominance of the bourgeoisie in most West European countries as the nineteenth century advanced was as much an imaginary creation of their opponents as it was a reality. Gains were made but the great diversity of the middle groups of society and the persistence of the aristocracy places in doubt the reality of a unified bourgeois hegemony.[20]

In two provocative essays on the German bourgeoisie in the nineteenth century, David Blackbourn and Geoff Eley decoupled what they reluctantly called the bourgeois revolution in Germany from liberal political success in imperial politics. Instead, a silent revolution occurred in Germany that encompassed a set of "material, institutional, legal and intellectual changes" that created conditions for the development of industrial capitalism and were mirrored in changes in civil society.[21] Such changes were pervasive in society and established a new social norm by stealth. The social impact of these changes in Germany was particularly apparent in cities, which engaged in a broad range of housing, public health, local financing, educational, social security, and labor initiatives.[22] Blackbourn and Eley point out that the forms of the bourgeois revolution were not the same from nation to nation.[23] Conditions in Russia differed from those in Germany in important ways, but elements of the silent bourgeois revolution of Germany with its pervasive norms and values were also apparent in Russia as urbanization, industrialization, and market relationships intensified in the early twentieth century.

The second obstacle believed to have impeded the growth of civil society in Russia was the divide in urban areas between educated society and the working class. Writing in the mid-1960s Leopold Haimson posited the existence of a "dangerous split" in urban centers between an obshchestvo, which had since 1905 reclaimed the great majority of the intelligentsia and was even attracting some elements of the worker intelligentsia, and the mass of industrial workers, who were dissatisfied with their lot and subject to the propaganda of revolutionaries. He argued that the trend among workers toward moderation after 1905 ceased in the summer of 1912 in the wake of the moral enormity of the Lena goldfields massacre.[24] Nearly 35 years later he supplemented but did not significantly change his opinion about the polarity in cities between educated society and industrial workers, although he justifiably regretted the way in which some of his arguments had become stereotypes in the literature.[25] Haimson's formulation has a compelling simplicity but fails to capture the social complexity of Russian cities by 1913. Moreover, his case with regard to the attitudes of the proletariat rested heavily, as he acknowledges, on St. Petersburg workers, in particular metalworkers. Neither their experience nor their actions, as we have already seen, were typical of workers generally.

Workers—Proletarians or Middle Class in Waiting?

Not all Russian labor historians have adopted Haimson's point of view. Nevertheless, it has left a profound mark on the historiography about worker radicalism and the way some loosely defined entity called obshchestvo related to workers. In her otherwise nuanced study of the Association of Southern Coal and Steel Producers, Susan McCaffray notes that although workers in the Donbass struck less often than workers in St. Petersburg and were less politically articulate, cases of labor disturbances, indiscipline, and violence "must have preoccupied the engineer-managers, even if they did not often make their way into the pages of their proceedings and reports." Here the absence of evidence is outweighed by the hypothesis of worker-society polarity. So powerful is it that everything can be read as a sign of the militant disposition of workers, even drunkenness.[26]

A great deal of effort over the years has gone into the search for evidence of proletarian or revolutionary consciousness among workers. For Marxists social classes and class consciousness were objective entities produced by forces embedded in history and capable of empirical evaluation. Whatever value Marxism retains as a tool of social analysis it has proven to be an inadequate guide to the nature of historical change and especially revolutionary causation. Capitalist factory discipline did not give birth to proletarian consciousness in the way that Marx understood it; advanced capitalism did not give way to the dictatorship of the proletariat, socialism, and communism as Marx believed it would. Proletarian consciousness was not an objective entity arising from historical necessity. Instead, intellectuals constructed a discourse of class war, proletarian consciousness, and revolution that they attempted to instill in a worker audience. Socialist ideologists positioned the proletariat as the driver of their own salvationist goals for mankind.[27] In Russia, a large proportion of workers, perhaps a majority, especially those who worked in small-scale or artisan enterprises, were subjected to little or no systematic exposure to this discourse. Other workers encountered it at various levels of intensity and assimilated it to their own perceptions and needs.

That the specific idea of a liberating proletarian consciousness was a construct of intellectuals and not the objective consequence of workers' historical experience should not be construed to mean that workers had no goals of their own or ideas about how to achieve them. The drive to organize in defense of workers' interests and the push toward individual improvement through self-help and mutual aid were characteristics of working-class movements everywhere. At times workers' ambitions led them into alliances with socialist intellectuals. Such alliances tended to be unstable and impermanent and advanced workers' interests far more than they forwarded the utopian plans of the intellectuals. Recent studies have rightly emphasized the agency of workers in pursuing individually and, at times, collectively the outcomes they desired for themselves. By 1913 what at least some workers wanted was becoming increasingly clear among the more articulate and better-paid segments of the working class.

1—Nicholas II and the heir, Alexei, at Livadiia in 1913

2—The Main Gate—Kostroma Tercentenary Exhibition Village

3—Street—Kostroma Tercentenary Exhibition Village

(left) 4—Agricultural Implement Display Shed—Kostroma Tercentenary Exhibition Village

(below) 5—View of the Heavy Industry Pavilions—Kostroma Tercentenary Exhibition Village

(above, left) 6—Agricultural train en route, 1913

(above, right) 7—A lineup for a lecture

(left) 8—Peasants and instructor in a display car

9—Peasant auditors in the train's lecture car

Reflecting on the mentality and behavior of European workers in the period of the revolutions of 1848, Alexander Herzen concluded that the worker was a future bourgeois. Bourgeois society, he complained, effaced individuality but "these effaced persons are better fed" and their "prosperity increases."[28] Herzen deplored, for aesthetic reasons, the mass society and culture that the triumph of the bourgeoisie entailed. His prediction, however, has largely been borne out as workers have entered bourgeois civil society, joined and made their own contributions to mass culture, and broadly assimilated to middle-class values. Even socialism served as a school of liberalism. Since for Marxists scientific and technological culture and culture in general were cumulative, they welcomed the assimilation by the working class of the cultural developments of the past and the discipline and values of capitalist organization. Such was the case in Russia, where in 1913 the Bolshevik newspaper *Pravda* hailed the proletariat as the guardians of the cultural heritage of Russia.[29] Similarly, Russian socialists, especially the Mensheviks, believed that civil and individual liberties were a precondition of a successful mass labor movement and promoted those quintessentially liberal objectives. Marxists believed that although workers assimilated the achievements of the bourgeoisie, proletarian consciousness would in time enable them to transcend their bourgeois teachers and overcome the exploitation of a class-based social order. For this reason, liberal and socialist cultural work among the masses had much in common. The culture and values, particularly the ideal of the self-conscious individual, which both liberals and socialists wished to instill in the masses, were strikingly similar, and their assimilation by the masses signaled success for parties representing both viewpoints.

City living gave birth to new skills and built self-confidence and self-respect among workers. Literacy opened their minds to new ideas and experiences. Consumerism fed both hopes for betterment and envy of those who had achieved it.[30] Above all urban life pulled some workers into the world of civil society. The desire of workers to take part in the larger cultural and social concerns of society found expression in numerous ways. Workers were participating in growing numbers in cultural and educational self-improvement projects. These included courses, lectures, and events organized by intellectuals for workers but also activities created and run by workers themselves. The most educated among workers did not seek to create a new culture or to perpetuate a folk culture but wanted to assimilate established intellectual culture, especially the realist tradition of the nineteenth century, a preference they shared with many in the lower middle classes. Like many among the intelligentsia, educated workers who promoted the cultural development of fellow workers deplored the effects of commercial popular culture on the masses.[31] Participation in "high" culture or noncommercial culture signaled, in their view, respectability and suitability for inclusion in full citizenship.

In order to assert their autonomy but also to underline the cultural values they shared with other classes, some workers began to organize their own cultural activities. An example was the theater. The performance of folk plays was a long-established aspect of factory culture in Russia. Young, skilled workers, however, rejected folk theater and formed groups to choose and perform their own repertoire from the Russian and foreign classics. These same workers were active participants in study circles and evening courses, read the journals of the intellectuals, attended the theater, visited museums, and joined literary-dramatic societies. One of the historians of worker theater, Anthony Swift, argues that it sought to "promote class solidarity and to signify the proletariat's cultural independence,"[32] that is, separation from other social groups. Later in the essay he comes closer to the mark in concluding that "For both actors and audiences, the performances were an affirmation of their identity as cultivated people who appreciated drama,"[33] that is, an affirmation of identity with educated society. The brief history of the Workers' Theater of St. Petersburg, founded in 1913 bears out the latter interpretation. The director, Pavel Sazonov, a professional actor, understood the mandate of the theater as the performance of "non-tendentious, classless art." The majority of members shared that view, but a minority wanted an ideological commitment. When in 1914 the company invited liberal literary critics to give lectures on the works of Gerhardt Hauptmann and M.E. Saltykov-Shchedrin, the minority resigned from the theater and founded a separate company.[34]

Worker poetry invites a similar interpretation. Not separateness but the smashing of barriers that perpetuated separateness was the goal of much worker literature. Mark Steinberg found that at the core of workers' ethical vision was the demand for dignity. Articulate workers believed in human rights and the equal worth of all individuals. The cult of the individual and individual rights stood at the very heart of the concept of the modern and was a quintessential bourgeois value. In that vein, worker poets developed a discourse of the suffering self. Workers suffered both from the physical pains of accident, hunger, disease, and premature death as well as spiritual loss and emptiness. The suffering was not the suffering of a class but of the injured self. Relief from suffering rested on the "determined self" and not on class struggle. Marxists condemned the focus on personal suffering in much worker poetry as un-proletarian. As Steinberg points out, the suffering in worker poetry dovetailed with the efforts of intellectuals in literature and journalism to document the suffering of the people.[35]

Worker poets did not usually write in popular language or forms but in the literary styles of the Russian classics.[36] Even the theme of individual suffering in their work evoked the alienation and moral struggles of the nineteenth-century literary hero. Class themes were not entirely absent from their work. Worker authors recognized the struggles of fellow workers and rejected an individualism that turned its back on others. Steinberg concludes that while worker poets tried to unite individual and collective themes, their goal was not to create a proletarian culture but to break down the "class barriers that deprived the workers of their full humanity."[37] Elsewhere Steinberg points to a new and growing emphasis in popular fiction and songs on the individual. In the years before World War I, worker writers edited journals for a worker audience that satirized vices such as drunkenness, gambling, and sexism. They portrayed these as moral evils that harmed the individual.[38] Individual failings were most often attributed in popular culture to moral degeneracy rather than to the social environment.[39] The moralistic themes of popular culture are more reminiscent of bourgeois attitudes about self-help, independence, and moral rectitude than of the social analysis of socialist intellectuals. Individualism, the virtue of self-help, legal rights, and other middle-class values were readily absorbed by articulate workers, who sought to enter the civil society that supported them and not to overthrow or transcend it.

The workers' aspirations to participate in civil society were embodied in repeated efforts to participate in public discussion of pressing social issues. Between 1908 and 1911 several unions sent delegates to a variety of congresses with social import. Among them were the Congress of the Representatives from Societies of People's Universities, the Congress of Cooperative Societies, the All-Russian Women's Congress, all in 1908, and the All-Russian Congress of Factory Panel Doctors of 1909. The authorities arrested 20 workers who attended the First All-Russian Congress on the Struggle against Alcohol in 1909–1910, however. The same fate befell worker representatives to the Second All-Russian Congress of Factory Panel Doctors in 1911. The arrests temporarily brought an end to worker representation at congresses and conferences.[40] Workers did not give up, however. In 1913 the Moscow Society of Workers in the Printing Arts petitioned for standing at the upcoming Congress on Public Education.[41]

The role of workers in preparing and implementing the legislation of 1912 that introduced a health insurance plan into large industrial enterprises also illustrates the aspirations of workers to participate in civil society and their willingness to collaborate with others within it. The health insurance law was formulated in St. Petersburg. Representatives from eight metalworking factories worked with employers to produce model rules for the operation of the insurance funds. As Alice Pate has shown, the majority of workers in St. Petersburg not only welcomed the law but their representatives had actively taken part in discussions about it with doctors and factory inspectors as well as employers since 1904.[42] The discussions drew workers into cooperation with other social groups and involved them in the larger sphere of civil society. Clearly, the alienation of workers from liberals as the result of the "liberal treason" of the 1905 revolution has been overstated.

The health insurance legislation mandated the election by workers of representatives to sit on the boards of insurance funds along with a number of state-appointed board members. The law required that elected representatives on the boards should outnumber appointed delegates by at least one. Tensions between appointed and elected members of the boards were endemic.[43] But the work of the boards went forward. In addition to the local insurance fund boards, each province established an oversight commission to monitor the functioning of the boards. The membership of the commissions included the governor, seven officials from concerned government ministries, two representatives of the provincial zemstvo, one of the city duma, two of the agricultural community, and two of the workers. The Insurance Council located in the Ministry of Industry and Trade in St. Petersburg was made up of fifteen bureaucrats, a member of the St. Petersburg city duma, a representative of the St. Petersburg provincial zemstvo, five representatives of appointed health insurance board members, and five representatives of board members elected by workers.

The elections to the local health insurance boards were troubled. Medical insurance was controversial among workers. The tradition that factory owners should provide social services for their workers was strong in Russia. Some workers were reluctant to forgo established benefits for the uncertainties of a new system and boycotted elections. Fearing that the boards would serve as organizing centers for worker dissatisfaction or as venues for socialist propaganda, some owners, especially in St. Petersburg, or as in Moscow where more liberal owners were willing to provide information, the police forbade meetings held to inform workers about the terms of the insurance legislation or its administration. Where workers were willing to hold elections, police often imposed restrictions and hindered balloting. The first large industrial concern in St. Petersburg to hold elections of worker representatives to a health insurance board was the Putilov works in early September 1913. The workers first voted to reject a boycott of the elections that the Social Democrats were advocating. Some eleven thousand of the fifteen thousand workers at the factory then took part in electing forty-five workers and four administrative staff to the insurance board.[44] By the end of 1914 most large-scale factories had functioning elected insurance boards. In 1914 in St. Petersburg alone the funds paid out 2,048,497 roubles in various benefits.[45] However imperfect, the boards were bridges between workers and management, and their operation brought workers into formal and sustained contact with health professionals and other representatives of educated society. The insurance law left many workers out. Workers in Siberia and central Asia were not included in the insurance, and those employed in small-scale operations and artisan workshops were excluded as well.

The health insurance legislation and elections to the insurance boards became bones of contention between the Social Democratic factions in St. Petersburg. Party factionalism was not welcome even to more militant St. Petersburg metalworkers in 1912 and 1913. In early summer 1913, delegates to a meeting of St. Petersburg metalworkers passed a resolution calling on the Bolshevik and Menshevik newspapers to end their polemics. The resolution neatly captured the disparity between the goals of workers and the dreams of intellectuals. The workers were especially critical of the Bolshevik paper *Pravda* which "often twists the meaning of certain decisions and resolutions of the workers out of internal considerations that in no way correspond to the interests and attitudes of the workers." They characterized the parties' presses as the "imaginary leaders of the working masses."

Particularly striking is the moderate nature of the issues the metalworkers singled out in the resolution as important to them. The first concern of the workers was the campaign against alcoholism, followed by the study of the political and economic condition of the country. The workers were especially concerned about the toll that the pending crisis of industry, arising from fuel shortages and the credit squeeze in Europe, might take on them.[46] During the health insurance election campaign Bolsheviks and Mensheviks struggled with one another to control it, going so far as to propose a counter insurance plan. The workers rejected both sides and adopted the original program. They resolutely elected representatives to the insurance boards who supported their interests as they understood them. Pate concludes that the results of the campaign do not support the idea of Bolshevik hegemony among workers. The factional battles of the intellectuals, however, did divert workers from the goal of unity but in no way prevented them from pursuing their real goal, full participation in the benefits of civil society.[47]

Russian liberals, with their commitment to individual over group rights, attempted to reinforce worker aspirations to full citizenship. They emphasized membership in the nation as opposed to a class, and they linked commercial growth and industrial development to the attainment of civil liberties. They appealed particularly to better-educated workers who, they believed, could see beyond the confines of class to the interests that they had in common with other social groups. They supported worker unions and tried to locate them within the larger union movement that incorporated educated society. They positioned liberal politics above class and stressed the need in Russia for political and social instruments for the mediation of social conflicts.[48] Persuading workers to participate in the democratic process was difficult. In the elections to the fourth Duma in 1912 only 20–30 percent of workers in engineering factories voted in the elections in their curia, although plants with higher-skilled workers had higher rates of voting.[49]

The working class in the Russian Empire in 1913 was characterized more by its features of diversity than its unity. The culture, values, and goals of the majority of workers owed little to Marxist intellectuals. The dynamics of urban life afforded industrial workers opportunities to interact in a complex environment with other social groups. The pressure urban life exerted on all social groups to cooperate for survival, growing literacy among workers, and exposure to the penny press, film and other commercialized forms of culture encouraged workers to assimilate to the culture and values of the larger society. While some worker youth were attracted to radical political activity, many more pursued self-improvement. Elite workers often shared the contempt of the intelligentsia for the culture of the middle class, but the majority of workers did not. Many did their best to embrace the new commercial culture that large segments of the middle class also consumed.

SUPPORTS OF CIVIL SOCIETY

The Press

The dissemination of middle-class values and civic virtue was widespread by 1913. A mass circulation press played a large role in creating a common frame of civic reference for the growing middle class and those who aspired to join it. By the beginning of World War I a majority of urban adults regularly read newspapers, and a large proportion of them had some exposure to magazines or journals as well. In 1913 there were 2,075 journals and magazines and 878 newspapers published in the Russian language in the empire. Another 468 journals and magazines and 280 newspapers came out in 25 languages other than Russian. Periodical publications in 1913 embraced 121 specialized topics from politics through humor and cinema to vegetarianism and cycling.[50]

Preliminary censorship of periodicals published in major cities had been removed after 1905, although it remained in force in the provinces. As a result the press, though regularly harassed with fines and occasional incarcerations of responsible editors, remained freer of administrative control than most other organs of public opinion. The censorship distinguished between papers for the educated and those for the masses and disproportionately focused on the latter. The workers' press and that of non-Russians received the lion's share of attention from censors. The periodical press was highly differentiated in content and ideological orientation. The government had its own press as well as tame news agencies that sought to shape the news, especially in the provinces. Some papers received direct government subsidies; others were regularly favored with commissions to print government announcements and decrees. The independent press ran the full range of ideological positions, from the reactionary *Zemshchina* to the conservative *Novoe vremia*, liberal *Russkie vedomosti*, and the Progressive Party's *Utro Rossii*. No socialist papers could be published legally but several came out regularly in any case.[51] The mass circulation press declined to serve narrow political interests and sought instead to advance a broad public interest through detailed factual reporting. In the prewar period journalists developed a different set of attitudes toward their readers from the old intelligentsia. The latter claimed to speak for the mass of readers; the former sought to speak to them. The old intelligentsia wanted to interpret the world for readers, whereas the new writers tried to observe it impartially. Unlike the old intelligentsia, journalists did not feel estranged from the life around them. They encouraged readers to make their own judgments about what they read.[52] They believed that the public had a right to know what the government hoped to conceal and felt a duty to report it. In the bourgeois spirit pervading prewar Russia, reporters promoted social mobility, the growth of individualism, and entrepreneurship. Generally the Russian press was editorially critical of capitalist consumerism but, through advertising and reportage on the modern and the innovative, abetted the spread of a consumer culture. Whatever concerns journalists expressed about the corrupting influence of commercialism on the press in Russia, they served to bridge the gap between the market and the reading public.[53] Advertising of a wide range of products in the major papers was extensive. Many advertisements offered grooming and health products; others focused on fashion and aids to self-improvement. Almost all appealed to upward mobility as the goal of consumption.

The press functioned to bring workers and the middle class together. It consciously strove to fill the gap between the better- and less-educated members of society. Publishers of the mass circulation press tried to build alliances by promoting the civil rights of all groups and defending the poor and underprivileged members of society. The penny press that arose after 1905 attracted new readers. *Gazeta kopeika* appealed to lower-class readers but in such a way as not to frighten a middle-class audience. It was the model for 29 other similar papers throughout the empire by 1911. All served as conduits from the middle class to the workers. The goal of papers like *Gazeta kopeika* was to help lower-class readers feel themselves a part of the larger society and assimilate to liberal attitudes and values. They encouraged women to join together to resist male dominance in society and supported the efforts of individuals to improve themselves and move up the social scale. They encouraged worker moderation and discouraged worker radicalism.[54] In 1913 the factory workforce in St. Petersburg numbered 216,000 and the circulation of *Gazeta kopeika* was 220,000. No figures on how many workers read the paper exist, but it is reasonable to suppose that many did.[55] Before World War I, therefore, the mass circulation press was a forum for the formation and expression of public opinion and a powerful force for political change. It drew workers and middle class into a shared cultural perspective and promoted the values of the middle class among the working class.

Religion

Religion also provided a bridge between workers and other urban groups, especially the lower middle class. Few workers abandoned their faith completely. The economic and time constraints imposed by urban and factory conditions often led, however, to the stripping down of some of the more elaborate Orthodox rituals around weddings or funerals that were common in the villages to their bare essentials in the cities. Most workers continued to baptize their children in spite of the high cost of obtaining a priest. A rise in common law marriages among workers in the early twentieth century signaled the exorbitant cost of formal marriage rites rather than a decline in faith. The rituals of a worker "civil marriage" might include a procession around a church or cathedral before adjournment to an inn for a wedding party.[56] From around 1908 the Orthodox Church witnessed a revival of religious observance among workers. Since women were more likely to practice their faith than men, the increase in church attendance from 1908 in part reflected a significant increase in the proportion of women in the industrial workforce. Observers of the religious scene in cities also noted a new phenomenon among the worker faithful. Increasingly workers sought to inject faith into their daily lives, to develop a critical attitude to religion, and to determine questions of faith for themselves. The desire for personal religious autonomy was accompanied by the wish for lay control in parish affairs.[57] The campaign to increase the role of the laity often brought workers into contact with others beyond their class in their own or nearby parishes.

Some workers did abandon Orthodox religious observance but remained caught up in the spiritual revival that swept through educated circles in the years before World War I. Workers often turned to alternative forms of religious belief after the revolution of 1905. The congregations of Baptists and Evangelicals swelled with lower-class worshippers. Religious topics at trade union lectures also drew large audiences. Sectarians preached temperance, the importance of family, and an end to violence in the family. Particularly influential among workers in the major cities were movements headed by charismatic Orthodox lay leaders. In Moscow, Ivan Koloskov and Dmitrii Grigor'ev formed the *brattsy* whose popularity among workers, servants, tradespeople, and store and office workers brought down anathema on them by the Church in 1910. The brattsy not only advocated temperance but promoted vegetarianism as well. A speaker at the Congress of Vegetarians in April 1913 estimated that thanks to their work there were around fifty thousand vegetarians among the workers of Moscow and St. Petersburg.[58] In St. Petersburg, Ioann Churikov, like the Moscow brattsy, had thousands of followers. His Sunday sermons on moral topics, with their focus on the here and now, spoke to the real needs of lower-class urban dwellers. Echoing the moralistic themes of popular culture, Churikov preached that misery and relief from misery rested on personal moral choice.[59] Even Marxists did not escape the religious fervor that gripped Russians in those years. In the wake of 1905 the God-building movement among Social Democrats sought to inject into socialism elements of emotionalism and the spirit of religion. The movement was formally dead by 1913 within Russian Social Democracy, but remnants of it remained as an important element of worker identity.[60]

The Orthodox Church tried to counter the influence of sectarians among workers by organizing debates with sectarian preachers. Large crowds, many among them factory workers, attended these debates. The challenges that the Church faced fostered a new clerical liberalism among a minority of priests. Among its goals were greater autonomy for priests from the hierarchy, the alleviation of the many social and economic problems of the priesthood, and the improvement of curriculum and conditions in seminaries and academies. Although the focus of clerical liberalism was relatively self-referential, not all of the priests' energies were turned inward. Their reforming zeal also found expression in a growing commitment to the needs of parishioners. For some priests, parochial service began to take precedence over ritual. Others started to participate in temperance movements or became involved in the setting up and running of consumer and credit cooperatives, among other activities.[61]

Urban Government

If some urban workers were seeking incorporation into civil society, elected officials of the cities in which they lived were increasingly addressing their needs. The governance of cities was complicated by overlapping administrations. In eight of the largest cities of the empire the elected duma had to compete with a state-appointed city administration (*gradonachal'stvo*), headed by a prefect (*gradonachal'nik*) with overriding supervisory authority. Provincial governors exercised similar powers in smaller cities. The revised Municipal Statute of 1892 had severely reduced the electorate for city dumas. Only the owners of income-producing properties were entitled to vote in urban elections. In 1910 only 3,757 people qualified to vote in the municipal elections of Kiev.[62] In Moscow in 1912 a mere 9,431 people had the right to vote.[63] The franchise in St. Petersburg was wider. Those who paid a set level of the state tax on apartments were entitled to vote.[64] The elected members of the city duma proposed two candidates for mayor from among their own numbers; the minister of the interior appointed one of them to the office. The mayor chaired an executive board that implemented policy, employed municipal workers, and administered urban activities and enterprises. The dumas had taxing authority and used the revenues to support a range of urban services like lighting, sewage disposal, water supply, and transportation. A major portion of city council budgets was allocated to education.

By 1913 urban governments were beginning to engage more aggressively with the physical and social problems that cities faced. As had occurred in Germany, a bourgeois revolution of sorts was taking place in many Russian cities by 1913. Several cities in the empire had by then attained a high degree of social complexity. The members of educated society were differentiated by social origin, occupation, status, and wealth, and the laboring classes displayed a bewildering diversity. Between them was an array of intermediate white collar, artisan, and service groups with their own interests and concerns. Most cities had some measure of ethnic diversity. Urban populations in border regions were often volatile admixtures of dominant ethnic groups and large vocal minorities. Such complexity renders notions of a simple polarity between "society" and "workers" untenable.

The municipal elections of 1912–1913 saw the removal in many cities of the old conservative guard and their replacement with parties of change. In preelection meetings, specialists like doctors or engineers discussed with voters the nature of city economies and the needs of the municipality. Such meetings occurred in Saratov, Iaroslavl', Kazan', Minsk, and Simbirsk, among others. Siberian newspapers also reported on the vitality of preelection meetings.[65] In Smolensk the governor refused to allow the progressive group to publish its program. In spite of the prohibition, the group won 44 of the 45 seats in the duma.[66] In Pskov the progressives' program included the broadening of the urban franchise; greater freedom from administrative interference for municipal organs of self-government; vigorous action on water supply, urban transport, sewage, and the health and education needs of residents; an end to costly obligations owed by cities to the state, such as support of designated state servants; and tax reform on the basis of socially shared responsibility.[67] Progressives swept the duma elections in Tula; in Viatka the governor overturned the elections when the progressive slate won; the election of progressives in Odessa also ended in dissolution and a new election, but when the second vote affirmed a progressive majority, the governor forcibly installed the conservative group; progressives in Ufa won a majority in the duma; a progressive slate also succeeded in Iaroslavl' city elections; in Saratov the authorities overturned elections in the second curia, but the "new.thinkers" won the reelection; and in Ekaterinoslav the Progressive-Octobrist coalition won 70 of the 75 municipal duma seats.[68] In addition to overturning elections to city dumas when progressives gained majorities, the imperial government in 1913 also refused to accept the election by dumas of progressive mayors. Mayors in Moscow, St. Petersburg, Odessa, and several other cities were refused confirmation in 1913.

Many of the progressive councilors came from the professions. Of 70 city councilors in Saratov, 40 had a higher education, including doctors, engineers, architects, and lawyers.[69] In Moscow a high proportion of councilors also had professional qualifications. There was little correlation between social estate and occupation and political orientation.[70] Although elected by a tiny proportion of the urban population, most councilors saw themselves as representing all urban dwellers. Their reasons were likely mixed. Some acted from paternalistic or charitable instincts or simply a sense of duty; others may have feared mass unrest unless social problems were addressed. Blair Ruble has argued that the very complexity of urban life before World War I, with its social fragmentation and pressing social problems, demanded broad toleration of differences among urban inhabitants and fostered a spirit of cooperation in the name of survival. This "pragmatic pluralism" prevented any one group from monopolizing power and promoted the formation of coalitions and inclusiveness in policy formation. Much of the necessary negotiation occurred outside of formal power structures in the interactions of daily life. Specialization and dependence on expertise in capitalist societies demanded cooperation among competing forces and compelled class compromises that gradually became embodied in institutional arrangements. It is out of such accommodation of difference and the pluralism it permits that civil society grows. In Russian cities the interference of central government officials in municipal affairs slowed but did not prevent this process.[71]

In Moscow the professional intelligentsia and the industrial-commercial bourgeoisie allied around a platform of modernization. We have already seen that in spite of regional and industrial branch differences, the business class of Russia had by 1913 reached a high level of agreement about the broad economic, political, and social needs of the empire and was publicizing its program through its institutional organs. A Moscow patriotism that was driven by competition with St. Petersburg, the fount and center of the administrative arbitrariness that progressives believed held the cities back, also motivated many among the city's activists.[72]

The Moscow city duma that was elected in 1912 was much more progressive than the one it replaced. For all that, the outgoing duma had already begun a program of the rapid expansion of city services around 1910 with the aim of better integrating the lower classes into the life of the city. In keeping with the civilizing goals of the elites, the duma provided a range of new cultural amenities. In 1904 a municipal People's House began to stage operas and plays and offered a teahouse and lecture hall. Half fares on railways enabled summer excursions that took children into the countryside beginning in 1912; during the summer of 1913, 2,700 children a day participated in organized street games. In 1913 the city spent nearly two hundred thousand roubles on school breakfasts for needy children. From the end of April to the beginning of May 1913, the city organized nightly concerts in a variety of locales to make them accessible to the many. The city created more public space by opening five new public squares and three new parks from 1911 to 1913. By 1913 the Society for Free Popular Literature operated 14 branch libraries. The society took pride in the fact that in 1912, 50 percent of its nearly twelve thousand users were workers.[73] The duma gave an annual subsidy to the Shaniavskii People's University. The university gave only evening classes and included a preparatory section for those lacking a middle-school diploma. Once accepted into the academic section, students took classes for two hours a night, five nights a week, for four years to attain a degree in history, law, languages, literature, or science. A practical section provided training in library science, pedagogy, cooperative administration, and local government. In the 1913–1914 academic year, 5,372 people attended classes. Fees ranged from six to twenty-five roubles, and some workers were among the students.[74]

The people's universities were also active in promoting workers' theater. In 1909 the Moscow Society of People's Universities set up a Section to Aid in the Establishment of Rural, Factory, and School Theater. Between 1 September 1913 and 1 September 1914, the number of theater circles under its auspices grew from 211 to 437, testimony to popular interest in cultural pursuits.[75] In 1913 the Society of People's Universities established a section to assist the development of factory and village theater. The society provided a list of about 150 approved plays, classified by subject, degree of difficulty in content, and complexity of production. They also mounted courses for directors and set up a drama school for workers. By April it had forty worker-students in attendance studying with six teachers.[76]

Moscow factory owners also began to participate in educational outreach to workers. Several of them helped to finance the work of the Society of People's Universities. In 1913–1914 factory owners enabled the society to set up 11 auditoriums in industrial centers in Moscow province as well as to present lectures in nine factory locales in Moscow. V.A. Morozova, a Tver' factory owner, was instrumental in establishing the Prechistenskie courses for workers and had built classrooms to house them in Moscow in 1908. The city duma provided a subsidy of two thousand roubles for the courses. More than forty-seven thousand people attended the lectures that season.[77]

Support for education for workers was part of a larger effort to address the hardship of the urban masses. The city administration had backed the savage suppression of Moscow workers in the December 1905 uprising. After the revolution, however, the endless harassment of nearly all social groups by state authorities fostered fellow feeling between workers and educated society and encouraged cooperation. State and city approaches to worker unrest began to diverge as early as 1906. From that year the city created public works projects to ease unemployment and to support employment bureaus. The police went on arresting the unemployed as before and deporting them to the countryside. In 1913 the Moscow Society of Factory and Mill Owners sent representatives to Western Europe to investigate the handling of strikes there, and in early 1914 it officially sanctioned trade unions and their right to negotiate on behalf of members.[78]

The tram workers' strike in Moscow in the late summer of 1913 illustrates the dynamic of social relations under stress in the city. The tram conductors and drivers called for a wage raise, rent allowances, and an eight-hour summer and six-hour winter working day with a maximum of twenty-four working days per month.[79] The drivers struck in support of the demands. The state-appointed city prefect ordered the arrest of their leaders. The duma administration immediately requested the release of the arrested workers, but the prefect responded with additional arrests.[80] The public was greatly inconvenienced by the strike but widely supported the workers. On 20 September the workers suspended the strike but asked once again for the release of the arrested men. Mayor V.D. Brianskii supported their request and tirelessly mediated between the two sides. When the request was denied the workers resumed the strike. Typographers and many factory workers joined them in sympathy strikes. Fearing an escalation, the prefect released some of the workers' leaders, but the drivers refused to end the strike until all of the arrested men were freed and their economic demands were properly considered.

The duma administration now took a hard line, perhaps to preempt an even harsher response by state authorities. They set 2:00 p.m. on 21 September as the deadline for a return to work and promised termination of employment for noncompliance.[81] Duma councilors supported the city administration's ultimatum but called for a review of the living conditions of all city workers and the feasibility of their unionization. They also agreed to consider the list of demands made by the tram workers. When the prefect promised that no further arrests would occur, the workers returned to work. The conductors, who had not officially joined the strike, now petitioned the mayor for equal treatment with the drivers.[82] The mayor continued to demonstrate good faith with the workers by repeatedly pressing the prefect to rescind the exile outside of the city of 10 of the drivers' leaders.[83] The actions of the prefect were intolerable, but the response of the elected city council and its administration and the support of the citizenry for the goals of the workers do not suggest deep and irreparable alienation of workers from the rest of urban society.

In spite of a concerted effort the city failed to provide sufficient housing for workers in Moscow. In 1912, 8.7 Muscovites shared each apartment compared to 4.3 Parisians, 3.9 Berliners, 4.2 Viennese, and 4.5 Londoners. In 1910 the figure for St. Petersburg was 7.4. Living conditions for many workers remained inadequate. About two hundred fifty thousand Moscow workers still lived in barracks in 1912. In 1913 only about two thousand people lived in publicly built and subsidized housing.[84] Plans to build inexpensive apartments were made but not realized before the war. By 1912 the city had built six overnight hostels with 5,650 places, but turned away 55,823 people from them in 1913. The prefect vetoed plans to provide hostels in the notorious Khitrov market in 1912 and again in 1913.[85] Although 60 percent of the Moscow population had indoor flush toilets by the end of 1912, sanitary conditions in the city remained poor; infectious diseases still devastated residents at rates higher than in most other European cities.[86] Moscow's record in elementary education was better than in housing. The share of education in the city budget went from 5.9 percent in 1901 to 7.9 percent in 1913. In the case of education, the city and central state worked effectively together to finance schooling. Class sizes remained large, however, and teachers' salaries low.[87]

Inadequate resources to cope with the flood of in-migrants and state interference arising from the government's fear of public initiative, rather than lack of will on the part of educated society, slowed the integration of the social classes in Moscow. What is striking about the Moscow experience is the breadth of the consensus across ideological divides within educated society about the need to address social issues in the cause of social peace. There is no support in the experience of Russia's second capital for the notion that liberal society abandoned the people after 1905 and attached its loyalties to the state. Liberals were, however, prepared to work with the state where cooperation around shared goals was feasible. The low level of labor disturbances in 1913–1914 in Moscow is testimony to the efforts made by both workers and middle class to accommodate one another. The misbehavior of state authority, rather than antibourgeois or anticapitalist feelings, sparked whatever militancy there was in Moscow among workers in those years.

Matters in Russia's first capital were more complex. In St. Petersburg the big industrial players were more closely attached to the state than were the textile manufacturers of Moscow. Although the state practiced in St. Petersburg and elsewhere an inconsistent policy of benevolence toward workers, repression was a more frequent response to worker protest than kindness, especially in the capital. The St. Petersburg Society of Factory and Mill Owners differed markedly from its Moscow counterpart. As already noted, the St. Petersburg society refused to recognize unions. When in 1914 the Moscow society accepted 1 May as a worker holiday, the St. Petersburg branch refused to go along. Long before then it had more or less severed relations with the society in Moscow.[88]

The consensus around the need to confront social ills was weaker in the St. Petersburg duma than in Moscow. Limited as its resources were, the Moscow duma had more to spend than the duma of the capital. Much property in St. Petersburg belonged to the government and was exempt from urban taxation.[89] I.I. Tolstoi, chosen as mayor in 1913, complained about the constant interference of the governor in duma business and the obstructions raised by the building-technical committee of the Ministry of the Interior in urban planning and housing.[90] Lack of resources and insufficient resolve meant that St. Petersburg lagged behind Moscow and other more progressive centers in dealing with social problems. A good example was primary education. With a larger population than Moscow, St. Petersburg still had only 56,378 children in elementary schools in 1914 compared to Moscow's record of 64,526 children in 1913.[91] Much of the militancy of St. Petersburg workers in 1913–1914 is explained not only by difficult urban living conditions but also by the absence of a consistent effort on the part of city councilors and industrialists to address the workers' concerns in the way they were prepared to do in Moscow. The rest was bred by the relentless pressure that the authorities exerted on workers' public lives.

Other cities struggled as well to meet rising social needs with limited resources. Some were more successful than others. By 1913 the reactionary mayor and council of Odessa were under fire from professionals who pointed to unaddressed problems in housing, sanitation, and public health. Unlike in Moscow, where municipal government grappled competently if not entirely successfully with pressing concerns, the city government of Odessa fostered disunity among the populace and dampened public-spiritedness.[92] In Kiev, the growth in the municipal budget lagged behind that of other cities. The city earned little from its municipal businesses. Public expenditure on housing was low and rents rose precipitously. Although liberal professionals had broken the hold of conservatives on city governance in Kiev by 1910, morale in council was low. Lack of a quorum resulted in the cancellation of 41 of the 100 council meetings scheduled in 1913.[93]

By 1913 an important difference from earlier years in major cities was the growing number of workers who brought their wives and families with them instead of leaving them behind in the village. Neighborhoods of working-class families were becoming more common.[94] Marriages of workers resident in cities were also on the rise. In St. Petersburg, for example, the heavily working-class district of Vyborg accounted for 5.7 percent of the city's total population in 1908 but celebrated 6.75 percent of all marriages in the city. By 1913 the figure had risen to 7.9 percent of all marriages.[95] The trend heightened the profile of the nuclear family in urban environments. Since many workers could not afford church marriages and contracted unofficial "civil marriages," the number of married couples was likely greater than these statistics suggest.

Russian cities experienced an epidemic of suicides in the prewar period.[96] After the revolution of 1905 the suicide rate had markedly increased. Although the figures are uncertain, contemporaries believed that St. Petersburg had the highest per capita rate of suicide in Europe. The newspapers in major cities reported in lurid detail on the more dramatic cases of suicide. The several explanations given for the frequency of suicide encapsulated the concerns and anxieties of the times. Some attributed the epidemic to the repressive political climate. Youth suicide in particular was seen as a product of the harsh climate of spying and control in schools.[97] Enemies of the market economy agreed that the well-to-do killed themselves as a consequence of the excesses of a market-driven culture, and the poor sought relief in suicide from the poverty their exploitation in the name of the market inflicted on them. The Pirogov Society of Russian Doctors in 1913 brought together a commission of doctors, teachers, lawyers, and social activists to study the causes of suicide in Russia, especially among young people, and appealed in newspapers for materials relevant to its work.[98]

Voluntary Associations

The work of charities significantly supplemented the efforts of under-resourced municipalities to address social ills. The earliest voluntary associations were charities, whose history dates back to the beginning of the nineteenth century. Toward the end of the century, the government created standard charters that greatly simplified the process of registering as a charity or other type of voluntary association. By the outbreak of the revolution of 1905, about four thousand charities were operating in the empire. In March 1906 the government issued the "temporary rules" on the formation of voluntary associations, which created an alternative route to the model charters for forming societies. Under the rules, citizens could form societies without permission if they were prepared to forgo the society's rights to hold property and to have a juridical personality. To attain those rights, societies still had to apply under a standard charter and gain the approval of newly formed provincial bureaus for the regulation of societies. The provincial governor chaired the bureau, and its members included formal representation from the noble estate, the courts, the zemstvos, and the dumas. Permanent rules proposed in 1910 aimed to strengthen the powers of governors over voluntary associations. The draft required the use of the Russian language in the daily operations of societies. Non-Russian voluntary associations also needed permission to own real estate. The rules did not, however, pass into law before the outbreak of World War I.[99]

Charities often served as points of contact between members of different social classes and occupations. The virtue of charity was deeply embedded in Orthodox practice. The great majority of charities were local in character and focus. Most were in cities, and their work was a matter of civic pride for the local population.[100] By 1913 professionals allied with local businessmen were most often the real driving forces behind charitable work. Businessmen brought to their philanthropic work the middle-class values of self-help through education and the rational employment of leisure time as well as industriousness, initiative, self-reliance, and autonomy.[101] In 1908 the All-Russian Union of Organizations, Societies and Activists in Public and Private Relief was organized. The union held its first national congress in 1910. Only a handful of the thousands of charities in the empire joined, however.

In the years immediately preceding the war, the activities of charities intensified. As Adele Lindenmeyr has written, "Volunteers in causes ranging from temperance, literacy and adult education to women's rights and antiprostitution joined doctors, scientists and other professionals in an unprecedented upsurge of nation-wide organization and activism."[102] The alliance of charitable funding with professional expertise marked a growing interest in Russia as elsewhere in Europe in discovering and addressing the root causes of social disorders rather than simply relieving its victims' sufferings. A good deal of charitable work involved social issues identified by workers as priorities; the campaign against alcoholism, literacy programs, and efforts to reign in prostitution were good examples. It has been said that philanthropy gave entrepreneurs and professionals stewardship over workers.[103] In fact, the values promoted by middle-class philanthropists were the very same values that the more articulate workers had adopted as their own: self-development through education, personal initiative, self-reliance, rationality in the use of leisure, and hard work. These were the values of the bourgeoisie writ large. Charitable causes were in some cases meeting grounds on which worker and middle-class social activists could cooperate to advance common concerns through shared values.

Charities were only one example of the larger world of voluntary associations in the empire. Although some reinforced existing group identities, others "cut across economic, religious, occupational, estate, class and gender lines," creating new communities.[104] Some were highly ambitious in their activities. The Society for the Dissemination of Technical Knowledge in Saratov, for example, organized excursions to Germany, France, Switzerland, Britain, Norway, and even Japan. Teachers paid a lower fee for the trips than others.[105] Many middle-class associations required membership fees that excluded members from the lower classes. Although social exclusivity remained powerful, after 1905 some associations began to attract a broad social spectrum.[106]

The city of Kazan' in the middle Volga region provides a striking example of the importance of voluntary associations in the building of civil society. The city boasted a host of charitable organizations by 1913. A society for aid to prostitutes operated an employment bureau for women and girls and supported a hostel for women seeking employment, a shelter for homeless women, tearooms and cafeterias, cheap apartments, and an artisan workshop as well as agricultural training institutions. The Alcohol Society functioned not only in Kazan' but set up branches in other towns in the province. The society provided reading rooms and presented a variety of entertainments, including highly popular magic lantern shows. The Red Cross and the Society for the Prevention of Cruelty to Animals also had branches in Kazan'. The Brotherhood of St. Gurii funded schooling for baptized non-Russians. These were only a few examples of dozens of charitable societies in the city and region.[107]

Kazan' also had a large number of mutual aid societies that supported the interests of a wide range of social and professional groups and insured and protected their properties. The oldest of the mutual aid societies in the city was the Clerks' Mutual Aid Society. It derived part of its income from merchants and industrialists as well as from members' fees. It was a large organization that provided cultural as well as financial benefits to members. The society owned a large property with tea and games rooms and a fine lecture hall. The clerks' society was only one of many mutual aid societies in Kazan': others included the Society of Commercial Employees, the Society of Employees in Administrative and Social Institutions, and the Society of Women Doctors. Doctors' assistants, booksellers, and teachers also organized their own mutual aid societies.[108] In addition to material support for members, mutual aid societies in Kazan' and elsewhere that could afford it built schools for members' children, provided scholarships for higher education, maintained libraries and reading rooms for members, and sought to provide improving recreations. The activities that they supported are testimony to the middle-class values and aspirations that they held and wished to promote among their members.

In addition to its numerous charitable organizations and mutual aid societies the city of Kazan' was home to many social clubs. Most notable among them was the New Club that the Society of Employees in Administrative and Social Institutions established. The club provided entertainment for its members through family dance evenings, concerts, and shows. In 1913 the Family Club opened to provide space in which families could convene, dance, play games, or read. Only men could be paying members of the Family Club. The club hosted balls and musical and literary evenings and staged plays. It subscribed to a number of newspapers and magazines for the use of members. The Muslim Club opened in 1907 to enable members and their families to pass their free time together in an enjoyable setting. The club put on musical and literary evenings, organized walks, subscribed to newspapers and journals, and staged checkers and chess competitions. Other social clubs included the Kazan' Society of Hunters, the Society for Domestic Fowl Breeders, the Society of Lovers of Equine Sports, the Kazan' Yacht Club, and the Kazan' Society of Cyclists. In the 25 years before World War I more than 100 social clubs operated in the region with varying duration.[109]

The emphasis on the family in the activities of these clubs is striking and an indication of the penetration of middle-class values into the organization of leisure activities. The family was central to the European bourgeois ideal. As Gay argues, the domestic felicity promised by the ideal was at best only partially obtained in most family unions. He concludes, however, that the family "made for an emotional intimacy that was more than merely rhetorical."[110] The dissemination of the ideal of family was also a defining characteristic of the middle segments of Russian society in the prewar years. The family was the focus of particular attention by Russian reformers in the late empire. William Wagner has documented the rise of the "affective ideal" of family life that arose in legal reform circles in opposition to the patriarchal family ideal of imperial law.[111] Reformers portrayed the family as a "moral community" bound by affection. Family members respected one another's rights as individuals and honored their mutual obligations. Each family member was committed to the personal fulfillment of the others and to the welfare and happiness of the whole. Laura Engelstein has shown how medical reformers teamed with jurists to reorder family relations in the interests of the needs and rights of individual family members.[112] In an unpublished doctoral dissertation, Julia Kinnear has traced the concern of educators with strengthening family bonds and mutuality through appropriate early child education within the family.[113] The evidence is strong that family and marriage reformers were found on both sides of the state-society boundary. The roots of the reform movement lay in the silent percolation into Russian consciousness of the bourgeois values of individual autonomy and the moral centrality of family life. Emphasis on the family points to the extent to which Russian elite values had moved toward those of the European bourgeoisie by 1913.[114]

Although some Kazan' clubs limited their membership, few were socially exclusive. The Merchant Club was for merchants only, but guests from other estates were welcome. The Nobles Club included nobles, military men, bureaucrats, honorary citizens, merchants, and well-known artists and professionals among its members. Other clubs were even more open socially. The New Club self-consciously appealed to all social groups and tried to create a society built around social, political, ethnic, and religious pluralism. Jews participated in clubs in Kazan' in proportions larger than their numbers in the population. Muslims were more inclined to stay in their own societies, but in the years before the war they, too, were becoming more active in general clubs. Foreigners were also prominent in club memberships in the province, especially Germans and Poles. Even the most elitist of clubs drew members from the nobility, bureaucracy, merchants, and professoriate. For all their openness the clubs incorporated into their membership only about 5 percent of the population of the city. Through their lectures, competitions, dances, and shows, however, they affected a much larger circle.[115]

A striking example of collaboration among the voluntary associations of the city of Kazan' for the social good was the establishment in 1906 of a people's university and its subsequent material support. The group established to found the university attracted a broadly based membership. It included many professional educators, but also the Clerks' Mutual Aid Society, the

Society of Commercial Employees, and nearly all of the professional mutual aid societies in the city. Professors from Kazan' University volunteered to lecture. The Clerks' Mutual Aid Society made available to the university its lecture hall four times per week, and the New Club provided lecture facilities for an additional two times each week.[116]

Rural areas experienced little of the social vibrancy and interaction characteristic of cities. But even small district towns had their social clubs for cards and family dances. The larger towns had noble and merchant clubs that opened their doors to the local public through balls, dance and musical evenings, plays, readings, and lectures. Most had small libraries and many carried out charitable work. The membership of associations in small towns tended to be socially narrower than in the larger centers where the erosion of the estate structure was more advanced.

Voluntary associations fostered a new sociability. Nobles, civil servants, industrialists, professionals, government employees, and others met together and produced and enforced social norms on an expanding circle of members. The supra-estate, supra-ethnic, and supra-sectarian socialization that occurred in many clubs fostered a new culture. Clubs brought social groups into new formations and promoted a process of social development that often nourished citizenship and democratic values. Participants formed multiple attachments and interests beyond their immediate group. Although they were relatively elitist in membership, clubs diffused new norms and values by example and through their outreach by means of events open to a wider public.[117] Compared to Germany, voluntary associations in Russia arose later and were fewer in number by 1913, but they placed Russia on a time line that by 1914 had raised it to the brink of a national bourgeois culture.[118] As associations generated new identities and social formations, the potential for conflict among them grew.[119] Contestation was, however, more a sign of the vitality of the new culture than of irreparable social fragmentation.

Joseph Bradley has observed that voluntary associations in Russia fostered "values" too often thought of as absent in Russia. They included "opportunity, individual initiative, autonomy, self-reliance, self-improvement, a spirit of enterprise, organizational skills, industriousness, rationality, the ability to control one's destiny, and a belief in science and progress."[120] Bradley limits his study to scientific learned societies, but by 1913 many of the values he describes were being promoted in a wide range of voluntary associations. In whatever milieu voluntary associations grew, be it working- or middle-class or across social divides, they taught their members the lessons of autonomous organization and self-management. Voluntary associations were built on principles of equality, were self-funded, made majority decisions on the basis of rational discussion, elected officers, rotated offices, and held leaders accountable to the membership. They provided an organizational model contrary to the autocratic paternalism of the regime.[121] The regime recognized the threat and sought to limit and control the activities of voluntary associations. Before the war the government interfered in the fund-raising campaigns of charities or restricted the scope of their relief work. It kept a wary eye on ethnically based associations and selectively opposed the organization of associations at the imperial level. Many associations carried out functions, however, that the state could not or would not administer itself but could not do without. The voluntary sector was increasingly setting the agenda for solving social problems before World War I.[122] Not only charities but all voluntary associations increased the scope of the public sphere, fostered public initiative, and promoted the growth of civil society.

LEISURE, READING, AND THE NEW CULTURE

A rapidly expanding popular consumer culture of leisure was helping to define new identities and blur old social distinctions. As James von Geldern has noted, "Consumers [of popular culture] cut across the lower middle range of Russian society and could be found in most classes."[123] Consumers of popular culture wanted to be entertained as well as informed. Entertainment was transformed into a commodity, and the masses increasingly became consumers of cultural products. The segmentation of the cultural market witnessed growing competition for market share. The producers of popular culture in Russia were not part of the ruling elite, who despised them, and were only marginally aligned with the cultural elite and the creative intelligentsia, who looked down on them. Capitalist production in any sector, including culture, rests on the simple, albeit temporary, appropriation of a market niche. Capitalist competitors are ever alert to early trends and changing needs and tastes among potential consumers. The relationship between the producer and consumer is reciprocal, contingent, and inherently unstable. Capitalism thrives not on a single market but on the multiplication of markets, which are susceptible to expansion through adept marketing. The proliferation of tastes, the very heterogeneity of the consuming middle class, in a word, market segmentation, is the essence of capitalist consumer economies. Success in the cultural marketplace does not rest on the partial or full sanction of the ruling elites or cultural gatekeepers but on the continuing vitality of demand in the market. The creative intelligentsia deplored the pressure exerted on culture by the market but found it hard to resist. As Catriona Kelly has pointed out, the elites seek to define popular culture as they observe and study it but are also influenced by it. Writers find inspiration in popular movements and themes, which they express in their own work whether or not they are writing for a mass audience.[124]

The leisure industry exerted a democratizing influence on the wider culture. The market encouraged consumption in pursuit of pleasure and fulfillment that also transgressed social divides.[125] Hunting societies campaigned for environmental protections and for more open social access to the hunt. The Bogatyr Society for Physical Education funded physical education for schoolchildren in St. Petersburg and by World War I had spawned branches in several other cities.[126] Some industries sponsored racehorses, while others organized athletic clubs to promote worker loyalty. The pursuit of leisure brought more women into the public sphere. Some women began to participate in competitive sports such as swimming, cycling, and tennis.[127] Actors and other performers became stars. When Anastasia Vial'tseva, a popular operetta singer, died in 1913, one hundred fifty thousand people joined her funeral cortege in St. Petersburg.[128] Tourism, assisted by half fares on railways and tourist companies offering group rates, expanded rapidly before the war. Companies linked tourism to physical fitness and education. The Russian Tourist Society in Moscow organized educational tours for teachers, students, and other groups of modest means.[129] Major cities developed a commercialized nightlife ranging from restaurants to clubs and cabarets. Before World War I urban Russians enjoyed a wide range of leisure activities for self-discovery and a breadth of cultural choice and freedom that was later sharply curtailed under Soviet power.[130]

Soccer rapidly widened its base as a spectator sport in the prewar years and attracted supporters across class lines. At first soccer matches promoted strong local identities built around one's factory or club. In Moscow an urban league made up of elite amateur sports societies included foreigners and well-to-do Russians. They imposed high fees to control club memberships. Worker soccer teams founded their own leagues and by 1913 matches between worker and elite clubs were not uncommon. Local teams gave their fans a sense of place and meaning. By 1913 improved transportation enabled regional sport competition. The emergence of all-city teams supplemented prior local loyalties and helped to build a wider urban loyalty and identity. Other cities also formed teams, and inter-city matches were common. The All-Russian Football Union boasted 155 clubs with around 4,000 players in 1913. Urban sports contributed to the breakdown of local rural identities among migrant workers. Children's teams began to form. Youth became enamored with soccer and lost interest in the traditional entertainments of their parents. By 1913 the cult of soccer was already creeping into the countryside.[131] Ice hockey was also gaining in popularity. In Moscow in 1913 the hockey league season opened on 30 November. The city league contained two divisions with teams of different levels of skill.[132] As sports professionalized, athletes became objects of popular consumption, as had already happened with popular actors and performers.

Amateur soccer played a large role in the entertainments of the summer *dacha* culture. The dacha phenomenon was emblematic of the formation of a broad middle class that spilled outside traditional social boundaries. The formation of suburban communities around major cities where urbanites flocked in the summer to experience rural living or simply to escape the city's high rents encouraged the crossing of social barriers and the cultivation of common activities among the various strata of the middle class. Dacha soccer leagues proliferated among middle-class vacationers. Five railway lines that radiated out from Moscow boasted their own leagues by 1913. In 1914 there were 55 dacha towns in the Moscow region that were members of soccer leagues. Players in the dacha leagues also made up a major portion of the spectators at urban league games when the dacha season ended.

Dacha communities had a long history in Russia. From the 1860s the dacha ceased to be exclusively associated with the nobility and began to embrace a wide social spectrum. A property boom in the late nineteenth and early twentieth centuries facilitated the rapid growth of the dacha experience. In 1896 the government made parcels of state lands available for long-term leasing for the construction of dachas. Dachas could be rented or owned; they ranged from peasant cottages to large houses. Some poorer urbanites found respite from the city by renting a single room in a dacha settlement. Dacha culture organized identities less around occupation and social status than around leisure activities. It was marked by its informality;

its primary rationale was leisure. Shared leisure activities permitted social mixing that would be difficult or impossible in the city. Dacha culture encouraged a range of social activities from country walks to cycling and tennis as well as amateur cultural events.

Group leisure activities promoted solidarity, but *dachniki* also organized to improve railway or policing services or to develop sanitation facilities in their summer communities. Dacha culture promoted individual self-fulfillment but also a new sense of community based on lifestyle and consumerism. Above all it brought together people from a variety of urban groups who otherwise would never have socialized. Tensions arose with locals over the refusal of summer visitors to pay taxes. Peasants near major cities participated extensively in the dacha economy, providing a variety of services and renting rooms and cottages to urbanites. Some critics thought that dacha settlements distracted peasants from their proper pursuits and encouraged dangerous modern attitudes and behaviors among them. Many among the creative intelligentsia disclaimed dacha culture in its bourgeois variant but readily took part in a dacha experience that they sought to portray as authentic and purposeful and not the artificial and frivolous experience favored by the less discerning middle class.[133]

The Russian book industry in the early twentieth century illustrates the response of cultural industries to new market opportunities. The book market in Russia was highly differentiated by 1913. Book publishers in that year put out 26,629 titles in Russian and 7,347 in other languages in 118,836,713 copies and 100 topic categories.[134] Serious literature continued to be produced but increasingly was forced to compete for readers with popular tales of brigands, detectives, and other action heroes. As the reading public broadened so too did the range of authors who served it. The largest single publisher in Russia was the I.D. Sytin firm, which in 1911 published 815 titles in 14,848,890 copies.[135] Charles Ruud has described Sytin as the archetype of the entrepreneur as defined by Joseph Schumpeter and argues that his example shows how much scope for free enterprise Russia afforded in the prewar years.[136] Sytin came from state peasant stock; his father served as a volost' and later as a zemstvo clerk. The young Sytin got his start in publishing by selling religious prints at the Nizhnii Novgorod Fair and from village to village for a Moscow publishing company. He proved to be a highly successful employee, but in 1883 he went into business on his own with a shop in Moscow. Sytin knew the potential markets well and cultivated both the popular commercial market of the *lubki* and the educational market. Sytin cooperated with L.N. Tolstoi to produce affordable works by respectable authors for simple readers. Sytin balanced high quality with affordability and enjoyed huge success. In 1913 he bought out his main competitor.[137]

The Vol'f Bookstores were among the largest distributors of books in the Russian Empire. In addition to selling books, M.O. Vol'f published the classics and the works of known contemporary authors. He was a brilliant marketer. He studied the characteristics of his readership by surveying customers in his stores. He tracked sales from around the empire and urged his employees to understand the tastes of customers. In 1897 he established a mail-order market, which he advertised through the *Vol'f Bookstore News*. The news provided reviews and lists of books for sale.[138] With the establishment of the *Literary Herald* in 1905 Vol'f began to reshape public perceptions of the book and the author. The journal portrayed reading as a high calling and raised the spiritual value of the book above other commodities. It also informed the public about the practical aspects of writing, such as authors' rights and copyright law. Vol'f portrayed authors as celebrities, drawing readers into the personal lives of writers and using the personalities of the cultural producers to tie his customers to them and their work. Vol'f also lionized the place of the publisher in the process of cultural transmission. Above all he stressed the role of public taste in driving cultural production. The *Literary Herald* encouraged readers to trust their own judgment in assessing the merit of literary works rather than submitting to the tyranny of the author or the authority of critics in establishing a canon of the best books.[139]

The freeing of taste from canonical restraints encouraged taste for a literature that combined elements of both the serious and popular. This new middlebrow literature did not aim to replace serious literature but rather to widen the appeal of literature to a larger readership. Beth Holmgren has noted that it legitimized the desires and the aspirations to respectability of the complex middle strata of Russian society. The new literature highlighted the civilizing power of informed consumption and validated material pleasures as productive of taste and refinement. It supported the commodity culture of which it was itself an important part. To the positive heroes of the classics, the new middlebrow literature juxtaposed colorful personalities who, Holmgren notes, tended to be "model consumers."[140] She goes on to rehearse the familiar argument that ethnic, religious, regional, and economic divisions prevented middle social groups from forming a single class in Russia. Since, as earlier noted, diversity marked the middle class wherever it had appeared, it is scarcely surprising that the Russian middle class was no exception. She goes on, however, to express some surprise that the critics writing in the *Vol'f Bookstore News* distinguished texts "according to criteria quite different from those of their highbrow predecessors and peers, as if they were anticipating a middlebrow aesthetic with its valorization of high emotion and strong personality."[141] In truth, by 1913 anticipation had given way to the reality of a middlebrow taste based on the valorization of consumption and individualism.

The effects of the market on the Russian frame of mind were profound. Jeffrey Brooks has shown that popular writers in the years leading up to World War I defined success as material advancement within a market economy. Their works showed readers alternative paths to pursuing careers and achieving their goals. Not wealth and status but education, persistence, initiative, and willingness to innovate were portrayed as the ingredients of success and social mobility. Brooks writes, "Such stories served to legitimize emerging patterns of wealth and status and to strip the legitimacy from the old hierarchy of social classes." He also notes reluctance in these stories, especially in women's fiction, to sanction extreme gaps in wealth.[142]

Film supported similar attitudes. The prewar film craze reached its height in Russia in 1913. Until 1908 French movies had dominated cinema in Russia, and foreign films still retained their hold on Russians in 1913. The first Russian-made movie, *Stenka Razin,* appeared in 1908. Its success brought Russian capital into the domestic movie industry. In 1913, 18 Russian movie studios turned out 129 movies, about 25 percent of which were full-length films with running times of around an hour. By that time there were roughly 1,400 movie theaters in Russia. An estimated 12 million regular patrons purchased 108 million movie seats in 1913. In St. Petersburg 130 cinemas operated and in Moscow another 67. The hit of 1913 was a screen adaptation of Anastasia Verbitskaia's sensational novel, *Keys to Happiness,* which came out in two parts.[143]

Film attracted a heterogeneous audience. It was popular among the urban upper classes. They were drawn to elaborate cinemas where they watched the screen from private boxes sometimes equipped with telephones.[144] Even the most fashionable movie theaters, however, had differential seating pricing that enabled the less well off to share the experience, if not the telephone, with the rich. Aleksandr Blok, the poet and critic, hated the downtown cinemas but haunted suburban film houses where the "real Russia" went.[145] Like much of popular publishing, the making and distribution of film was largely in the hands of middle-class entrepreneurs, and the bulk of filmgoers were of the middle class or aspiring middle class. Many of Lenin's hated labor aristocracy sought out in the movie house the lessons about conduct and deportment, culture and social mobility that the cinema had to teach them.

Many Russian-made melodramas featured a violent eroticism. Films made in 1913 depicted rape, murder, and suicide.[146] The themes of many films were drawn from the pressing concerns of urban life—the clash of classes, gender wars, and the dislocations of urban living. Such films provided outlets for the abstentions of middle-class life. As Peter Gay has argued, the bourgeoisie liked to read about adultery but preferred to honor the sanctity of the home.[147] Such films may have helped to fuel widespread rumors about "leagues of free love," in which young people were said to be schooled in the pleasures of sex.[148] The police were less concerned with the moral than with the political implications of the cinema. They were quick to grasp the potential of film for subversive goals. In 1913 they forbade the depiction in films of hardship among workers, management abuses, or anything else that might arouse worker discontent.[149]

The creative intelligentsia was even more ambivalent about the movies than about popular tastes in literature. Leonid Andreev accepted film as an antidote to the impoverishment of the theater that the struggle between symbolism and realism had caused. He noted, however, the widespread hostility toward the cinema among the elite levels of the intelligentsia.[150] The poet Zinaida Gippius despised film. Many saw cinema as merely mechanical and lacking in the organicism that they believed to mark real culture.[151] Defenders of the theater lauded the profundity of the stage and decried the superficiality of the screen. Others complained that film was fodder for the masses unlike the haute cuisine on which the social elites dined at the theater. Still others associated film with the public's endless taste for novelty and demeaned it as ephemeral and unimportant.

Others were more positive about the movies. The Futurist Vladimir Maiakovskii touted film as superior to the theater and literature and saw in the cinema the future of art. In 1913 he wrote on film in *Kine-Zhurnal* and drafted a film scenario. Fellow Futurists David Burliuk, Igor Larionov, and Natalia Goncharova attached themselves to film and collaborated in

1913 to produce *Drama in the Futurists' Cabaret 13*.[152] The Symbolists, too, found in the transient images on the screen an expression of their belief in the impermanence of the material world.[153] Symbolists like Blok linked their eschatological fears about the collapse of culture and the end of history and of the world both to the city with its dissonance, lack of permanence, and fragmentation and to the fleeting, dim, and ever-changing images in the movies. Andrei Bely saw in the cinema a place where through experiencing and feeling together an audience could achieve true community (*sobornost'*).[154] Before he died Lev Tolstoi had written for the screen. Both Andreev and Aleksandr Kuprin, the realist writer, had adaptations of their works on film by 1913. The movie studios defended film as best suited to capture a modern world in flux. Film, they argued, was democratic and made the world of literature accessible to a popular audience. It was also a tool for educating the public about the world.[155]

The history of film was similar in Russia and the West. The comfortable replication of the Western pattern in Russia points to the extent to which Russia was westernized before the war.[156] As in the West, film in Russia served to commodify culture. Filmgoers could learn to simulate social status through informed consumption and find on the screen models for civilized behavior, proper dress, public decorum, and table manners.[157] Film played an important role in socializing the new Russian middle classes and enabling those on the fringes to emulate their ways. It validated their love of consumption, self-improvement, the novel, and the modern. It is notable that while film supported the sales of merchants, the portrayal of merchants in film upheld the deeply engrained and unkind stereotype.

Theater was also developing new audiences with new forms in the years before the war. There were more than 200 regular theaters in the empire and 240 cabarets and miniature theaters.[158] In 1912, 125 cabarets and miniature theaters operated in St. Petersburg and Moscow alone.[159] By 1913 they had spread to Odessa, Vladivostok, Kiev, Baku, Kharkov, Rostov, and elsewhere. Although cabaret and miniature theater began as venues for the avant-garde and some retained their exclusiveness, others began to cater to a broader audience. They specialized in satirical forays against both innovation and convention in the arts and increasingly in society.[160] Their repertoire consisted of a variety of song and dance acts, short dramas, and vignettes that illustrated city life and captured the speed and discontinuity of urban living.[161] Cabarets and miniature theaters were often housed in movie theaters and shared the same audience. The heterogeneity of new audiences gave scope to stand-up comedians who used humor to diminish social distance, mediate new identities, and relieve social awkwardness. A popular act in 1913 was Willard, the man who grows. Willard, a happy American, appears on stage surrounded by spectators. Suddenly he starts to grow—one foot gets wider than the other; one arm gets longer; he grows one, then two heads taller and then regains his normal stature and appearance. At the end he says with entrepreneurial glee, "I'll grow like this for five more years and by then I'll have a half million in capital."[162] Even the emperor could not resist the sending up of revered art forms. Nikolai Evreinov's mock opera *Gastrol' Rychalov*, which was performed at the Crooked Mirror cabaret in 1913, attracted Nicholas's attention. He commanded a performance at Tsarskoe selo. The opera, which ruthlessly parodied the conventions of grand opera, left the emperor in stitches and the rest of the audience in suspense as they waited for Nicholas to stop laughing and lead the applause, as protocol required.[163]

Realism was by no means dead in Russian literature and drama. For all the advances of experimental theater, the commercial theaters of the empire, even in the capitals, were dominated by a realist repertoire in 1913.[164] The so-called neorealists of the day included Maxim Gorkii, Ivan Bunin, Aleksandr Kuprin, and the sometimes expressionist Leonid Andreev. Preference for the realism of classical Russian literature and drama and resistance to modernist experimentation remained strong among middlebrow readers and theatergoers. Middle- and lower-level white collar workers and culturally aspiring factory workers looked to literature as a source of self-improvement and hoped to find in it a shortcut to understanding the world and a model of the cultured and educated person. They were drawn to the nineteenth-century classics and chose realists from among contemporary writers. Among artists they preferred the realist Il'ia Repin, who was a loud critic of modernist art. A number of journals catered to these readers and from 1910 shaped their views about modernist writers and artists, whom they condemned for their erotomania, degeneracy, and elitism. The relative obscurity of its images, its metaphysical aspirations, and its exotic language limited the appeal of much modernist poetry to the reading public at large. The avant-garde scorned middlebrow audiences, whom they labeled the "pharmacists."

The "pharmacists" reciprocated with a powerful resentment toward the "aesthetes." Some modernists responded to public hostility by moving away from pessimism and mysticism and back toward classical realism. The extent to which these prerevolutionary lower-middle-class attitudes overlapped with later proletarian notions of culture is exemplified by the antimodernist campaign in the mid-1920s in the Soviet Union.[165]

Variety theater (*estrada*) was a vehicle for the dissemination of the new popular culture. The experience of urban life gave rise to new forms of song and singing styles. The art song and folk song made room for the more coarse and sensual urban song. The urban song expressed the new individualism that characterized the period. Gypsy songs, with their evocation of freedom, license, and open spaces, as well as longing and loss, had been popular in some circles since the 1860s but found a wider audience in the early twentieth century. The so-called cruel song of romance in the city also highlighted the individual experiences of the urban masses. The estrada stage embraced all of these forms as well as comic acts, operettas, and even adaptations of traditional rural fair shows. Cinemas often combined movies with estrada intervals.[166] The penetration of estrada entertainments as well onto the stages of the People's Houses, the popularity of adventure fiction among workers, and their fascination with the movies testified that the cultural tastes of workers and the petty bourgeoisie were converging.

The development of popular culture in Russia and the evolution of its uneasy relationship with elite culture, while exhibiting some native features, broadly imitated similar developments in the bourgeois West. The commercialization of culture was well advanced by 1913. Increasingly, a new urban-based commercial culture created new audiences and competed with the established arts for old ones. A sign of modernity in Russia was the wide differentiation of tastes, which the producers of culture competed to meet. Popular culture was a stimulus to market consumption and reflected the values characteristic of the middle class. The defenders of elite culture, faced with the challenge of consumerism, factionalized amid a flurry of manifestos, as elsewhere in Europe. They either retreated into disdain and the esoteric or, more often, began to grapple in their own works with the subjects and forms that spurred popular interest. A middlebrow literature was in the ascendant by 1913. Consumers of popular culture ranged across the social spectrum. They found common sympathies in their shared values within a variety of forms that catered to a wide range of tastes.

CONCLUSION

A civil society was well established in Russian cities by 1913 and supported a lively public sphere. A host of institutions and organizations capable of autonomous activity were in place. Urban assemblies and a vast array of voluntary associations nourished the skills of organization, democratic practice, and self-monitoring. The press had attained a level of competence and self-confidence that put the government on the defensive and brought a wide readership into the business of the nation. An expanding market, rising individualism, and the penetration into the wider culture of the middle-class values of family, work, self-improvement through education, and the rational organization of work and leisure marked the extent to which Russia had moved along the familiar economic and social path of West European nations. Far from being estranged from one another, social groups were increasingly enmeshed in a web of social policies and goals, especially on urban agendas, voluntary associations, the commercialization of entertainment and leisure, and the growth of a popular culture shared by an ever-widening audience from across the social spectrum. Obstacles to the effective functioning of civil society remained. The rule of law was not guaranteed. Powerful interests opposed the direction the country was taking. The head of state was out of touch with the mood of the country and unsympathetic to the institutions of modern statehood. Even greater was the challenge of including the great majority of the country in a still emergent civil society.

EXPANDING CIVIL SOCIETY

Early theorists of civil society and the public sphere linked their growth to the interaction of individuals and corporate groups, who represented the collective interests of individual members, in the realm of market exchange. They were aware that civil society excluded various social groups. Some groups either stood outside the sphere of market exchange or, if they participated in it, still lacked the corporate organization necessary to give them a clear public voice. Women, in particular, were largely confined to the private, family sphere. Few believed that the exclusion of some people from civil society was permanent. Hegel, as previously seen, maintained that the state could alleviate the bias in civil society toward particular corporate groups and enable a realm of civic freedom for all citizens. In Russia, the attitudes and institutions underlying civil society were relatively weak and vulnerable to state oppression and especially weakly represented among the large rural population. But by 1913 the potential for wider inclusion of the population in civil society was everywhere apparent. The growth of civil society, however, posed a potential threat to the empire. Historically, the appearance of civil society coincided closely with the rise of the nation-state. Could the institutions of civil society nurture a pluralism that embraced ethnic diversity, or would the development of the institutions of civil society within ethnic groups foster national rivalries and divisions?

WOMEN

Women had made striking inroads into membership in civil society by 1913, although they were far from equal to men in law and even less so in practice. Women's exclusion from civil society in Russia began to break down well before the beginning of the twentieth century. Women had been organizing to demand admission to the public sphere since the 1860s. By 1913 the female workforce across a broad spectrum of employment was large and growing. Earning their own living allowed women to challenge patriarchal institutions and traditions. What is striking about the gains and setbacks for women is the extent to which by 1913 they had entered the public sphere and women's issues had made their way high up onto the public agenda. They had also garnered widespread public and even institutional support, in the form of the majority in the State Duma, for even greater inclusion.

Entrepreneurs in Russia, like their counterparts in the West, had as early as the mid-nineteenth century identified urban women as primary consumers of luxury, and later, of mass-produced goods. Fashion magazines not only transferred to Russia the latest styles and tastes of Westerners, but also gradually introduced the West European middle-class ideals of domesticity and sense of self into Russian homes.[1] Well before the rise of the cinema, fashion magazines drew their readers into new and foreign worlds and enabled a Russian woman to "feel herself part of a modern, cosmopolitan community of women, who shared the same interests and tastes."[2] The sense of self that a new identity as sophisticated consumer provided, however, fell well short of the satisfaction of recognition in the public sphere.

The drive for recognition had begun in the 1860s. Women's most important early success was in higher education.[3] They were aided by the great need of a large population for education and the relative shortage of professionals in Russia to meet the need. Women presented their case for higher education not as a demand for equal rights with men but as a call to service. The strategy won them a good deal of support within state circles. The vocations that many entered, however, such as teaching, general medicine, and pharmacy, were relatively low-status occupations in Russian society. An attempt in the emancipation decade to open universities to women students soon failed, but in 1872 the government permitted the organization of the first Higher Courses for Women, the Guerrier courses in Moscow. Kazan' University faculty mounted women's courses in 1876, and St. Petersburg and Kiev universities joined the parade in 1878. Still others followed. The Petersburg Higher Women's (Bestuzhev) Courses were the best known. They offered courses in two faculties, History-Philology and Mathematics-Natural Sciences. University professors lectured in the courses. Although the higher courses did not confer a degree, the education was roughly equivalent to that given in the universities. Only in 1911 were woman accorded the right to sit for state examinations and receive degrees.

After the assassination of Alexander II in 1881, resistance to higher education for women strengthened in conservative and official circles. Critics associated highly educated women with radical political sympathies. The result was that by 1905 only the Bestuzhev Courses were still functioning. The revolution of 1905 inspired a fresh push for women's higher education. By 1914, there were twenty-five thousand students enrolled in women's university-level higher courses in ten cities.[4] For many educated women, finding employment commensurate with their level of education was difficult. Most women went into teaching. Until 1911 they were confined to the lower grades; the curriculum was basic and provided little intellectual stimulation; and opportunities to move up to more responsible positions in the educational system were mostly confined to men. In most jurisdictions women teachers who married had to resign. If they did so they lost their pension rights.[5] In 1913 the rule against marriage was abolished for women teachers in St. Petersburg but persisted elsewhere, as did restrictions on teachers' attire and enforcement of codes of social behavior.[6] Women were not allowed to teach in universities but from 1906 could teach in the higher women's courses.

Opportunities for women to obtain both education and meaningful employment were expanding rapidly in the years before the war, however. In the 1912–1913 academic year two-thirds of the 903 students of the Moscow Conservatory were women. Ninety women graduated from the conservatory at the end of the school year.[7] The growth of private industry and commerce provided one outlet for talented women. The expansion of journalism and publishing especially attracted women. The zemstvos provided professional work for many women, and by 1913 a wide range of lower-level bureaucratic support positions were also open to them. In 1906 the St. Petersburg Women's Technical Institute began to train female architects, designers, and engineers. The Department of Railways in 1913 opened employment in the railway system to graduate engineers from the institute but excluded them from responsible positions and limited their salaries.

In 1872 courses in medicine for women began in the Military-Medical-Surgical Academy in St. Petersburg. After further intensive lobbying by activists, the Women's Medical Institute opened in St Petersburg in 1897. Other such institutes appeared later in other university centers.[8] Between

1898 and 1916 the proportion of women among registered physicians rose from 3 percent to 15 percent.[9] However, women medical practitioners were disadvantaged compared to men. On average they earned about half the income of males.[10] In public service female doctors were restricted to pediatric, gynecological, and maternity hospitals as well as girls' schools and the police-medical service that examined prostitutes. In private practice and in rural districts, where many women worked as zemstvo physicians, they performed a much broader role.[11] Women also worked as fel'dshers (paramedics), dentists, pharmacists, and licensed midwives.

Cracking restrictions against women in the legal profession proved difficult. The relative success of women in medicine encouraged the drive to expand the rights of women lawyers. Women's law faculties had come into existence in 1906, but graduates were restricted to legal consultation and could not plead cases in court. In 1912 the State Duma passed a bill to allow women to serve as barristers in court. The bill went to a commission of the State Council in January 1913. The minister of justice argued that the widening of the role of women in the law was part of a larger attempt to promote women's rights and destroy the family. The majority in the commission countered that other professionals, such as actors and musicians, were more likely to be separated from families than lawyers. As well, not all women were destined to be married. To arguments of conservatives that women were not suited for the professions or that peasants would never seek out female lawyers, supporters of the bill replied that women doctors had proven the professional abilities of women, and peasants regularly went to them voluntarily. Peasants also routinely sought advice from women teachers. The commission forwarded the bill to the main body of the State Council. Crowds of women attended the debate on the bill in the council. They were disappointed. The majority rejected the legislation.[12] Further attempts to improve the access of women lawyers also ended with a State Council veto. Legislative attempts to allow women to serve as jurors also failed in the State Council.

In spite of such setbacks, women were making gains in other areas. In response to an inquiry from the Eisk stock exchange committee the Ministry of Trade and Industry ruled in 1913 that women could sit as members of stock exchange committees and could vote for responsible officers in them but not hold office themselves.[13] In Kazan' in 1913 a hundred Muslim women petitioned the library directorate for library access for women. The directorate granted access for one day per week. An attempt to establish a gymnasium for Muslim women, however, failed.[14] In 1913 the daughter of General Aleksandr Samsonov was the first Russian woman to receive a pilot's license, which she celebrated with a display of figure eights and barrel rolls over the aerodrome.[15] Her father was soon to command Russian troops at the catastrophic Battle of Tannenberg.

In March 1914 married women received the right to hold their own internal passports without their husbands' permission. The old law had required a woman to live with her husband in a place of his choosing. The new legislation enabled a woman to live separately from her husband. The bill was far from perfect. To the original clause permitting a woman to petition the courts to live away from her husband, the State Council added the phrase "under the condition that living with her husband is unbearable."[16] The State Council further amended the bill to eliminate a clause requiring a woman's consent to be included on her husband's passport and to drop other provisions that allowed a woman living with her husband to get a job, go to school, or take out a loan without his consent. Under the amendment women who were separated from their husbands retained those rights. As critics argued, the amendment encouraged women to leave husbands who resisted their wives' career or educational ambitions.

Another striking example of the evolution of attitudes to women's rights was the issue of female property inheritance. The Russian Women's Mutual Philanthropic Society had pressed for several years for a bill to make the inheritance rights of men and women equal. A new law passed in June 1912 and came into effect in 1913. The Ministry of Justice and the Council of Ministers agreed with the Duma in supporting the right of women to full equality of inheritance with male heirs. Ever vigilant in its primary concern to preserve the tradition of keeping landed gentry property intact, the State Council amended the bill to provide equality of inheritance of urban property but to preserve the traditional provision for a woman to receive one-seventh of rural property. Interestingly, the law retained the right of all female heirs to a share. Thus a settlement involving a widow with four daughters and four sons would result in the women of the family receiving five-sevenths of the property and the men the remaining two-sevenths. It was not clear whether the law applied to all rural property or only to that of large landed estates.[17]

The battle for women's suffrage that peaked in late 1905 and early 1906 did not die out completely in the years of reaction. Immediately before

World War I some fifteen thousand women belonged to suffrage organiza-tions.[18] In 1912 the League for Women's Equality petitioned the third Duma to amend the state electoral law to allow women to vote and be elected on an equal footing with men. The petition was consigned to a commission from which it never emerged. Late in 1912 a feminist meeting to press for votes for women organized in St. Petersburg by the Women's Progressive Party packed a large hall. In early 1913 the Kadets sponsored a bill in the Duma to introduce universal suffrage in all elections. After two days of debate the bill failed by a vote of 206 to 126. Another bill giving women the right to vote in elections to the proposed new volost' assembly passed in the State Duma but failed in the State Council in spring 1913.[19]

Russian women were also engaged heavily in the international women's movement. The International Women's Council was formed in 1888 to advance the rights of women. The council membership was made up of national branch organizations. Since the Russian state refused to permit the formation of an all-Russian women's organization, Russian women were by rule excluded. The council responded by naming A.P. Filosofova as an honorary vice president and permitted Russian delegates to attend its conferences and congresses. With Filosofova's death in 1912, A.I. Sha-banova assumed the honorary vice presidency. The Women's Progressive Party and several other women's political organizations formed close ties after 1905 with the International Women's Suffrage Alliance, which was founded in 1902, and regularly sent a delegation to its congresses. From abroad A.M. Kollontai, N.K. Krupskaia, and I.F. Armand spoke on behalf of Russian working women at meetings of the International Women's Socialist Secretariat. During 1913 Kollontai worked diligently to persuade female textile workers to choose a delegation to attend the next congress of the Secretariat in Vienna in 1914.[20]

It is easy to dismiss women's gains in education and legal status as the gains of an elite, with no impact on the lives of lower-class women. Class divisions were an obstacle to a unified women's movement, and the police regularly blocked whatever attempts middle-class women made to reach women socially beneath them. But gains across gender lines were gains for women regardless of class, as the long and painful history of feminism has shown. Moreover, middle-class women did try to press for reforms to benefit working women. The League for Women's Equality campaigned for a maternity law to protect the rights of women factory workers. It is notable

that the legislation for the factory health insurance funds did provide maternity leave for women workers in those factories under the jurisdiction of the
factory inspectorate.[21] The league also led the struggle to introduce female
factory inspectors. A bill went before the Duma in 1913 to create a female
factory inspectorate to oversee the enforcement of the laws on female and
child labor.[22] The Ministry of the Interior opposed it and nothing was done
to implement it before the war.

Socialist intellectuals, too, were dismissive of feminist initiatives and
worked to direct women workers into the proletarian struggle. That began
to change in 1912 when some social democrats began to appeal to women
workers directly. In 1910 the Socialist International had designated 8
March as International Women's Day. On 23 February 1913 by the old
style calendar, International Women's Day was celebrated in Russia for
the first time, with demonstrations in five cities. In St. Petersburg workers
organized a day on behalf of female workers. In the morning a full hall
listened to readings and songs. In the afternoon there were speeches and
more readings in a larger hall. The speakers were mostly women workers.
The police refused to permit the Social Democratic deputies in the State
Duma to address the crowd.[23]

Working women in cities occupied a wide variety of roles in the prewar
urban economy. Many were domestic servants. They had little free time,
earned next to nothing, and were largely isolated from each other. By 1913
there were well over two hundred thousand female shop assistants in the
country. They earned low wages and often endured harsh work and living conditions.[24] A growing portion of the factory workforce was female.
Mechanization and tightening restrictions on child labor brought more
women into the workforce. Women were paid less than men, and employers found them to be less likely to protest or strike. Women's participation
in trade unions was extremely low. With the implementation of the factory health insurance funds in 1913, however, women were elected to the
insurance fund boards in industries like textiles and tobacco, where the
workforce was mostly female.[25]

Peasant women were by 1913 beginning to assert themselves within patriarchal village society. They were taking work outside of the village more
frequently than in earlier decades. In particular, they preferred to work in
rural rather than urban factories. In the former, the dislocation from the
village was reduced but they were, temporarily at least, employees earning a

salary rather than the wards of fathers or husbands. Younger women often saw factory work as temporary, frequently as a means to acquire a dowry.[26] A growing market for crafts enabled both men and women to supplement agricultural incomes. The increasing role of the peasant woman as earner rather than as laborer was symbolized in the changing nature of a peasant bride's dowry. Traditionally brides had hand made their dowries to showcase their skills to prospective grooms. In the last decades of the empire brides more often bought urban manufactured goods as tokens of their capacity to earn. New brides were also instrumental in driving a trend toward dividing up extended family property, which enabled them to escape the traditional tyranny of the mother-in-law.[27]

Peasant women were also in growing numbers using the law to defend their rights. In June and July 1913, for example, one peasant volost' court heard two cases brought by wives against husbands for insult by violence. The husbands received seven- and fifteen-day jail sentences. Women also brought cases against other women to the courts and spoke for themselves before the judges. Such cases were commonplace in some jurisdictions by 1913.[28] Provisions in the land reform laws that greatly strengthened the legal authority of heads of households left widows vulnerable. A law of 1910 declared that property held by a woman and her children was the common property of the family and not of the woman head of household. Peasants were reluctant to give widows temporary usage of allotments that might lead to sale of the property. Many widows sought redress for such treatment in the volost' courts.[29]

The agricultural reform movement in the countryside enabled educated women to take leadership roles in rural development. In Odoev the chair of the Ivitsk Agricultural Society since its establishment six years earlier was a Mrs. Shetrovskaia. Under her direction the society had established an experimental plot, a tool and machine depot that included a winnower for separating weed seeds from seed grain, a credit society, and a consumer cooperative. At its most recent annual meeting, a motion put forward by Mrs. Shetrovskaia to enroll peasant women as members of the society had passed.[30] A certain S.A. Mak-tskaia arrived in the village of Tomilin in Sebezhsk district in 1910. In less than three years she established an agricultural society, opened courses in animal husbandry and milk production, and set up a dairy artel' and two furniture manufacturing artels. The correspondent of *Moskovskie vedomosti* reported that the local intelligentsia and the officials of the Main Administration for Land Reorganization and Agriculture had sat up and taken notice of her work.[31] Newspapers identified other women playing similar roles in rural areas. Female teachers in peasant classrooms were common by 1913, and women doctors practiced rural medicine through the zemstvos in growing numbers. Such women provided role models for female independence that were otherwise rare in patriarchal peasant society.

The public prominence of women was a source of male anxiety in 1913.[32] The rising proportion of women in the factory workforce, with their lower wages, provoked resentment among male workers. Writing in *Metallist'* in December 1913, a worker lamented that women were everywhere taking work away from men. In the eyes of some workers at the new Aivaz works, he wrote, "The factory has already begun to seem alien, like an odious 'women's' city...." He attributed the invasion to technological development, which capitalism ruthlessly drove forward.[33] In their protests male workers sometimes sought to limit mechanization that reduced work to mere routine, or more often, failing that, to prevent the placement of women in the new easier jobs.

The entry of women into the public sphere was by 1913 a subject for artists and writers. The portrayal of women in melodramatic films in many ways mirrored the gender issues of the time. The strong, independent woman, the woman as sexual predator, the female avenger, or the working woman of films catalogued not only the real gains that some women were achieving in the public sphere and in gender relations but also male anxiety about the new woman. Women in many Russian films of the day bought their independence at a high personal cost. As Denise Youngblood, a historian of the early Russian cinema, observed, the heroines of the screen finished ahead no more often than did women in life.[34]

The theater was also engaged with the woman question in 1913. A whole series of what some critics referred to as "misogynist" plays that year were the occasion for a number of debates and mock trials of the authors. In *Ekaterina Ivanovna* Leonid Andreev depicted a woman who is falsely accused of infidelity and shot at by her husband in the opening scene. She escapes unharmed and leaves the household with her children. She then commits adultery with the very man her husband suspected. In time the couple reconciles, but Ekaterina Ivanovna, who only wished to dance in life, as Andreev later explained, is jostled and elbowed by those who cannot dance. She loses her rhythm and whirls into infidelity and moral decline.[35] Late in the play she poses as Salome with the head of the Baptist in an urn and at the end goes off into the night in an automobile with a dissolute artist. No reference to her children is made after the opening scene. Many saw in the play a slander on women and found Ekaterina Ivanovna's decline highly implausible. Others sympathized with her refusal to become an "average person" (*srednyi chelovek*).[36] Andreev was astonished to learn of his mock trial in Moscow. Nor could he credit reports that women hissed during the performance of the play. The men, he insisted, must be the ones who hissed, for "Katerina *strikes them.*"[37]

Mikhail Artsybashev's play *Jealousy* kept the controversy alive. A reworking of *Othello,* the play is a condemnation of the institution of marriage and the sexual double standard, by which betrayal by a man is "like spitting from a window into the street, while betrayal by a woman is like spitting from the street into the house."[38] Marriage chains the partners together so that any move made by one disturbs the other. Conditioned from childhood to be attractive to men, Elena Nikolaevna, who is married to an author, Sergei Petrovich, collects the men in their circle and enjoys their attentions. She flirts, toys with their affections, but remains faithful to her husband. He notes her flirtations and reproaches her. He refuses to accept her reassurances. He storms in on a scene where one of her more determined admirers is attempting to rape her. His uncertainty and jealousy grow. He presses her again and again to tell the truth. She bursts into anger at his refusal to believe her and tells him that she has had dozens of lovers. Attempting to stop her words he strangles her in a kind of trance. In a debate in Moscow the artist Natalia Goncharova denounced the play as an artistically and psychologically negative phenomenon and strongly protested the depiction of women in it.[39] Some saw the wave of misogyny on the stage as an attempt to define women sexually in the face of the rise of women's rights. Others blamed the decline of romanticism and the dominance of positivism. Only a few grasped Artsybashev's point that it was men who still defined women and their appropriate roles in life.[40]

By 1913 upper- and middle-class women had gained significant ground in the struggle for membership in civil society. They had attained more equal property rights and won greater control over their own fates as individuals rather than as wards of men. Higher education was increasingly open to them, and in spite of certain restrictions on their activities women were practicing the professions in large numbers. Women participated in a range of voluntary societies as equal partners with men and had formed their own societies and political parties to advance feminist goals. They were active participants as well in international women's organizations. Although feminist and socialist women were reaching out to working women in cities, state repression and the cramped intellectual and physical lives of most lower-class women stood in the way of their organization and any significant improvement of their lot. Factory legislation, however, had not overlooked at least some of the needs of women in the workforce. A few working women were getting experience in public office through the health insurance fund boards. Peasant women were increasingly placing their selves ahead of marriage, family, and village. Although scarcely yet members of civil society, they were by 1913 acquiring some of the economic and legal tools needed to help them breach its walls.

PEASANTS

The peasantry as a whole was also showing signs of awakening to the possibilities of civic inclusion. The traditional structure of legal social estates, which was weakening in cities, remained a powerful economic and social determinant in rural areas. Nobles still owned a significant, if declining, share of rural land. The curia system of voting in the zemstvos assured the rural nobility of domination over local self-government. The official roles of marshals of the nobility and the land captains in rural administration and their informal ties with central government officials guaranteed their authority over the peasant majority. While much remained the same as in earlier decades, by 1913 three processes were well underway that were changing attitudes and relations in the Russian countryside. They were an increase in literacy, an intensification of urban-rural contacts, and the penetration of the market into the rural economy. The last two were uneven, heavily dependent as they were on geography; the first was more uniform, as central government, zemstvos, and church collaborated to bring the realization of universal primary education into sight.

The process of learning to read and write replicates a number of conditions and skills associated with modernity. In particular, the school separates learning from the traditional environment, teaches lessons of general application rather than skills attached to immediate and specific tasks, and inculcates discipline and constructed external order.[41] A literate individual has the capacity to move between abstract and concrete understandings of phenomena. Peasants had by 1913 broadly recognized the value of literacy and numeracy as assets in a changing world. Access to education topped the list of peasant demands in the revolutionary year of 1905; peasant delegates to the Duma regularly denounced the poor quality of education in church-parish schools and demanded their incorporation into the school inspectorate under the Ministry of Education. Peasant schools provided only a low level of literacy to most of their graduates. Schooling nevertheless enabled a minority of young peasants to access new general and technical knowledge that contradicted old beliefs and challenged traditional practices and techniques. Popular literature opened to some literate peasants an imaginative world that stood in sharp contrast to village conditions and norms.

Literacy in particular had an impact on the religious sensibilities of peasants. As the ability of peasants to read spread, devotional literature for the masses proliferated, and rural libraries became more common, the peasant faithful, like urban workers, formed a more engaged and self-conscious appreciation of their beliefs. Literacy nurtured a growing spiritual autonomy and promoted greater religious diversity. The clergy also began to revise its relationship with a more spiritually aware laity. Sermons became more common as priests sought to enter into a dialogue with their congregations. The Church hierarchy was itself divided about the role the laity should play in church administration and the centrality of the parish to church organization. A minority viewed the parish as the basic unit of the church. They aimed to secure the fundamental equality of all believers. In particular, they wanted to enhance the role of the laity by creating self-governing parish councils and assemblies that would manage church property in the parish and name their own priests. In their view, the laity and priesthood were separate but equal partners in the church community. The majority adhered to a bishop-centered view of church reform. They rejected the autonomy of the parish and viewed the priest as the representative of the bishop. Bishops, they argued, should go on appointing priests but should consult more widely with parishioners than they had in the past. The laity should have no formal role in the management of parish church property. The majority favored the election of parish church councils by parishioners with the priest as their chair but denied the equality of priesthood and laity. The former was the teacher and shepherd of the latter. Most priests favored greater freedom from the consistory of the diocese but not the election of priests by parishioners. Many of them also supported the right of priests to elect the bishop.[42]

Religious self-consciousness and growing awareness among peasants of the debate in the hierarchy about the role of the laity and control of the parish fostered the desire among parishioners to enter the discussion. Like the urban lower classes, peasants actively sought to play a larger role in parish affairs. They pursued their goals through letters and petitions to the chanceries of dioceses and to the Holy Synod in the capital. Peasant communications on religious subjects suggest that little difference existed between the beliefs of peasants and the hierarchy. They cast doubt on the idea, advanced by educated society, that Orthodoxy harbored two faiths (*dvoeverie*), an official, correct theology and a popular theology among the masses that combined elements of Orthodoxy with pagan beliefs. Religious activists among the peasantry were at least well informed by the early twentieth century about the orthodox interpretation of their faith. The struggle for parish autonomy conducted by peasants developed in them the habits and skills of independent organization and promoted their intellectual independence.[43]

Literacy combined with peasant mobility to bring other cultural changes to villages. There has been a tendency to exaggerate the economic self-sufficiency of the peasant village in the historical literature. Peasants routinely took part in a variety of economic activities that connected them to the larger economy.[44] Many peasants earned income from both agricultural and nonagricultural pursuits. The numbers varied from region to region, but between 40 percent and 70 percent of peasants engaged in trade or commerce.[45] Other households derived extra income from family members who had migrated to work in commercial, industrial, or mining centers. In Viatka province in the northeast, for example, 90 percent of households supplemented their income through handicraft production or remittances from migrant family members.[46] A few peasants ran manufacturing businesses of their own. The peasant trader, so vilified by the intelligentsia as a capitalist exploiter, was a regular and accepted figure in village life. Peasants did business in both rural and urban settings and acquired a broad familiarity with both local and national issues. Even stay-at-home peasants were regularly exposed to news of the world abroad by migrant workers, traders from other villages, returning soldiers, and increasingly the schoolteacher, the fel'dsher, or the village clerk. An important vehicle for commercial exchange was the trade fair that brought peasant traders from far and wide.

Here and elsewhere in their dealings they created a public sphere, in which they socialized widely, shared views, and formed opinions.[47] Their regular participation in market exchange carried with it the praise, respect, and approval that promoted selfhood as well as the mutual recognition of the interests and desires of others that were the foundation of civil society as Hegel understood it.

Peasants were often better apprised about affairs in Russia and abroad than the educated supposed. A rural correspondent of *Russkie vedomosti* recorded a conversation with a peasant father who had two sons of conscription age. The father turned out to be well informed about the situation in the Balkans and the tensions between Russia and Austria.[48] Literate peasants were a minority but their influence was large. They read a variety of publications and passed on what they read orally. Many villages subscribed to newspapers, which literate peasants read to those who were not. Jeffrey Burds has chronicled the proliferation of taverns and teahouses in the countryside in the last years of the nineteenth century. Places of respite and entertainment, they also served as information centers. Proprietors drew peasants to their inns by subscribing to newspapers and journals. When the mail came, peasants gathered to read or to hear the news read. In Moscow province 564 villages and 164 teashops subscribed to 1,395 and 283 newspapers and journals respectively. The more remote the area the more subscriptions were taken.[49]

Cultural changes in the countryside, particularly a growing sense of self among young peasants, were not simply a consequence of urban influence and the mimicking of urban ways. Urban cultural influences only reinforced cultural and social processes driven by the changing economy in rural areas. They were a product of forces at work simultaneously in city and countryside. Chief among them was the development of market relations. Semen Maslov, a strong supporter of the cooperative movement, noted that on the eve of the war the Russian peasant was very different from the peasant of a half century before. The main cause of the difference that he saw was the monetarization of Russian agriculture in most regions. Peasants, he argued, could no longer get along without the market.[50] Market penetration was most pronounced in areas near cities or along railway lines that joined cities or in regions linked to foreign agricultural export markets.

The rapid growth of the urban commercial and industrial economy in the last years of the empire increased city-village contact in a number of ways. The outreach of cities was growing. More middle-class citizens were buying rural properties for investment or recreational purposes. In the near hinterland of major cities the growth of the dacha phenomenon extruded urbanites and their culture into the countryside. The extension of the railway network established dynamic corridors along which the urban and the rural interacted. The number of fairs, at which urban-produced goods were available, intensified in district and volost' capitals. Stores selling consumer products proliferated in rural areas.[51]

The zemstvo was also exerting greater influence in villages. Hired zemstvo specialists, who were known as the third element, had shown radical political tendencies in 1905. By 1913, however, most of them were committed to a constructive and patient approach to the improvement of rural life. A.N. Naumov, who served as marshal of the nobility in Samara province, noted that by 1913–1914 the radicalism of the period of 1905–1907 had given way to "peaceful, measured work."[52] Not everyone approved of the change in the attitudes of the third element. One contemporary lamented the decline of what he called idealism among zemstvo professionals and regretted their turn to careerism.[53] The third element was fundamentally a middle-class group, and their employers, the zemstvos, were building the foundations of middle-class society in rural Russia with the creation of savings banks, hospitals and clinics, schools, and postal and telephone services. The third element served as a transmission belt, conveying middle-class ideas and values from the cities where they trained to the villages in which they worked.[54]

The impact on villages of urban contact in its various guises was considerable. After the emancipation reforms a culture of conspicuous consumption, fueled by peasant migrants to urban areas, developed. Peasants sought distinction and honor in the decorating and furnishing of their homes and in their personal appearance. More and more peasants saw consumption as the road to social mobility and were prepared to sacrifice to possess goods that conferred distinction.[55] Peasant dress and fabrics began to give way to urban fashions and machine-manufactured materials among women. Felt boots in winter and leather footwear in summer replaced bast shoes. The Tula peasant and Tolstoyan Mikhail Novikov remembered that when the young women and men came back from the factory for Easter it was no longer possible to tell by their dress which were the peasant and which the noble children. At village dances the factory youth introduced the villagers to songs from distant villages that they had learned from fellow factory workers. Novikov also recalled the arrival of sewing machines and gramophones in the villages.[56]

Mores also began to change. Peasant families were willing to tolerate more relaxed standards of behavior from women in return for the wages they contributed. A woman's earnings could allow a son and his wife to leave a father's house. Husbands with wage-earning wives often had to take on traditionally female tasks that further blurred established gender lines. These trends weakened the patriarchal extended family and pointed toward a more companionate type of marriage. There were still limits. Women who spent time in cities were deemed by many peasants to have learned habits of independence and unconventional behaviors that made them less desirable as peasant wives.[57]

There were other signs of the growing individuality and independence from tradition that changes in dress and generational relations suggested. The folk song, with its broad generic themes, was giving way in rural areas to the *chastushka,* which most commonly took the form of a four-line song in rhyme. The emotional life of the personality was at the heart of the chastushka. Instead of the permanence of tradition it captured the passing moods and changing experiences of the modern individual. Common themes in the chastushka were the desire of youth to marry freely and the rejection of constraints imposed by convention and authority. The influence of the city played a role in transforming the folk song, but other forces at work in rural life were of greater importance. The school exposed students to poetry that not only influenced the form of the new songs but introduced into them themes of individual loss, pain, and joy that characterized the literature of the educated. Cheap songbooks helped to spread the new forms as did itinerant workers and soldiers returning from service.[58]

Changes in peasant culture stirred fears among the authorities over the decline of morality among the rural masses. Concern about the spread of hooliganism, long an urban phenomenon, into rural areas reached a crescendo in 1913. The Ministry of Internal Affairs appointed the Lykoshin commission early in the year to recommend measures to control the hooligan menace, and the Church solicited reports from bishops on hooligan behavior. The bishop of Perm complained that young people went about at night playing harmonicas, singing scurrilous songs, and making a general uproar. The Holy Synod attributed such outrages to the broad decline of morals and religious principles in the rural population.[59] The hooligan activities of Perm's youth that the bishop deplored ranged from singing, rock throwing, and daubing graffiti on buildings to assault, rape, arson, and even murder. Insolence and lack of respect toward cultured, wealthy, or responsible people were marks of the hooligan. Hooligans were seldom organized in gangs: their acts were largely spontaneous and had little purpose other than to hurt a passing target. Rural hooliganism was more common among Russians than among non-Russians and more prevalent in areas with nearby factories where seasonal labor was common. Some experts saw a correlation between the incidence of rural hooliganism and proximity to urban life or to the factory experience, and they associated it with villages in transition from a traditional to an urban culture.[60] Frequent victims of hooligans were fellow peasants, especially those who had established khutors, which were more isolated and easily targeted.

The Ministry of the Interior proposed the use of the powers of reinforced security, which empowered authorities to use arbitrary measures against individuals or groups, and a return to corporal punishment to combat rural hooliganism. Many citizens were skeptical about such drastic measures. Some argued that most acts now labeled hooliganism were not new but had existed before in the criminal code under different names.[61] Peasants were reluctant to help the authorities apprehend hooligans or to condemn their behaviors in the volost' courts. Some peasants mocked public anxieties about hooliganism. In one instance, villagers, whom a zemstvo official had roundly cursed for refusing to vote an end to the commune, wrote to the local newspaper to ask why the official was not charged with hooliganism. The governor had decreed that cursing was a hooligan act and had set a fine of from 1 to 500 roubles or three months in jail for offenders.[62]

Others accepted hooliganism as a real phenomenon but rejected drastic remedies. The Constitutional Democrats opposed the use of administrative measures against rural hooliganism and wanted the regular courts to deal with cases on an individual basis.[63] The provincial zemstvo of Nizhnii Novgorod adopted measures to combat hooliganism that included educational programs, the prohibition of the sale of alcohol, and reform of the police courts.[64] The Riazan' district zemstvo sought an answer in schooling and after-school education for youth. A number of district congresses that were organized to discuss an Octobrist-sponsored bill on hooliganism in the Duma rejected corporal punishment as "inappropriate at a time when life is becoming more cultured" and recommended community work and cultural measures instead.[65] Only a tiny minority of zemstvos supported corporal punishment or administrative measures as a weapon against hooliganism. The overwhelming rejection in 1913 by respectable rural society of drastic repressive measures against hooliganism belies the view that the elites saw the peasants as dangerous or as an imminent threat to them or their property in the immediate prewar period.[66]

The impact of the land reform in reshaping peasant attitudes and practices was considerable. The land reform forced peasants into making decisions concerning their self-interests that they had never before faced. It also brought them into contact with outsiders, who provided assistance and mediation, in unprecedented numbers. An important, relatively new and controversial presence in the countryside in the prewar years was the agronomist. There were about ten thousand in the field by 1914, an increase from around five hundred in 1906. There were also another twenty thousand students attending agronomic schools in 1914. Most of the scholar agronomists were from intelligentsia backgrounds. Peasants accounted for no more than 25 percent of students in any advanced agricultural school. In Russia's 400 middle and lower agricultural schools, however, by 1914 one-half to two-thirds of students had peasant origins and more peasant graduates were poised to enter the rural workforce.[67] Peasant graduates often complained about their lack of influence, but their presence in the field in increasing numbers was beginning to narrow the social gap between the scientific specialist and the peasant farmer.

By 1913 a network of local agronomists was in place, although their numbers were inadequate to the need in most areas. Since the majority of local agronomists still came from nonpeasant backgrounds, peasants initially tended to view them as officials; few believed that agronomists had anything useful to teach them. Local agronomists lectured on agricultural techniques, conducted group discussions, and provided private consultations with individual peasants. They frequently managed equipment centers and credit cooperatives, taught peasants how to use new tools, and tested farming techniques on demonstration plots. At the district level most zemstvos had an agronomist, who managed an equipment depot that loaned equipment to local equipment centers, ran an experimental station and often the zemstvo credit bank, and supervised the local network of agronomists. Zemstvos also routinely employed agricultural teachers who went into villages to give lectures or assist with innovative projects.

Scientific agronomy had enormous potential to improve the tilling, sowing, and harvesting techniques of individual peasants whether they farmed communal or consolidated lands. Zemstvo agronomists were committed to the improvement of all peasant agriculture regardless of the form of land tenure, and from about 1910 the government tacitly acquiesced. Most provinces developed experimental plots and farms, where peasants could see in action: new crops; machines such as winnowers (which cleaned seeds of weeds) and other tools; and new methods, including the latest plowing and sowing techniques. The zemstvos in 1913 supported more than fourteen thousand model plots.[68] Scientific agronomists in general did not despise or dismiss traditional peasant practices. Rather, they tested those techniques against others on experimental stations. Frequently, but not always, they found them to be less than optimal practices.

Russian peasant agriculture in the prewar years was producing adequately but well below its potential. Peasants lacked the scientific knowledge that the agronomists could provide. Their own traditions could not (at least not quickly enough) keep pace with the demand for increased productivity. Rational choice for peasants was possible only when they had adequate knowledge of current, effective techniques and of their applications and costs.[69] The most common peasant explanation for the discrepancy between estate yields and yields on peasant lands was that the landlords had taken the best land. Since only 10 percent of all land was in estate tenure, this was at best a faulty rationalization. Traditional peasant agriculture did adapt to new techniques.[70] Most adaptation was the result of copying successful practices elsewhere. Peasants near large estates where innovations were in place sometimes imitated the techniques they observed there. From around 1900, peasants, for example, began to harrow their fields a second time before planting to kill newly sprouted weeds, a technique first developed on estate farms. In dry years, however, a second harrowing was undesirable because it further dried the soil. Most peasants, having incorporated the practice into their routine, did it anyway. Lack of knowledge often meant that innovations were not used to the best advantage but became matters of habit rather than of understanding.

Peasants generally lacked knowledge about how to adjust their tillage techniques to weather conditions. The timing of sowing crops is also weather-sensitive. Peasant observance of the Easter holidays often delayed sowing past the optimal time. The density of sowing, too, depended on weather and soil conditions. On average peasants sowed too densely, sometimes by a factor of six. Frequently they sowed less densely on poorer than on better soil, the reverse of proper husbandry. Peasants were resistant to the use of seed drills. They believed the spaces between the drills to be a waste of land. Since sowing in drills could produce yields of up to 30 percent more than hand sowing, their belief was mistaken. When choosing grain for planting, peasants paid little attention to seed size and frequently sowed the smallest grains. They did, however, recognize that new seeds germinate better than old ones. Peasants paid little attention to weed seeds in the seed grain. Winnowing machines, which blew out the weed seeds, were expensive and not common. Their use, however, was spreading by 1913.

If tillage and seeding techniques were faulty, peasants did little better at harvest time. Many peasants, who failed to understand the drying capacity of harvested grain, delayed reaping, resulting in lower-quality grain and losses of up to 50 percent because of dislodged grains from overripe stalks. The transportation of grain sheaves from field to threshing floor resulted in further grain losses, since few peasants took measures to catch falling grain. Once the grain was in the barn, mice and rats took their share. Although threshing machines were expensive, one machine served many peasants, since the time needed for threshing was greatly shortened. As a result, machine threshing was widespread by 1913.

Change in peasant farming techniques was painfully slow. Historically, Russian peasant farming had been extensive. Peasants looked for relief from shortages in an increase in land rather than in higher yields on existing plots. Many peasants believed their plots were too small to benefit from innovation and initially, at least, were convinced that the agronomists' knowledge applied only to large farms. Even peasants who took land as khutors or otrubs often continued to till, sow, and harvest in the old ways and to practice the traditional, unimproved three-field rotation. It was, however, not primarily the three-field system of rotation that prevented peasants from improving crop yields. It was poor tillage, sowing, and harvesting techniques on individual plots that reduced yields, and these were precisely the skills that agricultural science was able to teach.[71] By 1913 some peasants were beginning to realize that the new agronomy was not just for the landlords.[72] The proximity of demonstration plots enabled some peasants to see for themselves what different techniques could achieve and the impact that machines or new tools could have.

In many villages a few peasants were prepared to try something new. More peasants were willing to book private consultations with agronomists and to try out the techniques they discussed. Innovators tended to be the younger and better-educated members of the community. Often they were the same individuals who attended agricultural lectures and courses. Attendance at lectures and conferences on agronomy grew. In the Velizh district of Vitebsk province in 1913, for example, a 16-week course of agricultural lectures that emphasized practical demonstrations drew peasants from many district villages, some of them quite remote.[73] Seventy-nine provinces and *oblasts* in 1913 hosted 1,657 agricultural courses of varying lengths, an increase of 100 percent over 1912, with 98,704 participants. More than 60.4 percent of participants were between the ages of 20 and 40, and 88.6 percent were literate.[74]

In imitation of the practice in Canada and the United States, agricultural trains ran on several routes in Russia for the first time in 1913. The first was an 11-car train on the Vladikavkaz railway that carried demonstrations on field, garden, and viticulture cultivation. The Moscow-Kazan' agricultural train had twelve cars: an auditorium car for 60 to 90 auditors (sometimes they crammed in 120); two each for a museum, cattle, and poultry displays; four for machines and tools exhibits (one for fodder demonstrations, three to house the lecturers); and one for steam heat for the whole from a boiler. The train made three trips in 1913 with 45 stops. In all, 39,033 adults and 8,862 children attended the 1,650 demonstrations and 219 lectures.[75] A Siberian agricultural train in 1913 was on the road between Kurgan and Makushino stations for 178 days, during which 16,024 people heard 398 lectures.[76] To facilitate the marketing of grain, government and zemstvos cooperated in the building of grain elevators. These greatly assisted the storage and sale of peasant-grown grain. In earlier years large-scale producers, especially noble estate owners, had provided the bulk of grain for market distribution. Increasingly, small to middle peasant producers were assuming that role. By 1914 peasants were selling about 40 percent of their grain production on the market.[77]

For all the efforts of agronomists, only a distinct minority of peasants by the beginning of World War I had transcended the realm of routine; most continued to make choices rooted in tradition and superstition. But not all peasant resistance to agricultural innovation was due to ignorance. For many peasants the additional labor required to employ the new techniques was not worth the improvement the innovation brought in increased yields. Peasant choices were frequently governed by the availability of water or the amount of labor available within the family to carry out the tasks of farming. As well, higher yields of existing crops or a switch to new crops made sense only if a market for a surplus or for a new product was readily available. Commercial processing of crops locally was weakly developed in most regions but growing in the prewar years. As we have seen, industrial crops still represented only about 4 percent of all crops produced by the beginning of the war.[78]

Available evidence suggests that communes still practicing repartition were least capable of adjusting to new farming techniques. Change occurred where repartition had ended and the communes could no longer interfere in individual peasant decisions.[79] Moreover, peasants who consolidated their land tended to adopt better planting and reaping practices than did peasants who retained plots in communal tenure. Improvements in crop yields were the result. In light of annual variations in growing conditions across a vast territory, all-empire figures comparing previous yield totals to totals in 1913 are not very meaningful.[80] More helpful is the work of Peter Toumanoff. He compared the outputs of 14 crops in 1905 and 1913. He found that before the reform, repartition of communal lands led to a decrease in productivity. The reform did little to improve the situation on lands where repartition continued. But where communal ownership gave way to private land rights, productivity increased. He concluded that "The evidence is strong that communal ownership did have a negative effect on agricultural productivity and that Stolypin's reform was effective in improving productivity."[81]

A survey conducted in 1912 compared yields of two cereal crops on three different types of landholding. Khutors on average produced 65 poods of rye and 87 poods of oats per dessiatina; otrubs produced 45 poods and 73 poods respectively; and communal lands 35 poods and 51 poods.[82] A German government commission visited Russia in 1913 in order to assess the impact that the agrarian reform was having on productivity in Russian agriculture. The commissioners were deeply impressed. They reported to their superiors that if the reform continued for another 10 years, Russia would become the strongest country in Europe. The commissioners' conclusion is overstated, but it captures the extent of change in the Russian countryside. It also unduly alarmed the German government.[83] Bernard Pares concluded that the land reorganization program initiated a rapid economic transformation in the empire unprecedented in its history.[84] None of these testimonies definitively establishes the superiority of individual over communal farming in Russia before the war, but together they strongly suggest that something approaching a transformation was occurring in Russian agriculture.

The patient work of the zemstvo activists in providing agricultural aid and financial assistance to peasants began to pay off by 1913 in the transformation of peasant attitudes toward the zemstvo as an institution. No longer did peasants regard the zemstvo as a place for the nobles. Instead they began to look on it as a source of services and became more active in asking it to provide more agronomists, teachers, veterinarians, doctors, and fel'dshers. It is also worth noting the composition of the land commissions that settled land reorganization issues. The local marshal of the nobility headed the district land organization committee. The membership included several bureaucrats and a total of six elected representatives from zemstvo or volost' peasant assemblies. Governors chaired provincial land settlement commissions, which were made up of several more bureaucrats and six elected representatives of the provincial zemstvo assembly, including three peasants.[85] The inclusion of peasant voices in the important work of the land commissions was an important step forward in rural social relations.

As an instrument of periodic land redistribution, the peasant commune, already in decline before the reform, experienced an even sharper decline as a result of the reform. The ability of peasant families to withdraw their plots from communal tenure if threatened by repartition largely destroyed the economic and moral rationales for the repartitioning commune, although a number of its functions remained. What survived the reform was the village society. Peasants showed a clear preference for communal social organization and living. It was the survival of the village society and not of the commune that preserved a basis for group action against landlords and separators in the fall of 1917. The reversal of the reform late in that year said little about the peasants' attitude to land reform but spoke to the curtailment of market forces in the chaos of revolution and a temporary return to near-autarky in the villages as a result. It also underlined the long-standing conviction of the great majority of peasants that the handiest solution to their problems was more land. It was possible and certainly safer to appropriate land as a group than singly. In any case, with regard to land seizures during the revolution, peasants behaved differently according to their historical experience and condition, and generalization is difficult.[86] Soon the Bolsheviks sanctioned the seizures and annulled the legal basis for the land reform, but the agricultural aid program was resumed in the 1920s.

The land reform created a number of new problems. The transfer of land into the ownership of the head of the household not only helped to reinforce patriarchal attitudes, but also created severe tensions regarding inheritance. The peasant preference was to divide property equally among male heirs and to provide a smaller share for single women in the family. Although peasants could buy non-allotment land, few could afford it in quantity. In any case, the law prevented them from taking ownership of more than six shares of allotment land. By law, the size of the shares varied from region to region. Without single inheritance the land could become fragmented among heirs and soon become too small for sustainability. In 1913 legislation to provide for single inheritance combined with a cash payment for disinherited family members was under consideration but was not enacted before the war.[87] It was in any event an impractical solution for cash-poor farmers. The law also proposed to set a minimal limit on the size of a khutor or otrub.[88] Such properties, whether made up of former allotment land or land purchased from the Peasant Bank or with the aid of the treasury, could not be divided in such a way as to fall below norms established for each province and district.

Historians have pointed out that the land reform conferred personal property rights on the peasants but not private property rights. Peasants who took allotment land into hereditary title, for example, did not qualify as private property owners in zemstvo elections but continued to vote in the peasant curia. Peasants holding former allotment land experienced certain restrictions on its use and could sell it only to other peasants.[89] Of far greater significance, peasant owners could not mortgage their property or use it as collateral for loans. The Main Administration for Land Reorganization and Agriculture campaigned ceaselessly on behalf of the peasants to change this restriction but other ministries stood in the way. Many reasons for the restriction were advanced at the time. One was that the treasury could not afford the burden of peasant mortgages. When the agricultural minister proposed a bank with joint government and private participation, the prime minister, who was also the minister of finance, rejected such a partnership.[90] A potent reason for the ban on individual mortgages also underlay the resistance in some government circles and among the conservative nobility to the creation of a volost' level zemstvo that aimed to eliminate the estate structure in voting for local elections and replace it with a single property qualification. Noble lobbyists opposed any measure that would weaken estate distinctions. The leveling of property rights was unacceptable to them. Outside of government, many members of the intelligentsia believed that mortgages would open peasants to the exploitation of peasant traders and other petty capitalists or that peasants were simply too incompetent to be trusted. As a result peasants could only secure loans over a certain limit on the guarantee of a cooperative.[91]

The limitations that peasants faced in the disposition of their properties did not prevent them from developing some sense of property rights. Their tendency was to understand use as the equivalent of ownership.[92] Paying for the land they had in use from the commune through redemption payments encouraged many to regard the use of the land, if not the land itself, as permanently theirs.[93] With the passage of time and generations, however, that distinction was fading. Many of the attributes of private ownership applied to personal peasant ownership: peasants could sell their land to other peasants and bequeath it to heirs. Peasants clearly distinguished between the property of others and their own. They made use of the volost' courts to secure their possessions and economic assets from others and occasionally to settle property disputes over land title.[94] The courts, however, had little central guidance to inform their decisions about property. Instead, they applied local understandings rather than a widely shared legal norm. The failure of government to define property law left disputes over land in limbo between custom and law. A failure to get redress in one jurisdiction pointed to seeking it in the other.[95]

The issues the reform raised spurred the representatives of peasants in 1913 to voice on the national stage their aspirations to full rights of citizenship. Late in the year the nonparty peasant faction in the State Duma adopted a program on rural reform. It called for the equalization of peasant rights with those of other citizens and an end to all legal disadvantages affecting the peasantry; the reform of the zemstvo franchise and of zemstvo and volost' institutions of self-government; the extension of the zemstvo to all areas where it did not presently exist; the facilitation of everything necessary to achieve land reorganization; the reform of the Peasant Bank to aid landless peasants and petty peasant proprietors; treasury assistance for the purchase by peasants of land from private sellers; treasury assistance for resettlement; universal, compulsory, and free primary education and the construction of a network of upper-level elementary schools in villages; the right of individuals to open schools, libraries, and other educational institutions; a progressive income tax and abolition of indirect taxes; reorganization of church parishes to improve conditions for the clergy; antialcohol measures; broad development of cooperative organizations; and the reorganization of production with the widest participation of the population.[96] In sharp contrast to the intelligentsia-dominated press that clamored for the withdrawal of the land reform legislation, the independent peasant delegates in the Duma gave their full support to the process and encouraged its acceleration.

The program of the independent peasant deputies was firmly anchored in developments in the countryside and reflected the wishes of many of their constituents. The land reform was only one of several important stimuli to peasant awareness of the larger world and their connectedness to it. Many other factors were at play to reinforce peasants' civic consciousness. Contemporaries referred to the effects both of the cooperatives and of the zemstvos in ending the centuries-old "eternal silence" of the villages. Zemstvo expenditures on a host of social institutions and initiatives such as schooling, experimental plots, and lectures in agronomy knitted the rural community more closely together.[97] The cooperatives poured new energy into peasant life and released long stifled initiative and creativity. Yearly, the cooperative movement was reaching out to embrace more peasant households.

Initially, the cooperatives were managed by members of the intelligentsia, who also dominated at cooperative congresses and conferences. They controlled the membership of the cooperatives and did their best to manage peasant elections to cooperative boards. It has been said as well that peasants were largely excluded from the podium at congresses.[98] Ample evidence exists, however, that their voices were heard. *Russkie vedomosti* reported that at the congress of representatives of cooperative organizations of Iaroslavl' province, the majority of the three hundred attending delegates were peasants. Peasants took the initiative in discussions. One member proposed that the agenda of future congresses be circulated in advance to member villages so that peasants could formulate their views and charge their representatives. Another proposed that the cooperatives should form a unit to initiate discussions in villages about the workings and purposes of cooperatives and to disseminate literature about them. The literature, the delegates urged, should not be distributed for free because peasants did not take handouts seriously. The theme of the literature should be to inform villagers that each member of the cooperative was entitled to take part in defining and directing the policies of the cooperative. Another peasant proposed that member cooperatives should fund a school for the study of the cooperative movement.[99]

At the first congress of western Siberian cooperative activists in Tomsk in June 1913 nearly every village in the region sent a delegate. Although many of the peasants were not used to speaking in such circumstances, they expressed their commitment to the movement and to social improvement.[100] In Chistopol district in Kazan' province the majority of the one hundred delegates to a meeting of the representatives of petty credit institutions were peasants.[101] At the local level peasants elected cooperative boards. Although it was said that some peasants had no idea that they belonged to a cooperative, more often peasants clearly understood the importance to them of the cooperative movement; factions among them vied for control of the boards. If peasants elected board members unacceptable to them—peasant traders were especially regarded with hostility by the peasants' self-appointed mentors—the intelligentsia managers of regional cooperative offices could overturn the elections. Peasants often elected traders because they respected their experience and acumen. Frequently, they reelected the very members that their superiors had just removed. Such behavior does not point to peasant passivity or resignation in the face of intelligentsia tutelage. It is noteworthy that by 1 January 1917, 85.4 percent of the members of cooperative boards and 83.5 percent of members of cooperative auditing commissions had an elementary education only, suggesting a large preponderance of peasants in the board membership.[102]

Many peasants took advantage of cooperative services. They deposited savings, took out small loans, and bought and sold goods under cooperative auspices. The cooperative network linked peasants to one another from village to village and across entire regions and broadened their identity beyond village bounds. The rhetoric in which some of the intelligentsia indulged about peasant ignorance and incurable incompetence made little difference to peasant perceptions of themselves or to the benefits they chose to derive from the cooperatives. Moreover, such rhetoric among the intelligentsia did not pass unchallenged. One commentator remarked that since the emancipation of the 1860s, the peasants had changed dramatically. But the attitudes of other social groups toward the peasantry had remained the same. He noted all sorts of survivals of the serf mentality among the nonpeasant classes and called for the recognition of peasants by their fellow citizens as men like others.[103]

Experts on the cooperatives, writing in *Russkie vedomosti* and other papers, did express concerns that better-off peasants would benefit unfairly from the cooperatives. They saw the solution, however, not in tutelage by the intelligentsia, who had slight contact with the village and no ability to successfully combat kulaks, not in control by bureaucrats, who knew little about agricultural methods or equipment, and not in supervision by the zemstvos, which had other work to do. Instead, the cooperatives had to be led by peasants educated in the ways of cooperativism, as had occurred in Germany, where "every small society was under the direction of experienced people."[104] Unfavorable comparisons of the situation in Russia with the cooperative movement in Scandinavia, where farmers shared control with educated experts, fail to take into account the far higher literacy and numeracy rates of Scandinavians than Russians and the long experience of Scandinavian farmers in the self-management of their properties, which provided them with management skills applicable beyond the farm economy. Russian peasants were just beginning to acquire that experience and the skills it taught.

Other initiatives also created public spaces where people from various estates and conditions could meet, collaborate, and develop the associations and fellow feeling that are at the heart of civil society. Closely allied to cooperatives was the drive to fireproof peasant dwellings and the provision of fire insurance. The movement began in the 1860s and intensified in the years leading up to World War I. Between them the zemstvos and the government had 2,300 specialists in fire-resistant construction in the field by the end of 1914.[105] Fire prevention measures and insurance brought peasants into contact with outsiders and schooled them in habits of responsibility for their property and that of neighbors. Peasant participation as members of volunteer fire brigades in villages brought them into rural civil society. As Cathy Frierson has noted, firefighting brigades served as models for "rational, modern organization." Some peasants occupied administrative posts and learned basic managerial skills as a result of the campaign for fire prevention. Noble paternalism encouraged collaboration between rural estates, further broadening the basis for civil society.[106] A noblewoman in Poltava province established the first permanent kindergarten in Russia for peasant children. Countess N.B. Musin Pushkina recalled visiting her aunt

Rain'ka, who ran the family estate near Smolensk after her husband's death. She built and maintained a school and hospital and "actively took part in the life of the peasantry."[107] Princess Varvara Dolgorukaia and her husband collaborated in 1913 with the local zemstvo in building a hospital on their estate. The plan called for the Dolgorukii family to pay for the construction of the building and of housing for the doctor. The zemstvo was to pay the salaries of the hospital staff.[108]

Growing peasant awareness of the benefits to them of the zemstvos served to awaken their interest in the outcomes of zemstvo elections. Peasant participation in zemstvo elections varied greatly from region to region. In district zemstvo elections in Kremenchug, where progressives were in a struggle with a slate of rightists, peasants showed a strong interest and elected peasant representatives who sided with the progressives. In Pskov, on the contrary, peasants continued to choose illiterate peasants and even village drunks as their zemstvo representatives.[109] Administrative interference in peasant elections was still common in 1913. Local officials pressured peasants to elect preselected candidates who could be counted on to support the official line. When peasants failed to elect the chosen slate, the authorities often annulled the elections and ordered a new round of voting. The result was often peasant indifference to the electoral process and an invitation to opportunists to gain administrative posts and favor.

By 1913 peasants in some jurisdictions were starting to fight back against outside manipulation of elections. In the Iaroslavl' district zemstvo elections, peasants turned out in large numbers at meetings to select electors and defeat officially supported candidates. In a lengthening list of districts, peasants responded to annulled results by reelecting the same slate with even greater majorities.[110] In some areas local cooperatives took an interest in elections. They put up candidates for peasant electors, organized preelectoral meetings to discuss local issues, and encouraged participation in electoral meetings. Their interest sometimes stimulated wider peasant participation in the electoral process.[111] In Rostov district zemstvo elections candidates chose active cooperative members to represent them at the electoral meetings. When the administration overturned the results, they elected the same people again.[112]

The representatives of peasants in zemstvos were also becoming more effective in securing policies beneficial to the villages. In the Kherson district zemstvo in 1913, peasants drew attention to the small part of the zemstvo budget designated for public education. The assembly agreed and instructed the executive to bring forward proposals for the expansion of schooling in the next budget cycle.[113] In the Umansk district of Tambov province the district zemstvo assembly voted increased funding for the zemstvo periodical *Vestnik Umanskogo Zemstva*. Peasant representatives insisted on the increased funding because their peasant constituents had expressed a strong interest in the periodical and benefited from the information it provided.[114]

Peasants residing in districts that included urban agglomerations were learning to seek out alliances with other voters to press for common interests. In the Riazan' district zemstvo peasant representatives allied with a bloc of urban representatives to press for greater expenditure on public education, student excursions to Moscow, the presentation of public entertainments, and the building of a school for artisans. They also helped progressives in the zemstvo to pass a new law on more equitable property assessments for taxation purposes.[115] In the Iuknovsk district zemstvo in Smolensk province, peasant and second curia urban representatives united to demand both sweeping changes in the way peasants were elected to the zemstvos and equal representation of peasants on land reorganization commissions, zemstvo administrative bodies, and provincial zemstvo assemblies.[116]

A few examples of growing peasant political awareness and savvy in using representative institutions not only for their own benefit but in alliances with others in the interests of the public good does not prove a wholesale commitment of the peasantry to democratic institutions and legal, incremental change. Peasants in growing numbers were willing to seek out outsiders to the village to resolve their problems and were forced to consider new understandings of the nature of rights and property. As Corinne Gaudin writes, the willingness of peasants to bring lawsuits and to appeal court decisions suggested growing peasant confidence in public institutions.[117] Peasant participation in a broadening range of administrative and social organizations with other groups points to a deepening acceptance of social pluralism among them and dispels notions that peasants had no interest in political or social participation beyond the confines of the village. Some peasants sought out and effectively participated in organs of self-administration and voluntary associations. The notion that peasants were fixated on isolation from outsiders, economic autarky, land seizures, and an illusive freedom (*volia*), if ever true, was no longer the case in 1913.[118]

By 1913 civil society was still rudimentary in the Russian countryside. The memories of the revolution of 1905 and the terror that followed remained deeply imprinted on the minds of rural dwellers. The land reform drove wedges between neighbors and sharpened competition and jealousy in villages. It is a measure of the integrating forces at work that the reform caused as little disturbance as it did and that well-off rural residents had few fears about peasant revenge by 1913. Divisive factors were more and more offset by forces and institutions that encouraged cooperation, broadened horizons, and complicated identities. More and more peasants were recognizing the value of agricultural education and were prepared to learn from the experts they had formerly derided. Market forces increased interdependency. Whatever their faults, the cooperatives were a response to capitalism that helped to secure for petty producers more control in a competitive economy and encouraged broad collaborations. Jane Burbank concludes that the cases heard in the volost' courts turned on the bourgeois values of the market, honoring of contracts, and external regulation of family relations.[119] Traditions were eroding and a more uniform popular culture was breaking down regional barriers. In most districts the intercourse between city and country was intensifying. A culture of conspicuous consumption of manufactured products was well established in villages by 1913. Although decades in arrears, the same forces that were promoting the growth of civil society in urban areas were working their magic in the Russian countryside as the war clouds began to gather.

NATIONALITIES

Ethnic, national, and religious tensions in the empire were high and rising by 1913. The Fundamental Laws of 1906 facilitated the growth of nationalist tendencies by sanctioning the formation of national organizations and communications within national groups. The emergence of national consciousness among many non-Russians brought into question the old ideal of a united and indivisible empire. The imperial government had developed no consistent or unified nationality policy or practice over the centuries and no single approach to governance. Instead, ad hoc administrative measures characterized Russian rule in the empire rather than a generalized body of colonial laws. No clear separation of domestic and imperial policy had emerged in Russia, and distinct colonial institutions did not exist.[120] Legal categorization of the population by estate or ethnicity played an important part in preserving cohesion in the empire. By recognizing the diversity of the groups that made up the emperor's subjects, imperial administration afforded a measure of self-rule that encouraged the loyalty of regional elites to the throne. The usual practice was to recognize established local power and social arrangements and place them under the supervision of viceroys, governors-general, and governors. Since they reported to the emperor, the personal nature of imperial rule persisted. The state also incorporated members of non-Russian elites, often educated in Russian language schools, into the central bureaucracy. The bureaucracy had traditionally promoted an inclusive Imperial Russian (*rossiiskii*) identity in preference to a narrow ethnic Russian (*russkii*) identity. In the last years of the empire, however, officials began more often to classify the peoples of the empire according to their ethnicity in addition to the older designations by estate or religious affiliation. Ethnicity increasingly emerged as a measure of relative loyalty to emperor and country.[121]

Historians have argued that Russian expansion into occupied lands followed by Russian peasant settlement, especially in the south and east, had generally been so gradual that the elemental nature of the process obscured for Russians the fact that they lived in a multinational empire. Instead they believed that they were building a nation-state.[122] Others have recently challenged this view. By the late eighteenth century Russian intellectuals accepted the growing romantic national consensus that historically a people that was characterized by a common language, customs, shared history, and religion, also occupied a corresponding territory. They began vaguely to identify a space that was Russian surrounded by a non-Russian periphery. Since, however, only Russians lived over the whole territory of the empire, they regarded the empire as in some sense Russian as well.[123] In the nineteenth century the idea of a Russian national territory within the larger empire spread to the ruling elite. For the most part nationalists did not see the empire as a nation-state. Instead, the imperial and national processes, though overlapping, remained distinct. The project of building the Russian nation was expansionist but did not aim to embrace the whole empire. Nationalists across state and society lines differed over the boundaries of the Russian national space, however.

The imagining of the Russian nation took place in encounters with other national groups in the empire. By 1913 some of them were engaged in their own nation-building projects.[124] As Andreas Kappeler observed, "The national movements, which were closely linked to modernization, gradually remodeled the horizontally divided estate-based societies into vertically integrated and culturally conscious nations, which now began to make political demands."[125] Of the many nationalities within the empire, only a few had reached such a high degree of national consciousness. Poland, Finland, and, to a lesser degree, the Baltic peoples and the Armenians and Georgians in the Caucasus were among them. The first two enjoyed special constitutional status in the empire and the others had strong local elites that had been co-opted to the central state through various accommodations.

The flexibility and adaptability that characterized Russian imperial rule had served the empire well. The recognition of diversity had, however, coexisted uneasily since the eighteenth century with an impulse toward standardization. The long established instrument of extending distinctively Russian rule in the midst of ethnic diversity was administrative russification. It was designed not to impose cultural uniformity within the empire but to extend Russian administrative practices and, to a lesser degree, Russian laws throughout the land as well as to secure the Russian language as the language of governing.[126] But varying conditions from region to region had compromised even that goal. Sporadically during the nineteenth century the state engaged in a more aggressively assimilationist policy of cultural russification. Cultural russification was most often intended to block competing assimilation projects—Polish in the western provinces, German in the Baltic region, and Tatar along the Volga.[127] Such an ambitious undertaking could only result in cultural conflict with the periphery as well as intensifying ethnic Russian identity in the Russian heartland and within bureaucratic circles.

The greater complexity of regional administration, the emergence of new elites who contested old power arrangements, and the growing demands that populations placed on government for services had by 1913 made the old system of administration through local elites no longer workable. New notions of a united and equal citizenry under a common law contradicted the principle of group diversity on which the viability of the empire rested.[128] No adequate means to replace it was found, however.[129] The very persistence of estate and ethnic groupings was an obstacle to the reform of governance both in Russian and non-Russian areas. Legally sanctioned estate and ethnic groups resisted changes that might diminish self-rule. Not only officials but often local groups were resistant to elected popular representation as an alternative to administrative rule.[130]

The original franchise granted in the Fundamental Laws for elections to the State Duma provided significant representation to non-Russian groups that might have supported a federalist solution to imperial tensions. Although Russians were significantly overrepresented in the first and second State Dumas, many more of the non-Russian peoples were represented in them than in the last two Dumas. The revised electoral law of June 1907 greatly diminished the number of non-Russians elected to the third and fourth State Dumas. In the fourth Duma, Ukrainians, who made up 17.8 percent of the population, held only 2.1 percent of the seats; Poles and Belorussians comprised 6.3 percent and 4.7 percent of the population respectively but seated only 3.9 percent and 1.1 percent of Duma representatives. Only Germans, who made up 1.4 percent of the population but held nine seats (2.1%) in the fourth Duma, exceeded their entitlement. Many nationalities such as Bashkirs, Buriats, Chechens, Chuvash, Kalmyks, Kazakhs, Turkmen, and Uzbeks were altogether excluded from the fourth Duma. With 44.3 percent of the population, Russians held 83.4 percent of the seats in the legislature in 1913.[131] At a time when the desire for political representation was growing, the sharp decline in the entitlement of non-Russians to Duma seats was particularly harmful to the cause of federalists. It is noteworthy, however, that non-Russians who were elected as deputies to the Duma gained prestige and authority among the people they represented, a measure of the important place the Duma had assumed in the politics of the empire.[132]

A lightning rod for ethnic conflict throughout the empire was the language of instruction in elementary schools for non-Russians. Language in schools remained a complicated, divisive, and unresolved issue to the end of the empire. It had been a matter of contention since the 1860s. In the Kazan' school district in the 1860s and 1870s the educator and scholar of Islam N.I. Il'minskii had worked out a system of instruction for non-Russians that included teaching in the native language transliterated into the Russian alphabet in the first two years of schooling, with Russian as an oral subject of study. In subsequent years instruction took place in Russian. Religious instruction, Il'minskii believed, should be in the native language throughout elementary schooling. Originally intended to slow apostasy among baptized non-Russians in the Volga region, peoples who had no written language of their own, the Il'minskii method was soon extended to Russian schools for Muslims in the Volga area and later in the central Asian steppes and the Caucasus.[133] By the early twentieth century it was also in limited use in elementary schools in the western provinces.[134]

Russian nationalists had contested Il'minskii's approach to native school-ing from the beginning. The Holy Synod and the Ministry of Education had broadly supported his method, however, as did the Ministry of the Interior, whose interest in stability in border regions trumped other concerns. By 1913, under pressure from nationalists, the Il'minskii method was falling into disuse at the discretion of local officials, despite heroic efforts on the part of its proponents to defend it. The Ministry of Education was softening its support for the Il'minskii method as well. New regulations issued by the ministry in June 1913 omitted Il'minskii's original assertion that the native language was an "indispensable tool" for the education of non-Russians. Although the revised regulation preserved the essentials of the Il'minskii method, it diminished the status of the native language as a learning tool and required for the first time that teachers should only be "familiar" with the native language of the children instead of fluent in its use.[135]

Duma members on the center and left introduced numerous interpella-tions in 1913 calling the government to account over its failure to enforce its own directives on non-Russian education. In January 1913, for example, the Social Democrats registered an interpellation asking the minister of educa-tion to investigate the teaching of non-Russian children in the Caucasus school district in the Russian language from day one of their education, in violation of a directive of 1881 that mandated teaching in the native lan-guage for the first two years of study.[136] In the fall of 1913 the Riga city duma contested a circular from the curator of the school district that forbade the teaching of German and Latvian in the first two years of schooling as illegal. Authorities in the Ministry of Education replied that the circular was legal because the teaching in German and Latvian harmed Russian interests: the languages of instruction excluded Russian children from attending such schools. It made no difference to the curator that of the 87 classes available in Riga, 50 were in Russian, 30 in Latvian, and seven in German.[137]

Public support for teaching in the native language remained strong. The press section at the Agricultural Congress in September 1913 called for teaching in the native language in elementary schools and for the publica-tion of agricultural journals, newspapers, and books in local tongues.[138] At the end of the year teachers at the All-Russian Congress on the Question of Public Education strongly supported the use of the mother tongue as a fundamental and powerful tool for the education of children. They recom-mended that education should begin in the mother tongue of pupils. In the third year the study of Russian should be compulsory, but the native language and literature should remain subjects of study.[139] The program of the independent peasant State Duma representatives also supported elementary instruction in the native language of pupils.[140]

The teachers' congress also recommended that the government should legalize the establishment of private schools that taught in the local language. In the eastern parts of the empire the main competitors to the state-sponsored schools were the Muslim religious schools. Most of these maintained a traditional religious curriculum taught in Arabic. By the 1880s, however, a Muslim school reform movement was underway. In the *jadid* (reform) school, modern subjects as well as religion were taught, and instruction was in the Turkic languages of the region. The reform schools also taught Russian as a subject of study. At first the government supported the reform movement, which it believed would weaken Muslim "fanaticism." The rise of the pan-Islamic and pan-Turkic movements, however, which linked Russian Muslims to modernizing movements in the Ottoman Empire, frightened the authorities. They withdrew support for Muslim reformers, sought to restrict links between mullahs and Muslims abroad, and interfered less in the traditional schools, which they now saw as bulwarks of conservatism.[141] In the west, Polish and German private schools were common. Here the government faced a dilemma. If private schools were forcibly closed, they could move across the border into Austria or Germany.[142]

The fourth Duma was badly divided over the nationalities question and the language of school instruction. On the far right the Union of the Russian People maintained that Russia was one and indivisible. Schoolteachers should be Russian and Orthodox and non-Russians should, if possible, be placed in classrooms with a majority of Russian students. In the borderlands the language of instruction should be Russian. Native languages should be confined to family, literature, and religion.[143] Toward the center right of the political spectrum, nationalism took on a variety of forms. The Nationalists, a party formed in the interests of Russian landowners in the western provinces where Russians were the minority, saw in limited constitutional government a basis for Russian nationalism. They wanted further to strengthen Russian representation in the Duma and establish the zemstvo in the western provinces on the basis of national curiae that privileged the Russian minority of the region. The Nationalists identified strongly with the Orthodox Church and upheld the parish rather than a secular local zemstvo as the appropriate center of education and social welfare. The more centrist Octobrist party was committed in its party platform to the unity and indivisibility of the Russian Empire founded on loyalty to the state. Their platform opposed laws that discriminated against non-Russians and supported the legal equality of national minorities, who should be fairly represented in the parliament. In practice, the Octobrists tolerated local autonomy to the degree that it furthered the unity and indivisibility of the empire and served the best interests of the Russian population of the region in question.[144]

Further to the left, the Constitutional Democrats (Kadets) also took a statist approach to the nationalities but softened it with promises of cultural autonomy. They envisioned a federation with full civil liberties and cultural self-determination for minorities, including autonomy for Poland and Finland. They supported the use of local languages in public life and educational and cultural institutions designed to preserve and develop the language and culture of minorities. They upheld Russian as the language of central institutions and the army and navy. The Kadet platform left elementary schooling in the hands of local authorities but made it clear that all schools should teach Russian if their students aspired to places in institutions of middle and higher education, where Russian would prevail.[145] Parties on the left, such as the Socialist Revolutionaries and Social Democrats, advocated national self-determination for minorities, but by no means unconditionally. Only if an aspiring national polity provided a minimal standard of political rights or protected the interests of the lower classes would their Russian mentors permit them self-determination. Across the political spectrum, few Russians doubted their civilizing role among the so-called little, nonhistorical peoples of the empire, whether through assimilation or paternalistic tutelage.

The state refused to recognize Ukrainians and Belorussians as non-Russians. It therefore forbade teaching in or of Ukrainian. In Belorussia, however, the government wanted to weaken the hold of the Catholic Church and the use of the Polish language in schools. In the years leading up to the war, therefore, the imperial authorities began to encourage the development of the Belorussian language and culture. The prohibition on the Ukrainian language went far beyond the elementary school classroom. During summer courses for teachers in Kiev the lecturer on educational psychology, when asked his opinion on teaching in native languages, replied that teaching should be not only in the native language but in the district dialect of the language. The school administration acted quickly, promising new measures to root out "Ukrainian separatism" among participants in the courses. A few weeks later the authorities closed the courses, which, they said, were infected with a Ukrainophile mood.[146] An article in *Moskovskie vedomosti* mocked the very idea of a Ukrainian "literary language." The author called it an ugly monstrosity that consisted of distorted Russian and Polish words and unfortunate neologisms.[147]

Imperial officials clearly understood the relationship between Ukrainian language and ethnic institutions of civil society, and they diligently sought to stamp them out or to curtail their development and activities. In Kiev the government banned reports in Ukrainian at the Rodina club and prohibited the registration of new Ukrainian clubs. They also declined to register the Ukrainian dramatic society Kobzar and the Ukrainian Art Society. Additionally they banned Ukrainian books from school libraries. The railway police in Poltava prohibited the sale of Ukrainian newspapers at the railway station.[148] In Borzen the administration closed the Ukrainian drama circle on the grounds of its recent "inactivity" and banned theater notices in Ukrainian; in Voronezh officials compelled the Ukrainian Literary-Dramatic Society to cancel a planned evening to honor the fiftieth anniversary of the death of the Ukrainian national poet T.G. Shevchenko. The bishop of Podol'ia banned a memorial service for Shevchenko "in light of its democratic character," and the rector at the Kiev Theological Academy prevented the reading in Ukrainian of the New Testament at Easter.[149] The pressure on Ukrainian cultural institutions was unrelenting. Ukrainians, sometimes with support from liberal Russians, fought back as best they could. For example, during a public holiday toward the end of the year, the Ukrainian Club defiantly flew Ukrainian flags over the club building.[150]

While harboring Russian nationalists, probably in growing numbers by 1913 as trust in the loyalty of non-Russians declined, the bureaucracy generally resisted the more virulent expressions of nationalism by any ethnic group. State bureaucrats regarded nationalism as disruptive and a threat to the peace and security of the empire. That position brought them into conflict over a number of issues with Russian nationalists in the State Duma and State Council. The more extreme Russian nationalist agenda of the far right did not win the favor of a majority in the Duma, but even moderate nationalists made their views and their discontent with the nationalities policy of the state clear in Duma debates. The State Council was a more conservative and more Russian body than the State Duma and in the last years of the empire emerged as a bastion of Russian nationalist opinion. A bill initiated by the Council of Ministers to extend urban self-government to Poland included the right of councilors and city administrators to use both Polish and Russian in the conduct of city business and in the city council. The bill passed in the Duma but was turned back by the State Council. Although the emperor supported the bill and the State Duma passed it a second time, the State Council defeated it again in 1913. The exclusion of the Polish language from urban local self-government prompted Polish newspapers to urge Polish members of the State Council to vote against a bill to extend the zemstvo to Poland. They argued that self-government was unworkable unless Polish was permitted as a language of business and debate.[151] The government also banned the Society for Polish Culture on the grounds that it was a vehicle for the dissemination of socialist ideas.[152]

On most issues, however, government policy concerning minorities and the wishes of Russian nationalists had converged by 1913 and differed more in degree than in principle. By that year the government had given up plans to russify the larger national groups of the empire. Instead it aimed to place limits on their autonomy with the goal of preserving state unity and protecting the interests of the Russian majority. Government measures to resist Finnish aspirations for greater autonomy won the support of nationalists in the Duma from the Octobrists on the center right to the extreme right. Beginning in 1908 a number of actions were taken to reduce Finland's special status. Any law passed in the Finnish parliament had to go to the Council of Ministers for scrutiny. If the council deemed that the law affected the interests of the empire as a whole it required state approval. Any law passed for the empire as a whole no longer required reference to Finnish legislators for it to have effect in Finland. In 1912 the government rejected the establishment of a separate Finnish army, while refusing to permit Finns to serve in the Russian military. Instead, the Finns were required to pay a special levy to support the imperial armed forces.[153] In 1913 the government proposed to fix tariffs on Finnish-Russian trade without reference to the Finnish parliament.[154] In the same year a bill to impose the imperial criminal code on Finland was working its way through the committees of the Duma with the backing of the Nationalists and rightists as well as right-wing Octobrists.[155]

Elsewhere in the empire, tensions were mounting as well. In August 1913 Governor-General Count Vorontsov-Dashkov reported on the situation in the Caucasus at the end of his eight-year term. The earlier confiscation by the state of a number of Armenian Church properties, he pointed out, had set off disturbances and fueled a terrorist movement. The return of the properties had quieted the resistance. In Georgia nationalists were exploiting the resistance of the Orthodox Church to granting autocephalous status to the Georgian Church. Muslim religious leaders in the Caucasus, the governor-general granted, were under the influence of Islamic governments across the border, but he doubted that the Muslim masses had much interest in separatism. Pan-Islamic and Pan-Turkic sentiments in the region were not widespread, he reported.[156] Commenting on this report, the editors of *Russkie vedomosti* opined that for the people of the Caucasus, Russian was the language of culture that all aspired to acquire. The cultures of nearby Persia and Turkey were alien to them.[157] This complacent view was widely held among Russian liberals, whose main contacts among non-Russians were with the assimilated or partly assimilated elites educated in Russian schools.

The insensitivity of imperial officials was reaching new heights before the war. In central Asia officials in Ashkabad decided to deal with what they perceived as a drinking problem among the Turkmen population by banning them from bars and restaurants altogether.[158] Further east the intensive settlement of the Kirgiz steppe by Russians was destroying nomadic agriculture and creating antistate feelings. In retaliation Kirgiz were taking the cattle of settlers and moving them across the border into China.[159] In Priamur province in the Far East, nationalist policies that restricted free trade with China and put a tariff on the import of grain from Manchuria had alienated the local Chinese population and threatened it with dire poverty.[160] Most Russians were oblivious to the harm they inflicted on local inhabitants. An editorial in *Moskovskie vedomosti* praised the settlement policy beyond the Urals. First, the editor declared the east to be uninhabited. Then, without regard to the previous claim, he spoke of Russian settlement as needed to raise the cultural level of the indigenous peoples. Russians, he said, hurt nobody's interests and displaced no one. On the contrary, Russian cultivators brought only benefit with their farming skills that the local population lacked.[161] It is not surprising in light of such views, which were widely shared among Russians, that there were few places on the periphery in 1913 where relations between Russian authorities and the non-Russian population were friendly.

Ethnic tensions between non-Russian groups were also common. Clashes between Armenians and Azeris in the Caucasus during the revolution of 1905 had left deep wounds on both parties that still festered in 1913. Many cities were increasingly sites of ethnic and religious discord. The oil boom in the region of Baku attracted both Armenians and Muslims to the city for work from areas where conflict between them was endemic. The imported tensions aggravated existing disputes on the ground. Conflicts with their employers could temporarily unite Russian, Armenian, and Muslim workers, but inter-ethnic conflict among oil workers was commonplace.[162] The rapid growth of Riga since the 1860s radically altered the ethnic balance of the population of the city. The proportion of Germans fell from nearly 50 percent of the total to around 16 percent. The Latvians rose from 24 percent of the population to a clear majority. Russians, Jews, and Poles also increased their shares at the expense of the Germans. Although the city's social elite remained German, a Latvian middle class with a flourishing Latvian national consciousness had emerged by 1913. Latvian patriots regarded Germans as aliens. Russians competed with Latvians to replace the Germans as the dominant group. Pressed from all sides the Germans began to assert their own nationality more aggressively, especially through the establishment of a network of private German schools.[163] Voters in elections to the city duma polarized along ethnic lines.[164]

In Odessa, Jews made up 33.5 percent of the population and controlled 61 percent of artisan shops, 64 percent of industry, and 69 percent of trade and commercial businesses. Their economic power did not, however, translate into political effectiveness. Jews were excluded from the urban franchise. Memories of the pogroms that had scarred Odessa in 1905 were still fresh and the dominance in municipal politics of the Union of the Russian People, with its openly anti-Semitic views, further exacerbated ethnic relations in the city. The Jews of Kiev had also suffered pogroms in 1904 and 1905. As in Odessa, Jews in Kiev were excluded from the urban vote. Officially, around eighty-one thousand Jews lived in Kiev in early 1914, but many more lived in the city illegally. Nearly sixty thousand Poles made their home in Kiev as well. The wealthier among the Poles could vote in duma elections and used their numbers to thwart the Russian Nationalist Party's ambition to control the city council. As a result anti-Polonism ran high among Russians in the city. The Ukrainian population of Kiev was only around 17 percent of the total, although many Ukrainians had assimilated as Russians. The small Ukrainian intelligentsia of Kiev was increasingly asserting cultural nationalist views.[165]

Ethnic and religious conflict was part of the daily reality of life in the empire. But the news was not always bad. Left to their own devices local populations could bridge ethnic and religious barriers. In the Crimea, Russian and Tatar farmers amicably cooperated in 1913 in putting on an agricultural exhibition. Far more remarkable was an incident in Simferopol. Slav and Greek residents of the city organized collections for relief of the wounded in the Balkan conflict. Banned legally from doing the same for Muslim wounded, local Tatars organized an illegal fund. When a local merchant began to sell Slavic flags to raise funds, a Muslim Tatar asked him for a Turkish flag. One was found and the man paid a hundred roubles for it, which the Slavic committee turned over to the illicit Muslim relief committee. Fired by his example, a local women's club held a bazaar to raise funds for both sides. The Tatars reciprocated by hosting an event to raise funds to aid the wounded of all nationalities. The event drew Tatars from across Simferopol and from the whole of the province.[166]

The Jews of the empire had long been subject to a set of discriminatory laws that restricted their movements and rights of residency and limited their numbers in educational institutions. The last two tsars, especially Nicholas II, were openly anti-Semitic and set the tone for the rest of society. Many Russians resented the successes of Jews in commerce and industry. Even small Jewish shopkeepers and other petty businessmen, especially in the provinces of the Pale, were generally disliked by resident Russians, Ukrainians, and Poles. Conservative Russians in particular associated Jews with capitalism and despised both. Even the workers' health insurance funds could not totally escape religious division. In Vilno the typographic industry created two insurance funds, one for Christian companies and a second for Jewish establishments.[167] The waves of pogroms that periodically devastated Jewish communities in the 1880s and 1890s had subsided after the revolution of 1905, but occasional outbursts kept the threat alive. In 1913 official policy on Jewish residency and property rights and the infamous Beiliss trial imposed huge strains on the Jewish population and further poisoned relations with the tsar's other subjects. The Orthodox Church was often in the forefront of anti-Semitic activity. The Holy Synod requested the Senate to rule on the legality of Jews' bearing Christian names. Early in 1913 the Senate ruled that the law was silent on the matter and went on to ask rhetorically how the Synod proposed to distinguish between Jewish and Christian names.[168]

In 1912 the government approved a plan to resettle most Jews living in the interior provinces of the empire to the Pale. The Pale was created in the reign of Catherine the Great as a place where Jews were permitted to live. It roughly embraced what today are Belarus, Latvia, Lithuania, Poland, and western Ukraine. Its purpose was to limit Jewish commercial competition with Russians and protect Russians from what officials saw as the pernicious influence of the Jews. Although the vast majority of Jews were confined to the Pale, by 1913 a small minority were living outside it. The regulation on resettlement came into effect on 1 January 1913. The law permitted Jewish merchants outside the Pale to remain, provided they registered with provincial authorities. In many cities, however, no registers existed or if one did the police refused individuals the right to get on it. As early as 8 January *Russkie vedomosti* reported that the "number of expulsions from St. Petersburg were daily rising."[169] The law bore heavily on Jewish students. Jews attending private schools outside the Pale were allowed to remain until Easter.[170]

Inside the Pale, where Jews could live in certain cities only with permission, residency permits were now severely scrutinized. When the Ministry of Trade and Industry granted 1,700 Jewish students the right of residency in Kiev as free auditors at the Kiev Commercial Institute, the local police denied the authority of the ministry to make such concessions and forced the students to resettle. In Odessa the women's medical courses attracted 40 Christian and 50 Jewish applicants. Although many places remained unfilled only six Jews were admitted.[171] In November 500 Jews studying dentistry in Kiev were deemed not to have residency rights and summarily sent away. Students in the Kiev School of Music and in a number of technical schools had already suffered the same penalty.[172] A ruling of the Senate on 22 August 1913 rescinded a law of 1879 that permitted Jewish pharmacist assistants, dentists, fel'dshers, and midwives, who were allowed to live outside the Pale without permission, to trade on the side in order to supplement their meager salaries. The minister of trade and industry intervened and persuaded the Council of Ministers to request that the Senate grandfather all those who held the right of trade before 22 August.[173] In the State Duma a coalition of rightist deputies proposed a bill to ban the kosher slaughter of cattle as cruel, unsanitary, and unnecessarily costly to poor Jews.[174]

Russian institutions of civil society often resisted government restrictions on Jews when they could. Foreign Jews could now attend international congresses in Moscow or St. Petersburg, but the participation of

Russian Jews at national congresses remained contentious. When the All-Russian Congress of Dentists met in Moscow in April, 12 Jews were in attendance. At first the authorities had refused to allow any Jews to take part, but when the congress organizers threatened to move the congress to Odessa, the authorities compromised. For some the compromise was insufficient; the Odessa Society of Dentists refused to attend.[175] The organizers of the Fourth All-Russian Congress of Commercial Employees engaged in a lengthy struggle to persuade the government to allow Jews to take part in the congress. Eventually the government permitted limited Jewish participation. When the police closed the congress, they also unceremoniously hustled the Jewish delegates out of the city.[176]

The organizers of the All-Russian Congress of Clerks in Ekaterinoslav also threatened to move their conference to the Pale if Jews were banned from the interior. The government proposed that Jews could elect delegates to the congress provided none of those elected was Jewish. After further negotiations, 10 Jews were allowed to attend.[177] When the Ministry of the Interior circulated a questionnaire to factory and shop owners requesting them to report on the number of Jews and foreigners in their area and to detail the harmful influence of Jews on the local population, the chairman of the Nizhnii Novgorod fair replied on their behalf that "We are citizens first and merchants second" and not "police first."[178] At the imperial level the All-Russian Stock Market Congress resolved that all commercial schools should be open to auditors of all faiths and that Jewish students registered at the Kiev Commercial Institute be permitted to complete their studies. They also resolved that the quota on Jews in the school be raised to 10 percent of total enrolment.[179] A few weeks later the city duma of Minsk, which was in the Pale, cheekily announced that its project to honor the tercentenary of the Romanov dynasty was the establishment of a commercial institute with no restrictions on Jewish enrollments. The city voted twenty thousand roubles for the new institute and the local merchants donated another thirty thousand roubles.[180]

In spite of such courageous stands, anti-Semitism among the general populace was high. In 1913 Poles organized a boycott against Jewish shops. Its defenders described it as pro-Polish and not anti-Semitic.[181] As their contribution to the boycott the Polish pharmacy students at Warsaw University refused to take examinations in the same group as the Jewish students.[182] In Lodz a peasant woman brought two children to a Jewish fel'dsher for treatment. The oldest wandered off and the mother raised the alarm. Before a peasant found the girl in the street and returned her safely to her mother a pogrom had ensued; several Jewish shopkeepers were badly injured and their shops destroyed.[183] A speaker at the Monarchists' Union meeting in Moscow in November called for the expulsion of Jews from the empire "by means well known to the Russian people."[184] When, at last, 21 of 41 men accused of instigating a pogrom in Ivanovo-Vosnesensk in October 1905 were convicted and sentenced in 1913 with great leniency, the Ministry of Justice reduced the sentences even further.[185] In Vilno a Jewish miller asked his young Polish employee to deposit one hundred roubles in the bank. The employee claimed to have been attacked by three Jews and robbed and wounded. A pogrom loomed, but police found the roubles, which the employee had stolen and hidden, in time to prevent the outburst.[186]

Some incidences had more sinister causes. In Kovno, a Christian woman bought an onion bun in a Jewish bakery. On examining it she saw something red on it and supposed it to be blood. She screamed; people came running; the bun was dispatched to the police for analysis. It proved that a bit of red onion skin had stained the bun.[187] In Smolensk, *Russkoe znamia*, the newspaper of A.I. Dubrovin, an extreme right-wing leader, published an article accusing a Mrs. Pinkus, a Jew, of bleeding a Russian girl by inflicting tiny wounds on her to obtain Christian blood for Jewish ritualistic purposes. Although the chief of gendarmes quickly determined that the marks were flea and tick bites and after several months the procurator dismissed the case as frivolous, *Russkoe znamia* pursued the matter in its pages. Mrs. Pinkus then sued for libel. The libel case dragged on in court in spite of the fact that the responsible authorities dismissed the newspaper's accusations as libelous.[188]

Blood and ritual murder were much on the minds of Russian subjects in the summer of 1913. The trial of Mendel Beiliss, a Jew accused of murdering Andrei Iushinskii in 1911, began in September 1913. The alleged motive was to collect Christian blood for ritual purposes. The charge from the beginning was murder and not ritual murder, for which the law had no provision. In fact, the police knew that Andrei was killed by a gang of robbers when he discovered that the mother of one of the gang was storing goods stolen by the gang in her house. The superiors of the two young policemen who had discovered the truth of the murder fired them. The fired policemen went to the press with their story, but authorities widely suppressed or discredited it. The Minister of Justice and the tsar, himself, knew that Beiliss was innocent, but the trial proceeded. The state paid witnesses and the judge constantly intervened to lead the jury to convict. He later received a special medal for his work. The Kharkov Medical Society among others roundly condemned the medical testimony. Only a fraction of the testimony at the trial was related to proving responsibility for the murder. The rest focused on Judaism with the aim of proving the historical reality of Jewish ritual murder. So-called experts on Judaism solemnly affirmed the necessity of Christian blood for Jewish worship. The mostly peasant jurors saw through the charade and acquitted Beiliss. They found that the victim bled to death but gave no support to the claim that the crime was religiously motivated. The prosecution loudly claimed, however, that the trial had once and for all established Jewish ritual murder as a fact.[189]

Condemnations of the trial poured in from abroad. The hierarchy of the Church of England denounced it as a throwback to the age of black magic and witchcraft. In Vienna five thousand people staged a protest march against the case.[190] A group of Czech writers condemned it as a tool by reactionaries to trigger pogroms.[191] In Russia, even some of the conservative press found the trial objectionable. The independent conservative journalist V.P. Meshcherskii called the Beiliss case "a page from the records of an asylum" and the reactionary newspaper *Kievlianin* questioned the legality of the trial proceedings.[192] Even the Orthodox Church divided on the matter. On one side, the bishop of Astrakhan publicly announced that there was no basis on which to accuse the Jewish people of such a crime and wished for Beiliss's acquittal. On the other, after the trial, Bishop Dmitrii of Riazan' accused Jews of buying or intimidating witnesses at the trial to secure an acquittal and urged his congregation to "fight with all our strength against this tribe cursed by God."[193] The prosecutor of the case averred in the Noble Assembly of St. Petersburg that, in spite of the verdict, he had no doubt about Beiliss's guilt; with remarkable disregard for the truth, he said that he took satisfaction from the fact that in his mind the jurors had recognized the ritual nature of the murder. The assembled nobility cheered him as he left the hall.[194] Liberals saw the trial as a condemnation of the legal system, which could so easily be manipulated. The total lack of independence of the investigators of the case and the exclusion of defense lawyers during the investigation cast a shadow over the provisions of the judicial reform of 1864 that restricted the pretrial role of defense counsel. Calls for a new judicial reform quickly followed.[195]

The Beiliss trial deeply stained the reputation of official Russia at home and abroad. But it also galvanized social protest against the arbitrariness of the regime. The problem of nationalities was a severe test not only for the government but for Russia as a nation. On nearly every front official policy alienated non-Russians. The policy was driven, at least in part, by pressures from Russian nationalists, who resented the successes of others and sought special protections for Russians. By the end of 1913 the rise of national consciousness among Russians and, to varying degrees, among other peoples in the empire—and the institutions of civil society that accompanied this rise—were already placing strains on the integrity of the empire. Historically the development of civil society has been closely linked to the emergence of the nation-state. A certain level of cultural homogeneity that enables mobility and facilitates communication in a mass society has characterized modern societies.[196] The instruments of civil society that were emerging in parts of the empire and promising new levels of civic engagement posed a threat to the integrity of the whole. They were certain to exert even more centrifugal pressure as time passed.

The Russian Empire was not on the brink of general disintegration in 1913. Only a few of its constituent parts by then had the capacity or the will to achieve independence. Even they had to deal with internal ethnic and class divisions and tensions that slowed their own nation-building projects. The traditional methods of ruling the disparate parts of the empire were inadequate by 1913. New methods of governance were needed in order to integrate the parts and promote common feelings of loyalty to the whole. The weight of the past, however, stood in the way of reform. The historical division of the population into legally recognized social estates or ethnic groupings, all with their own arrangements and concessions that they were loath to lose, hampered the process of liberal democratic reform that the October Manifesto had promised. The belief among Russians of nearly all political persuasions in the primacy of the Russian people and language in the empire made a federalist outcome difficult but not impossible to negotiate. The future loss of parts of the empire such as Poland and Finland was likely, but the challenge of accommodating subject peoples would have remained and unavoidably continued to reshape imperial institutions.

CONCLUSION

The public sphere and the institutions of civil society within the Russian Empire were far from inclusive in 1913. Urban males of the middle and lower middle classes were participating in the institutions and adopting the attitudes of civil society in growing numbers. Workers were seeking access to the public sphere for themselves and their children through education and organization. The consumption in common of commercial culture created a public cultural sphere of reference that narrowed differences between workers and the lower middle classes and reshaped middle-class and even high culture. Although still disadvantaged compared to men, women were entering the public realm as well. By 1913 they had joined the professions in large and growing numbers, though restrictions on their practice remained. The growth of the market economy created more and more opportunities for women to gain a measure of independence from men through employment. Inheritance laws were changing to protect the interests of female heirs, and women were gaining legal identities distinct from fathers and husbands. These changes laid siege to the patriarchal family. Middle-class women took part in a multitude of voluntary associations, from charities to political parties, often in leading roles. In spite of their sustained efforts the franchise still eluded them. Urban working women had few organizations of their own to speak for their interests in the arena of civil society. Middle-class feminists and a few socialists advocated reforms on their behalf. There were some successes. The hours of work for women were restricted under factory legislation and the inclusion of maternity leaves in the factory health insurance funds signaled recognition by fellow workers and the authorities of the special needs of women.

In rural regions urban influences and market-driven changes within the village were combining to reshape the circumstances and attitudes of peasant men and women. After the revolution of 1905 the activities of many zemstvos increased dramatically and the number of personnel that they employed grew. Peasants were beginning to press the zemstvos for increased services. The land reform brought agronomists into contact with peasants in growing numbers and the development of the cooperatives further intensified relations between villagers and urban educated outsiders. Traditional peasant hostility to "officials" gradually was eroding as more and more peasants grasped the benefits that expertise could provide them. Membership in cooperatives and cooperative unions fostered new identities beyond village confines. Participation in fire insurance programs and volunteer fire brigades taught attitudes of civic engagement. The land reform divided villages but also exposed peasants to new opportunities. Some grasped them more readily than others. Peasant women were showing signs of greater independence from family and village. Their willingness to participate in legal actions in defense of their rights pointed to the growth of legal consciousness in peasant society as a whole. As older mechanisms to resolve disputes within village society were undermined by provisions of the land reform, peasants in general were forced to seek resolutions in the larger legal public sphere. The issues and language of the peasant courts were increasingly those of the bourgeoisie. Unfortunately the legal instruments provided by the state were inadequate and continued to hinder the integration of peasants into the larger society. Not only Russians but also other ethnicities were experiencing the rise of individualism and the growth of institutions of civil society. Some civil society organizations cut across ethnic lines and reinforced multiple identities. Others coalesced around national cultural objectives that clashed with the objectives of others in the empire. A few national groups actively aspired to independence, although their own national projects were fraught with divisions and tensions. Existing imperial administrative and political institutions were poorly constructed to integrate the disparate parts of the empire. The legacy of the past, rule through corporate bodies, retarded the growth of an equal citizenry and popular acceptance of liberal participatory democracy. A rising tide of Russian nationalism, which harbored strong antialien feelings, fostered resentment among non-Russians and began to erode the commitment of the bureaucracy to a measure of ethnic proportionality in its composition. Although the rise of competing nationalisms within the imperial territories challenged its integrity, the Russian Empire was far from facing total disintegration into its ethnic components in 1913.

STATE AND SOCIETY

Looking back in 1928, A.A. Kizevetter, the accomplished historian of Russia and Constitutional Democratic Party activist, reflected on the "most important elements" of the political situation in Russia immediately before World War I. "State power and society (obshchestvo)," he wrote, "here were 'we' and 'they,' and a bridge between them could never be."[1] Kizevetter was not the only one to think so. Both before and after the revolutions of 1917 other members of obshchestvo and the intelligentsia promoted a narrative about the profound gulf that divided society and state before the revolution. The existence of a gulf separating state and society in the Russian Empire before World War I was once a staple of the historiography.[2] In this reading a more or less monolithic state confronted a determined but unstable society, a struggle that culminated in 1917 with victory for neither side. More recently historians have begun to record both real divisions over policy among state actors and also collaborations between state and society in pursuit of common goals.

Kizevetter had in mind the narrow meaning of obshchestvo, defined by the principled opposition of educated society to the state. In reality, obshchestvo in this sense was only a part of the larger educated public. Many members of the public interacted extensively and regularly with state officials both in public and private capacities. Even those among the public who liked to identify with obshchestvo often found it convenient to consort with civil servants to advance particular causes or simply to further their careers. By 1913 formal cooperation between the state and bodies of local self-administration on a range of issues was common, and individuals and groups among the public put their energy and resources into advancing, along with the bureaucracy, a number of state-led initiatives. Bureaucrats often participated as private citizens in civil voluntary associations. Cooperation between state and public coexisted with sharp tensions that sometimes pitted officials against the public or more often spawned rival camps whose members were on both sides of the line between state and society. Such collaboration was hardly surprising. Members of obshchestvo often had an education in common with state personnel, frequently in the same schools, and many had relatives or friends in state service.

The state was far from presenting a united front to the public. Several factors combined in the early twentieth century to produce wider divergences of opinion among state officials about policy and to bring state and social actors into common causes. Among them were rapid economic and social change; constitutionalism; the crisis in a broad range of institutions and practices, which established a clear agenda for reform; the complexity of modern governance, which compelled a measure of cooperation between the state and the public; a near consensus among the elites about the need to extend education and disseminate culture to the masses; and changes within the bureaucracy itself. Policy differences about complex matters within the bureaucracy drove many bureaucrats to look for allies among the public in order to advance their plans. The introduction of representative government, limited as it was, and the relative freedom of the press after 1905 brought the educated public nearer to the process of governance, fostered a new pragmatism, and encouraged some among them to work with moderates in the state structure to effect desired reforms.

A number of incidences in 1913 illustrated the cracks developing within the state and the convergence of the views of some state actors with public opinion around specific issues. In July 1913 news broke that the former governor of Kostroma province, P.P. Silovskii, had now resigned from his post as governor of Olonets province, loudly citing as his reason thae fact that it was no longer possible to work honorably and constructively in the provinces given the disorder in recent years within the Ministry of the Interior, and especially in its department on general affairs. The last two ministers, he complained, appointed people to the department who did not know its mandate. Silovskii had clashed with the ministry before. The emperor had approved his transfer from Kostroma to distant Olonets on the grounds that the people of Kostroma hated him. When those same people invited him back to Kostroma to take part in the exhibition to celebrate the Romanov tercentenary, the interior minister forbade him to leave Olonets. Silovskii tendered his resignation. Although he was scarcely the first governor to resign in anger, Silovskii chose to make his reasons for quitting highly public. His target was not the whole administration, but his rebuke was squarely aimed at its largest, most powerful, and most conservative ministry. The liberal press made much of his resignation.[3]

In March 1913 students and professors of the Military-Medical-Surgical Academy protested a decision by the government to end the autonomy of the academy and place it under the control of the Ministry of War. When the protests persisted the Council of Ministers forced the temporary closing of the academy. Public opinion, led by a broad spectrum of the press, deplored the proposed changes. A majority in the State Duma also opposed the reform. The ministry persevered and brought new statutes for the academy before the Senate for promulgation into law. The Senate refused to discuss a matter that had not come to it through normal legislative channels, and the Ministry of War withdrew the measure. After much talk over the summer about the use of article 87, which empowered the government to pass legislation while the Duma was not in session, the government decided instead to implement the new regime at the academy without either the retroactive sanction of the Duma, which the constitution required, or the approval of the Senate.[4]

Early in 1913 Senator S.S. Manukhin, whom the government had appointed to investigate the massacre of workers in the Lena goldfields of Siberia in 1912, submitted his report to the Council of Ministers.[5] The ministers were themselves publicly divided over the causes of the slaughter. The minister of the interior, A.A. Makarov, defended the soldiers who, he told the Duma, had justifiably fired on unruly workers out of loyalty to the regime. The minister of trade and industry, S. Timashev, stated in the Duma that the foreign management of the Lena Company was in violation of the law and had been repeatedly warned to mend its ways.[6] Manukhin found no evidence of political motives among the strikers. Instead, he blamed the British management of the gold mines, whose ill treatment of the workers precipitated the strikes, and local Russian officials whose negligence and brutality led to the massacre. He stressed the peaceful conduct of the strikers during confrontations with authorities. Although a majority in the Council of Ministers initially accepted the findings, no actions were taken against the offending officials. The right-wing press strongly criticized the report because Manukhin had failed to reveal the role of revolutionaries in stirring up the Lena workers.[7] The council came to share that view and ordered a new investigation into the massacre. In spite of official obstacles to its publication, the contents of Manukhin's report were widely publicized in the press.[8]

None of these events signaled a severe crisis in the Russian state. Silovskii was complaining about changes in the way the bureaucracy did its business and in the personnel who conducted it but not about its raison d'être. The Senate's refusal to promulgate one arbitrary government decree did not nec-essarily mark its wholesale conversion to the rule of law. The government's miscalculation in appointing Manukhin to investigate the Lena events, though from its point of view unfortunate, was manageable. Nonetheless, those occurrences and several others like them in 1913 exposed for the Russian public various divisions within the state apparatus that deepened as the complexity of governance in a changing world increased. Reports in the press and debates in the State Duma made it impossible for the state to maintain an appearance of unity. Silovskii used the press to air his griev-ances; the Senate, for whatever reasons, allied with public opinion against changes to the statutes of the Military-Medical-Surgical Academy; and internal rivalries within the government prevented the suppression of Ma-nukhin's report. The myths of the unity of the state and of the barriers that separated it from the public were no longer sustainable by 1913.

The Institutions of Government

The revolution of 1905 had pitted a broad but unstable coalition of social forces against the bureaucratic autocracy that was Russia's historical legacy. The revolution ended in a compromise, proclaimed in the October Manifesto of 1905, which the Fundamental Laws of 1906 embodied. The Fundamental Laws provided a constitutional order in Russia and defined the rights and freedoms of the population. The new laws conferred on the emperor supreme autocratic authority and made him answerable only to God. They also, however, required the emperor to exercise his authority in unity with two new legislative institutions, the State Duma, an elected lower house of peoples' representatives, and the State Council, an upper house of delegates half of whom were elected by a variety of corporate groups and institutions and half appointed annually by the emperor. The Fourth State

Duma was elected according to the narrow franchise laws of 1907. Overall, the franchise of 1907 greatly overrepresented large landowners, vastly underrepresented peasants, and largely disenfranchised non-Russians. Although many city dwellers were excluded from voting, the urban share of representation in the Duma was relatively generous in relation to the proportion of urbanites in the whole population. Laws required the approval of both houses of parliament and of the emperor in order to come into force. The emperor also had the authority to prorogue the State Duma and the right to legislate when it and the State Council were not in session; the two legislative bodies in turn had the right to confirm the legislation when they reconvened. The emperor retained the sole right to declare war and proclaim peace and to conduct negotiations with foreign governments.[9] The constitutional constraints that the creation of new legislative organs imposed on the emperor further limited an authority already restricted by the bureaucratic complexity of a modern state and rambling empire.

The constitutional powers and prerogatives enjoyed by the State Duma made it, along with the State Council, an integral part of the government of the Russian Empire—its legislative branch. The moderate liberal V.A. Maklakov, a member of the Constitutional Democratic Party, strongly defended what more radical members of his party called a "false" constitution. In his memoirs he argued that in the few years of its existence the constitution taught members of both the state and public the lessons of legality and the subordination of authority to the law.[10] The Duma exercised its authority both formally, through its right to discuss and approve all laws and to scrutinize the budget, and informally, through public opinion at home and abroad. Foreign leaders and investors were attuned to opinion in the Duma and widely sympathetic to it in its struggle with the ministers and the court. The inexperience of Duma members in formulating legislation, sharp ideological divisions among its members, and the casuistry of some of the people's representatives, who were more committed to using the Duma as a rostrum for radicalism of the right and the left than as an instrument for reform, all slowed the passage of important legislation, hampered the Duma's effectiveness as a legislative body, and undermined its credibility among the public.[11]

Public disappointment about the inability of the Duma to legislate as effectively as voters wished should not be interpreted as public indifference to the role the Duma played in the governance of the empire. Electorates chronically grumble about the ineptness of their parliamentary or congressional representatives. Many Russians desired the reform of the State Duma in more democratic directions; only a few saw it as irrelevant or wished for its abolition. The Duma did succeed in passing a large amount of important legislation and did establish itself in the minds of the growing reading public as an integral part of the governing process. The newspapers with the highest circulations reported extensively on Duma debates, especially those on the state budget. Those debates revealed to the public the broad dimensions of national economic and political life and helped to educate it in the responsibilities and complexities of governance. As the journalist and liberal activist Ariadne Tyrkova-Vil'iams observed, "Gradually the State Duma re-educated the bureaucracy, the opposition, public opinion, the whole country, the whole people. The Duma debates were a safety valve."[12] The British observer Bernard Pares agreed. The Duma, he remarked in his memoirs, "rather permeated than attacked the existing order of things...."[13] The diplomat Nicholas Basily noted the extent to which the "educated classes, the majority of the military cadres and even the bureaucracy had embraced the Duma as an indispensable part of the political order." He contended that the Duma had entered the fabric of the political structure of the country so completely that even many who had formerly opposed representative government tacitly accepted it. Even the parties of the right, having tasted participation in law-making, were prepared to defend their right to legislate.[14]

TENSIONS WITHIN THE STATE

The Russian state had never been a monolith, and the new constitutional arrangements that came into effect in 1906 only exacerbated its divisions. Emperor Nicholas II generally supported legality in the bureaucracy but resisted full bureaucratic independence from the throne or legal accountability. He did not trust bureaucrats and the state institutions they represented; he preferred instead to rely on family members and favorites for advice and appointment.[15] Russian "serving persons," as bureaucrats were known, could not be held directly accountable to the law in the courts. Instead, complaints against their behavior could be made to the bureaucracy itself, which would then decide whether to take any action. The third Duma passed legislation providing for bureaucratic accountability, but it was still stalled in the State Council in 1913.[16] The bureaucracy strongly resisted the legislation.

If Nicholas did not trust officials they, for their part, deplored personal rule. After the reforms of the 1860s, legal consciousness among civil servants steadily grew. It was not, however, primarily in the broad authority of law and the courts but in narrow bureaucratic procedure and regularity that most imperial state servants placed their hopes for limiting personal autocratic power. In particular, they attached to the Council of Ministers and the prime minister a mediating role between emperor and subjects that would effectively limit the emperor's authority. Nicholas, however, fought off all efforts to reduce the throne to a symbol of authority; he escaped the subordination to the law that constitutionalism implied and continued to exercise real power.[17] As a result, the monarchy was in near constant tension with its ministers. The emperor's plenipotentiaries in the provinces, the governors, and the extraordinary powers they exercised on his behalf helped him to resist submission to administrative control. But the ministries also exercised authority in the provinces. As Governor Silovskii's outburst illustrates, provincial administration was a potential site of intragovernmental conflict.

The new constitutional order had not changed the right of the emperor to appoint his own ministers, who remained individually accountable to him for their actions. Although there were provisions for interministerial discussions, the Council of Ministers had little sense of shared responsibility for the policies of individual ministries. As long as the prime minister exercised considerable influence on whom the emperor appointed to various ministries, a measure of coordination was feasible. By 1913, however, Nicholas was more aggressively making his own appointments with little or no consultation with ministers. The result was a cabinet in 1913 that was less cohesive than any since the 1905 revolution. The removal of Count Kokovtsov as prime minister in early 1914 and his replacement with Ivan Goremykin put an end to any lingering hopes for a united cabinet.

The conduct of foreign policy in Russia illustrates the drawbacks of the new constitutional arrangements. The Fundamental Laws of 1906 conferred exclusive power on the emperor in foreign relations. The Council of Ministers had few constitutional tools to influence foreign policy and, as in other policy areas, had no sense of shared responsibility for its conduct. The prime minister, Count Kokovtsov, requested from the emperor special permission to discuss important matters of foreign policy in the Council of Ministers. Although such discussions did take place on a couple of occasions in 1913 and 1914, Nicholas preferred to work through his foreign minister S.D. Sazonov, who shared the emperor's view and rarely briefed fellow ministers on foreign policy issues.[18] Consequently, the mechanism of foreign policy formation and implementation in Russia was handicapped by its centralization in the hands of the emperor and the Foreign Ministry and by an absence of ministerial collegiality. No office existed to coordinate and reconcile the policies of external relations with other interested parties in government. Coordination, such as it was, was mostly by the emperor, who did not even employ a secretary for the purpose.[19] Communication between the military and the diplomats was minimal. In the dangerous years preceding World War I the Russian high command had almost no firm knowledge of the diplomatic objectives or treaty obligations of the empire they served. On their side, the makers of foreign policy were badly informed about the preparedness of the military for war.

Although the State Duma had no constitutional role in the making of Russian foreign policy, many of its members took a keen interest in the external relations of the empire. They often used the privileges of office and access to the press to advance their views. Paul Miliukov, the leader of the Constitutional Democrats, was especially active in 1913 in seeking resolution of the conflict in the Balkans, and traveled to the region several times amid extensive coverage by the liberal press. Unlike many members of the Duma, Miliukov had concluded that the Slavs of the Balkans could arrange their own affairs without Russian interference. It is notable that in spite of his hostility to the existing constitutional order he strongly supported the moderate line of the Ministry of Foreign Affairs on Balkan diplomacy. Other Duma members were less restrained. Cut off as they were from detailed knowledge of diplomatic matters, Duma representatives were frequently ill-informed about the Russian position on affairs abroad. They often spoke at odds with official policy. By 1913, the State Duma was home to a boisterous Russian nationalism that posed dangers to an imperial state in desperate need of an extended period of peace in which to complete its defense preparations.

The fragility of international relations in 1913 and the lack of coordination and consensus-building in the making of Russian foreign policy were sources of further instability in the Russian imperial state. The French were strongly committed to the Russian alliance that had been forged in the 1890s and to supporting a military buildup in the empire. In late summer 1913 the French government extended 400–500 million francs in credits to strengthen the military capacity of the railway network of the empire.

Russian diplomacy aimed to contain German power through strategic alliances in order to buy the time needed to complete a rearmament program. The Balkan wars of 1912 and 1913 highlighted the fragility of the peace. The Russians knew that neutrality was not an option for them and from 1912 sought even closer ties with France and Britain in case hostilities broke out. A second objective of Russian diplomacy was to defend the position of the empire in the Balkans, especially by maintaining the strength of its main ally in the region, Bulgaria. The annexation of Bosnia-Herzegovina by the Austro-Hungarian Empire in 1908 had compromised Russia's claim to be defender of the Slavs of the Balkans and outraged Russian nationalists. In 1912 the Russians failed to prevent the Balkan states from seizing Turkish territories and failed again in 1913 to prevent them from attacking one another over the spoils. Russian initiatives in the Balkans placed strains on the all-important British-French alliance.[20]

Of even greater concern for the Russians was the future of the Straits. In 1912–1913 the Straits closed briefly as a consequence of the Balkan conflict. In the period from 1903 to 1912, 37 percent of all Russian exports and 75 percent of grain exports passed through the Straits. Regardless of whether alternative routes were available, the Russians were alarmed at the prospect that the Straits might close again.[21] In 1913 Germany dispatched a military mission to Turkey. The activities of the German officers on the mission convinced the Russians that Germany was conspiring to control Turkish foreign policy and take over management of the Straits. By fall 1913 the Turks had also achieved naval superiority in the Black Sea. Russian forward plans included the placing of three or four new dreadnoughts in the Black Sea and the deployment of a naval squadron in the Mediterranean Sea with the capacity to inflict damage on Constantinople in case of war. Still anxious to maintain the peace, the Russians requested that the German mission either alter its activities in Constantinople or move to a locale outside the Turkish capital. They requested French and British support. In November 1913 their allies, more reluctantly than the Russians could have wished, agreed on a joint note to Germany supporting the Russians' request. Elsewhere, Russia annexed territories in northern Persia and northern Mongolia in 1907. In 1913 Outer Mongolia came under Russian authority. In the Far East Russia's partners in the Entente were competitors for spheres of influence in China. There, Russian and Japanese interests converged. Both feared a resurgent China and worked to weaken the newly established Chinese republic.

The pressures of maintaining national security in an uncertain world put Nicholas at odds with a growing section of the army officer corps. The emperor neither understood nor welcomed the new professionalism among a growing segment of military personnel. Like Minister of War V.A. Sukhomlinov, Nicholas supported the ideal of a dynastic army that served the interests of the emperor. Some officers concurred, but many army professionals wanted to build a national army that served the national interest. Many field officers preferred an army led by a professional officer corps that included national and religious minorities, among them Jews.[22] They opposed policies designed to preserve the dominance of Russians and the Orthodox. The army had friends in the State Duma. Many elected representatives better understood the technical needs of the military, if it were to avoid a debacle, than did the emperor. Assistant Minister of War A.A. Polivanov headed a group of officers that sought closer ties with the State Duma, indicating a stronger loyalty to nation and constitution than to the dynasty. He was fired in 1912. By 1913 the ministry had moved to isolate officers who identified more strongly with the Duma than with the emperor.[23] Professionalism in the military was far from total in 1913 as officers of the old school continued to occupy leading roles and ethnic and religious restrictions remained. As a result, Russia entered World War I with a divided and semiprofessional officer corps, one in which the deeper loyalties of the most able within it were to army and nation rather than to the emperor who commanded them.

If tensions existed between the throne and the bureaucracy, strains within the bureaucracy were equally apparent. Ministries in the past had proposed rival policies and strategies. After 1905, however, the pace of change quickened and public scrutiny of government, thanks to a relatively free press and debates in the Duma, intensified. Officials in the ministries used the press to publicize their positions and manipulate public opinion in their favor. Three social elements coexisted uneasily within the state bureaucracy. The numbers of landed gentry had fallen into steep decline by the end of the nineteenth century, and their representation in the civil service declined proportionately. Various schemes to augment their participation failed or were rejected. The dominant group in the bureaucracy was the hereditary service nobility, who had attained rank solely through service. In 1913 the nonlanded service nobility dominated the middle and upper levels of most state departments. A third group was on the rise, however. Its members were the beneficiaries of growing educational opportunities for a larger public and increased demand for expertise. They came from a variety of backgrounds, especially the new entrepreneurial and professional classes.[24]

The balance among these three groups varied from ministry to ministry. The more traditional elements of the mix were heavily represented in the Ministry of the Interior. The newcomers were more often found in the newer economic ministries—Finance, Industry and Trade, and the Main Administration for Land Reorganization and Agriculture—and to some extent in Justice. Increasing social and cultural diversity within the bureaucracy inhibited the growth of civil service cohesion. Expertise vied with amateurism; personal power and favoritism frequently trumped process. The creation of new ministries for modern tasks exacerbated ministerial rivalry. Ministers' reliance on imperial favor did little to enhance the coherence of policy across government, in spite of the mechanisms for interministerial consultation that were in place.[25]

Examples of interministerial conflict in 1913 abounded; many of them were aired in the press. Kokovtsov was not only prime minister but minister of finance as well. His priority was to restructure the imperial budget the better to extract more government revenues and also to build the economic, particularly the industrial, strength of the country. He was also a strong advocate of keeping the peace in Europe and was no friend of a military buildup at the expense of his economic priorities. Although he did not starve the war and navy ministries of funds, he tried to reduce their overall share of the budget.[26] The military turned to its supporters in the State Duma. In early 1913 the Ministry of War requested a closed session of the Duma budget committee. Ministry officials briefed the committee members on the military inferiority of Russia to Germany and requested 500 million roubles over three years to enable the army to match the technical level of the German forces. The credit was granted. One member afterwards doubted that the Germans would wait for three years to let the Russians rearm.[27] For its part, the leadership at the Ministry of War unwisely saw little strategic advantage in a policy of industrialization. Minister Sukhomlinov resented expenditures on industrial development that he saw placing undue constraints on the military budget. In 1913 he tried but failed to persuade the Council of Ministers to exclude the Ministry of Finance from any role in military allocations.

The military was also shaking off obligations that it regarded as beyond its purview and competence but within the jurisdiction of the police. During the repressions of the counterrevolutionary period that followed the revolution of 1905, officers had resigned in large numbers rather than take part in the killing and arrest of civilians. In 1910 the government raised officers' pay, a step that had helped to replenish the ranks of officers by 1913.[28] The use of the military to suppress internal dissent and to carry out extensive policing duties was deeply resented by officers and Ministry of War officials. To protest against these perceived abuses, the army began to resist the established practice of drafting civilian troublemakers into the military as punishment. The ministry also stepped up complaints about policing duties, including the guarding of prisons and banks. By 1912 the army had secured a ban on the internal spying on the military conducted by the security police. During the strike movement of 1912–1913 that followed the Lena goldfields massacre, the army played almost no role in suppression of the strikers, although a military unit was involved in repressions in St. Petersburg in early July 1914. In July 1913 the government freed the military from guard duty at 39 prisons, and in October of that year the State Bank relieved the army from guarding its many branches.[29] By the beginning of 1914 the army had won its battle with the Ministry of the Interior, was free of nearly all of its former civilian roles, and was able to concentrate more fully on its military functions.

As was the case with foreign policy, the absence of collective cabinet responsibility proved to be a hindrance to forging a coherent policy on labor. The Ministry of Trade and Industry and the Ministry of the Interior developed opposing points of view and fought with one another over control of labor policy. The latter opposed any form of worker self-governance. It blamed revolutionaries and employers for stirring up worker militancy; opposed unions, whose growth and discussions it sought to limit; and saw all political strikes as illegal. It preferred a paternalistic approach to labor-management relations and often remonstrated with factory owners and managers about poor working conditions. The interior ministry was particularly hostile to the law on workers' health insurance. The ministry feared that the insurance boards set a precedent for autonomous worker organization and provided a vehicle for socialist propaganda. The contribution of the Ministry of the Interior and the police to the generation and perpetuation of labor political militancy, especially in St. Petersburg, was immense. Contemporaries clearly understood the damage the ministry's actions toward labor posed to social peace.[30] So did the Ministry of Trade and

Industry. It strongly supported the health insurance program and worker participation in administering the insurance funds. It, like the Association of Industry and Trade, looked on strikes as a normal worker response to the economic boom that the country enjoyed from 1909 and had little sympathy for its rival ministry's fears about revolutionary agitators.

In 1913 the minister of the interior, N.A. Maklakov, proposed the establishment of mediation courts to adjudicate worker-management disputes. The courts would be made up of appointees from the factory inspectorate, the provincial bureaucracy, the local police, and members of the Gendarme Corps as well as officials from the Ministry of Justice. Their task was less to mediate disputes than to study the life of workers and propose changes to the law to deal with the unsatisfactory aspects of factory life without regard for the views of either workers or management. The Ministry of Trade and Industry made a counterproposal. In order to succeed, its minister warned, mediation chambers would have to enjoy the confidence of both sides in labor disputes. The way to secure it was to permit labor and management to elect representatives to the courts, as was the case in the rest of Europe where labor mediation bodies functioned.[31] The Council of Ministers split over the matter and took no immediate action to set up the mediation courts.

The struggle between the Ministry of the Interior and the Main Administration for Land Reorganization and Agriculture over the implementation of the land reform also pointed to sharp differences within the government. The former encouraged separations from the commune with the long-term aim of its destruction; the latter favored land reorganization and agricultural education regardless of forms of land tenure. The Main Administration found an ally in the zemstvos, which promoted group land reorganization over separation as the way forward. With new legislation in 1911 that encouraged group land reorganization, the Main Administration won its case.[32] By 1913 the Ministry of the Interior had tacitly acquiesced in the new direction.

The above clashes pitted the economic ministries, two of them new or newly reorganized, against older, more traditional departments. Both were responding to new economic and social realities but in very different ways. The former increasingly recognized and tried to manage change and enlist new social actors through accommodation and cooperation. The latter accepted change only grudgingly and, even when moved to promote it as in the case of the land reform, sought to assert top-down control using traditional administrative means. The differences reflected the balance of bureaucratic forces within the ministries as well as the relationship of individual ministries to the modernization agenda that was imposing itself on the empire.

The existence of the State Duma and the State Council as integral parts of the legislative process complicated the task of policy-making. Emperor Nicholas was at best uncomfortable with the emergence of the civic nation that the new parliamentary order implied. So great was his contempt for representative government that he scratched out in the draft of the manifesto on the tercentenary of Romanov rule the words that pledged him to "unity with those elected by the people to participate in legislation."[33] As early as 1909, Nicholas had privately spoken about reducing the Duma to consultative status. In October 1913, when Maklakov proposed to Nicholas the prorogation of the fourth Duma, the Emperor agreed and went on to suggest the abolition of the legislative powers of the parliament. The Council of Ministers refused to consider the idea, however, and Nicholas temporarily dropped it. He returned to it in June 1914. Again the Council of Ministers turned him down.[34]

In 1913 Prime Minister Kokovtsov warned that any attempt to limit the role of the Duma would alienate allies and investors abroad and harm Russia's diplomatic and economic position. That was reason enough for the Council of Ministers to reject Maklakov's proposal, but the ministers had other reasons for preserving the legislature. Like the minister of war, who had successfully used the Duma to gain additional funds, most of the ministers agreed that the Duma was useful and even necessary. Maklakov remained intransigent, however. He became minister of the interior in December 1912 and made his hostility to the Duma known immediately. In January 1913, he withdrew a bill on religious toleration from Duma consideration; in February he withdrew his ministry's support for the bill on volost' reform, which the State Duma had approved and which was under discussion in the State Council. He arbitrarily increased the powers of governors to arrest so-called hooligans and hold them without trial for three months. He proposed a press bill to the Council of Ministers that reintroduced preliminary censorship and extended liability for violations of the press law to typographers and bookshop owners. The Council of Ministers told him to revise it. The ministry stubbornly brought a similar bill to the Duma in the fall.

On the pretext of an insulting remark by a right-wing deputy, Maklakov initiated a ministerial boycott of the Duma in May that lasted through most of the year.[35] The boycott of the Duma by ministers did not mean that all legislative work halted, but only that subordinates rather than ministers attended sessions.[36] In December the president of the Duma, M.V. Rodzianko, put a brave face on the situation when he announced that a great deal of the work of the fourth Duma so far had taken place in its commissions. The Duma as a whole, he said, had dealt with a few of the bills earlier prepared in its commissions, but the great majority would come forward in the next session in early 1914.[37] Paul Miliukov later recalled that bills under review in Duma commissions in 1913 included one on civil liberties first prepared in the second Duma, and others on freedom of conscience, the rights of unions, and freedom of assembly. Only a bill on universal suffrage, which included the female franchise, had failed to win Duma approval for forwarding to its commissions.[38] The ministerial boycott, therefore, by no means threatened the constitutional standing of the Duma. The budget discussions of that year were vital, and although few major pieces of legislation passed in 1913, a host of small and useful acts won approval and went forward to the State Council.[39]

The ministerial boycott nonetheless demoralized members of the Duma. Absenteeism rose. By early November the Duma member who had caused the boycott with his ill-judged rhetoric had apologized for his remarks and cleared the way for the resumption of normal relations between ministers and parliament. Maklakov's heavy-handedness on a range of issues damaged his authority among his fellow ministers and senior bureaucrats. His refusal to confirm the election of several mayors during 1913 and, in particular, his decision to appoint B.V. Shtiurmer, a non-Muscovite and stalwart of the extreme right in the State Council, to the post of mayor of Moscow angered responsible state servants. Even Shtiurmer demurred. Such a reaction from a wide range of officials, who had no wish to alienate moderate public opinion, rattled Maklakov and made him more receptive to renewed cooperation with the Duma. By the end of the year he indicated his readiness to appear at Duma sessions in January. The Minister of Justice, I.G. Shcheglovitov, also had a stormy relationship with the Duma. The effect of Duma debates on public opinion also moved the government to propose an order to limit the publication of Duma debates in newspapers.[40] Diplomat Nicholas Basily regretted in his memoirs that reactionary ministers like Maklakov and a couple of others refused to come to terms with the Duma, unlike most of the ministers.[41]

The State Council had emerged as a thorn in the side of both the State Duma and ministries seeking reform. The vulnerability of appointed members to dismissal at the end of each year made the State Council in the recollection of one of its university-elected members, M.M. Kovalevskii, the most "amoral" of any legislative body in Europe. Its members voted against their conscience in consideration of "what we Russians call state interests and needs."[42] On much legislation the State Council was to the right of the rest of the government and was by no means a rubber stamp for government-sponsored legislation. The Council of Ministers was itself divided over policy, and the State Council often served to block legislation supported by a majority of ministers in the council but opposed by its more reactionary members. Legislation that passed in the Duma, even with the support of the Council of Ministers, often failed or was drastically amended in the State Council.

There were many examples of effective vetoes by the State Council. The government and the Duma had reached a compromise in 1912 on a bill to transform the peasant volost' into an all-class primary institution of local government to be elected on the basis of a property qualification. The bill went forward for debate in the State Council. The conservative nobility strongly opposed any reform that threatened to eliminate the estate system on which their predominance rested. In defense of the estate principle the State Council tied up the bill in committee. After Maklakov became minister, the Ministry of the Interior withdrew its support for the volost' bill. In May 1914 the State Council voted not to debate it and the bill died in committee.[43] Calls to abolish the appointment of members to the State Council and for election of counselors on the basis of zemstvo and Duma elections were made in the Duma and the press. But the State Council was entrenched in the Fundamental Laws, which lacked any provision for amendments.

Since the reign of Peter the Great the Holy Synod had governed the affairs of the Orthodox Church. The synod was a body of clergymen but was headed by a layman, the procurator, appointed by the emperor. Orthodoxy was the state religion, and in many ways the church functioned as a department of state from the time of Peter. In 1913 the Church received nearly 46 million roubles in state support, up from 30 million in 1908; about half of it went to the funding of church-run elementary schools, which both the Duma and the zemstvos were increasingly unwilling to support.[44] The official status of the Church brought it under the scrutiny of the State Duma. The sitting

Duma in 1913 was particularly critical of church officials for allowing the Orthodox Church to be used by the state to influence the Duma elections of 1912 by instructing clergy to support designated candidates. An interpellation condemning the Church's part in the elections won overwhelming support among Duma representatives from all factions. Clergy elected to the Duma pressed the Church for the reform of the Code of Religious Consistories and the religious courts, and condemned the practice of rapid promotion in the hierarchy, regardless of merit or conviction, of selected youth from the academies.[45]

Peasant members of the Duma expressed widespread popular dissatisfaction with the fees that priests charged for basic religious services. They wanted to regulate the salaries of priests. Delegates from the peasantry along with many center and left representatives sought as well to abolish the church-parish schools, which they blamed for a host of problems in villages, including hooliganism.[46] The Ministry of Education also wanted a unified school system under ministry control. The fourth Duma supported numerous interpellations regarding violations by church and state of religious toleration. The procurator of the Holy Synod, V.K. Sabler, responded to the Church's critics by proposing in September 1913 that all legislation relating to the Orthodox Church be removed from the purview of the State Duma and State Council provided it did not entail new funding.[47] He also refused to put the Church's plan for parish reform before the Duma or even the Council of Ministers. The Council of Ministers disagreed, but Sabler won Nicholas's support. The council acquiesced and the plan escaped the scrutiny of the Duma. But the ministers also declined to publish the concession or to permit it to be cited, thus preventing it from serving as a precedent.[48]

The relationship between policing and the law was in 1913 a subject of dispute in the empire. It was an issue on which the State Duma and the Council of Ministers fundamentally disagreed. A bewildering variety of police forces operated in Russia. There were mounted police, foot police, and criminal investigators; factory, mill, railway, port, river, and mountain police; secret police, and others. Despite the proliferation of police forces, Russian per capita expenditure on policing in 1913 was less than half that of France and Italy and a quarter of spending on policing in Germany. Police in Russia carried out a variety of functions in addition to the prevention and investigation of crime. Duties included the collection of taxes, implementation of government legislation and military decrees, enforcement of health and safety laws, inspection of roads and buildings, collection of statistics, monitoring of public opinion, and broad supervision of public morals.

The main arm of central state policing in the empire was the Gendarme Corps. Eight gendarme regions maintained a network of local stations throughout the empire in 1913. The corps had six sections performing a range of tasks. The Gendarme Corps, whose officers had military rather than civil rank, was linked to but also distinct from the Department of Police, which was a branch of the Ministry of the Interior. It, too, contained a number of sections. Among them were the secret police (*Okhrana*), who worked closely with the Gendarme Corps but were organized separately from it. In the years preceding World War I the so-called Special Section of the Department of Police evolved into an agency for the collection of detailed information about revolutionary groups and individuals. The Fourth Section of the department assumed the responsibility for active surveillance and responses to revolutionary activities. The success of security police methods in tracking revolutionaries spilled over into other branches of policing. Russian criminal investigation units by 1913 had developed highly professional standards and made use of sophisticated modern equipment. They began systematic record-keeping of the photos of felons, their fingerprints, and verbal descriptions of their appearance, characteristics, and habits. In 1913 the International Congress of Criminologists in Switzerland named the Moscow Criminal Investigation Section the best in Europe.[49]

The chaos and relative thinness of policing in the empire prompted calls for reform that reached a crescendo in 1913. Both the Ministry of the Interior and the State Duma put forward plans for the reform of policing. Both plans sought a more united police force and called for a target of one policeman for every four hundred inhabitants. Otherwise the plans sharply diverged. The ministry wanted to devolve police services onto lower administrative bodies and concentrate policing on the battle against crime, in which it included what it referred to as subversion. Its reform plan called for the supervision of local policing by the head of the provincial gendarme administration, who would be appointed as assistant to the governor on police affairs. The plan also proposed to increase the powers of local police to impose fines and short sentences on petty offenders without reference to the court system. In other words, the ministry intended to diminish judicial supervision while augmenting police powers. The Duma bill proposed to abolish police authority to impose fines and to confer supervision of police on civilian provincial boards created for the purpose. In this way the Duma hoped to remove the Ministry of the Interior and the governors from their direct roles in policing. The matter remained unsettled before the war.

On most matters of substance it is difficult to speak of imperial government policy in 1913. Faced with rapid change that posed a vast array of policy choices, unprecedented exposure to publicity, an articulate, if handicapped, lower legislative organ, a recalcitrant upper house, and a monarch jealous of dynastic prerogatives, various ministers developed their own agendas and pursued their goals in a variety of ways. A common theme in the ministries was the desire to devolve more authority onto organs of local self-government without relinquishing overall bureaucratic control. That contrasted with the wish of many in the legislative branches of government to pass control fully into the hands of elected bodies of government. That fundamental division has led some commentators to believe that state and public were irrevocably separated and that no grounds for cooperation and exchange between them existed. Educated people on both sides of the state-public divide, however, shared a number of objectives. Common objectives promoted communication. The frontier between state and public was porous, and collaborations between state and public actors was not uncommon.

CENTRAL AND LOCAL GOVERNMENT

The organs of local self-administration, the zemstvos and city dumas, played an increasingly significant part in the delivery of public services. The former came into existence by statute in 1864 and the latter in 1870. They were bodies of local self-administration elected by curia loosely based on the social estates. By 1913 the zemstvos functioned in 40 provinces of European Russia. There were two levels of zemstvos, district and provincial. The district zemstvos provided an array of essential services at the local level, increasingly in partnership with the central government. They levied taxes and with the revenues attended to a variety of local concerns, including building and maintenance of roads and bridges, schooling, hospitals, clinics, veterinary, and other agricultural services such as seed and machine depots, experimental plots, and agricultural courses. Many ran institutions of petty credit. Provincial zemstvos served to coordinate district zemstvo activities within the province. By 1913, however, many zemstvo activists had come to regard the provincial zemstvos as superfluous and a drag on resources and local initiative. Projects mandated by the central government to provincial zemstvos drained 37 percent of the budgets of district zemstvos annually.[50]

Both zemstvos and dumas received about 10 percent of their funding from transfers from the state. Most of the rest came from taxes and city-run services. Municipal governments found ways to increase their revenues rapidly in the last years of the empire in spite of obstacles. Between 1870 and 1914 the Moscow city budget grew by 700 percent, a far greater increase than in the population of the city. The budget of Riga soared by 900 percent in that period. In search of revenues many cities municipalized city services. Trams, electrical power, and water supply were the main revenue earners. Many cities borrowed money for urban projects from abroad and accumulated debt. Many also ran deficits. The budget deficit of Moscow in 1912 was two million roubles, and in 1913 Nizhnii Novgorod ran a similar deficit.[51] The zemstvos, too, were rapidly increasing their revenues by 1913, but growing demand for services kept them under chronic financial pressure. The budgets of dumas and zemstvos were small compared to local governments elsewhere in Europe. Local government spending as a proportion of national government expenditure was only 15 percent in Russia, far below the proportion in Western Europe. In 1913–1914, for example, total local government expenditures in Belgium and England exceeded the national budgets.[52]

There were strains in the relationship between the state and elected bodies of local self-government, but a high level of engagement also prevailed. Many in the government preferred to think of the zemstvos and dumas as state organs rather than as independent entities. The election of zemstvo representatives and their powers of taxation made them, however, sufficiently autonomous to pursue their chosen agendas. The thinness of the central bureaucracy meant that the government depended heavily on the bodies of local self-administration to deliver public education and other services. On their side many zemstvos were by 1913 more disposed to cooperate with the government around specific reforms. Contemporaries noted that with the zemstvo and duma elections of 1912 and 1913, which brought significant turnover among representatives in some districts, many of the old hostilities between rightists and moderates had diminished. A businesslike and purposeful mood prevailed, and plans for practical reform dominated assembly agendas.[53] Although the autonomy of bodies of self-administration from the state remained a major concern of members of dumas and zemstvos, few rejected collaboration with the state as a partner in reform. Cooperation between state and local organs of self-government on the largest and most important project of change in the period, the land reform, was extensive by 1913. In 1912 the Main Administration for Land Reorganization and Agriculture hosted a conference that brought state agricultural officials and zemstvo activists together to coordinate their activities and to establish rules and procedures for subsidizing zemstvo initiatives in agriculture and agricultural societies by central government agencies. One result was a green book guide to the conduct of relations between the Main Administration and the zemstvos.[54]

A large proportion of funds to support the administration of the land reform and agricultural education programs already came from the zemstvos. It was their financial leverage that enabled them to reshape the land reform away from its original focus on individual landholding and toward group projects and land use education programs. As well as contributing financial support to agriculture from their own budgets, in 1913 the zemstvos and agricultural societies disbursed 50.1 percent of central government funding for agricultural assistance under the new rules worked out in 1912. The rest was disbursed by government agencies. In 14 provinces all funds for agricultural assistance were disbursed by the zemstvos, and in another 11 provinces government agricultural aid funds were expended according to the zemstvo plan.[55] By the end of 1913 the government was preparing legislation to transfer the responsibility for providing loans to peasants for land reorganization and improvement entirely to the zemstvos. Under the plan, funding would flow from the treasury through the zemstvos to lending institutions in their regions.[56]

Central government officials had greatly increased state funding for agricultural assistance and education beginning around 1910. By 1913 government and zemstvos were increasingly coordinating their efforts to inform peasants of scientific agricultural techniques and to enable peasants to adopt them. Assistance took many forms. Institutes and schools to train agronomists steadily increased enrollments. In 1913, there were 6,397 land surveyors at work as well as 9,935 local agronomists, 3,100 of whom were supported by zemstvos. Local authorities developed machine and tool depots where peasants could get access to new tools without the need to purchase them and could learn their uses. Depots often made seeds available, especially to promote the use of clover crops as a more efficient substitute for the practice of fallowing of the third field each year. Organized excursions to plots, farms, and exhibitions were common. In 1913, there were 217 major experimental institutions supported by 4.5 million roubles from government and 2 million from the zemstvos.[57]

Government and zemstvo agricultural assistance work included support for cottage and rural artisan production. Central and local authorities jointly encouraged the creation of marketing artels and cooperatives for cottage producers and facilitated access to credit for small-scale production. To highlight the products of rural artisans, zemstvos organized regional exhibitions of rural manufactures, and in March 1913 the Second All-Russian Artisans' Exhibition, with 5,958 exhibitors and an attendance of nearly 200,000 people, took place in St. Petersburg.[58] The Main Administration for Land Reorganization and Agriculture fully and publicly acknowledged its partnership with the zemstvos in land reform and land improvement: "A review of the activities of the department in 1913 would be incomplete if it did not acknowledge the continuing close collaboration [sotrudnichestvo] of the department with local social forces."[59]

Except on the drafting boards of a few planners, there was little that was utopian about the land reform. It was not an attempt to force a rational schema on an unenlightened peasantry. Instead, the reform recognized long-term processes that were largely driven by economic change in the empire and attempted to give them a legal foundation. As the reform unfolded, a three-way negotiation began among government officials, representatives of local self government, and the peasantry. On the ground, different compromises were reached in different regions. The agricultural aid program was based not on the premise that peasants were congenitally incapable of learning and perennially incompetent, but that their potential for learning was well worth a major investment of time and resources. It is not condescending to provide peasants with a wider range of knowledge and options than their experiences has given them.[60] In the perspective of the long and painful transition from Soviet agriculture after 1989, a process that is still years from completion at the time of writing, the land reform and agricultural education projects of the prewar years were remarkable for their achievements and highly promising in their potential to modernize the empire's agriculture. The success was the product of large-scale collaboration between state and social forces.

Another area of public service on which nearly all parties were able to agree was the municipalization of pharmacies under duma or zemstvo ownership and state regulation. The Duma passed a bill conferring owner-ship of pharmacies on municipalities and the State Council concurred. The emperor approved the law in 1912.[61] More divisive was proposed legislation on the organization of medical-sanitary administration in the empire. High rates of death by infectious diseases and high infant mortality moved the government in 1911 to set up a commission to look into the organization of public health and sanitary affairs. G.E. Rein, who had for years pressed for a review of medical-sanitation organization, chaired the commission. Rein had been a zemstvo activist and was elected as an Octobrist to the second and fourth State Dumas. Like many other professionals he was prepared to move from the private into the state sphere to effect needed change. He resigned from the Duma when named chair of the commission. Rein had been deeply disillusioned with the failure of the first three Dumas to address medical and sanitary questions. He had also witnessed conflict between provincial and district zemstvos over control of sanitary regulation, which slowed reform.[62] The commission that he chaired included representatives of the government and of the zemstvos and dumas. It also sent question-naires to bodies of local government soliciting their views.

The commission recommended the establishment of a Main Administra-tion for State Health Protection with 13 regional medical-sanitary depart-ments through which to manage the delivery of medical and sanitary ser-vices. It also proposed that the present medical inspectors in the provinces, who reported to the governor, be replaced by a provincial medical-sanitary administration that included a broad spectrum of provincial medical workers. Commissioners argued that the complexity of modern life and disease management required the full engagement of the organs of local self-government along with their coordination from the center. Finally they recommended that medico-sanitary councils be set up in each province to bring together state provincial administrators and personnel from the organs of local self-government.[63]

Although the Rein commission favored the coordination from the center of medical affairs in the empire, it divided various responsibilities between central and local offices. The commission proposed a bill on contagious diseases and their containment that placed the onus on local authorities to identify and isolate cases. The bill on leprosy made it the responsibility of the state to build special hospitals for lepers. A bill on the administration of medical institutions proposed direct management by doctors. Another piece of prepared legislation provided for the independent practice of fel'dshers in communities where there were insufficient numbers of doctors.[64] The commission's legislative proposals gained the approval of the Council of Ministers in May 1913 but made no further progress before World War I when the work of the commission died.

The Rein report was based on wide public consultation. Its recommendations envisaged shared responsibility among the central state, local governments, and medical professionals. It delimited the role of the central state and defined the responsibilities and authority of local bodies. The principal organization of doctors in Russia, the Pirogov Society, denounced the Rein report at its congress. The interest of the state in medical-sanitary matters, in the view of its members, ought to be restricted to the armed forces, prisons, state railways, and resettlement projects. The rest should be entirely in the jurisdiction of dumas and zemstvos.[65] The majority of doctors did support community medicine as advocated by the Pirogov Society but were poorly organized to win the day. The resistance of the Pirogov Society was, however, more political or ideological than practical. National standards and coordination of disease control with clearly assigned responsibilities for local and national actors were preferable to a hodgepodge of local jurisdictions. In any case, Rein's recommendations afforded both local authorities and medical professionals significant areas of competence that many doctors found sufficient. The debate over medical-sanitary administration did, however, galvanize dissenting doctors to work to revive the corporate organization of the profession that had atrophied after the shock of the 1905 revolution.[66]

The central government had by 1913 recognized that several provisions of the Municipal Statute of 1892 hampered the work of municipal governments both financially and administratively. Under its provisions, cities had to contribute to the costs of quartering troops. They also paid for urban policing but did not control it; the police reported to the prefect or governor and not to the city council. Urban coffers also supported the salaries and living expenses of employees of the Special Office on Urban Affairs and of court officials. In large cities the state imposed a parallel urban administration through the office of the prefect and the Special Office on Urban Affairs. In smaller cities governors and officials from various ministries exercised powers that paralleled the authority of city councils. Urban government in St. Petersburg especially suffered from the interference of state officials in planning and financing urban development.

In 1913 the central state assumed the salaries and living costs of court employees and officials of the special offices of urban affairs. As of 1 January 1914 the state also absorbed half of the costs of urban policing. Legislation in 1913 provided as well for a rebate to urban governments of 1 percent of state tax revenues levied on urban properties. At the same time that it refused to allow the zemstvos to hold a national congress to discuss zemstvo financing, the government permitted a conference in Kiev in summer 1913 on the improvement of urban finances. This concession reflected the recognition by the state of the centrality of urban life in the future of the empire in a changing world.

The foregoing examples illustrate both the tensions between the central state and organs of local governance and civic groups, and the level of engagement and intercourse among them. Zemstvo and duma representatives proclaimed their right to be consulted about public policy. In particular, they pressed the government to permit regional and national meetings to discuss questions of common interest and coordinate their activities. The government turned down a request from the zemstvos to meet jointly to coordinate planning for the Romanov tercentenary but did allow adjacent provincial zemstvos to meet for that purpose on a regional basis. The congresses in Kiev in 1913 on agriculture and on urban finances were the result of zemstvo and duma lobbying and signaled recognition within the government of its need for social support in policy-making and implementation.

STATE AND PUBLIC

A critical interface between state and public was the law. The Russian Empire was far from being lawless in 1913, but the laws were not yet fully independent of will. The Judicial Statute of 1864 had created the basis for a comprehensive legal system and the rule of law. It challenged the state's assumption that law served administrative goals, and fostered instead a legal culture based on the notion of individual rights that vied with state rights. The statute created a system of regular circuit courts and judicial chambers and justices of the peace. Later the courts of the justices of the peace were suspended in most parts of the country but continued to function in some large cities. The reform provided appellate courts and entrenched the Senate as the supreme court of the land, with civil and criminal departments. It mandated trial by jury in criminal cases and provided that only a lawyer could represent individuals in court. The statute also regularized the legal profession. It created regional bar associations, called councils of the bar, which regulated entrance into the profession, set professional standards and codes of behavior, and disciplined their members. Lawyers had to graduate from a law faculty and undertake a five-year apprenticeship under a patron lawyer. At the end of the apprenticeship they entered one of the regional bar associations. By 1913 the legal network was expanding, with the creation of new courts and additional judicial districts. In 1913 the Ministry of Justice restored the courts of the justices of the peace, first in 10 southwest provinces where, it believed, the population was sufficiently mature not to abuse them.[67]

The Fundamental Laws of 1906 conferred a wide range of individual rights on the empire's citizens. They included the freedoms of religion, movement, assembly, speech, and association. The law regulated prosecution for criminal acts, gave homeowners the right to withhold consent for searches and seizures, provided compensation for property confiscations, guaranteed freedom to travel abroad, and assured the right to acquire and transfer property. Citizens could express their ideas freely and circulate them in the press. The emperor's subjects could also hold peaceful meetings and form societies and unions, provided their purposes were "not contrary to the law." The state exploited that phrase to limit many of the promised freedoms in practice.[68]

Although many state officials clung to the established notion of the role of law as the basis of administrative order and not the guarantor of individual rights, legal officials serving the state were trained in the same schools as lawyers, with whom they functioned together in the new legal culture of individual rights. Both sides shared values and principles contrary to the traditional values of the state. The court system oversaw discipline for state legal officials; judges enjoyed immunity from arbitrary removal from office; prosecutors answered to the Ministry of Justice. The state obstinately created barriers to the effective functioning of the system it had sanctioned. It limited the number of councils of the bar, excluded non-Orthodox subjects from the legal profession, interfered in disciplinary matters, and harassed judges and prosecutors deemed to be too independent in their judgments. The state blocked the formation of a national council of the bar and chronically denied lawyers the right to meet in national congresses. This began to change in 1906. In that year the state allowed the establishment of six new councils of the bar. It also relaxed prohibitions on the admission of Jews to the bar.[69]

Legal order clashed with the extraordinary powers granted under the measures on reinforced security, introduced in 1881 by Alexander III, which empowered governors to take punitive measures without reference to the laws or regular legal procedures. An important element of reinforced security was the power to transfer prosecutions, especially of crimes threatening security, from civilian to military courts. The conduct of cases moved to military courts was by no means arbitrary, however. Most such trials were open to the public and were conducted on the basis of the adversarial system. Military lawyers normally represented defendants, but in civilian cases the court often allowed civilian defense lawyers to act for the accused. All cases were open to appeal to the Supreme Military Court. Legal personnel in the military trained at the Alexander Academy of Military Justice, where they studied Western law and constitutional forms of government under civilian, often liberal, faculty. Most military legal personnel shared the legal ethos of their civilian counterparts. Like many army officers, they resigned from office in considerable numbers during the repressions of 1906–1907 rather than compromise their standards of justice. Around 14 percent of the personnel of the Main Administration of Military Justice resigned between January 1905 and March 1907. Others refused to submit to pressure from above, subverted prosecutions, and preserved due process.[70]

By 1913 the maintenance of reinforced security was a major issue of contention between state and public as well as a matter of debate within the Council of Ministers. The provincial press reported extensively on arbitrary measures taken under the security provisions. The minister of the interior, Maklakov, not only renewed reinforced security in areas where it was already in place, but also requested the Council of Ministers to extend it to other parts of the country. The council refused and even lifted it in some areas. Critics pointed out, however, that the governors' powers remained so extensive that the lifting of reinforced security made little practical difference.[71]

Although the Imperial Russian state resisted subordination to the law, it was not averse to law as the foundation of relations among its citizens.[72] The law increasingly served as a site where state and social actors attempted to restructure social relationships and to reshape social values. In matters such as property and inheritance law and in the contentious example of marital separation, the law was responsive to changing circumstances and public opinion. In Russian practice, churches administered divorce according to their own norms. The Orthodox Church made divorce particularly difficult. A public debate ensued that by 1914 had brought about significant changes in marital separation laws and support for separated women. State officials actively participated in the debate, one that was argued in the language of individual rights and freedoms. The debate did not pit state officials against the public. Rather, sides formed across the state-public boundary along conservative and liberal lines. The process was slow and incremental but the pattern of responsiveness to social needs and public opinion was clear. William Wagner, who has explored the history of the marital separation laws, maintains that the alienation of the state from society and its resistance to liberalizing reform have been overstated. The state was neither as isolated from society nor as united within itself as formerly thought. Instead, bureaucrats and social activists formed alliances to advance their common ideological preferences.[73]

Many professionals welcomed collaboration with the state. Historians have argued that in Russia, as elsewhere in continental Europe, the state played a significant role in fostering the professions through specialist schooling and state-sponsored professional organization.[74] Although Russian professionals shared in some measure with the intelligentsia the ethos of service to the people, they were also inclined to seek empowerment by partnering with the state in advancing their agendas. The willingness of many professionals to cooperate with the state in the years before World War I was prompted in part by a reaction against the excesses of the revolution of 1905.[75] Whereas before 1905 many professionals emphasized the struggle for the autonomy of their profession and competed with government to gain control of the economic and social agenda, in the postrevolutionary period they tended to pursue both broad social and narrow guild objectives through cooperation with like-minded colleagues or potential allies inside the state structure. Movement from the private to the state sector and back was common not only for lawyers but for others as well.[76] Tensions between the state and the professions did not cease, but the locus of debate shifted from control of policy to debates over policy alternatives.

Frustration with cumbersome government regulations, bureaucratic conservatism, and interministerial conflict was endemic among professionals. The greatest obstacles to the practical aspirations of professionals to improve material conditions in the empire were the slowness of the state to adapt to changing conditions and chronic rivalries among ministries. The struggle to bring electricity to Russia provides a good example. Electrification was seen by many as an effective means to bring about fundamental social, economic, and political change. From the beginning, government regulations failed to keep up with new technologies in the field. Lengthy waits for permissions, reviews that inhibited the diffusion of technologies, weak local governments, and a legal framework that worked against native entrepreneurship conspired to slow the process of electrification. By 1913 the Ministry of Transport and Communications was interested in assisting companies to develop hydroelectric power. In that year it made an effort to resolve right-of-way issues for transmission lines. But the Ministry of the Interior held a completely different view of land and water ownership, compensation, and the nature of oversight. As a result the Council of Ministers blocked the plan of the transport minister.[77]

Engineers and technicians played an important role in a critical area of often uneasy collaboration between the state and the public: the development of Russian aviation. By early summer 1913 Russia stood second in the world behind France in the number of military aircraft it possessed. By that time the air force had 18 aviation detachments with 112 planes in service. Ninety more planes were ready for deployment and another ninety-six were scheduled for delivery within weeks.[78] The navy had taken an early interest in seaplanes, and by 1913 Russia stood at the leading edge of float plane technology. The pioneering flight of Louis Blériot, the French aircraft designer and pilot, across the English Channel in 1909 set off in Russia as elsewhere in Europe a delirium of enthusiasm for the airplane. Both the state and informed members of the public quickly recognized the challenge that aviation posed to the empire's capacity for modernization. The progress of the industry became a kind of bellwether of Russia's cultural standing in the world. Many saw in the airplane a means to master the vastness of Russia and accelerate modernization. The Grand Duke Aleksandr Mikhailovich in 1909 grasped the importance of cooperation between the state and the public in nurturing an aviation industry. He established the Committee for Strengthening the Fleet through Voluntary Contributions. Although private donations in Russia did not match those made to similar organizations in Western countries, the committee raised enough money to have purchased 77 aircraft from abroad by 1913.[79] The Ministry of the Interior and the Okhrana opposed the importation and construction of airplanes, which they feared could become weapons of revolutionaries.[80]

The Imperial All-Russian Aero Club was founded in 1908. It boasted a broad membership, including members of the imperial family, society nobles, bureaucrats, wealthy merchants, and even actors and opera singers. The press criticized the club for its celebrity membership's lack of accomplishment in advancing Russian aviation. But the club did develop a network of flying clubs that stretched from St. Petersburg to Vladivostok in the east and Odessa in the south. Through air shows and flight competitions it whetted the public appetite for flight. In time its membership deepened to include aviation technicians and commercial representatives of the aviation industry. Other civil associations that promoted aviation in Russia were the Moscow Society of Aeronautics and the Odessa Aero-Club.[81]

Early Russian invention in aviation rested on close collaboration among state, military, and public actors. Dmitrii Riabushinskii, a Moscow industrialist, had in 1901 funded the construction of an experimental laboratory at Kushino near Moscow. It included in its facilities the world's first wind tunnel. The laboratory forged close ties with the Moscow Higher Technical Institute. Both civilian and military engineers and technicians used its facilities. Civilian inventors, engineers, and builders collaborated closely with the military in this period. D.P. Grigorovich built a number of seaplane prototypes for the Russian navy; Joseph Gakhel contributed several new designs for military aircraft.[82] Igor Sikorskii made the greatest contribution. In 1912 he won the Moscow military competition for his S-6b fighter plane.

In 1913 Sikorskii stunned the aviation world with the test flight of his multiengine aircraft, the Grand, soon to be renamed the Russian Warrior, over St. Petersburg. Engineers had previously thought that multiengine flight was impossible; they believed that a failed engine would twist the plane violently in the direction of the surviving engine. Among the 15 people on board the Grand's pioneering flight were members of the State Duma. To demonstrate the reliability of the plane, Sikorskii left the cockpit and joined his passengers in the cabin during the flight. He also shut off the engines and glided silently over the emperor's summer palace.[83] The Grand or Russian Warrior was 60 feet in length, and had a wingspan of nearly 90 feet and a 100-horsepower engine. It could remain in the air for several hours. The Warrior was a prelude to the larger multiengine aircraft, the Il'ia Muromets, which Sikorskii flew from St. Petersburg to Kiev in June 1914.[84]

The Russian Warrior and Il'ia Muromets were built in the Russo-Baltic Carriage Works with the financing of its director, M.V. Shidlovskii, a state counselor. The first plant to assemble airplanes in Russia was the Shchetinin plant in St. Petersburg. It assembled Blériot monoplanes, from parts manufactured in France, for public sale. The plant also built the Rossiia, the first Russian-designed production aircraft. By 1913 the largest aircraft plant in Russia was the Duks factory in Moscow. The Lebedev factory in St. Petersburg and the Anatra factory in Odessa also built planes.[85] What united all those engaged in the establishment of the Russian aviation industry was the recognition that successful competition with Western rivals required civic engagement. It signaled not only the rise of civic consciousness but also the interdependence, whether welcome or not, of state and public in advancing the agenda of modernization.

There were many points of formal contact between the state and public organizations. An important link was employers' societies. They had come into existence in the 1890s on government initiative. The goal was to create representative commercial and industrial branch organizations of entrepreneurs to articulate their needs and interests. Businesses also participated in interbranch commercial and industrial congresses, formed stock exchange committees, and created employers' unions. The government imposed strict controls on these organizations, and they depended on the state financially. Ministries approved and oversaw all of their activities. Congresses could petition for action, but the government had no obligation to follow their recommendations. The participation of ministry representatives in their congresses and the culture of bureaucratic dependency in general assured a measure of compliance by these organizations with the wishes of the state. Although the State Duma considered bills to make employer societies financially independent, a majority of members feared that if congresses of businesses gained autonomy from state regulation, they would transform themselves into price-controlling syndicates.

Although the initiative of employers' societies was strictly limited, these organizations provided a vital line of communication between government and business. Delegates to commercial and industrial congresses discussed tariff policy, interregional trade, transport, infrastructure improvements, and commercial insurance.[86] They also learned organizational and cooperative techniques and negotiating skills and formed alliances, not only among like businesses but with a variety of regional commercial and industrial enterprises. The participation of middle-level bureaucrats in the so-called Economic Dialogues in Moscow from 1909 to 1912 strikingly illustrated the

evolution of government and business contacts. The dialogues were organized by a number of Moscow industrialists, who later formed the nucleus
of the Progressive Party. They brought together businessmen with academic
experts to discuss issues related to the Russian national economy and attracted government officials into their circle.[87] The dialogues may also have
sown the seeds of the War Industries Committee of World War I.

CONGRESSES

Congresses also created venues for contact and exchange between state
officials and the concerned public. The year 1913 was one of congresses,
both national and regional. Their competence ranged from urban finances,
public education, cooperatives, and agriculture, through gynecology and
midwifery, manufacturing, and electro-technical engineering, to publishing
and bookselling, vegetarianism, dentistry, cottage industry, and juvenile
courts. Many of these congresses brought together representatives of state
and society to discuss in public major issues and future policy directions.
The very fact that they took place points to the need for the government to
harness a broad range of expertise and to build social and political consensus
around critical issues that could no longer be suppressed or ignored. The
congresses also, however, signaled the scarcity of more regular institutional
channels of communication between state and public.

A good example of the breadth of participation in congresses and conferences was a conference in October 1913 on land improvement in northern
regions of the country in Moscow. It brought together experts on agronomy,
State Duma and State Council representatives, academics, zemstvo activists, the chairs of zemstvo administrations, and a range of representatives
of concerned government ministries along with members of the industrial-
commercial classes. The discussion ranged over many sensitive topics,
including problems with the land reform, state-zemstvo relations, and local
governance.[88] The agricultural congress in Kiev, despite its support for anti-
government resolutions, heard reports from a large number of government
specialists. In the same month delegates from 14 provinces participated in a
congress on fire insurance and prevention. The zemstvos sponsored it, but
delegates represented a broad spectrum of interests from cities, fire prevention societies, mutual insurance societies, universities, scientific societies,
and state institutions. The conference adopted resolutions to support new

legislation on credit for fire-resistant buildings, funds to educate peasants on fire prevention and control measures, and additional fire brigades.[89]

Few congresses on major matters passed without conflict between state security and social forces. The Congress of Cooperative Societies was policed extensively, and police representatives frequently halted discussions and blocked resolutions.[90] The congress was attended by representatives of peasant cooperative groups. Observers noted its sharply democratic character.[91] Such a gathering was likely to garner special attention from the police. But police closely supervised more respectable representatives of society as well. At the September Congress of the Representatives of Municipal Government in Kiev, police imposed a strict censorship. The Ministry of the Interior had earlier forbidden city dumas to reply to a State Duma questionnaire about the reform of the municipal statute. It imposed the same prohibition on congress delegates.[92] For all their vigilance the police could not prevent A.I. Guchkov, former president of the third Duma, from cataloguing in his closing speech before the congress a long list of needed reforms and demanding the full realization of the promise of the October Manifesto. Delegates applauded the speech; even *Novoe vremia*, an independent conservative newspaper, endorsed Guchkov's outburst.[93]

Voluntary associations served as points of contact between state and public. Charities not only addressed social problems in conjunction with local elected authorities but also conferred with the state on matters of national concern. Penal reform was one area of collaboration between the state and the public. In the 1890s patronage societies (*patronaty*) were created to oversee the reintegration of ex-convicts into society. The societies were sanctioned by government but freed from its interference. They financed themselves largely through membership fees. The early results of the experiment were disappointing. The societies were purely voluntary and provided few inducements to individuals to take part. Social activists attributed the lack of interest in the patronaty to crippled social development and a dearth of *intelligenty* free to participate in such causes. Ironically, a survey of governors also blamed a lack of social independence for the problems with patronage.[94] Government concern about independent social activity, the revolution of 1905, and the dark years of reaction from 1906 to 1907 inhibited the development of the patronage movement.

Attitudes toward the punishment of criminals and their rehabilitation did not stand still, however, either in society or the bureaucracy. Prison overcrowding was acute by 1913. In June 1909 the state had begun to address the problem by creating provisions for parole and creating a medal to award those who made outstanding contributions to *patronatstvo*. In December 1912 the state agreed on a formula to subsidize patronage societies. In 1913, 117 patronaty and 38 related prison aid societies were serving a small percentage of parolees from the prison system. Although the system had its critics—parolees sometimes took the opportunity to flee—the historian of penal reform in Russia concluded that "[b]y 1908–1914, bureaucrats, professionals, and amateurs had arrived at similar views of criminality and corrections. There is every good reason to think that they would have continued to work together."[95] As in the case of marital separation, a convergence of views in society and government circles around a pressing social issue, the reentry of criminals into society, created sufficient grounds for collaborative action. Like its parent organization, the Society for the Patronage of Juveniles had a slow start. A system of courts for juvenile offenders was established in 1912. The aim of the society was to facilitate the rehabilitation of juveniles who passed through the court system. The authors of the society expected a flood of people to join such a good cause, but by early 1913 memberships were few.[96]

More successful was the Guardianship of Popular Temperance. The inspiration for the guardianship was a coalition of temperance groups. They enlisted the financial backing of several industrialists. The guardianship also received a subsidy from the Ministry of Finance, whose revenues benefited greatly from the spirits and wine monopoly. The guardianship promoted temperance in a variety of ways. Most important was its support for popular theater. The guardianship expended millions of roubles on thousands of performances of theater and opera for the masses. The goal was to lure the folk from the saloons into more rational and cultured pursuits and to develop in them a taste for the high achievements of the Russian arts.[97]

Voluntary associations other than charities also brought together individuals in their private capacities who shared a common interest and sought to advance common objectives. Often they were places where individuals from the state and private sectors came together as concerned citizens in pursuit of shared goals. In his recent study of learned societies, Joseph Bradley has pointed out that, especially in St. Petersburg, government officials made up a significant proportion of the membership of scientific societies.[98] A good example was the St. Petersburg Parents' Circle. The Parents' Circle was founded in 1884 in association with the Pedagogical

Museum of Military Educational Institutions, which in turn was under the jurisdiction of the Ministry of War. Its initial purpose was the advancement of early family education. Although the ministry took a broadly tolerant attitude towards the circle's activities, members increasingly chafed under the restrictions imposed on them. In March 1906 the circle attained independence as a voluntary association. By 1913 its membership included men and a significant number of women from education, medicine, the arts, and journalism. Membership in that year totaled 239. Of the 175 members for whom detailed information exists, 36 were employees of a total of 26 government ministries or other official institutions. They included the ministries of education, finance, interior, justice, and war. Several of those bureaucrats were also members of other voluntary associations.[99] It is apparent that civil servants in their capacity as private citizens routinely played central roles in the voluntary institutions of civil society. Bradley observes that in spite of the role of officials in such societies, they were not viewed by liberal society as being of the government.[100]

Dependence on a variety of social institutions for information, consensus-building, and policy implementation by no means cured the Russian state, especially its coercive branches, of fear of public initiative. The more conservative branches of the state sought to manage public initiative where it was needed and to crush it where it was not. State authorities had ample means available to suppress public opinion, intimidate social activists, and repress outright dissidents. The most drastic tool was imprisonment and administrative exile. The exile system was a hotly debated issue in 1913. A failed escape attempt in 1913 by Ekaterina Breshko-Breshkovskaia, later celebrated as the grandmother of the Russian revolution, and the poor state of her health drew the attention of the press to the living conditions of exiles.[101] The amnesty in February 1913 in honor of the Romanov tercentenary aroused weeks of speculation about its principles and extent before it was announced and weeks of complaints about its limitations afterward. City dumas and zemstvos called for a far-reaching amnesty and the liberal press joined the chorus.[102] The Ministry of the Interior banned discussion of the amnesty in bodies of local self-government on the grounds that it exceeded their legal mandate. The amnesty eventually freed more than 6,000 administrative exiles and released 1,252 of 3,074 inmates of St Petersburg prisons. By the end of 1913 only about one thousand political exiles remained, and the number of political hard labor convicts was reduced to about two thousand by January 1914.[103] People sentenced under article 102 of the criminal code, which was used to incarcerate anyone belonging to an illegal political organization, were excluded from the amnesty. Excluded also were those accused of crimes against religion. In their case the amnesty made provision for the possible reduction of their sentences by one-third.[104]

The authorities also had at their disposal fines for an array of offenses. Failure to pay the fines could lead to imprisonment. The press was particularly subject to fines, and editors to prison. In one estimate the press in 1913 received 340 fines totaling 129,775 roubles.[105] It is not clear how many responsible editors found themselves in prison in that year, but one of them wryly observed that if he were jailed for every cited violation he would need to be Methuselah to complete his sentence. Much was left to the discretion of local authorities. An editor of a paper in the Amur region was arrested for reprinting an article from a newspaper in the capital about the number 13. The article recounted events that occurred in the year 13 beginning in 1313 and graded them as lucky or unlucky. The original had elicited no comment from censors in the metropolis.[106] Authorities especially targeted the socialist press. Critics rightly warned that suppression of the legal press only encouraged the spread of illegal publications.[107]

Not only did the Ministry of the Interior attempt to control the content of the press and to punish editors for overstepping arbitrarily set boundaries, but it also tried to limit the distribution of opposition papers while secretly subsidizing and promoting rightist publications. Newspaper sellers who rented kiosks at railway stations were required to stock at least as many copies of right-wing organs as of other newspapers. The sellers protested that the obligatory rightist newspapers did not sell. Whereas progressive papers were returned to the publisher at the rate of 6 to 10 percent, right-wing papers went back at a rate of from 40 to 80 percent.[108] Governors ordered restrictions on the kinds of publications district zemsvos should distribute to the local population and required the widespread distribution of officially sponsored papers.[109] In a bizarre example of personal initiative, General P.K. von Rennenkampf ordered that officers under his command should read only newspapers from an approved list and took disciplinary action against readers of *Rech'*, the Kadet publication. The army newspaper *Ofitser* condemned the order as harmful to the independence of officers.[110]

The Council of Ministers had concluded by 1913 that the existing press regime was inadequate to protect state interests. In that year it introduced a bill to reform the press law. The bill proposed to force newspapers and other publications to submit copy up to three days in advance of publication. No newspaper could function under such conditions. The bill met the widest condemnation of most parties in the State Duma. The conservative press strongly opposed it, and even some ministers had severe reservations about its advisability. Lev Tikhomirov, the highly conservative editor of *Moskovskie vedomosti*, lamented that the proposed law assumed that the press was the enemy. "Strictly speaking," he wrote, "this is not really a statute about the press but a statute about measures for the suppression of a criminal press."[111] Public opposition to the bill prevented it from passing.

Books were also targeted. The Ministry of the Interior maintained an index of forbidden books. Many of them were published in Russia only to be subsequently banned. Most of Lev Tolstoi's nonfiction works and pamphlets were on the list, but his fiction, a part of the nation's great literary tradition, was not. Ukrainian editions of the works of the great Ukrainian poet Taras Shevchenko were unacceptable but translations were sanctioned. A Russian translation of Jack London's collected works with a foreword by Leonid Andreev that was published in Russia in 1912 made it to the list, as did Renan's *Life of Christ* and, curiously, Herbert Spencer's *The Right of Land Ownership*. The list also specified passages that should be excised from certain books. All information about sexuality and contraception and many religious references were among them. Some of the poems in Walt Whitman's *Leaves of Grass* were to be blacked out by local authorities.[112]

Access to books was also contentious. Moved by complaints from the reactionary organization the Union of the Russian People, the Ministry of Transport and Communications proposed to oversee book inventories at railway kiosks.[113] In 1913 local zemstvos waged a war with the schools inspectorate over control of libraries. A law transferred supervision of school libraries, which also served the general public, from zemstvo school boards to the curators of school districts, who reported to the Ministry of Education. A purge of the holdings quickly followed. The revolt against the law began in Ufa province. The provincial zemstvo ordered that all of the libraries in its lower schools be closed and recommended that the books in them be used to form new independent village public libraries or be transferred to existing public libraries. Seeing the danger in this bold move, the ministry persuaded the Council of Ministers to forbid the initiative.[114] Other jurisdictions followed the example of Ufa. In Viatka the district zemstvo assembly closed all school libraries and opened independent ones with the books from the closed libraries. The governor seized the books but announced that they would have to be purged before going back to the schools, a lengthy process.[115] In Novocherkassk the local Women's Society had sponsored the creation of a network of school libraries. Under the new regime of the Ministry of Education 90 percent of the books in them were removed. The women declined to place any more of their libraries in schools but planned instead to open a new network of public libraries.[116] The protest against ministry control of school libraries grew throughout the summer. In addition to closing or moving libraries, a number of zemstvos and city dumas took legal recourse and filed complaints with the Senate about the legality of the ministry's takeover of school libraries.[117]

State officials could also close organizations and societies that they deemed to have overstepped the limits of their charters. Examples of closings were numerous in 1913. One victim was the Third Women's Club in Moscow. It was closed in early November for holding a meeting on 29 October of a political nature. In addition certain books in the club's library were found to be undesirable. The Mutual Aid Society of Notaries was closed in Moscow at the same time for holding political discussions.[118] A national scandal resulted from the closing of the Kharkov Medical Society. During the notorious trial of Mendel Beiliss for the crime of murder with blood ritual as its leitmotif, the society publicly condemned the medical experts called by the prosecution and scoffed at the pseudoscientific efforts made by other so-called experts, who testified to the existence of ritual murder in Jewish religious tradition. The governor shut the society down. The Society of Tver' Physicians joined the protest and suffered the same fate.[119] The societies were reinstated when they agreed to alter their charters to exclude outside guests from meetings.[120] Nevertheless, the Kharkov society challenged the legality of the closure in the Senate. As we have seen, the power to close or to refuse registration to societies was particularly useful in suppressing organizations that fostered ethnic identity. In Ekaterinoslav the authorities refused to permit branches of the Ukrainian society Prosvite to form in a number of towns. In Vilno the governor even refused to allow a group to call itself Ukrainian because, he said, "Ukrainians are in L'vov but here they're Little Russians."[121]

Meetings were also strictly regulated. The law distinguished between public and nonpublic meetings. Nonpublic meetings were those attended by members of the society concerned without the presence of outsiders. Such meetings did not require prior authorization. Public meetings included people unknown by the organizers but also embraced all meetings held in theaters, public halls, and other public spaces. Police agents sat in on public meetings to catch deviations from previously submitted and approved agendas. Police also vetted in advance the topics of public lectures and monitored them for faithfulness to the original. If in the agent's opinion the meeting strayed into territory not previously approved or the subject matter of a lecture became too controversial, he could halt the proceedings and enforce compliance or close the meeting or lecture entirely. The distinction the law drew between private and public meetings forced members of societies to meet in private gatherings without outsiders. This greatly curtailed public discourse and exchange. The authorities required applications for meetings and lectures and the use of public venues well in advance. They regularly delayed approval until the eve of the event, often affecting attendance.[122]

Interventions in the proceedings of conferences were commonplace in 1913. At the first congress of the representatives of petty credit of western Siberia in June, the chairman, a state official, refused to allow discussion of the effects of the government liquor monopoly on the population. He also blocked discussion of the need for the introduction of zemstvos into Siberia and prevented a resolution on universal education.[123] In Moscow officials prevented discussion of a wide range of issues at the congress of the Society of Merchants Employees and early in July closed it altogether.[124] In August the Moscow Society of Metalworkers held a general meeting with a theme of worker solidarity. The police representative refused to allow discussion of the reasons for worker arrests or of organizational problems at various factories. Shortly afterward the police ended the congress.[125] At a banquet for six hundred guests in celebration of the anniversary of the founding of the progressive newspaper *Russkie vedomosti*, a speech of welcome by a Duma liberal prompted the closing of the affair by the presiding police representative. In revenge, newspapers throughout the country printed the text of the speech in full.[126] The line between private and public meetings was thin. In Chernigov eight electors in a by-election to the State Duma sat down in a hotel room to discuss the election. The police burst in and charged them with holding an illegal meeting. As the police captain read the charge that "eight men are sitting around a table, on which there is not a trace of tea or hors d'oeuvres," the hotel management wheeled in a samovar. The captain blustered that the refreshments had arrived too late.[127]

Another ploy used to limit public participation in civic institutions was to set high standards for legitimate elections. A good example was parent committees in schools. The law required that a quorum of two-thirds of all the parents of children in the school be present before an election of representatives to the parent committee could take place. If a quorum succeeded, the ministry then declared that the law really meant that two-thirds of the parents in each class had to be present. Despite these obstacles parents persisted. Whereas in St. Petersburg in 1912 only three of seventeen secondary schools had managed to elect parent committees, in 1913 eight succeeded. Of 55 schools in the capital's province, 21 elected parent committees in 1913, again a steep rise over 1912.[128] In other cities as well parents made a point of providing quorums. Schools in Riazan', Kostroma, Ekaterinoslav, and many others had successful elections in 1913.[129] The curators of the school district, who represented the Ministry of Education, had the power to confirm all elected members to the committees within a stipulated period. Nevertheless, they routinely let months go by before confirmation. Often the school year ended before the confirmations came through. A certain Flerovskii from Tambov brought a complaint to the Senate that the curator of the school district had refused to confirm his election as chair of the Lebedianskii gymnasium parent committee. At the hearing, minister of education L.A. Kasso testified that Flerovskii had been elected by the "low levels of the population" and held extreme leftist convictions.[130]

The power of the authorities not to confirm those elected to offices of all kinds was extensive. People elected to dumas and zemstvos were commonly rejected and new elections ordered. When I.I. Tolstoi, the mayor of St. Petersburg, complained to Maklakov, the minister of the interior, that the ministry vetoed the election of every useful member to the city duma, the minister replied that anyone with even the remotest association with an illegal party was not confirmed as a matter of form.[131] The law required approval or rejection within two weeks of the appointment. As in the case of parent committee nominees, officials commonly ignored the statute of limitations. One district zemstvo in Voronezh province fought back. It brought a case to the Senate against the governor accusing him of ignoring the two-week period. The Senate supported the zemstvo and ruled the governor's lack of action illegal.[132]

State repression and control were facts of life in Russia in 1913. Public resistance to repression and control through passive resistance, legal avenues, or heroic efforts to leap barriers erected by the government was, however, also an increasingly prevalent fact of life in Russia in 1913. Symbolic acts were highly meaningful. In Serpukhov the city administration established four scholarships, two for the men's and two for the women's gymnasiia, in the name of the novelist and excommunicant Lev Tolstoi. The Ministry of Education, as the Serpukhov city administrators intended, was compelled to reject the scholarships in the full publicity of a watchful press.[133] The press played its role by publicizing repressions widely, and the Duma launched a campaign of interpellations in 1913 that demanded, though rarely elicited, bureaucratic accountability to the law.

Some members of the government were by 1913 showing signs of re-thinking the role of coercion in governance. Late in 1912 V.F. Dzhunkovskii became deputy minister of the interior for police affairs. Dzhunkovskii was a former popular governor of Moscow in whose honor workers named a block of residences. He undertook a sweeping reform of security policing during 1913. Between May 1913 and February 1914 he abolished most of the provincial and regional security bureaus and transferred their functions to the gendarmes. In St. Petersburg and Moscow the security bureaus re-mained active. Even in the capitals, however, their role diminished as legal methods of protest gained ground over subversion among socialist organi-zations. In March 1913 security police ended the recruitment of informers in the military and banned their use in secondary schools after the arrest of two high school students earlier in the month created a public uproar. Dzhunkovskii disliked the long-established practice of perlustration, the interception and opening of mail, but did not end it. He tried, however, to limit it by improving the training of perlustrators.[134]

Without diminishing the importance of the suppression by authorities of public debate, it is well worth pointing out what matters they did allow to be discussed in public forums. The list is long. The Congress on Women's Education was a good example. Delegates discussed a range of technical and political questions concerning education in the empire. Topics included the relation of schools to the state, the struggle between the ministry and parent committees in secondary schools, police supervision of students outside the schoolroom, and women's attendance at universities.[135] At the All-Russian Agricultural Congress in Kiev in September, a speaker called for full civil equality for peasants and an all-class zemstvo at the volost' level. She also provided a long list of rights violations in villages. At one session of the congress, participants unanimously supported a resolution calling for the full implementation of the October Manifesto that had promised constitutionalism in Russia. Later the plenary session of the congress adopted the same motion.[136] Authorities observed little consistency from time to time or place to place in what was permitted. Even bureaucrats wholeheartedly committed to preventing all public discussion of matters of state lacked the means to carry it out. Many in the civil service had no wish to do so.

By 1913 social activists were publicly recognizing progressive elements within the bureaucracy and wooing them as allies in the reform process. Speaking at the Octobrist Party congress in November 1913, the party leader A.I. Guchkov blamed a palace camarilla for placing barriers between government and public. He excluded the bureaucracy and most of the nobility from the lists of the reactionaries. He identified within the bureaucracy "no small number of gifted people, who with pleasure bring their enormous experience in governance into service to the solution of great tasks."[137]

Conclusion

By 1913 the Russian state was deeply divided over both matters of policy and the critical issue of the appropriate relationships among the state, institutions of local self-government, and civil groups. The absence of institutionalized means to coordinate government policy and the complexity of the modernization process provoked deep disagreements over policy among ministries. The need to incorporate new social elements into the bureaucracy prompted further internal division and disagreement. Expertise formed a bridge between state and society. Forced more and more to rely on autonomous or semiautonomous social organizations to formulate and implement policy, the government struggled to balance control with effectiveness. Some might wish to end the legislative authority of the State Duma, but most found it useful in attaining their own objectives. Some resented the growing independence of the zemstvos and city dumas, but others accepted their autonomy and forged partnerships with them in order to advance common goals like education and agricultural reform.

As attitudes among the public evolved, so too did attitudes within the state. Interested parties on both sides of the state-public divide allied with one another to effect institutional and legal change. A variety of institutional and informal venues enabled state and social actors to meet, communicate, and work together. Distrust of the other on both sides was still much greater than mutual confidence. But the separation between state and public had significantly diminished since the confrontation of 1905. The narrowing of the gap alarmed conservatives in both camps and displeased many radicals on the left. Their reaction roiled the waters of state-society relations in 1913. It should, however, be noted that every initiative taken by the state to reassert control of the press or to limit the authority of representative institutions was thwarted either by lack of unanimity in state circles, public resistance, or a combination of the two. If it had ever existed, the barrier between state and society had been markedly breached by 1913.

6

DISCOURSES

Several discourses vied for dominance in the Russian Empire by 1913. Some were competitive with one another; others were mutually reinforcing. Almost all were in tension with the economic and social developments that were transforming the emperor's realm in the years before the war. Conservative defenders of the old order struggled to reconcile their principles with the new reality. Some rejected change outright. Many progressives welcomed change but disliked the direction in which the country was moving. The rapid expansion and transformation of the old intelligentsia, ideological differentiation among its members, and the incorporation of more and more of them into the work of legal cultural, economic, and social development by 1913 signaled the gradual absorption of the intelligentsia into the broader middle class. An important rump of deeply disaffected intelligenty remained in 1913, however. They dominated the leadership of left and center-left political parties, were heavily represented in the progressive press, and set the tone in literary and artistic circles. They also inhabited the demimonde of revolutionary conspiracy and politics.

The dislocation between much public progressive discourse on the one hand and change on the ground on the other was profound. The dominant progressive discourse, that is, a discourse that was committed to opposition to the status quo and to change in a democratic direction, distrusted or was openly hostile to capitalism and despised the bourgeoisie and its values. In the face of this ideological barrage, many educated Russians were reluctant to embrace fully the transformation through which Russia was passing. There were exceptions. Among them were the Marxists, who saw capitalism and its institutions as a necessary but only transitory prelude to a utopian future, and a growing but still small band of moderate liberals. Others in varying degrees rejected the path along which the economy and society were moving. Against the new realities of the empire—the strengthening of the market economy and the economic and social pluralism it nurtured and on which civil society was built, the emergence of a rights-based liberal order founded on the rule of law, and the consolidation of representative parliamentary government—they mounted campaigns of ideological resistance. Anticapitalist and antibourgeois attitudes were widespread among supporters of both the right and the left on the political spectrum. Many dreamed of creating a "symphonic society" in which difference was subsumed in a higher harmonious moral or traditional order. Their frequently apocalyptic visions promoted illiberal outcomes either in defense of a vanishing past or in pursuit of an uncertain future of beauty, justice, and truth.

RUSSIAN INTEGRALISM

Anticapitalist and antibourgeois discourses were symptoms of a larger anti-Western discourse in Russia. It was rooted in notions of Russian exceptionalism that most conservatives and many radicals harbored. A directive from the Ministry of Education in 1913 to teachers of history in the gymnasiums and compilers of history textbooks required them to state that the historical development of the Russian fatherland "in no way corresponds to the paths of development of western states."[1] The philosophical origins of Russian exceptionalism lay in Slavophilism. In Russian Orthodoxy the Slavophiles discovered communalist principles that separated organic Russian civilization from the individualism and class hostilities characteristic of West European civilization. Orthodox sobornost' (communalism) was an attribute not only of the church but of the whole of society and particularly of peasant social organization embodied in the commune. In the Slavophile ideal, sobornost' pervaded both church and state and governed their relationship; it also fostered an ethic of social reconciliation founded on inner moral conviction.

The deeper roots of Russian exceptionalism lay in Russian Orthodoxy itself. The Church had traditionally associated rationalism with the Catholic West and stressed the balance between reason and faith achieved in Orthodox belief. The culture of wholeness or integralism was also deeply imbedded in Orthodox theology.[2] Orthodoxy held out the possibility of the unity of man and God and saw in beauty the apotheosis of wholeness. V.S. Solov'ev built his philosophy of Godmanhood around the integralist doctrines of the Church. Godmanhood directly reflected the Orthodox notion of total unity. Solov'ev sought to reconcile science and religion and dreamed of a theocracy under a Christian ruler.[3] By 1913 conservatives were disillusioned with the direction of church-state relations, but the integralist ideas of Orthodox theology informed much of their thinking. Many hoped to renew the church through the reestablishment of the patriarchate and recover the culture of wholeness that constituted Russia's mission in the world.

A secular version of antiwesternism and Russian exceptionalism dates at least to the powerful influence of Alexander Herzen in the mid-nineteenth century. Disillusioned with a West in the clutches of the bourgeoisie following the revolutions of 1848, Herzen turned to the Russian peasant commune as the antidote to similar developments in Russia. Already lost to the West, the commune had by chance survived in Russia. In its communalist principles and practices, Herzen saw the seeds of the very socialism that Western socialists were striving but unable to realize in the face of the triumph of the bourgeoisie. Herzen mounted a passionate assault on the aesthetic and moral failings of the Western bourgeois order. He founded an anticapitalist tradition that the political left and sometimes the right in Russia drew on and elaborated over the decades. Herzen's disdain for the bourgeoisie and his hopes for the socialist future of the peasant commune became pillars of populist faith in the people (narod).

An integralist outlook was antipathetic to liberalism in church and state and to the flourishing of civil society in Russia. As we have seen, a thriving civil society is pluralistic and is dominated by no single idea or authority. In the years before the war, a few Russian liberals were beginning to understand the threat to the development of a liberal society in Russia that integralist thinking posed. A central theme of the *Vekhi* collection of 1909, which launched a stinging critique of the radical intelligentsia, was the dangers of integralism.[4] In 1913 the liberal theologian and philosopher Evgenii Trubetskoi in a study of Solov'ev's worldview called for a break with integralism, the separation of church and state, and the independence of the church within society.[5] The attraction of integralism was powerful, however. Nikolai Berdiaev, one of the contributors to *Vekhi,* abandoned his liberal outlook shortly after its publication. He, too, adopted an integralist approach, inspired by the tradition of Orthodoxy, to society and politics. He began to voice his dislike of rights based on laws and to privilege spiritual development and wholeness over material well-being.[6]

Legal discourse in Russia was also not conducive to liberal order and civil society. The promise of the triumph of legality was considerable by 1913. The Fundamental Laws of 1906 had provided a foundation for individual rights in Russia that had not previously existed. Lawyers did make use of existing laws in defense of clients' rights as a matter of routine. The workings of the volost' courts were instilling in parts of the peasant population respect for their rights and for the rights of others as well as providing a stable mechanism to defend them. Workers, too, were finding the justice of the peace courts, where they existed, to be a useful protector of their interests against the powerful.[7] The refusal of the regime to recognize the primacy of law and guarantee the rights promised in the Fundamental Laws, however, undermined appreciation of the law as the final arbiter of social conflict.

The primacy of law was not deeply ingrained in Russian intellectual traditions. The Slavophiles in the nineteenth century rejected the notion of a social contract embodied in laws and denounced Western legalism as coercive and external compared with the inner moral harmony contained in Orthodox sobornost'. Most conservatives in 1913 elevated the will of the monarch above the rule of law or confounded the monarch's will with legality. Many liberals viewed the law not as a means of defending an already existing state of being but as a value in a future reality. As Marc Raeff has argued, they did not see "legality as a system of norms and practices guaranteeing the effective and equitable application of the law but as an instrument by which the intelligentsia could define and champion the ethical principles of a future society."[8] Few among the educated grasped the necessary relationship between external law and inner spiritual freedom.[9] The legal practices of the regime and the legal discourse among many makers of public opinion were inhospitable to the advancement of liberal order in the country despite major gains in legal consciousness among large segments of the population. So was integralism. Few of the dominant discourses in the empire in 1913 were free of the exceptionalist mentality.

Dynastic Discourse

The interpretation by Emperor Nicholas II of the events around the selection and coronation of Michael Romanov in 1613 was emblematic of the dynastic discourse. Nicholas fixed his gaze on the day that young Michael was crowned. For him the coronation conferred divine sanction on the dynasty and justified personal rule. The tsar was subject to God alone. Conversely, supporters of representative government stressed not the coronation but the day a zemskii sobor elected Michael to the throne, an act in their minds of popular sovereignty. Nicholas's interpretation excluded popular sovereignty and left no room for the idea of the civic nation. Instead, he posited a mutually reinforcing bond of unity between the throne and an idealized people. In Nicholas's idyll, the tsar mystically embodied the nation, incorporated and defended all of its attributes, and alone spoke on the nation's behalf.[10]

The emperor failed to grasp the need to promote good relations between the elites—apart from a few sections of the military—and the crown, or to advance reform in the interests of both old and new elites. On the contrary, he saw the representatives of the elites in the State Duma as barriers standing between the crown and the people. Nicholas believed that the narod shared his view of the Russian monarchy. He was gratified by the emotional outpourings of ordinary Russians as the imperial procession made its progress along the Volga River in May during the tercentenary celebration. Interestingly, the royal progress alerted him to the problem of alcohol abuse among the peasantry and strengthened his resolve to end the state spirits and wine monopoly.[11] Throughout the Beiliss trial Nicholas firmly believed that in their innate wisdom the peasant jurors would see beyond the protests of liberals and the dubious evidence and pronounce Beiliss guilty in the name of a deeper national truth. Beiliss's acquittal spoke to the common sense of the Russian peasant and exposed the illusions of the tsar.

In spite of his hostility to representative government, Nicholas for the most part reconciled himself to the constitution embodied in the Fundamental Laws of 1906. He rationalized the new order as a gift of the monarchy for the good of the people.[12] A royal album issued in the tercentenary year neatly summarized the emperor's expectation of the Duma: "The work of the national representatives, being new in Russia, could not for a long time get things right. But one can hope that in time, when the State Duma marches hand in hand with the government, its work will proceed more specifically to the benefit of the throne and the fatherland."[13] Even here the dynasty preceded the nation in Nicholas's mind.

Nicholas identified with the military, or parts of it, and promoted the ideal of the emperor as conqueror. The vision of a conquered empire again excluded the ideal of an inclusive civic nation and underlined the subordination of subject peoples. In contradiction to the long tradition that made a virtue out of the diversity of territory and peoples in the empire, which had been such an important part of the imperial bureaucratic ethos, Nicholas valorized the Great Russian heartland. He had by 1913 come to identify powerfully with Great Russian culture. Like his father, Alexander III, Nicholas surrounded himself with the symbols and artifacts of the Russian (russkii) cultural tradition and diminished the older, more inclusive ideal of the Imperial Russian subject (rossiiskii). Royal architecture celebrated ethnic Russian styles of the past at the expense of imperial styles and symbolism. The architect of the Tercentenary Church, built in 1913 in St. Petersburg, wrote that in it he wanted to "create an entire corner of the seventeenth century."[14] At Tsarskoe selo, the Fedorov village reproduced an ideal miniature of old Muscovy, a model for a reborn Russian nation.[15] Nicholas's ideal was deeply religious and ran counter to the growing secularism of modern Russian culture.

As the head of a European great power in a dangerous and unstable world, Nicholas also had to reconcile himself to a measure of the industrial development of the country that was transforming the traditional social order and rural economy that he believed himself to embody. He understood the state interest and pursued it as narrowly as prudence allowed. While upholding the ideal of the ethnic Russian past within the empire, Nicholas disliked state nationalism and bellicose nationalist rhetoric. His acquiescence to some aspects of modernization and his anti-xenophobic caution, on the one hand, deeply disappointed many conservatives. On the other hand, the emperor's refusal to embrace and openly sanction economic, social, and political change both alienated and stigmatized the bearers and beneficiaries of modernity.

It is possible to explain Nicholas's choices as head of state as a product of his education and family loyalty, although his cousins and peers on or near the thrones of several European states scarcely left him bereft of alternative role models. His historical role, however, cannot be lightly dismissed. Leadership matters. Few doubt that the effective leadership of a Peter the Great or a Lenin was an important or even decisive factor in determining the outcomes of their day. By 1913 most of the elements necessary for the birth of the civic nation in Russia, though weak, were in place. The commitment of the still powerful dynasty to popular representation and the civic nation, while no guarantee of a successful delivery, would have greatly enhanced the prognosis. The withholding of Nicholas's wholehearted support for the new order was as critical to its future as his endorsement of it would surely have been. By the opening of World War I the dynastic discourse, which Nicholas expounded with ever growing vehemence, had alienated even the most loyal supporters of monarchy, including the best of the emperor's own ministers.

CONSERVATIVE DISCOURSES

Loyalists to the principle of strong monarchy within the bureaucracy were by 1913 deeply pessimistic about the future of the empire. The famous memorandum of P.N. Durnovo, submitted to Nicholas II in February 1914, warned the emperor of the dangers of war with Germany. It also set out Durnovo's views on the Russian masses, educated society, and elected representation. In 1913 Durnovo was an appointed member of the State Council but had spent most of his career in the bureaucracy. He had headed the Department of Police within the Ministry of the Interior and in 1905–1906 served as the minister of the interior. Durnovo believed that the Russian masses unconsciously subscribed to socialist principles. They neither understood nor desired political rights. "The peasant," he wrote, "dreams of obtaining a gratuitous share of somebody else's land; the workman of getting hold of the entire capital and profits of the manufacturer. Beyond this they have no aspirations." The educated could provide no leadership to the masses. The gulf of misunderstanding and distrust between the intelligentsia and the common people was, in his view, unbridgeable. Were the electoral franchise universal, the masses would not elect a single intellectual, he predicted. The State Duma did not enjoy the confidence of the people. Moreover, he contended, since the authorities had created the Duma, the idea that the government should be responsible to the legislature was absurd. The government should make no attempt to appease the opposition. Instead, it had to be crushed in order to prevent the socialists from getting a toehold.[16] Such false readings of the capacities and desires of ordinary Russians and contempt for representative institutions were common among conservative bureaucrats, especially in the powerful Ministry of the Interior. The damage done by such views to social relations in the country is hard to calculate.

Durnovo rejected nationalism in favor of a thoughtful Realpolitik. Among many conservatives, however, nationalism was deeply internalized by 1913. Closely allied with the dynastic discourse, but at the same time strangely distanced from it, was a rightist nationalist discourse that grew out of the constitutional settlement following the 1905 revolution. During the nineteenth century the theorists of "official nationality," a conservative body of thought that emerged in the 1830s during the reign of Nicholas I, portrayed the Orthodox monarchy as the embodiment of the nation, uniting the peoples of the empire and imbuing them as subjects with Russianness. The role of the state, according to the official nationalists, was to further the divinely ordained mission of the monarchy. Opponents of bureaucratic monarchy during the nineteenth century expressed their dislike of the state and identified Russian nationality with the communalist religious values of the peasantry. Many nationalists deemed the westernized elite to have lost a Russianness that only the common people could redeem.[17] Although such Slavophile views survived into the twentieth century and had spokesmen before the war, most Russian nationalists in the twentieth century did not reject the institutions of the state as had the early Slavophiles. Instead, they looked on the state as a potential instrument of Great Russian domination in the empire. Although critical of the administration of the Church, Russian nationalists on the right identified with Orthodoxy, supported its special status in the empire, and often rejected the policy of religious toleration that the state had embraced in 1905.[18]

While divided over a variety of issues, the political right in Russia was united in its commitment to the principle of unrestricted monarchy. Most rightists adjusted well after 1905 to the new order of parliamentary work, journalistic propaganda, and mass politics. Their ideological discourse, however, remained locked in a nineteenth-century time warp that rendered their program for change largely irrelevant to Russian reality.[19] They rejected any suggestion that the Fundamental Laws limited the absolute authority of the emperor. In Article 87 of the laws, which enabled the emperor on the request of the Council of Ministers to enact legislation when the State Duma was not in session, as well as in his right to approve all legislation, they saw the guarantee of his absolute authority. Although most conservatives accepted some form of national representation, they continued to see the monarchy as the locus of all authority in the state and did not understand popular representation as popular sovereignty.

Although no group on the right raised representative institutions above the monarchy, many accepted the State Duma as a useful body of mediation between the people and the crown. Russian conservatives widely despised the bureaucracy, which they viewed as dominated by non-Russians hostile to the Russian national idea and indifferent to the interests of the

Orthodox Church. Many supported some form of popular representation as well as local self-administration as counterweights to bureaucratic domination of governance. While some among them would have preferred a Duma with consultative responsibilities only, others saw the legislature and elected bodies of local self-government as constraints on bureaucratic rule and even advocated the expansion of the electorate. Although some conservatives adopted a populist rhetoric, their discourse was at heart profoundly undemocratic. Lev Tikhomirov, the former populist turned archconservative, in his farewell editorial as editor of *Moskovskie vedomosti*, lamented the decline in Russia of great national goals and the rise of political pluralism. Only in the harmonization of popular consciousness with politics was the well-being of the nation possible. He called for an organic politics that united authority with the voice of national feeling (*oshchushenie*) and saw in political parties the greatest obstacle to the clear expression of the national ethos. Parties, he argued, were attached to particular interests and disregarded general principles and their obligations to the whole country.[20]

Modernization was marginalizing the social groups from which many of the active and committed members of the Russian right originated.[21] They frequently had rural roots and were committed to the defense of agriculture and the old estate order of the Russian countryside. They deeply resented the success of others in the new order. In the years before World War I Russian nationalists aggressively voiced their resentment toward what they saw as the disproportionate representation of non-Russians in the bureaucracy and the economy. Many on the right supported economic measures designed to discriminate against non-Russians in business and finance. Resentments about the grip of others on the national wealth extended as well to foreign companies and investors. Conservatives tended to believe that the foreign debt and the interests of foreign investors had gained precedence over the interests of Russians and had condemned Russia to foreign domination. Government fiscal and economic policies that favored big private industrial over agricultural interests were to them proof of their worst fears.

Anticapitalism most often complemented the antialien and antidemocratic views of the Russian right. Conservatives associated capitalism with Jews and other non-Russians and with foreigners from the West. The extreme right deputy in the State Duma N.E. Markov dismissed the stock exchange committees as cabals of Jews and denounced all merchants as thieves.[22]

Like so many Russians before them, conservatives did not see capitalism primarily as an economic mechanism for the production and distribution of goods but as a social system. Drawing on a long tradition that went back at least to Herzen's antibourgeois cri de coeur during the revolutions of 1848 in Europe, conservatives in pre–World War I Russia associated capitalism with a westernizing bourgeoisie. In their view, the bourgeoisie was avaricious, selfish, and un-Russian. The marks of the bourgeois were narrow materialism, lack of principle or ideals, and willingness to compromise for short-term gain. Bourgeois society, it was widely held, promoted conformity and mediocrity at the expense of developed personality.

A dilemma for conservatives as for the emperor was the tension between the economic benefits of industrialization and improvements in agriculture that fostered market relationships, and the destruction that economic modernization meant for the old way of life. Most conservatives accepted the need for industry as a condition of national power and security; most grudgingly agreed on the necessity of the policy of tariff protection for industry that the government was pursuing. Many on the right rejected, however, large-scale capitalist industry, which they associated with private trusts. Instead, they preferred state-monopoly industry or middle or small-scale artisan or artel' forms of rural or semirural production. Others were critical of industry of any sort. They believed that it grew at the expense of the village by transferring capital and talent from country to city. Conservatives were also divided over the land reform. Some welcomed the support for rural private property that the reform promoted. Most, however, linked the commune to the traditional way of rural life and rejected the land reorganization program. The great majority supported agricultural aid as a means to improve the overall performance of Russian agriculture.

Although a handful of rightists saw some benefits in capitalism as a prop for the ideal of property, even they understood the concept of capitalism narrowly. It was best contained within small enterprises, cooperatives, and mutual aid societies. Only a very few conservatives took a larger view. They supported economic freedom and preferred private enterprise to state-managed industry. A majority on the right was alarmed by the rise of a proletariat and the socialist movement that capitalism fostered. Capitalism engendered a working class, on the one hand, but also was a bulwark of private property in the face of the socialist menace on the other. Rightists had little sympathy with the demands of workers, which they dismissed as the whining of the mediocre against the successful. They believed that it was the role of the state to manage labor relations and generally opposed concessions to workers.

The right often portrayed Russian industrialists and merchants as parasites, who pursued short-term material gain at the expense of the nation. They also associated capitalism with political reform, which in turn they linked to revolution. The bourgeoisie sought to replace the old elites by imposing a constitutional order on the nation. Bourgeois rights and freedoms were simply tools by which capital seized political power in the state. Bourgeois parliamentarianism was, in the right's view, alien to Russia. A leading rightist, S.F. Sharapov, wrote that "the world mission of Russia and constitutional democracy as the basis of the state order are a glaring contradiction."[23] The critique by the right of Western parliamentary institutions was closely akin to the hostility of the left and of cultural modernists to national representation. Populists and Marxists as well as many modernists in the cultural avant-garde also saw the parliaments of the West as instruments of powerful economic interests rather than as defenders of the common good.

An uncomfortable sense of the failure of Russian foreign policy in the last three wars that the empire had fought was prevalent among Russian nationalists in the prewar years. Relations between conservative nationalists and the Council of Ministers were particularly strained during the Balkan wars. In March 1913 mounted police broke up a demonstration in St. Petersburg in celebration of the capture of Adrianople by the Bulgarians.[24] I.I. Tolstoi, awaiting confirmation as the mayor of St. Petersburg, admitted to a shiver of schadenfreude at the sight of the same people who usually urged the police to beat progressive protesters finally coming under the whip themselves.[25] A later demonstration staged by the United Slavic Societies passed without incident.[26] The minister of the interior continued, however, to scold the nationalists publicly for speeches at banquets that condemned Russian foreign policy. Such speeches, he said, were inappropriate on the lips of those who truly upheld the monarchical principle. He forbade further demonstrations or banquets in support of nationalist goals.[27]

Nationalists nevertheless persisted. In April 1913, after further demonstrations in St. Petersburg in support of the Bulgarians and Serbs, the editor of the Moscow conservative newspaper *Novoe vremia* complained about the "spiritual bankruptcy" of Muscovites who, unlike the patriots of the capital, publicly demonstrated no support for the Slav cause in the Balkans.[28] Germanophobia was strong among Russian nationalists as diplomatic tensions mounted in the prewar period. Many officials and a wide segment of public opinion believed that Germans viewed Slavs as inferior to other races. Such attitudes fueled an aggressive nationalism that ill accorded with Russia's war readiness. Nationalist rhetoric in the Duma helped to fuel in Russia the prowar psychology that was prevalent in other European nations by 1914 as well.

Russian conservative nationalists publicly revered the monarchy and privately despaired of the incumbent on the throne. Their ideal monarch was a man of action who through resolute will led his subjects on a course decreed from on high. Instead, they were saddled with a leader lacking in initiative and apparently indifferent to their preferred policies.[29] By 1913 their disillusionment with Nicholas was almost complete. The Empress Alexandra also inspired contempt. Whispers about the "erotomania" of the empress and of the whole royal family and of the decay of the dynasty were heard. The access of Rasputin to the royal persons deeply offended conservatives. The staunch foe of liberal reform B.V. Nikol'skii had concluded by 1913 that Rasputin's assassination was essential to the realization of conservative hopes for the future.[30] There was even talk among rightists about the removal of Nicholas and his replacement by a nationalist leader in the mold of Stolypin. But attachment to the ideal of monarchy effectively ruled out such a solution.[31] By the beginning of the war the alienation of much of the right from the dynasty was nearly total.

With few exceptions, the discourse of Russian conservative nationalists embraced antialien, antibourgeois, anticapitalistic, antidemocratic, anti-Semitic, and anti-Western sentiments and promoted notions of Russian national exceptionalism within the empire and in the world. It was a discourse profoundly at odds with the realities of Russia as World War I approached. Although in most details their discourse paralleled and reinforced the dynastic discourse, Russian conservatives were deeply alienated by the actions of the reigning monarch, who fell far short of their ideal autocrat.

The Middle Class and Liberal Discourse

The Russian middle class was a vibrant and growing force before World War I. The great majority of the Russian intelligentsia by 1913 was middle-class, many by social origin, nearly all by socioeconomic position. The cultural differences between the intelligentsia and the commercial classes had narrowed significantly by 1913. The children of merchants moved comfortably into intelligentsia roles and identified strongly with intelligentsia values. Commerce now engaged people from all social estates. A broadly based urban middle class, which incorporated a wide range of commercial groups, white collar salaried employees in business and public administration, and the professions, was in the making before the war. The cadres of the middle class in the countryside were also growing as the market developed and public services through local governments expanded.

Antibourgeois and anticapitalist views were by no means a monopoly of the right and left in Russia, however. Many in the Russian functional middle class were in denial about their social status and resisted self-identification as a Russian bourgeoisie. Estate identities often abetted their denial. The press played a large role in sustaining a discourse that narrowly defined the bourgeoisie as the commercial-industrial class and stigmatized business and businessmen. Refusal to identify with the bourgeoisie was by no means confined to Russia. Historically, the term *bourgeoisie* passed through a number of definitions. In the Middle Ages it applied to inhabitants of cities. With the rise of the commercial-industrial class, the term became attached to them. By the end of the nineteenth century it embraced a much wider group of commercial, professional, and white-collar salaried individuals. Few members of the middle class willingly embraced the label *bourgeoisie*. Its modern usage arose in France after 1815 and from the start carried a negative connotation, which later socialist discourse reinforced. No group called itself bourgeois or claimed for the bourgeoisie cultural or political significance, although few rejected the bourgeoisie as foreign, as was often the case in Russia.[32]

In Russia, the liberal intelligentsia maintained a critical and mildly patronizing distance from the bourgeoisie as they defined it. An anonymous author, writing in the liberal newspaper *Russkie vedomosti* about the role of the Russian bourgeoisie in contemporary political life, limited the application of the word *bourgeoisie* to the industrial and commercial groups.[33] The editors of *Russkie vedomosti* acknowledged the sea change that Russian industrialists and merchants had gone through in recent decades and the demise of the "dark kingdom" of Dobroliubov's invention. Although nearing political maturity, however, the Russian bourgeoisie, in the eyes of the editors, had not yet arrived. They criticized the Moscow merchants for their lack of assertiveness.[34]

Russkie vedomosti cautiously defended the bourgeoisie from charges on the left that it was counterrevolutionary and a greater threat to democracy than the defenders of autocracy. Public opinion might blame industrialists for the fuel shortage and rising coal and oil prices during 1913 and condemn industrialists for hoarding materials, conspiring with foreigners, and exploiting the Russian working class.[35] But the editors noted that not all industrialists were the same. Those attached to the state economy feared democracy and supported government oppression. Those who served the national market, however, were themselves the victims of the monopolists of raw materials and fuel. Their fundamental interest lay in the development of a domestic market through an intensification of peasant agriculture. The latter could, the editors hoped, form the basis of a future bourgeois opposition to state economic policy.[36]

The commercial-industrial class had little control over its image in the press and even less in literature. Although a few balanced portraits of Russian businessmen appeared in fiction before the war, most writers remained hostile and badly informed about the evolution of the class that they vilified. In his play *The Zykovs*, completed in early 1914, Maxim Gorkii betrayed an earlier expressed fondness for the self-made businessmen, who had risen from the lower classes and through determination and work established a successful enterprise. He liked them for their Russianness. In *The Zykovs* he admires the father but dislikes the son, who is portrayed as soft and westernized. He contrasted the Westernized capitalists that he had earlier portrayed in *Enemies* unfavorably to homespun entrepreneurs like Zykov and his sister.[37] Opposition newspapers and journals continued to drum the anticapitalist message into the public. Lev Tikhomirov, the conservative editor of *Moskovskie vedomosti*, deplored merchants who played with liberal ideas. They needed, in his view, to shake off their westernism and return to their national roots.[38] Such tirades in the press inhibited the outreach and effectiveness of a moderate liberalism, rooted in the commercial-industrial class that was just finding its feet.

Tikhomirov was not entirely wrong about an earlier tradition among the Russian merchants. Russian industrialists and merchants in the past had distanced themselves from their Western bourgeois counterparts. Seduced by notions of Russian exceptionalism advocated by Slavophile publicists, the commercial class, especially in Moscow, had since at least the 1860s cultivated a strong Russian national identity. It was rooted in a belief in the existence of fundamental differences between Russia and the West, in particular the nature of the Orthodox faith that promoted social reconciliation in Russia rather than the class struggles of the West.[39] The closing of the cultural gap between the commercial class and the intelligentsia, with its ethos of public service, only reinforced the tradition of social responsibility among many industrialists and merchants in spite of a widespread public discourse that condemned them as selfish materialists.

The absorption of much of the intelligentsia into a broad middle class in the early years of the twentieth century enhanced the potential for the growth in Russia of a liberalism that was less inspired by ideology and more rooted in pragmatism. The formation of a middle class and the proliferation of the institutions of civil society that gave it public weight were engendering a moderate Russian liberalism that was just beginning to find a voice in the press and in the State Duma. Russian commercial groups had gained in confidence and acquired a clear political voice by 1913. They were far more prepared to embrace the label *bourgeois* than they had been in the past and, rhetorically at least, were claiming a leading role in Russia's future. The social conscience of the commercial classes found an outlet in the publications of the Association of Southern Coal and Steel Producers. In the years preceding World War I, the association was articulating a vision of a form of welfare capitalism, in which business played a leading social role.[40]

In 1912 the Progressive Party formed to give an organized political voice to Russian businessmen. The party was the inspiration of P.P. Riabushinskii, a leading representative of the Moscow merchant class, and other Moscow industrialists. It also attracted support from businessmen in other parts of the country. Initially, politically minded businessmen had found a home in the Octobrist Party. But the complacency of many Octobrists about the political status quo and their readiness to cooperate with the government made many future progressives uncomfortable. The Progressive Party was strongly nationalistic and supported a vigorous foreign policy. Its members believed in strong state authority embodied in the rule of law, but combined it with a liberal approach to representative government and economic and social questions.[41] The Progressive Party program was closely linked to the welfare capitalism espoused by the Association of Southern Coal and Steel Producers. It incorporated, however, a Russian nationalism largely alien to the more cosmopolitan association. In particular, the founders of the party retained traces of the mentality of the Slavophile capitalism of the second half of the nineteenth century. While committed to industrialization through capitalist development and to the extension of civil rights, like their Slavophile predecessors, they harbored notions about the underlying spiritual unity, in Orthodox communion, of employers and employees.[42]

Members of the Progressive Party were as dissatisfied with the radical liberalism of the Constitutional Democratic Party as with the complacency of the Octobrists. The anticapitalist rhetoric of the Kadets, their strong association with the parties of the left, and their ambiguity about critical liberal tenets like the sanctity of private property and the primacy of law alienated many moderate liberals. Several of the more intellectual newspapers in the capitals and other major cities had links to the Kadets, and their editorial policies reflected Kadet attitudes. Although reporters maintained a measure of detachment in their reporting, their leftward leanings were often apparent and influential among middle-class readers.[43] The radicalism of many of the Kadets that irked the Progressives arose at least in part from the legal status of the party and its organizational isolation from the population at large. The government declared the party to be illegal in 1907. Bureaucrats were forbidden to join illegal parties; many professionals who supported the Kadets did so only in secret. In particular they avoided serving on local Kadet commissions. The Kadets had urban and regional committees in St. Petersburg, Moscow, and Kiev but almost none elsewhere. Their illegal status also prevented them from holding broadly based party congresses. They managed to stage a number of party conferences, but the participants included little more than the Duma caucus and a few others who dared to attend. The party had no formal method of selecting conference delegates.[44] Unlike the Progressives, who were firmly rooted in a defined constituency, the Kadets were adrift, leaders without clear followers. Their platform was more a body of principled abstractions than a digest of the needs and wishes of a constituency. It did not at all reflect the newfound vitality and interests of the middle class in the years before World War I.

In the Russian countryside liberal anticapitalist discourse found expression in the antipathy of the intelligentsia to the peasant trader as well as to the kulak. Self-appointed guardians of the peasantry feared not only that kulaks, peasant traders, and village moneylenders would exploit ordinary peasants, but also that they would take unfair advantage of the petty credit and other opportunities that the new capitalism offered. Especially demonized in the progressive press were the *khutoriane*, the separators from the commune who established individual homesteads. Stephen Frank has written that "Separators, in effect, came to be viewed as a social basis for cultural renewal, enlightenment and order in the countryside."[45] It is not clear from the evidence just who viewed them in this way or how widespread the sentiment was. Without doubt a broad consensus existed among the elites that the Russian peasantry needed education and cultural development above all. Some supporters of the land reform harbored hopes that the improvement of the economic condition of the peasants through separation from the commune would in the long term raise their cultural level.

Although a few progressives among the public may have seen the independent homesteader as the agent of civilization in rural Russia, the great majority did not. On the contrary, in contrast to the North American image of the sturdy homesteader taming the wilderness and extending the frontier of civilization, the Russian homesteader was portrayed as base, cruel, and ignorant. The normally judicious *Russkie vedomosti* reported on horror stories about individual incidents on homesteads as if they were typical of homesteaders' behavior in general. A rural correspondent, a doctor, described the murder by a homesteader of his wife over a quarrel about a child from a previous marriage, then the murder of his own father who tried to intervene, and finally the killer's attempted suicide. He goes on, "From everywhere the same news comes." In vindication of the commune he recounts an incident in which villagers still living communally rescued another wife from a murderous husband when she ran to the door and shouted for help. "You can't do that on a khutor," he pronounces.[46]

In July *Russkie vedomosti* reported on an article in *Severnye zapiski* about the isolation of the homesteader on the steppe. Cut off from the village, he focuses on the land and forgets the sky, the sun, and people. If hooliganism should penetrate onto the khutors, the newspaper predicted, "It will grow into such a dark, savage force that it will be terrible to walk or drive on the roads. There are no people more embittered than those who live on khutors." The editors of *Russkie vedomosti* added that loss of social connectedness was only one aspect of life on the khutor. Separation from the commune brought a host of psychological and cultural consequences. Intellectual interests atrophied, children had the benefit of neither company nor school, people on homesteads became more savage, husbands beat their wives, and mothers their children. In the interests of objectivity, the editors continued, "Of course there are exceptions, but in general this

life, according to the author's testimony, is hard, dark and half animal."
They concluded, "And the new rural order carries within it these elements
of gradual but real barbarization (*odichanie*)."[47]

Russian liberals had in any case traditionally doubted the suitability for
rural Russia of full-blown laissez-faire capitalism. One of the early voices
of Russian liberalism, K.D. Kavelin, writing in the 1850s defended private
property, but argued for the retention of a form of peasant communalism as a
refuge for those unable to prosper in the capitalist world.[48] Little had changed
in much liberal thinking on the subject by 1913. Liberals wished to protect
the peasantry from both rural proletarianization and exploitation as workers
in capitalist industry. Bogdan Kistiakovskii, one of the contributors to the
liberal collection *Vekhi* in 1909, envisaged a socialist economy without private property or class distinctions situated within a liberal *Rechtsstaat*.[49] An
editorial in *Russkie vedomosti* in November 1913 captured the ambivalence
of Russian liberals toward rural capitalism. Writing of the changes affecting Russian agriculture, the editor noted the "awakening of individualistic
tendencies among our agricultural population," which he saw as "in the final
analysis an inevitable consequence of the embarking of Russia on the path of
capitalist development with all its positive and profoundly negative effects."
He concluded that economic individualism was a necessary part of Russia's
economic evolution. He hoped, however, that the cooperative movement
would mitigate the effects of capitalism and "protect the social collectivist
tendency from extreme individualistic pressures."[50]

The Kadet newspaper *Rech'* responded to this relatively balanced assess-
ment of Russian economic development in the countryside with an angry
denunciation of the assertion in the editorial of *Russkie vedomosti* that the
principle of individualism had to be incorporated into Russian economic
life and particularly into the agricultural sector.[51] A few leading Kadets such
as N.N. Kutler and L.I. Petrzhitskii did support privately owned peasant
properties. Others, however, such as I.I Petrunkevich and V.E. Iakushkin,
advocated national ownership of the land. The party platform compromised
by promising land given in use but not in ownership and allocating state
lands to villages.[52] Many Kadets vigorously defended communal property
against the land reorganization program. In his memoirs, Paul Miliukov, the
leader of the Kadet party, acknowledged the defects of the commune and
recognized the trend among the peasants toward individualism on which
the editors of *Russkie vedomosti* had remarked. Nevertheless, he continued

to defend the opposition of the Kadets to the land reform because they believed that only the commune could prevent the seizure of all of the land by powerful members of the village. The fact that no such seizures occurred apparently in no way altered his deeply ingrained conviction even years later.[53] The attraction of populism convinced many liberals that Russian liberalism differed fundamentally from its Western equivalents. The Kadets' fondness for peasant communalism tied them to the nonliberal left and posed a major obstacle to an alliance with their natural allies in the center of the political spectrum. Their attachment to the left fatally weakened Russian liberalism at a critical juncture in its history.

PASTORALISM AND MODERNITY

Peasants like Mikhail Novikov welcomed much of the change in village life and culture, which he associated with a new prosperity in the prewar years.[54] Many among educated urbanites did not. The elites were highly ambivalent about change in the Russian countryside. On one side was the discourse of elevating the cultural level of the masses. On the other was deep concern about the loss of folk traditions and communalist habits. Tolstoyan notions about the corruption of the city and the simple virtue of the peasantry were deeply engrained in the consciousness of the urban middle classes. The decline of traditional expressions of peasant culture and the spread of the new commercial popular culture into the villages especially alarmed many intellectuals. They imagined a peasant past that was less complicated, more clearly defined, and less threatening, which they hoped to restore. They attributed the perceived decline of peasant morality, generational tensions in the peasant family, and the degeneration of peasant customs to the influences of urban popular culture,[55] rather than to structural changes in the rural economic and social order.

They attempted to remedy the problem by, on the one hand, propping up those aspects of traditional peasant culture of which they approved and, on the other hand, trying to replace other, less desirable features of peasant life with an enlightened culture of their own making. And so they organized peasant choirs to sing the old folksongs and dance troupes to revive the old dances. They also sought not only to resuscitate fading traditional peasant leisure pursuits but to reorganize the leisure activities of villagers more rationally. They deplored the drunkenness and disorder of peasant holiday festivities as barbaric and elemental. They tried to limit the number of peasant holidays, which in recent years had increased in many districts, prevent unsupervised gatherings of youths, and ban drinking on Sundays and holidays. They organized antismoking and temperance campaigns and created new holidays to supplant older ones that they could not control. Concerts, supervised dances, sporting activities to replace village fistfights, and by 1913 even movies in district towns became tools of the civilizing campaign in the countryside.[56]

As well as organizing theater for urban workers, the elites sought to extend the civilizing influence of drama to peasants. In particular they wished to replace the cruder entertainments of the popular shows that traditionally toured the Russian countryside. The government supported temperance theaters not only in cities but in the country, and intellectuals organized theaters and sometimes traveling troupes to play in rural areas. Some tried to stimulate the formation of peasant amateur theater societies. Peasant audiences found the forms and situations of the classics of drama hard to understand, prompting attempts by respectable authors to craft plays they regarded as more accessible to peasants. Ironically, modern theater was a poor tool by which to defend traditional peasant mores and the spirit of communalism. As Gary Thurston has pointed out, the moral self lies at the center of modern drama. The theater promoted individualism in its audiences. Self-control and the mastery of emotions were keys to the bourgeois notion of civilization. Theater was a powerful force in acculturating peasants to these modern values.[57]

Closely allied to nostalgia for a simpler rural past was anxiety about the perceived disintegrative effects of modernity that was associated with urban living. The cult of progress and the pace of change destabilized the present and rendered the future uncertain. Fears about the future were accompanied by a sense of disconnectedness from the past and the loss of direction and guiding values. Feelings of loss were by no means unique to Russia. The unraveling of the old order in various European countries as modernity advanced had, since the beginning of the nineteenth century, spawned a rich literature of loss and nostalgia for bygone mores and values. Alienation was rooted in feelings. Social emotions were a subject of public discussion in prewar Russia. Writing in 1913, the critic A. Kugel declared that the intensification of feeling in the tango was the characteristic feature of the age.[58] Mark Steinberg has argued that, in St. Petersburg at least, feelings of loss and the pathos they fostered were not confined to the elites as in the West but percolated into the wider public discourse. The sense of loss was expressed in a mood of pervasive melancholy. The source of the emotion of sadness was seen to be the modern condition. It included disenchantment or disillusionment, a sense of disorder, disorientation, and tragedy. Some attributed the rash of suicides in the country to the disorders of the modern.[59]

The mark of modernity was pluralism, which most educated Russians of nearly all ideological stripes saw as a threat to the integral or symphonic societies of their imaginations. The advance of pluralism within Russian society in the years before the war was alarming to many. The past in Russia, however, also remained present, and daily mingled with the modern. The institutions of civil society were too recent and the attitudes of toleration of difference that they supported too underdeveloped to anchor confidence in modernity and dispel the attachments to the securities of the past that motivated folk revivalism. Melancholy was no doubt among the emotions that the Russian public experienced before the war. The press identified it and gave it prominence. There was, however, a hint of fashionable posing around sightings of the putative ruling emotion. Dmitrii Merezhkovskii, roaming the streets of St. Petersburg in 1908, commented on the expressions of melancholy he saw on people's faces.[60] An epidemic of melancholia that infected the entire population of a city, improbable as it seems, was as likely to be rooted in the vagaries of the weather, especially in St. Petersburg, as in the afflictions of modernity. By 1913 the opportunities provided by the economic boom that began in 1910 must have etched smiles on at least a few faces in the streets of the capital.

SOCIALIST DISCOURSES

The populist sentiment that many educated Russians shared took a more ideological form in Populist socialism. Russian socialism had its roots in the intellectual debates of the 1850s and 1860s and had become a movement by the 1870s. The early Russian socialists were influenced by Herzen's rejection of the bourgeois West and his hopes for the Russian peasantry. They saw in the peasant commune the kernel of a socialist order of the future. They believed that Russia could achieve an agrarian form of socialism and avoid the exploitative capitalism of the West. Russian agrarian socialists became known as Populists. Populism was a complex movement.

Some populists sought to abolish the state; others desired to use state power to impose a socialist order in Russia before capitalism became entrenched. The populists believed that Russia's backwardness relative to the West was an advantage rather than a liability. The survival of the commune in Russia would enable the country to skip the capitalist phase of socioeconomic development and achieve an agrarian socialism in combination with small-scale, largely rural artisan industrial production.

Peasant violence before and during the 1905 revolution disillusioned many among the intelligentsia about the unique potential of the Russian peasantry for socialist organization. Though diminished in the postrevolutionary period, the populist discourse was nevertheless still powerful in 1913. In particular, populist sentiment underpinned the resistance among educated Russians to the central feature of the Stolypin land reform, land reorganization that undermined communal tenure, in spite of the high rates of peasant participation in the reform. They continued to see the peasant repartitional commune in some form as a unique and desirable feature of rural life in Russia and a basis for a future that was qualitatively different from the capitalist West. The Socialist Revolutionary Party, the main successor to the populist movement, enjoyed the support of a significant segment of the radical intelligentsia. The SRs remained committed to the realization of an agrarian socialism built on the foundation of peasant communalism in the empire through either peaceful or revolutionary means. The Trudovik Party in the Duma also supported agrarian socialism and attracted a strong following among the intelligentsia.

The fledgling liberalism of the commercial classes in Russia, which was gaining confidence and support in 1913, was not the only voice supporting the capitalist development of Russia. The Marxist-inspired Social Democrats rejected the populist contention that the peasant commune was a sufficient basis to allow Russia to develop socialism without passing through a capitalist stage of economic development. In their view the peasantry was fundamentally petty bourgeois. The only truly revolutionary socialist class was the industrial proletariat. As early as 1898, V.I. Lenin had sung the praises of capitalism, which he embraced as a progressive phenomenon that increased the productive powers of labor and socialized the labor force. Capitalism drew the masses "into the whirlpool of modern social life."[61] It destroyed the patriarchal isolation of women and juveniles, stimulated their development, fostered their independence, and liberated them from patriarchal immobility.[62] Even the Social Democrats, however, could not ignore the peasantry. The Bolshevik faction of the party, in particular, expected that the development of a market economy in the countryside would augment an exploited rural proletariat and supplement the revolutionary potential of the industrial workforce. Beginning in 1905 Lenin became convinced that the Russian peasant was becoming a conscious actor in the revolutionary drama. He placed his faith in a dictatorship of the proletariat and peasantry. Although the party platform adopted at the Bolshevik Party Conference in November 1913 omitted all references to the role of the peasants in making a socialist revolution, Lenin returned to the theme during the war.[63]

Russian Marxists were well aware that the conditions Marx envisioned as prerequisites to a successful proletarian revolution did not exist in Russia. The capitalist cycle had only recently begun there; the proletariat was a tiny minority and not the significant majority of the population that Marx had in mind; Russia remained a semi-autocratic state and not the bourgeois democracy that Marx believed to be the cradle of socialist politics. The Menshevik wing of the Russian Social Democratic Party envisaged a long period of maturation of Russian capitalism and collaboration of socialists with other progressives to establish liberal democracy in the country. Bolsheviks or future Bolsheviks were more inclined to except Russia from Marx's formula for revolution. Leon Trotskii argued that capitalism developed differently from one country to the next. "The new Russia," he argued, "acquired its absolutely specific character because it received its capitalist baptism in the latter half of the nineteenth century from European capital, which by then had reached its most concentrated and abstract form, that of finance capital."[64] The result in Russia was a weak bourgeoisie and the endowment of the Russian proletariat with the revolutionary energy that elsewhere was associated with the bourgeoisie. He concluded that in the age of imperialism the time for national revolutions was over. The struggle had moved to one between the whole idea of the bourgeois nation, on the one hand, and the international proletariat, on the other.[65] With the outbreak of World War I Lenin quickly adopted a similar position. Russia, he argued, was the weakest link in the imperialist chain and could lead the way to international revolution in spite of the absence of Marx's conditions for socialist revolution.[66]

Marxism ultimately rejected capitalism and the bourgeoisie but not the values of work and labor discipline, respect for the individual, human rights, and rational organization that capitalism taught, values that Social

Democratic activists conveyed to workers in their propaganda. In 1913 the Social Democrats in Russia were weak and divided among themselves and enjoyed scant support except among a handful of workers. The Marxist discourse was, however, well established in intelligentsia circles. In addition to advocacy for capitalist progress, Marxism provided a powerful vocabulary of class war and social conflict or, in a more simplistic version, of the high (*verkhi*) and low (*nizy*) and the comic book specter of the exploiting bourgeois (*burzhui*), a discourse that the horrors of World War I, the regime collapse of 1917, and Bolshevik propaganda at the front rendered dominant among workers and especially soldiers in the fall of that year.[67]

CREATIVE INTELLIGENTSIA

In the early twentieth century, the creative intelligentsia, writers and artists, experienced disillusionment with politics and the social orientation of the nineteenth-century intelligentsia. While rejecting the positivism and narrow social agenda of the old intelligentsia, writers and artists in 1913 continued to believe in the high purpose and transformative power of art. The challenge of a popular culture that diminished the cultural authority of the creative intelligentsia and a new materialistic consumerism fostered a discourse of loss, resentment, and cultural despair among them. Many interpreted the growing economic and social pluralism of the country as a sign of social disintegration and disarray. The drive to create a synthesis of the arts that animated many of the projects of the World of Art movement was rooted in a perception of impending cultural and social fragmentation in the last decades of the empire.[68] The search for inner national unity and harmony had been a preoccupation of the intelligentsia since the 1840s. The Russian Symbolists reanimated the modernist search for spiritual unity with the injection into it of the integralism of Russian religious thought derived primarily from the influence on them of Solov'ev.

The Symbolists transferred the cult of wholeness from the religio-philosophical realm into the aesthetic sphere. Modernists charged art with the task of building national unity and social harmony through the creation of a community of convictions and feelings. Art should both liberate and unite its audience. The goal was the creation of a new myth capable of the aesthetic transformation of humanity, a new art to support the myth, a new morality for the new human being, and a new politics for a transfigured world.[69]

Fedor Sologub, a leading Symbolist, argued that seemingly accidental phenomena were in reality part of a world process, directed by a single will. The new physics had shown the relativity of relationships in time and space. But the Symbolists, he continued, "recognize something indivisible (*edinoe*), to which all objects and all phenomena are related. Only in relation to this entity does everything that is manifest, everything that exists in the world of objects acquire meaning." Art expresses itself through the national. Hence it is in national life, he maintained, that one must discern the eternal.[70]

By the beginning of the twentieth century, the struggle for control of culture for the masses between the creative intelligentsia, who saw itself as the guardian of the purity and moral purpose of culture, and popular producers of culture, who appealed to popular tastes, was well under way. Jeffrey Brooks documented the struggle in literature and concluded that the intelligentsia failed in its efforts to turn the commercial book market into an instrument to educate and uplift new readers.[71] Forms of popular culture other than literature also incurred the wrath of the guardians of the purity of artistic creativity. They complained that the commercialization of art robbed it of its high calling. Speaking of the cinema, the writer Kornei Chukovskii condemned the vulgar, mass tastes that compelled high culture to come down to the tastes of consumers in order to remain marketable. Culture, he complained, if driven by the market became the creation of the public. But authentic art, he argued, was possible only when the artist controlled the audience.[72] Modernists spearheaded the assault on popular culture and upheld the autonomous artist as the sole savior of culture from the vulgarity of the mass market. In declaring the cultural capitalist the enemy of art, the creative intelligentsia joined the anticapitalist chorus that dominated the public discourse of the empire.

Russian writers and artists in the early twentieth century were part of the larger movement of modernism that animated European culture from the mid-1860s to the end of the 1960s. Nothing signaled the basic cultural affinity of Russia with the West more clearly than the embrace of modernism by its creative intelligentsia. Modernism began as a revolt against the classical and academic traditions of art. It was a response to change in the nineteenth century and sought to reflect a world characterized by change rather than by tradition. Writing in 1863 the French poet Charles Baudelaire defined modernity as "the transient, the fleeting, the contingent; it is one half of art, the other being the eternal and the immutable."[73] Modernism initially embraced the realist school of literature and art but was marked by a spirit of change that made it the champion of a succession of avant-garde movements that replaced realism.

By the end of the nineteenth century, modernists had become disillusioned with positivist philosophy, with its faith in the powers of science to address human needs and its reliance on reason as the basis of knowledge and understanding. Although modernists rejected reason as a sure guide to knowledge, they also expressed deep dissatisfaction with traditional religious faith and other established ideological orthodoxies. Inspired by Friedrich Nietzsche's *Birth of Tragedy from the Spirit of Music*, modernists looked to art to release emotional spontaneity in humans and bring them into contact with the eternal and immutable, which Baudelaire identified as the other half of art. Their preference for the spontaneous over the cultivated or civilized awakened their interest in the primitive. Modernism encompassed the avant-garde and intellectual striving toward liberation, often through acts of individual rebellion. It is most often confined in the history of ideas to the realms of art and philosophy. Modris Eksteins, in his penetrating study of the birth of the modern age, argues that the impulse of modernism toward revolt extended beyond the artistic and into the political and social arenas. Eksteins posits a link between the cultural avant-garde and political extremism in Germany after World War I. In Germany, he argues, the war widened and deepened a tendency already embedded in the culture of the prewar years. "Introspection, primitivism, abstraction, and myth making in the arts," he writes, "and introspection, primitivism, abstraction and myth making in politics, may be related manifestations."[74] In Russia the avant-garde propagated its own myths and abstractions in rejecting the status quo and helped to stamp the mark of rebellion on the wider culture.

Russian modernism in the years before World War I was a stew of movements and influences. It shared with modernists in the West the drive toward synthesis, not only of the various branches of the arts, but also of art and science. The essence of modernism lay in the desire to transform matter into its essence through the creation in art of forms intuitively derived.[75] A main ingredient of the modernist recipe was the thought of Nietzsche. Nietzsche extolled the transformative powers of art. Art could give birth to a new consciousness, new men, a new culture, and a new world. It was the vehicle of myth, which was an instrument for the mobilization of the masses and the building of a new culture. He believed that the rationalist quest for knowledge emasculated creativity and destroyed myth. Only new myths could restore the emotional, spontaneous, and spiritual to culture. Nietzsche posited the myth of the Superman, who in the future would imbue culture with new value. The coming of the Superman would take place amid upheaval and apocalyptic convulsions. Myth transcended words and best found expression in music. Language imprisoned humans within established morality and power relationships. Release depended on a new word or even forms of expression that surpassed words.

Like Herzen before him, Nietzsche hated the bourgeoisie, with its attachment to the safe and comfortable. Nietzsche dreamed of new men who embodied beauty, freedom, creativity, and hardness. The source of evil in the world for Nietzsche was individuation. His new world was a world of unity and not of pluralism or individualism. The role of art was to restore oneness to men and nature. Individual freedom, in his view, was secondary to creating the conditions necessary to produce a man of the higher type. Aesthetic transformation transcended the ethical in Nietzsche's view. Only human will can build meaning in a meaningless universe. The new man shakes off conventional values and shapes himself in a new mold. Morality should be creative, self-affirming, and liberating rather than passive and repressive.[76]

An important addition to the modernist stew in Russia was élan vital, the central tenet of the thought of Henri Bergson. For Bergson reality was in a continuous state of becoming. As a reflective process, reason could apprehend reality only secondarily. The immediate and direct perception of reality occurred through imagination and intuition. The task of art was to unmask the conventions and prejudices that concealed reality and to enable humans to apprehend reality directly. Bergson was interested in simultaneity in time and space, the interpenetration of mind and matter, and the ordering of reality through subjective response. Bergson's notion of intuition was accompanied by a revival of the Naturphilosophie of Friedrich von Schelling and his philosophy of identity. These postulated the fundamental unity of God, man, and nature. Theosophy added spice to the mix. The theosophists believed in the possibility of an understanding of nature that was deeper than the knowledge attainable through science. Religious doctrines were external expressions of the deeper essence of nature. Theosophy drew its adherents to alchemy, astrology, occultism, and mysticism in search of keys to the door of nature. Another essential ingredient of the modernist recipe was Arthur Schopenhauer's notion of World Will. Together with Nietzsche's will-to-power, it fueled the idea of the poet who, through his art, imposes his will on the cultural and social order.

Russian modernists incorporated indigenous ingredients into the stew as well. The importance of will in shaping social outcomes had a long tradition among the Russian intelligentsia. As already observed Russian Orthodoxy rejected Western rationalism as one-sided and stressed the inner harmony of the spiritual community. Orthodoxy posited a universe of dynamic becoming and incorporated a powerful doctrine of the transfiguration of soul and body.[77] The Slavophiles passed the essential tenets of Orthodox faith into the mainstream of Russian philosophy. Russian modernists were thoroughly steeped in the integralist impulse of Russian religious belief and the philosophy of Solov'ev. All of these native ingredients melded with the flavors of Western thought to produce an intoxicating dish.

Modernism in Russia was fragmented by 1913, but its several camps had a number of features in common. Modernists turned away from prosaic visible reality and retreated into introspection. They sought both to create new forms and to recover lost forms from the past. Rather than seeking truth in the objective world, modernists examined human consciousness about the world. They also looked into the unconscious and delved into the worlds of fantasy, myth, and legend, in which they believed a higher reality lay concealed. Solov'ev had seen the real world as a mere shadow of a higher existence. The philosopher Lev Shestov called "the fantastic more real than the natural."[78] Like their Western counterparts many of the Russian modernists were interested in the archaic and primitive. They sought out the spontaneous and unadorned, unspoiled by the dead hand of rational-istic culture and moral self-denial. Others were fascinated by the new, by transience, impermanence, fragmentation, and speed, and their effects on human perception and consciousness.

The modernists mounted a far-reaching critique of Russian reality. Speaking at a debate on contemporary literature in St. Petersburg in January 1914, the writer Sologub maintained that the task of the Symbolist was to love life. But, he continued, one cannot love life as it is "because in its gen-eral direction contemporary life is completely unworthy of it." Life requires transformation. "In this hope for transformation art must go before life, because it will show life beautiful ideals by which life can be transformed if it wishes to be; and if it does not wish it, it will stagnate."[79] Georgii Chulkov followed Sologub to the podium. A Symbolist, he argued, reevaluates the reality given to him not in light of the external data of time and space but in its essence. Such a reevaluation is rebellion in the most profound sense of the word. He concluded, "You see, to adopt symbolism means to light a noble bonfire, which will illuminate the dark night of reality!"[80] Here the theme of rebellion crossing from the cultural into the social was made explicit.

Modernists also rejected the devotion to service to the people through social action that formed the ethos of the old intelligentsia and of many of the new professionals. In its place modernists enlisted art in a religious crusade to discover the soul of the nation and forge a new national community linked by the deepest emotional and spiritual ties.[81] The end of social tendentiousness in art did not render it antisocial or amoral, at least in the eyes of the Symbolists. Speaking at the Polytechnical Museum in Moscow in November 1913, Sologub maintained that morality in art rested on its truth, its sincerity, and the import of its message. Aesthetics and ethics were inseparable. In his view, only Symbolism was both fully moral and fully free. The true measure of art was its rejection of literary canons and the affirmation of life as a creative process.[82]

By 1913 Russian art and artists were an integral part of the larger world of the arts in Europe and elsewhere. The Ballets Russes had for several years before 1913 charmed Western audiences. The Russian basso Fedor Chaliapin, already well known to audiences in Italy and the United States, debuted in London and Paris in 1913, where he not only performed on the opera stage but, under Sergei Diaghelev's direction, developed as well a popular repertoire of Russian folk songs. In 1913 the theater director Vsevolod Meierhold traveled to Paris, where he staged a production of Gabrielle D'Annunzio's "Pisanella" at the Paris Opera. In January 1914 the founder of Italian Futurism, Filippo Tommaso Marinetti, visited Moscow. In painting, the new Russian avant-garde sought out native themes but also maintained strong ties with contemporary Western artistic circles. Vasilii Kandinskii was one of the founders of the Blaue Reiter group in Munich in 1911. Natalia Goncharova exhibited in the Blaue Reiter show of 1912. In 1913 Vladimir Tatlin visited Picasso and began his own Cubist experiments. Whereas Paul Gaugin traveled to the South Pacific to find the unspoiled and native, Natalia Goncharova, Mikhail Larionov, and Kazimir Malevich journeyed to the Russian and Ukrainian countryside and into the world of children's art in their own search for the naïve and natural.[83]

In spite of the close ties of the Russian avant-garde to trends in Western art and philosophy, struggle with the West was by 1913 deeply embedded in Russian modernist discourse. Russian writers and artists were torn between fascination with Western art forms and the wish for greater independence. Their tortured engagement with the West signaled their growing self-confidence and the maturity of the Russian art scene. The clash of the principles of East and West was a common theme. Russian modernists both feared and courted Apocalypse. Andrei Bely's novel *Petersburg*, which was serialized in 1913, portrayed Russia's westernized capital as an industrial nightmare and its inhabitants as ghosts with smoke-ravaged bodies and withered souls. He envisaged a cataclysmic conflict between East and West: "And Petersburg shall sink." "Europe will fall under the heavy Mongolian heel" and "on that day the ultimate Sun shall rise and dazzle the earth."[84]

In March 1913 the Target exhibition of painting was held in Moscow. Mikhail Larionov organized the show as a venue for his and Goncharova's Rayonist works. Rayonism was itself deeply influenced by Italian Futurism but aspired to even greater abstraction. The exhibition came complete with a manifesto that denounced the influence of the art of the West and a plea for a new art based on experiment in color and form. In his manifesto proclaiming Rayonism, Larionov identified Russian art with the Orient and denounced the West for "vulgarizing our Oriental forms."[85] Goncharova denied that she was European and vowed that she could not make effective art under a European influence. Only in Russia and the East, she said, could art become "all-embracing and universal."[86] Il'ia Zdanevich, a close associate of Larionov and Goncharova and theorist of neo-primitivism and the art of everything (*vsechestvo*), also celebrated Russia as the "avant-garde of the East" and embraced the Golden Horde and the Tatars as Russia's own. He drew a link between the struggle in art for national autonomy and political independence from Western forms. "The struggle with [the West]," he wrote in 1913, "is the issue of our day in politics as in art."[87] The notion of Eurasianism was to grow stronger after the war, but its embrace of antiliberal and authoritarian politics and irrationalism is already apparent among Russian modernists in 1913.

Modernism exhibited a powerful populist strain. Chagall, Goncharova, Larionov, and Malevich among others looked for the primitive and colorful in the peasant villages and fields or in the shtetls of the Pale. For Viacheslav Ivanov, ordinary Russian folk were the new barbarians charged with revitalizing Russian culture. The theater as a site of national spiritual harmony was central to his theory of drama, which deeply influenced a number of Russian composers.[88] The Symbolist poet Aleksandr Blok contrasted folk culture with the culture of civilization. The former embodied the creative forces of the Dionysian as Nietzsche understood it. The folk was destined to destroy Apollonian bourgeois civilization and with it the effete intellectualism of the intelligentsia.[89] Though populist, Russian modernism was far from democratic. Chukovskii's belief that cultural profit-making destroyed true art by transferring control of the artistic product from artist to consumer was widely shared by modernists. Sologub rejected democracy in art. Free creativity rested on the subjection of the audience to the will of the artist. The dramatist Nikolai Evreinov agreed. The audience must surrender its will and freedom to the artist if unity is to be achieved.

Important weapons of the modernists against social fragmentation and the spread of bourgeois culture were the will of the artist and the instincts of the elemental folk. The theater brought them together. Sologub wrote of a theater of one will, in which ritual united audience with performers. Art, he said, should reconcile the artist and the masses and revitalize the unifying spirit of the nation.[90] The theater was the key to the success of the modernist strategy, a gateway into a higher form of life. Evreinov believed that humans were inherently theatrical and spoke of the will to theatricality.[91] Ivanov advocated a democratic or communal theater. Invoking the Slavophile tradition, he argued that a Western-style parliament could achieve only an external and coercive national consensus whereas a communal theater would reveal the internal consensus of the people itself.[92] For Vasilii Chulkov the theater was a bridgehead against bourgeois individualism and a defense against property.[93]

Following Nietzsche, modernists believed that music was the key to understanding the universe. Bely believed that music carried humans above time, space, and place.[94] Igor Stravinsky sought to meld various art forms on the stage. Aleksandr Skriabin set his sights even higher. A blend of theosophy and Nietzsche's notions of the artist superman who creates himself and the world through the expression of abandon, pleasure, and rapture in his art inspired Skriabin. In 1913, he was at work on a grand musical called at the time *Mysterium*. *Mysterium* brought religious rite into the theater. Spectators were transformed into performers and would participate in the ritual through ecstatic Dionysian dance. The composer's goal was to embody in theater and music the creative principle of the universe.[95] The project was intended not only as an apotheosis of the theater but also as a site of Nietzschean transfiguration of national life.

Sologub's play *Hostages to Life,* which was staged at the Aleksandrinskii Theater in 1913, captured the Symbolist notions of myth and the word, their rejection of the utilitarian social-oriented ideology of their intelligentsia predecessors, their dislike of convention in social relations, their disdain for the family, and their dream of the transformation of life. As an exemplary expression of the modernist ethos before the war, the play is worth outlining in some detail. The action of the play extends over 12 years. Katia, who is 16 years old when the play opens, is in love with Mikhail, an 18-year-old gymnasium student who wants to be an architect. They come from different social milieus. Katia's family is a heavily indebted remnant of the provincial landed nobility; Mikhail is the son of a zemstvo doctor and his activist wife. Sologub ironically labels them "intelligentsia proletarians." They expect their son to marry a "proletarian." Katia's parents have in mind for her a husband worthy of her social station and able to pay off their rising debts. Their choice is a certain Sukhov, a recent property owner and rising star in the state service, who fervently courts Katia. In the background is the mysterious Lilit, a 15-year-old who seems without parentage or roots. She describes herself as a fable (*skazka*) of the forest and the moon. The young Katia and Mikhail reject their parents' hopes and lifestyles. They agree, however, that they cannot pursue their own paths until they are strong. With that goal, Mikhail leaves to pursue his studies in the city.

Four and a half years go by. In order to save her parents' estate from the bailiffs, Katia at last agrees to marry Sukhov on condition that he permit her to leave whenever she might choose. She tells Mikhail that they are hostages to life, but "tomorrow we will conquer."[96] Lilit, who has declared to Katia her love for Mikhail, goes to the city to live with him. Another eight years pass. Mikhail is successful as a builder and has designed a fine house for himself. His mother complains that he has not paid his debt to the people. He replies that a man's first social debt is to be strong and happy because only such a person "can build a happy and rational world."[97] Katia leaves Sukhov and goes to Mikhail. Sukhov is shattered. She tells him that she never pretended to love him. It was he who was deceived by his "male authority" and the power of traditional words and concepts. When Sukhov sends their two young children to persuade their mother to return to him, she sends them away with a box of candy. As the play ends, Lilit, who has promised to leave when Katia comes, appears at the top of a stairway, crowned with a golden diadem. "I have called one man to my side," she says, "but have a long road to travel."[98]

Hostages to Life vividly captured the modernists' disdain both for the old social order of Russia, with its debts, noblesse oblige, and pretensions, and for the old intelligentsia, with its earnest dedication to service to the people. Sologub made his contempt for bourgeois marriage and the family plain. He placed his hope for the future in the wills of individuals like Katia and Mikhail, who have the patience and courage to grow strong and defy the status quo. Lilit, the woman without a background or history, who remains free through self-denial and free will, is the future, the ideal toward which modernists strove. Rejection of the family, which was at the heart of the bourgeois ethos, was common among Russian modernists. They, like modernists elsewhere, sought to rebuild the world in nonfamilial and nongenerational ways. Blok believed that the ties of family served to bind the artist to the past and to stifle creativity. Like most of the Symbolists Blok had no children. Like them as well he rejected traditional marriage and the bourgeois family.[99] The anxiety of modernists about the penetration of the major themes and mores of the middle class into the Russian ethical mainstream further underscores the extent to which bourgeois concerns dominated the cultural consciousness of educated Russians by 1913.

Russian Symbolists sought to transform reality by revealing the higher mystical truth of existence. The Futurists attempted to close the gap between existence and theory by integrating word and deed. The goal was to elevate intuition over cognition and life over the forms that mind imposed on it.[100] They, like the Symbolists, sought unity in music and sound and wished to create a "symphonic society" that resolved all social conflict.[101] Like the Symbolists, the Futurists sought a new myth of the nation and a new language in which to embody it. Whereas the Symbolists attempted to reproduce musical sound in language, the Futurists labored to capture sound in words that went beyond meaning. Like other modernists, the Futurists wanted to bring art, science, and philosophy into a new synthesis. They were deeply influenced by the new physics that was subverting the old Newtonian understanding of nature and the universe. The Symbolist Andrei Bely, inspired by Solov'ev, sought to combine religion with science and art into an integrated worldview.[102] The Futurist poet Elena Guro, like several of the Cubo-futurists, used the scientific techniques of observation, analysis, and research to penetrate the forms and colors of nature and the relation of nature to space and time. Velemir Khlebnikov, in the spirit of Bergson, aspired to use mathematical laws to undermine existing understandings of nature and forge a new unity of nature and man.[103]

Joan Neuberger has linked both Futurism and the urban hooliganism that spilled into the public spaces of Russian cities in the early twentieth century to the rejection and public mocking of bourgeois propriety and philistinism. Both Futurists and hooligans used the streets to reach their intended targets, and both sought to shock the respectable public. The Futurists staged performances and exhibitions in the streets designed to shock conventional public mores and to challenge the institutional confinement of the old arts.[104] The Futurist opera *Victory over the Sun* embodied most of the elements of the Futurist project in a single work. Mikhail Matiushin composed the music, Aleksei Kruchenykh wrote the script, Kazimir Malevich designed the costumes and sets, and Khlebnikov contributed a prologue. The opera played at the Luna Park theater in a suburb of St. Petersburg in December 1913, apparently on a couple of nights. Maiakovskii's drama *The Tragedy of Vladimir Maiakovskii* accompanied the opera, either on the same evening or on alternate nights. The work shared with World of Art performances the desire to synthesize all of the art forms into a single whole. Much of the opera was spoken; there were arias that parodied the style of Verdi and musical effects at various stages in the work. The producers deliberately employed amateur actors. A well-known professional tenor from the local People's House, however, sang the leading role of Aviator. The first performance was sold out. One of the actors later described the audience as "scandal lovers from the St. Petersburg demimonde" and "fashionable and philistine bourgeois." The chief of the city police attended and police agents saturated the neighborhood.[105]

Victory over the Sun was an exegesis on the works of Nietzsche. Underlying the nihilism of the text was Nietzsche's proclamation of the death of God and the loss of order and meaning that it implied. The god of the sun was Apollo and his capture and "boarding up in a concrete house" signaled the demise of Apollonian rationality, clarity, and logic and the ascendancy of Dionysian freedom, frenzy, spontaneity, and intuition. The victory over the sun brings not only darkness but an end to time, space, and gravity. It frees men from necessity and achieves the highest goal of the Futurists, the disappearance of the past. The Chorus exults:

We are free
Broken sun...
Long live darkness!
And black gods
And their favorite pig![106]

Kruchenykh later wrote, "The point of the opera is to destroy one of the greatest artistic conventions, the sun in the given instance." Humans, he noted, think according to established conventions. He continued, "The Futurists wish to free themselves from this ordering of the world, from these means of thought communication, they wish to transform the world into chaos, to break the established values into pieces and from these pieces to create anew."[107] A world without the sun is a world of chaos. All is upside down and inside out. But chaos is merely the death of the old conventions. Now humans are free to construct a new meaning and new order based on a stern aesthetic. Freedom is terrifying: "Some tried to drown themselves, the weak ones went mad, saying: we might become terrible and strong you see." The play abounds in Nietzsche's cult of hardness. Futurelandman, who pronounces the prologue, and the two Strongmen do not fear being terrible. In Nietzschean fashion the Strongmen predict vast upheaval with "Plenty of blood/Plenty of sabers/And gun bodies."[108] Elocutionist also has no fear. He rejoices at the loss of the past and looks to a future "with danger but without regrets" where mistakes and failures are forgotten.[109]

The new men of the Futurists are Ivanov's peasant barbarians. They exult in their youth, health, bravery, and elemental creativity. As the figure of Aviator suggests, they are committed to the technology of the future. Futurelandman and the Strongmen appear in Cubist costume with hard flat surfaces and sharp angles. They were the progeny of the peasants that Malevich had earlier painted as steely robotic figures in rural landscapes. They were the marriage of the primitives of Goncharova and Larionov with the modern trolleys, cars, airplanes, and ships that the two artists had recently embraced as the symbols of modern times.[110] They moved slowly and ponderously and spoke with long pauses between syllables and words. They were not humans but transformed humans. The words they used abounded in consonants in order to stress their hardness and courage. In parts of the opera the playwright eliminated feminine word endings. Traveler boasts that "Everything became masculine/The lake is harder than iron/Do not trust old measurements."[111] The First Strongman delivers a message of violence: "Nothing matters to us/The sun has been slaughtered!"[112]

Committed as they were to a new myth, the Futurists sought a new word to bring it into being. They chose the language of *zaum*, or beyond meaning. Sound was more significant than sense. Attentive Worker says to Fat Man: "Do not dream they won't spare you! Why figure out yourself—speed you know is effective, if one puts the wagon filled up with old boxes on each of two molars and powder it with yellow sand and put all this in action then you will see yourself...."[113]

Meaning did not lie in the conventional sense of words but in the speed and intensity of their delivery and the patterns of sounds. Early in January, Matiushin reviewed his own work in a Futurist journal. He excoriated the press for failing to understand what was happening in literature, music, and the visual arts. *Victory over the Sun*, he explained, marked the "disintegration of concepts and words, of old staging and of musical harmony." It was a "new creation, free of old conventional experiences and complete in itself, using seemingly senseless words...."[114] To many in the audience the result was gibberish and a large portion of them was prepared to say so. There were catcalls, whistles, and much good-natured comment, although an actor recalled an errant piece of fruit that passed by his ear.[115] Kruchenykh was delighted with the reaction of the audience and pronounced the opera a huge success.

In the Futureland of the Futurists as in the imagined worlds of the Symbolists, there was little place for individualism, pluralism, liberalism, and the rule of law. Modernists lionized the strong and independent personality but deplored a rights-based individualism. Symbolists such as Viacheslav Ivanov feared that the rise of individualism threatened social unity. Many modernists in Russia were not only hostile to the democratization of culture but to democracy in political and social life as well. There were almost no liberals among the Russian modernists and few democrats except in a narrowly populist sense. Evreinov believed that democracy was at best undesirable. Ivanov was more receptive to democratic principles but understood democracy as the expression of the universal spirit of the nation, which only an art that bridged the gap between the poet and the people could reveal.[116] Not only the Symbolists but many representatives of other modernist schools in Russia were ambivalent about democracy or openly hostile to it. The trappings of liberal democracy—parliaments, political parties, the rights of individuals, and the courts and laws—in their view, as in the opinion of many on the political right, stood in the way of the spiritual unity of the nation and undermined social cohesion.

Some modernists adopted an apolitical stance. Georgii Chulkov, for example, argued that Symbolism is not good because a symbolist poet sings about civic-mindedness—he might or might not—or good because it sometimes serves the democratic interest of the fleeting moment. Symbolism is good when it provokes profound upheaval, which can give rise to new, meaningful developments. Symbolism as an aesthetic phenomenon proves nothing, he went on, unless life changes.[117] In their separate spheres, however, modernists and other critics of Russian life in 1913 opposed the same things. They also shared a discourse of national wholeness and spiritual unity. Like other Russians who opposed the changes transforming the empire, the modernists perceived the spread of the market, the rise of individualism, and the healthy differentiation and multiplication of social groups and institutions, which are the essence of civil society and pluralist liberal order, as social fragmentation and the end of national unity.

It should by now be obvious that the primary target of the modernists was not the old regime but the emergent culture of the new Russian bourgeoisie. Cultural modernists were profoundly antipathetic to the development of a Russian bourgeoisie and a middle-class culture and its values. The Russian literary avant-garde, like its counterparts elsewhere in Europe, sought separation from the crowd in bohemian exclusiveness, esotericism, and, in the case of the Futurists, *epatisme*. Many even rejected strongholds of the avant-garde like the Stray Dog cabaret in St. Petersburg, where Vladimir Maiakovskii staged his first public reading in November 1912, as tainted by the bourgeois "pharmacists."[118] In their concerns about the direction that Russia was headed they formed a tacit alliance with other critics of the new Russian middle class and its culture and values.

In retrospect the greatest beneficiary of the integralist discourse was Social Democracy and especially its Bolshevik faction. Many modernists, particularly the Futurists, later threw in their lot with Bolshevism, at least initially, although most were soon disillusioned with it. Perhaps they realized, too late, what George Santayana later understood, when he assessed the future of Nietzsche's Superman, "that the misguided hero, like a Damocles or like a poor ghost-seeing and witch-hunting Macbeth, will lose his soul in gaining a sorry world, and his wishes once attained, will horrify him."[119]

Marxism lent itself readily to the integralist ethos prevalent in Russia in the years before World War I. It was rooted in the long tradition of millenarianism. The Marxists dreamed of overcoming class conflict and establishing the rule of the last class, the proletariat. In their analysis the cause of class conflict was the alienation of man from the fruits of his labor. The revolution would end alienation and restore men's original harmony with nature and one another by returning the means of production to the ownership of the producers. The end of alienation entailed not only recovery of the means of production but also of the original goodness of natural man, of which alienation had deprived him. The end of alienation signaled the transfiguration of humanity, the reuniting of man and nature, a new morality, and an end to discord and disharmony in a new world of unity and wholeness. Many Marxists were quick to inject Social Democracy in Russia with the apocalyptic strains of Russian thought. Although World War I was the main crucible of cruelty, the Futurist discourse of blood, hardness, masculinity, and violence reinforced the Marxist notion that only through violent revolution and the extirpation of the capitalist and bourgeois could the workers' paradise be born.

Conclusion

In the years between 1907 and 1914 several discourses that served a variety of narrow elitist interests competed for dominance. They frequently contradicted the major social, economic, and political developments taking place in the empire. Capitalism had established itself by 1913; a sense of individual worth and the rights of the individual were developing among all social groups, as was legal consciousness; the institutions of a pluralist society were emerging and performing many of the tasks of civil society; popular representation, while weak, was putting down roots at both the local and national levels. The repressive actions of the state enfeebled but did not destroy the associations and mechanisms for social mediation that liberal pluralism must have to survive. A popular culture that appealed to a wide range of middle-class tastes and supported the values of the middle class was already commercially successful, but was still too weak to displace the discourses of the old cultural elites, who controlled influential media outlets.

The clearest measure of the growing strength of the challenge to established interests from cultural, economic, social, and political change, however, was the mounting opposition to change from the dynasty, the political right, much of the left, and the cultural intelligentsia. All of them understood just how far Russia had by 1913 traveled down the bourgeois capitalist path. Most of them strongly opposed the very forces that were creating in Russia the economic and social pluralism on which civil society and political liberalism are based. The opponents of civil society harbored integralist visions of an alternative future Russia to be founded on one or another imagined version of the people's will.

Conclusion

During the first six months of 1914 the strike movement, especially among workers in St. Petersburg, intensified. Of the 3,534 strikes recorded in 1914, 2,401 were classified as having political objectives.[1] A strike supported by the Bolsheviks in the capital in July to protest against police repression of oil workers in Baku sparked scenes in the city's working-class districts reminiscent of the revolutionary days of 1905. Unlike in 1905, however, workers in only a few branches of industry, especially metallurgists and machinists, participated in the strikes of 1914 in large numbers. Moreover, the intensity of the strikes in the capital was not felt elsewhere in the empire. Neither faction of the Social Democratic Party, Bolshevik nor Menshevik, devastated as they were by police repression, was able to provide ideological leadership to workers, who in any case were chary of intelligentsia tutelage. The goals of the strikes remained ill-defined. Not only the great majority of workers but other social groups failed to join in the strike movement.[2] The police, who in late 1916 proved to be so prescient about the coming revolution in February 1917, did not predict revolution in July 1914.

The apparent isolation of the workers in July 1914 has given sustenance to the idea of the alienation of the workers from the educated groups of society and the political authorities before World War I. Leopold Haimson has recently stated the case most strongly. Workers' insistence on equality and separateness, he maintains, was "a distinctive feature of worker consciousness" in the years before the war. He went on, "...practically every day, every hour, every minute of this experience confirmed the Russian workers in the instinct, and ultimately in the conviction, that they were locked in an irreconcilable conflict with all authority—with all those who stood politically, socially or economically over them in the factory, on the streets of their industrial slums, and on the broad and elegant sidewalks of the Nevskii Prospekt."[3] Few historians of the period would be so unequivocal, but the clash between the "verkhi" and the "nizy," which is seen by many as a critical factor in the Bolshevik successes of the autumn of 1917, has cast a long backward shadow onto the historiography of Russia before the war.

A Social Democratic activist in the prewar period, Nikolai Valentinov, took a very different view of the situation in Russia as World War I approached. Although he granted that sharp differences still remained within the society as a whole, almost no one wanted a repeat of the revolution of 1905 and no one in 1913 or 1914 seriously thought about another revolution. Much of the working class remained aloof from the strike movement, which was largely confined to St. Petersburg. Peasants who had acquired land as property rejected revolution as well. The large commercial and industrial interests opposed revolutionary action and the urban petty bourgeoisie was drawn to left-leaning liberal reform rather than to revolutionary socialist influences. Valentinov attributed the containment of social antagonism in the empire to widespread opposition to the forces of the past, among whom he listed the court of Nicholas II, the State Council, the United Nobility, and the bureaucracy. Opposition, however, fell well short of revolution; 1905 was a time of war and economic depression. The period immediately preceding the war was a time of peace, economic boom, and improving material conditions among the working classes.[4]

Research in the past 20 years has exposed the extreme reductionism of an interpretation that sharply polarizes workers, educated society, and the state. Workers were diverse in their attitudes, conditions, and experiences. They lived within an urban society that was highly complex. A whole range of groups, many of which have been poorly or not at all studied, stood between workers and the educated, and interacted with both. A differentiated functional middle class had come into existence by 1913, consisting of a commercial-industrial group of large and petty producers drawn from all social estates, a range of salaried employees in the private and public sectors, professionals, and others. While they disagreed on any number of practical issues, as middle classes do, shared values of education, family, sobriety, social mobility, and work united them around a broad social agenda. Many workers, especially those who were better educated, internalized these values and aspired to the respect and recognition that they conferred. The pressures of urban living forced compromise and accommodation on city residents. Urban governments, especially outside of St. Petersburg, did not turn their backs on workers but sought, with very limited resources, to improve living conditions and provide education for workers' children and amenities for their recreation. In spite of relentless repression by the police, some workers participated or persistently sought to participate in the public sphere. They worked with reformers to create health insurance funds in industry and persistently sought representation at conferences dealing with social issues.

The rapid growth of a commercial popular culture in the years before World War I further weakened social barriers by creating widely shared cultural references. Popular and middlebrow literature and film promoted consumption and served as schools for the transmission of middle class dress, mores, and ways to the lower classes. Peasants shared in the culture of conspicuous consumption. Many among the cultural and political elites and even cultured workers deplored popular culture and promoted, with limited success, both high culture and folk traditions as antidotes to commercialism. Some writers were themselves drawn to the themes of popular literature or to the allure of the silver screen. Spectator sports also helped to forge common local or regional loyalties. Soccer games between factories or local clubs could spark local rivalries, but intercity, interregional, and international matches shaped common identities across larger spaces. The popularity of soccer and ice hockey also helped to displace traditional games and sports.

A vibrant public sphere existed in the Russian Empire by 1913. It was supported by a plethora of institutions of civil society. Newspapers and periodicals catered to a wide range of interests and tastes in many languages. They reported extensively on political and social life in the empire and built communities of shared beliefs and values among their readers. Newspapers and journals were read widely not only in cities but also in rural areas where villages or taverns subscribed to them in surprisingly large numbers. A penny press that espoused middle-class values and ambitions was widely available to workers in urban areas. A whole range of voluntary associations from charities and clubs to professional and mutual aid societies gave an organized voice to a host of interests and concerns; it also taught participants the habits of self-governance and democratic practice. These voluntary associations were by no means the domain of educated society only, but involved many levels of urban populations. Nor, as the examples of Kazan' and Saratov show, were they restricted to the two capitals. Conferences and congresses also contributed to the maintenance of the public sphere. The government needed the public input into policy formation and popular consensus around major reforms that congresses could provide. It sought to control congresses' agendas and to manage debate but could neither do without nor completely suppress public opinion. The needs of state and society also contributed to the steady improvement of the status of women. Not only did women secure a stronger legal identity after 1905, but educated women also gained access to several professions in numbers that matched or exceeded their counterparts in many West European countries. The benefits of the growth of civil society and the public sphere still significantly favored men over women, however.

The countryside, where the legal social estate structure still predominated, lagged well behind cities in terms of the development of the public sphere. Change, however, was also endemic in rural areas, and a more open society was in formation. The penetration of the market, greatly assisted by the growth of the cooperative movement and an increase in petty credit, was beginning to create the economic and social diversity and individual relationships on which civil society is based. Cases in the volost' courts captured both the growing sense of peasant individualism, expressed in the defense of dignity and rights, and the values of the market, expressed in the defense of property and contracts. By weakening the traditional instruments of mediation in the village, the Stolypin land reform significantly changed the relationship of peasants—even those who did not directly take part in the reform—with the outside world. To resolve their disputes they sought out courts and other bodies of mediation and accepted their decisions. Not only peasant men but women as well used the courts to protect their property and rights. Not peasant attitudes but the regime's ill-defined laws of property and inheritance as well as other concerns important to peasants slowed the transition to a stable rural legal order.

The growth of literacy among peasants and the penetration of urban fashions, mores, and ways of thinking into the villages were both a consequence of and stimulus to the development of market relations. Literacy not only opened peasants' minds to new ideas and experiences, but also enabled them to engage more effectively with the public sphere. The best example of such engagement is peasant participation in the struggle for the reform of church parishes. Some peasants were also beginning willingly to take part in zemstvo elections and politics in defense of their interests. Public subscriptions to newspapers and journals and communal readings of the news extended the outreach of literacy to many who could still not read. Though still subjected to a measure of tutelage by intellectuals, peasants in the cooperative movement gained a sense of belonging to a larger enterprise that connected them with peasants beyond their villages. Peasants who ran for elected positions on cooperative boards acquired basic but valuable administrative and financial knowledge. Other relatively new rural institutions, such as local fire brigades, provided similar experiences.

Expertise from urban-trained specialists was also infiltrating the countryside at an unprecedented rate in 1913. The numbers of the third element, the specialist employees of the zemstvos, had steadily grown since the 1880s. To the expanding list of teachers, doctors, feld'shers, midwives, statisticians, veterinarians, and others, a large and rapidly increasing number of agronomists were added, especially after the introduction of the Stolypin reform. Many were in the employ of the zemstvos but others worked for the Main Administration for Land Reorganization and Agriculture. Peasant distrust of experts and officials was slowly beginning to erode by 1913. Peasant delegates to the zemstvos were demanding more of the services that the zemstvos could provide, especially primary schooling. A small but growing number of mainly literate peasants was willing to attend agricultural exhibits and courses to learn new techniques of cultivation and animal husbandry. The cooperative movement encouraged contacts between peasants and the educated. The values of the experts were the same middle-class values that were growing in the middle and lower orders of urban society. The surprisingly peaceful peasant response to the land reform in most areas—and the widespread rejection by rural elites of punitive measures against rural hooliganism—pointed to a sea change in social relations in the countryside since 1905–1907. Many obstacles to rural social integration remained but progress was being made.

Change in peasant agriculture remained slow in 1913. Peasants who separated to form khutors or otrubs did not necessarily adopt new crop rotations or improve their habits of cultivation. Communal peasants whose land passed into individual ownership under the law of 1910 often continued traditional land use practices. The zemstvos and agronomists were quicker to grasp than was the central government that agricultural education was no less important than changes in land tenure in improving yields on peasant lands. Where, however, there was land reorganization that was more than nominal, peasants were more receptive to agricultural education.

The evidence is inconclusive but suggests that yields were poorest where the repartitional commune survived and highest on average on khutors and otrubs. What is certain is that more and more peasants were open to learning from scientific agronomy and prepared to seek out expertise.

Competition among the great powers combined with internal economic and social pressures to set a modernizing agenda for the Russian Empire before the war. Education, better health services and conditions, greater productivity in industry and agriculture, legal regulation, taxation, and other modern concerns left state and public only limited choices about what was to be done. Differences arose over ways and means and especially over control of the reform process. Some, both in the state and public, deplored change but found it hard to prevent. The pressing needs of the country fostered a pragmatic approach to reform that witnessed compromise and collaboration across state-public lines. The emperor's ministers and their officials disagreed among themselves about the need for and direction of reform. So did articulate interests among the public. Ministers sought out allies in the public to advance their agendas, and members of the public worked within and alongside ministries to achieve shared objectives. Central and local governments worked out protocols for collaboration. The disbursement of funds for land reorganization and agricultural education was one example; shared costs for primary schooling was another. The development of Russian aviation, the reform of the marriage separation laws, and the creation of the parole system were illustrations of various modes of cooperation between state and society.

In spite of collaborations and movement between the state and private sectors, tensions between state authority and the public were endemic. The powerful Ministry of the Interior, at times abetted by the Ministry of Justice and the Holy Synod and with the backing of the majority in the State Council, crippled the reform process with a regime of suspicion and repression in the name of the failing interests of a doomed old order. The toll of repression was especially drastic in the development of labor and management relations. The emperor proved unable to free himself from an imaginary past that he felt obliged to defend; ultimately he was an accomplice in the distortions and resulting incalculable damage to Russia that were wrought by the modernization process.A middle-class discourse that reflected the economic and social evolution of the country was developing in Russia. It flourished in popular writings and in the works of middlebrow literature as well as in the popular press, which had a broad audience that included literate workers. It also found a voice in the journals and newspapers of the associations of the commercial-industrial class. It was a broadly liberal discourse, but one with a strong social element reminiscent of European social democracy after the war. It found an ambivalent exponent in *Russkie vedomosti* and a committed one in *Utro Rossii*, the newspaper of the Progressive Party. It was a progressive discourse, one committed to the full implementation of the October Manifesto, the rule of law and protection of individual rights, cultural development, social mobility, balanced economic development through the market, and publicly supported social and health services. It valued individual enterprise and self-help, sobriety, and work as well as family life. Some progressive newspapers, however, expressed ambivalence about the suitability of capitalism for Russia, which divided liberalism at a critical moment in its development.

The newness of the discourse of the middle class and the relatively small numbers of its bearers compared to the population as a whole condemned it still in 1913 to a muted voice in the larger public discourse. It had to compete with a number of other established discourses that for the most part contradicted or actively opposed the growth of liberal capitalism, commercial culture, and parliamentary democracy in Russia. The ambiguity of personal identities caught between class and economic function, on the one hand, and social estate, on the other, and the long-established intelligentsia tradition of service to the narod stood in the way of the acceptance by many educated Russians of the new economic and social realities of their country. Conservatives also rejected much of what history had piled up in Russia by 1913.

Although the discourses of right and left in the empire differed significantly from one another they also had several features in common. All were anticapitalist, some more than others, and, at root, antidemocratic. All were built on ideas about Russian exceptionalism. Opponents of liberal, rights-based democracy despised and feared the economic and social pluralism that is at the heart of civil society. They associated diversity with social disintegration. Instead, they supported various versions of an integral or "symphonic" society. Most anchored their vision of society in imagined qualities of Russia that were best exemplified by the narod. Only in unity with the people could all Russians together realize their nation's true role in the world. At work in these discourses as well was an idea of a reified nation that ill accorded with the imperial reality of Russia in 1913. The growth of institutions of civil society not only strengthened Russian national consciousness but stirred national sentiments in other peoples in the empire as well. Some of them had by 1913 constructed ambitious national projects of their own.

If Russia was still far from becoming a liberal capitalist democracy in 1913, it was even farther from socialist revolution. Severe stresses and tensions remained but the clear trend before the war was toward cooperation and integration. The passage of time in peaceful circumstances would likely have strengthened the middle-class liberal discourse at the expense of its opponents. Nevertheless, as long as the monarchy supported, however tentatively, opposition to the economic and social direction that the country was taking, the transition would remain incomplete. The coming of the war and its disastrous course inexorably altered the environment for change. The experience of war weakened the forces of social integration from within that were at work in the prewar years and created conditions conducive to the advancement of forces and ideas that had opposed prewar trends.

In spite of important advances in the historiography over the past 20 years, much of the complex history of Russia between the revolution of 1905 and the outbreak of war in July 1914 is yet to be written. The great diversity among workers, the very different experiences of peasants from region to region, the multiple urban groups situated between workers and educated society and the associations and societies that they built, and a detailed look at the lives of servants or of female shop assistants, among several others, are only a few of many largely unexplored subjects for further study. If this book has succeeded in drawing attention to the complexity that was Russia in 1913 and providing an alternative, less reductive framework in which to examine it, it will have more than fulfilled its purpose.

Glossary

artel'—an association for common work in which members shared production costs and/or jointly sold their product

brattsy—an offshoot of the Orthodox Church, led by laymen, that originated in Moscow; the brattsy stressed through sermons and other activities the moral responsibility of individuals to lead good lives. They attracted thousands of followers and were anathematized by the Church in 1910 but continued their work.

buntarstvo—a term used by revolutionary ideologists to describe undisciplined or spontaneous acts of protest or rebellion among workers or peasants

burzhui—bourgeois; the term emerged as an epithet, particularly during World War I.

chastushka—a four-line rhyming verse, usually sung, that expressed individual emotion and the passing mood

dacha—a summer home in semirural and rural areas ranging from a room in a peasant cottage to large homes

dachniki—people who owned or rented dachas

dessiatina—a measure equivalent to 2.7 acres

duma—an elected city council created by the municipal reform of 1870 and headed by a mayor. When capitalized, "Duma" refers to the State Duma, Russia's lower house of the legislature.

dvoeverie—literally "dual faith," dvoeverie was the belief among educated Russians that Russian peasants had retained many features of pre-Christian paganism, which they incorporated into their Orthodox beliefs and practices.

estrada—variety theater or vaudeville

fel'dsher—paramedical practitioners who worked as assistants to doctors or in many remote areas worked independently. The designation was also applied to veterinarians' assistants.

gradonachal'nik (gradonachal'stvo)—a state-appointed official in charge of the oversight of urban administration in eight designated cities in the empire (and his office)

inorodtsy, adj. inorocheskoe—originally the term applied to the non-Russian peoples of the northern, eastern, and southeastern parts of the empire. By 1913 it was used loosely to refer to all non-Russians in the empire.

intelligent, pl. intelligenty—a member of the intelligentsia. By 1913 the intelligentsia in its wide meaning incorporated all educated Russians. More narrowly it referred to those who opposed the regime and were, in some cases, prepared to use violence to end it.

jadid—a reform movement within Islam that sought to reconcile Islam with modernity, especially through the reform of Muslim school curricula and teaching methods

Kadets—the Constitutional Democratic Party

khutor—a farmstead on which peasant proprietors (khutoriane) had their homes

kulak—literally "fist," the term referred to wealthy peasants, especially in intelligentsia discourse.

kustar'—handicraft industry largely conducted from peasant cottages

lubki—simple illustrated booklets and prints for popular consumption

meshchanstvo (meshchane)—an urban social estate that incorporated small urban traders and shopkeepers and some artisans (and its members)

narod—ordinary people, especially the peasants, in whom many educated Russians detected special features that denoted essential Russian-ness and/or communalism

nizy—those of lowly estate, originally defined as those who paid the poll tax; the tax no longer existed in 1913 but the designation lingered in the social consciousness.

oblast'—an administrative territory, a region or district

obshchestvo (obshchestvennost')—society in the sense employed by sociologists, but in Russia the word refers as well to a social movement of educated people who self-consciously opposed the autocratic regime in the name of service to the people. Obshchestvennost' is sometimes translated as "public-mindedness."

obshchina—a peasant community as well as the peasant commune that administered the community

otrub—a consolidated farm with a peasant proprietor who lived away from it in the village

patronatstvo—a form of charitable organization in which individuals bought memberships and volunteered work in charitable societies (patronaty) in support of causes such as criminal rehabilitation

pood—a weight equivalent to 36 lbs avoirdupois or 16.4 kilos

praktiki—workers who preferred legal means to improve conditions for labor and supported cultural and educational work among workers

rossiiskii—an inclusive term for subjects of the Russian Empire

russkii—a Russian, usually a Great Russian, but sometimes including Ukrainians and Belorussians

samosud—peasant summary justice

sobornost'—a powerful sense of community founded on shared inner moral and spiritual conviction, sobornost' was closely associated with Orthodox theology

soslovie, pl. sosloviia—a legally constituted social estate that conferred on its members both privileges and duties as well as corporate institutions

starosta, pl. starosty—the village elder or head, usually elected by villagers

verkhi—those of higher estate; groups exempt from the poll tax; the tax no longer existed in 1913 but the designation lingered in the social consciousness.

verst—a measure equivalent to approximately a kilometer or a bit less than two-thirds of a mile

volia—literally "freedom" or "will," the term was frequently used to describe the longing of peasants for an end to interference in their affairs by officials, landlords, and other defenders of the status quo.

volost'—an elected body of local peasant governance; a township. Attached to the volost' was a court in which disputes among peasants were adjudicated by peasant judges according to local peasant legal traditions and norms.

zaum—literally "outside of mind" or "outside of reason," the term was used by the Futurists in Russia to describe a language that communicated through sound, cadence, and rhythm rather than through defined meaning.

zemskii sobor—an institution of sixteenth- and seventeenth-century Muscovy that brought together representatives of various service groups to build consensus around state policies. A zemskii sobor met in 1613 to name Mikhail Romanov as the new tsar.

zemstvo—an elected body of rural local self-government established in 1864. By the end of 1913 zemstvos operated in 40 provinces of European Russia. District zemstvos were elected according to a curia system, and provincial zemstvo representatives were elected by representatives of the district zemstvos from among their own numbers. Zemstvos had taxation powers and were responsible for maintaining a wide range of services in their jurisdictions.

Notes

List of Abbreviations

AHR — American Historical Review
CSP — Canadian Slavonic Papers
HJ — The Historical Journal
IstSSSR — Istoriia SSSR
JfGOE — Jahrbücher für Geschichte Osteuropas
JoMH — Journal of Modern History
JoSH — Journal of Social History
JoSpH — Journal of Sport History
MV — Moskovskie vedomosti
RH — Russian History
RR — Russian Review
RV — Russkie vedomosti
SR — Slavic Review
VopIst — Voprosy Istorii

Introduction

1. *RV*, no. 24 (29 January 1913), 4.

2. *MV*, no. 210 (11 [24] September 1913), 2–3.

3. *RV*, no 84 (11 April 1913), 5.

4. Ibid., no. 190 (18 August 1913), 1 and no. 290 (17 December 1913), 7.

5. *MV*, no. 234 (11 [24] October 1913), 3.

6. Ibid., no. 101 (3 [16] May 1913), 3.

7. Ibid., no. 7 (9 [22] January 1913), 2.

8. Ibid., no. 105 (8 [21] May 1913), 1; see also *RV*, no. 52 (3 March 1913), for a liberal view of the issue.

9. *RV*, no. 275 (29 November 1913), 4.

10. *MV*, no. 89 (19 April [2 May] 1913), 3.

11. Ibid., no. 45 (23 February [8 March] 1913), 1.

12. Ibid., no. 47 (26 February [11 March] 1913), 1.

13. Ibid., no. 45 (23 February [8 March] 1913), 2.

14. Count V.N. Kokovtsov, *Out of My Past. The Memoirs of Count Kokovstsov* (Stanford, 1935), 361.

15. *RV*, no. 48 (27 February 1913), 2 and M.V. Rodzianko, "Krushenie imperii (Zapiski predsedatelia Russkoi Gosudardstvennoi Dumy)," *Arkhiv russkoi revoliutsii*, xvii (Berlin, 1926, reprint The Hague, 1970), 60–61.

16. I.I. Tolstoi, *Dnevniki, 1906–1916* (St. Petersburg, 1997), 427 and Princess Lydia Wassiltchikoff, "Vanished Russia. Memoirs," Hoover Institution ms., Stanford University, 202.

17. Tolstoi, 428.

18. Aleksandr Nikolaevich Naumov, "Iz utselevshchikh vospominanii, pt. 7, 1909–1914 gg.," Hoover Institution ms., Stanford University, 1814.

19. Ol'ga Nikolaevna Golovina, "Iubelei Doma Romanovykh, 1613–1913," *Vestnik Khrama—Pamiatnika*, nos. 145–46, 5.

20. Naumov, 1813.

21. Richard S. Wortman, *Scenarios of Power: Myth and Ceremony in Russian Monarchy*. Vol. 2, *From Alexander II to the Abdication of Nicholas II* (Princeton, 2000), 476.

22. *MV*, no. 116 (21 May [3 June] 1913), 1.

23. Seminal works supporting this analysis were Alexander Gerschenkron, "Agrarian Policies and Industrialization in Russia, 1861–1917," *Cambridge Economic History of Europe*, 6/2 (Cambridge, 1965) and his *Economic Backwardness in Historical Perspective* (Cambridge, Mass., 1962); and L.H. Haimson, "The Problem of Social Stability in Urban Russia, 1905–1917," *SR* 23 and 24, nos. 4 and 1 (1964–1965): 619–42 and 1–22.

24. An important exception is the recent textbook by Catherine Evtuhov et al., *A History of Russia Since 1800. Peoples, Legends, Events, Forces* (Boston and New York, 2004), especially Chapter 13, which paints an unusually nuanced portrait of Russia on the brink of war.

25. William G. Wagner, "Civil Law, Individual Rights, and Judicial Activism in Late Imperial Russia," Peter H. Solomon, Jr., ed., *Reforming Justice in Russia, 1864–1996. Power, Culture, and the Limits of Legal Order* (Armonk, 1997), 22–25; ibid., "Ideology, Identity, and the Emergence of a Middle Class," Edith W. Clowes, Samuel D. Kassow, and James L. West, eds., *Between Tsar and People: Educated Society and The Quest for Public Identity in Late Imperial Russia* (Princeton, 1991), 149.

26. Haimson, "The Problem of Social Stability in Urban Russia, 1905–1917," pt. 2, 2.

27. Edward Acton produced an influential synthesis of the state of the historiography about the Russian Revolution by the end of the 1980s. He looked at the Soviet, libertarian, liberal, and revisionist schools of thought about the revolution and its coming. The work was broadly dismissive of the liberal interpretation, critical of Soviet and libertarian views, and sympathetic to a revisionist interpretation that underscored peasant land hunger and worker militancy in the immediate prewar years, the ineffectiveness of liberal reform before the war due to "profound divisions within the middle classes," the unlikelihood of the development of "rural capitalism," and social and political factors that "pointed firmly towards a revolutionary upheaval likely to be fatal to tsarism and liberalism alike." Edward Acton, *Rethinking the Russian Revolution* (London, 1990), 82.

28. Useful collections include Harley D Balzer, ed., *Russia's Missing Middle Class. The Professions in Russian History* (Armonk, 1996); Clowes et al., eds., *Between Tsar and People: Educated Society and The Quest for Public Identity in Late Imperial Russia*; Mary Schaeffer Conroy, ed., *Emerging Democracy in Late Imperial Russia* (Boulder, 1998); Olga Crisp and Linda Edmondson, eds., *Civil Rights in Imperial Russia* (Oxford, 1989); Susan P. McCaffray and Michael Melancon, eds., *Russia in the European Context 1789–1914. A Member of the Family* (New York, 2005); and Theodore Taranovski, ed., *Reform in Modern Russian History. Progress or Cycle?* (New York, 1995). An important essay is by Joseph Bradley, who also made valuable contributions to several of the collections listed here.

Joseph Bradley, "Subjects into Citizens: Civil Society and Autocracy in Tsarist Russia," *AHR* 107, no. 4 (October 2002): 1094–1123. On charities and voluntary associations, see Adele Lindenmeyr, *Poverty is Not a Vice. Charity, Society, and the State in Imperial Russia* (Princeton, 1996) and ibid., "Voluntary Associations and the Russian Autocracy: The Case of Private Charity," The Carl Beck Papers in Russian and East European Studies, no. 807 (Pittsburgh, 1990).

29. An exception is Joseph Bradley, who emphasized not constraints but "opportunities for public action…." Bradley, 1105.

30. The chronological boundaries of late imperial Russia are vague. Sometimes it includes the whole period from 1881 to 1917, but 1890 to 1917 appears as well. An example is John F. Hutchinson, *Late Imperial Russia 1890–1917. Seminar Studies in History* (London and New York, 1999). A host of articles, collections, and monographs contain "late Imperial Russia" in their titles but usually specify no dates.

CHAPTER 1

1. *RV*, no. 133 (11 June 1913), 3.

2. A.P. Korelin, ed., *Rossiia 1913 god. Statistiko-dokumental'nyi spravochnik* (St. Petersburg, 1995), 35. From 1908 to 1913 the value of the industrial sector grew by 41%. Ibid.

3. Korelin, ed., 26. Between 1897 and 1914, 875,000 people emigrated and 4,282,200 relocated to Central Asia or Siberia. The total number of those who returned from emigration or places of relocation is hard to determine.

4. *RV*, no. 205 (5 September 1913), 2.

5. Korelin, ed., 18–22. These figures were published in the *Russian Statistical Yearbook* in 1915. R.W. Davies and his fellow researchers argued that the Central Statistical Bureau overestimated the rate of population growth between 1897 and 1914. They estimate the population of the empire on 1 January 1914 to be around 167,500,000. R.W. Davies, Mark Harrison, and S.G. Wheatcroft, eds., *The Economic Transformation of the Soviet Union, 1913–1945* (Cambridge, 1994), 59.

6. Peter Gatrell, *The Tsarist Economy, 1850–1917* (London, 1986), 57.

7. Korelin, ed., 359–60.

8. V.G. Tiukavkin, *Velikorusskoe krest'ianstvo i Stolypinskaia agrarnaia reforma* (Moscow, 2001), 35.

9. Ibid., 23. The average was around 15%. By the definition of "urban" adopted in the 1897 census, the urban population in 1917 rose from 12.4% of the whole in 1897 to 14.65% in 1914, and by a revised definition in the 1926 census from 15% to 17.5%. Comparable figures for several European countries just before the war are: England and Wales, 87%; Norway, 72%; Germany, 56.1%; USA, 41.5%; France, 41.2%; Italy 26.4%; Hungary, 18.8%.

10. Andreas Kappeler, *The Russian Empire* (Harlow, 2001), 288.

11. Robert W. Thurston, *Liberal City, Conservative State. Moscow and Russia's Urban Crisis, 1906–1914* (Oxford, 1987), 21–22.

12. Joseph Bradley, "Moscow. From Village to Metropolis," Michael F. Hamm, ed., *The City in Late Imperial Russia* (Bloomington, 1986), 14.

13. Gatrell, 32–33 and 59–60. Davies records an infant mortality rate of 273 per 1,000 in 1914. Davies et al., 59.

14. The figures were 29.4 per 1,000 inhabitants in Russia compared to 24.1 in Austro-

Hungary, 21.8 in Italy, 20.4 in the United States, 19.8 in Germany, and 16.0 in Great Britain. Margaret Miller, *The Economic Development of Russia, 1905–1914*, 2nd edition (London, 1967), Appendix, 30.

15. Paul R. Gregory, *Before Command. An Economic History of Russia from Emancipation to the First Five-Year Plan* (Princeton, 1994), 23.

16. Michael Hamm, "Continuity and Change in Late Imperial Kiev," Hamm, ed., *The City in Late Imperial Russia*, 87.

17. James Bater, "Between Old and New. St. Petersburg in the Late Imperial Era," Hamm, ed., *The City in Late Imperial Russia*, 49–50.

18. Daniel R. Brower, "Urban Russia on the Eve of World War One: A Social Profile," *JoSH* 13, no. 3 (Spring 1979): 424–36.

19. Korelin, ed., 342.

20. Ibid., 327.

21. Ibid., 326. A one-day census of schools in 1911 found that roughly 43% of all children between the ages of eight and twelve were in school on that day. Ibid., 343.

22. Ibid., 288.

23. Only 9% of property owners and 27% of renters had a secondary or higher education. Brower, 433.

24. The Ministry of Education oversaw 80,801 of them, the Holy Synod managed another 40,530, and other jurisdictions shared the remaining 2,414. Korelin, ed., 326.

25. Another 7% were being educated in private general or private ethno-religious schools and 0.8% attended private secondary level boarding schools. Ibid.

26. Local authorities offered 147 summer pedagogical courses for practicing teachers in 1913 as well. Ibid., 344 and 330.

27. *RV*, no. 1 (1 January 1913), Supplement, 35.

28. Ibid., no. 194 (23 August 1913), 1.

29. Davies et al., 83.

30. Korelin, ed., 347–48.

31. Ibid., 155.

32. Ibid., 337–39.

33. Ibid., 272–75 and 345.

34. Blair A. Ruble, *Second Metropolis. Pragmatic Pluralism in Gilded Age Chicago, Silver Age Moscow and Meiji Osaka* (Cambridge, 2001), 185.

35. In Moscow in 1913 12 free public libraries held 80,000 volumes and achieved a circulation of 800,000 volumes. Another 28 libraries operated by educational charities in the city held 70,000 volumes and reached a circulation of 450,000 volumes. In all, 45,000 Muscovites made use of public or charitable libraries in that year. B. Zaks, "Neskol'ko dannykh po statistike russkogo bibliotechnogo dela. (Eksponaty Obshchestva Bibliotekovedeniia na Leipzigoi vystavke 1914 g.)," *Bibliotekar'*, vyp. 3 (1914): 313.

36. The budget for 1913 projected 821 million roubles from the monopoly and the sale of 95.5 million vedros of vodka alone. *RV*, no. 100 (1 May 1913), 2.

37. Korelin, ed., 155. Another 139 million roubles for military-related programs were channeled through civilian ministries in 1913. The year 1913 was a one of high expenditure in Russia's military buildup before World War I. Ibid., 156.

38. The servicing of the state debt absorbed 13.7% of the budget in 1913, down from 18.3% in 1900. Ibid., 152–55.

39. Miller, 121–22. In 1913, 7.1% of the state budget serviced domestic loans and

5.4% went to service loans abroad. Korelin, ed., 157.

40. A.V. Ignat'ev, *Vneshniaia politika Rossii, 1907–1914* (Moscow, 2000), 17.

41. Gregory, *Before Command*, 9 and 36. Elsewhere Gregory maintains that by international standards Russian growth rates were high in the 1861–1914 period and that even its per capita and per worker growth rates were at least average by international measures, exceeded as they were only by Belgium, Norway, Sweden, the United States, and Denmark. Paul R. Gregory, *Russian National Income, 1885–1913* (Cambridge, 1982), 158. Gatrell, 161.

42. Gregory, *Russian National Income*, 31.

43. The economy grew on average between 1885 and 1913 at a rate of 3.25% annually. Gregory, *Before Command*, 27. Only the United States, Canada, and Japan in their highest periods of national output exceeded the rates of increase that Russia achieved in its highest period of national output growth during the 1890s.

44. From 1870 to 1913 the annual per capita output rate of increase was 1.6%, which was roughly comparable to the per capita output growth rates of the major Western states in the same period. Gregory, *Russian National Income*, 158–59 and 163.

45. In the 50 European provinces in 1913 the average income per person was 107 roubles compared to the average of 136 roubles per head achieved in Poland, the Caucasus and western Siberia. Gatrell, 34.

46. Korelin, ed., 210.

47. Exports to China and Mongolia in 1913, at about 2% of the total, were in fact down from the 3% reached in the years 1904–1908. Ibid., 214–15.

48. Ibid., 216–17.

49. Ibid., 212–14.

50. Tiukavkin, 32 and 35.

51. Davies et al., 1–2.

52. Gregory, *Before Command*, 54.

53. Lazar Volin, *A Century of Russian Agriculture. From Alexander II to Khrushchev* (Cambridge, Mass., 1970), 110.

54. In the decades before the 1905 revolution, real wages of hired agricultural laborers rose by 14%. By 1913 real wage rates for hired agricultural labor were from 23% to 64%, depending on the region and sector, higher than the 1901–1905 average. Gregory, *Before Command*, 42–48; Volin, 111.

55. Gatrell, 202.

56. Andrew Verner, "Discursive Strategies in the 1905 Revolution: Peasant Petitions from Vladimir Province," *RR* 54, no 1 (January 1995): esp. 80–83.

57. Tiukavkin, 293.

58. Gatrell and Gregory share these conclusions. Gatrell, 44 and 137–39; Gregory, *Before Command*, 43–49. Elsewhere Gregory concludes, "Thus the Gerschenkronian (and Lenin) depiction of the Russian economy as a dual economy comprised of a dynamic modern factory industry and a backward and traditional peasant agricultural sector does not appear to be accurate, at least as judged by the period 1885–1913." Gregory, *Russian National Income*, 170.

59. N. Valentinov, "Russkaia derevnia i sel'skoe khoziaistvo za period 1906–1917," Hoover Institution Archives ms., Stanford University, 3.

60. Corinne Gaudin, *Ruling Peasants. Village and State in Late Imperial Russia* (DeKalb, 2007), 17–20.

61. Ibid., 156.

62. Ibid.

63. Korelin, ed., 67–68.

64. In all 26 provinces with large Great Russian majorities, the average figure was 61.5%. Tiukavkin, 173. Gaudin, using the examples of Tver' and Riazan' provinces, contends that the methodology used by the Ministry of the Interior in deriving these figures exaggerated the decline in repartitions, but he does note a sharp decline of repartitions in those provinces after 1906. Gaudin, 182–86.

65. Judith Pallot, "The Stolypin Land Reform as 'Administrative Utopia': Images of Peasantry in Nineteenth-Century Russia," Madhavan K. Palat, ed., *Social Identities in Revolutionary Russia* (Basingstoke, 2000), 117.

66. Tiukavkin, 196 and 204–5.

67. B.V. Anan'ich, *Vlast' i reformy. Ot samoderzhavnoi k sovetskoi Rossii* (Moscow, 1996), 593.

68. Valentinov, 40–41.

69. Ibid., 6. Merchants and honorary citizens by 1915 also owned only 86.9% of what their holdings had been in 1905. Ibid.

70. Between 1906 and 1913 village societies bought 1,125,969 dessiatinas of land, partnerships bought another 3,839,946 dessiatinas, and individuals bought 3,493,833 dessiatinas. Ibid., 41–42.

71. On 1 January 1915 individual peasants owned 16,843,126 dessiatinas of private land, village societies privately owned 4,609,944 dessiatinas, and peasant partnerships owned 12,483,706 dessiatinas. Ibid., 63. Dorothy Atkinson maintained that between 1905 and 1915 private land held by peasant individuals declined from 54% to 49% of all private land owned by the peasantry. Dorothy Atkinson, *The End of the Russian Land Commune, 1905-1930* (Stanford, 1983), 82. My data do not support this claim. In addition, many peasants who purchased land in partnerships used it as individual proprietors.

72. Yaney notes that between 1907 and 1914, 79% of all land sold either to groups or individuals went into consolidated tenure and 93% of purchasers were individuals. From 1908 the Peasant Land Bank cut back on land purchases and concentrated on aiding poor villages to acquire more land directly from private sellers. George Yaney, *The Urge to Mobilize. Agrarian Reform in Russia, 1861-1930* (Urbana, Chicago, and London, 1982), 285–86.

73. B.F. Egorov, "Kooperativnoe dvizhenie v dorevoliutsionnoi Rossii (novyi vzgliad)," *Voprosy istorii*, no. 6 (2005): 14–15.

74. By 1 January 1914, 538 regional unions of petty credit institutions were in place. Korelin, ed., 169–70 and 193.

75. A.D. Bilimovich, *Kooperatsiia v Rossii vo vremeni i posle Bol'shevikov* (Moscow, 2005 reprint), 62.

76. Korelin, ed., 194.

77. Valentinov, 14.

78. N.A. Roubakine, *Qu'est-ce que la Révolution Russe?* (Geneva and Paris, 1917), 216. That was about 18% of the incoming group.

79. *RV,* no. 63 (16 March 1913), 5.

80. Gatrell, 155.

81. The United States led with 35.8% of world industrial production, Germany followed with a 15.7% share, and Great Britain and France contributed 14% and 6.4% respectively. The Russian Empire and the Austro-Hungarian Empire were roughly equal producers of industrial goods by the end of 1913. Korelin, ed., 51.

82. Davies et al., 131 and 2.

83. Gatrell, 158.

84. Ibid., 163–64.

85. Davies et al., 133.

86. N.A. Ivanova, *Promyshlennyi tsentr Rossii, 1907–1914* (Moscow, 1995), 279–81.

87. Korelin, ed., 47–49.

88. Ibid., 177–79.

89. Ibid., 183 and 192.

90. John P. McKay, *Pioneers for Profit. Foreign Entrepreneurship and Russian Industrialization, 1885–1913* (Chicago and London, 1970), 74.

91. Gatrell, 46.

92. The breakdown was 22% by French investors, 16% by Germans, and 5% by the British. McKay, 234.

93. Korelin, ed., 185–86.

94. By contrast, in the same period foreign-owned companies in the chemical sector grew from 11 to 13 and their capital from 7.5 million roubles to just over 9 million roubles. Ibid.

95. Ibid. These figures come from the Ministry of Trade and Industry. L.E. Shepelev, using figures from the Congress of Representatives of Industry and Trade, found that there were 2,263 stock companies in Russia early in 1914 with a total capital of 4,639,000,000 roubles. This compared to 5,488 stock companies in Germany with capital of 8,038,000,000 roubles. L.E. Shepelev, *Aktsionernye kompanii v Rossii* (Leningrad, 1973), 232.

96. René Girault, *Emprunts russes et investissements français en Russie, 1887–1914* (Paris, 1994), 531.

97. V.S. Diakin, *Germanskie kapitaly v Rossii. Elektroindustriia i elektricheskii transport* (Leningrad, 1971), 150 and 206–7.

98. McKay, 276.

99. Iu.A. Petrov, *Kommercheskie banki Moskvy. Konets xix v.-1914 gg.* (Moscow, 1995), 247.

100. Ibid., 246. The private banks held a total balance of 6,285,300,000 roubles compared to the 4,624,000,000 roubles in the State Bank. Cooperative credit societies had a balance of 1,059,700,000 roubles and urban society banks held another 261,300,000 roubles.

101. 70% of bank savings books were held by town dwellers. Miller, 89–90.

102. Korelin, ed., 169–70.

103. Petrov, 141.

104. Girault, 514.

105. Miller, 85.

106. McKay, 294.

107. Ibid., 237.

108. Shepelev, 281.

109. In 1914, 28% of registered Russian stock companies were headquartered in St. Petersburg, 20% in Moscow, 5% each in Warsaw and Kiev, and 2% in Riga. Ibid., 235.

110. Ibid., 230.

111. Those companies represented 21% of all Russian corporations or 27% of companies with capitalization over 500,000 roubles, which were legally enabled to trade shares. Ibid., 238.

112. McKay, 236.

113. Thomas C. Owen, "Doing Business in Merchant Moscow," James L. West and

Iurii Petrov, eds., *Merchant Moscow. Images of Russia's Vanished Bourgeoisie* (Princeton, 1998), 32.

114. On pending reform of corporate law, see Shepelev, 261–63 and 270.

115. Teodor Shanin, *Russia as a 'Developing Society.' The Roots of Otherness: Russia's Turn of Century*, vol. 1 (London, 1985), esp. Chapter 5, makes a strong case for Russia as a developing society. Shanin calls Russia in 1914 a "semi-colonial possession of European capital." Ibid., 188.

116. Ibid., 110–11.

117. Alexander Gerschenkron, *Economic Backwardness in Historical Perspective: A Book of Essays* (Cambridge, Mass., 1962).

118. Davies et al., 3.

119. L. Iurovskii, "Torgovaia politika," *RV*, no. 1 (1 January 1913), Supplement, 43.

120. Peter Gatrell, *Government, Industry and Rearmament in Russia, 1900–1914. The Last Argument of Tsarism* (Cambridge, 1994), 326.

121. McKay, 78.

122. Fred V. Carstensen, "Foreign Participation in Russian Economic Life: Notes on British Enterprise, 1865–1914," Gregory Guroff and Fred V. Carstensen, eds., *Entrepreneurship in Imperial Russia and the Soviet Union* (Princeton, 1983), 140–44.

123. McKay, 7 and Gregory, *Before Command*, 60.

124. Korelin, ed., 110–12.

125. Ibid., 156, note 9.

126. Ibid., 32–33. The total national wealth created in Russia in 1913 was just under 70 thousand million roubles. The combined contribution to the national wealth of large-scale industry and of the transport and communications industries at the end of 1913 was around 13.3 thousand million roubles by most estimates.

127. Ibid., 156, note 9.

128. Girault, 554–56.

129. Gatrell, *The Tsarist Economy*, 214.

130. L.E. Shepelev, *Tsarizm i burzhuaziia v 1904–1914 gg.* (Leningrad, 1987), 156.

131. Korelin, ed., 110–14.

132. In Russia 71.3% of all phones belonged to cities, 13.9% to the central government, and 12.8% to the zemstvos. Ibid., 149–50.

133. *MV*, no. 204 (4 [17] September 1913), 2.

134. Dominic Lieven, *Empire. The Russian Empire and its Rivals* (London, 2000), 211 and Ekaterina Pravilova, *Finansy imperii. Den'gi i vlast' v politike Rossii na natsional'nykh okrainakh, 1801–1917* (Moscow, 2006), 368–69.

135. Pravilova, 370.

136. Kappeler, 321 and Pravilova, 369.

137. Malcolm Falkus, "Aspects of Foreign Investment in Tsarist Russia," *The Journal of European Economic History* 8, no. 1 (Spring 1979): 5–36 provides a good overview of the challenges to Russian economic development.

138. Shanin, 187.

139. Gatrell, *The Tsarist Economy*, 232.

140. Gregory, *Before Command*, 64.

141. See, for example, L. Iurovskii, "Promyshlennyia perspektivy," *RV*, no. 1 (1 January 1913), Supplement, 30.

142. Gregory, *Before Command*, 82–84.

CHAPTER 2

1. On the estates, see Elise Kimerling Wirtschafter, *Social Identity in Imperial Russia* (DeKalb, 1997). On the persistence of the estate system, see Gregory Freeze, "The Soslovie (Estate) Paradigm and Russian Social History," *AHR* 91, no. 1 (1986): 11–36.

2. A.N. Zorin et al., eds., *Ocherki rodskogo byta dorevoliutsionnogo Povolzh'ia* (Ul'ianovsk, 2000), 46.

3. Wirtschafter, 146.

4. Freeze, 11–36.

5. On the post-emancipation nobility, see Seymour Becker, *Nobility and Privilege in Late Imperial Russia* (DeKalb, 1985).

6. Percentages based on the 1897 census figures. A.P. Korelin, ed., *Rossiia 1913 god. Statistiko-dokumental'nyi spravochnik* (St. Petersburg, 1995), 219.

7. Geoffrey A. Hosking and Roberta Thompson Manning, "What Was the United Nobility?" Leopold H. Haimson, ed., *The Politics of Rural Russia, 1905–1914* (Bloomington and London, 1979), 142–83.

8. *RV*, no. 59 (12 March 1913), 2, and ibid., no. 62 (15 March 1913), 1.

9. Ibid., no. 157 (9 July 1913), 5.

10. Ibid., no. 174 (29 July 1913), 4.

11. Wirtschafter, 34.

12. S.E. Kryzhanovskii, *Vospominaniia* (Berlin, n.d.), 139.

13. B.V. Anan'ich, *Vlast' i reformy. Ot samoderzhavnoi k sovetskoi Rossii* (Moscow, 1996), 597–98.

14. For a study of the condition of the nobility after the emancipation, see G.M. Hamburg, *Politics of the Russian Nobility, 1881–1905* (New Brunswick, N.J., 1985).

15. Of 182 members of the State Council, 153 had noble backgrounds; in the State Duma the membership in 1913 was 437, of whom 299 had noble origins. Korelin, ed., 235–38 and 246–53.

16. Ibid., 245.

17. Aleksandr Nikolaevich Naumov, "Iz utselevshchikh vospominanii, pt. 7, 1909–1914 gg." Hoover Institution Archive ms., Stanford University, 1783–84.

18. N.G. Kusova, *Riazanskoe kupechestvo. Ocherki istorii xvi-nachala xx veka* (Riazan', 1996), 12 and 35.

19. *RV*, no. 278 (3 December 1913), 2.

20. Quoted in *MV*, no 190 (18 [31] August 1913), 1.

21. *RV*, no. 190 (18 August 1913), 2, and ibid., no. 214 (17 September 1913), 3.

22. Ibid., no. 190 (18 August 1913), 2.

23. Kusova, 120–21.

24. Daniel R. Brower, "Urban Russia on the Eve of World War One: A Social Profile," *JoSH* 13, no. 3 (Spring 1979): 433.

25. Princess Lydia Wassiltchikoff, "Vanished Russia. Memoirs," Hoover Institution Archive ms., Stanford University, 187–88.

26. N.A. Dobroliubov, "Temnoe tsarstvo," *Izbrannoe* (Moscow, 1970), 43–178.

27. Bernard Pares, *My Russian Memoirs* (London, 1931), 259–61.

28. Irina V. Potkina, "Moscow's Commercial Mosaic," James L. West and Iurii A. Petrov, eds., *Merchant Moscow: Images of Russia's Vanished Bourgeoisie* (Princeton, 1998), 43.

29. Thomas C. Owen, "Doing Business in Merchant Moscow," ibid., 30.

30. Peter Gatrell, *The Tsarist Economy, 1850–1917* (London, 1986), 210–11.

31. Ekaterina Pravilova, *Finansy imperii. Den'gi i vlast' v politike Rossii na*

natsional'nykh okrainakh, 1801–1917 (Moscow, 2006), 370.

32. Ruth AmEnde Roosa, *Russian Industrialists in an Era of Revolution. The Association of Industry and Trade, 1906–1917* (Armonk and London, 1997), 28.

33. Ibid., 29–48 *passim* and 82.

34. Robert B. McKean, *St. Petersburg Between the Revolutions. Workers and Revolutionaries, June 1907–February 1917* (New Haven and London, 1990), 276.

35. Heather Hogan, *Forging Revolution. Metalworkers, Managers, and the State in St. Petersburg, 1890–1914* (Bloomington and Indianapolis, 1993), 161 and 229–30.

36. McKean, 279–80.

37. Ibid., no. 176 (30 July 1913), 1.

38. Susan P. McCaffray, *The Politics of Industrialization in Tsarist Russia. The Association of Southern Coal and Steel Producers, 1874–1914* (DeKalb, 1996), 73 and 199–200.

39. L.E. Shepelev, *Tsarizm i burzhuaziia v 1904–1914 gg.* (Leningrad, 1987), 157–60.

40. *RV*, no. 20 (24 January 1913), 3.

41. Ibid., no. 31 (7 February 1913), 3.

42. Teodor Shanin, *Russia as a 'Developing Society.' The Roots of Otherness: Russia's Turn of Century*, vol. 1 (London, 1985), 119.

43. Cited in Roosa, 144.

44. McCaffray, 131.

45. Ibid., 225–26.

46. Shepelev, 157.

47. Roosa, 52.

48. Shepelev, 244–45.

49. Roosa, 146.

50. *RV*, no. 169 (12 July 1913), 1.

51. McCaffray, 198.

52. Ibid., 200.

53. Roosa, 62–67.

54. *RV*, no. 268 (20 November 1913), 5.

55. Ibid., no. 59 (12 March 1913), 4.

56. Ibid., no. 110 (14 May 1913), 5.

57. Ibid., no. 156 (7 July 1913), 4.

58. Ibid., no. 262 (13 November 1913), 4.

59. Ibid., no. 300 (31 December 1913), 3.

60. Ibid., no. 82 (9 April 1913), 2.

61. Ibid., no. 85 (12 April 1913), 4.

62. Ibid., no. 114 (18 May 1913), 4–5.

63. Ibid., no. 166 (19 July 1913), 4.

64. Ibid., no. 243 (22 October 1913), 5.

65. Ibid., no. 146 (26 June 1913), 1.

66. Ibid., no. 154 (5 July 1913), 1 and 3.

67. Ibid., no. 264 (15 November 1913), 5.

68. Ibid., no. 121 (28 May 1913), 6.

69. Ibid., no. 284 (10 December 1913), 2.

70. Ibid., no. 143 (22 June 1913), 5.

71. Ibid., no. 71 (27 March 1913), 5.

72. Susan McCaffray makes a strong case for the effects of change on elite cooperation. McCaffray, xvii–xviii.

73. See Harley D. Balzer, "Conclusion: The Missing Middle Class," Harry D. Balzer, ed., *Russia's Missing Middle Class. The Professions in Russian History* (Armonk, 1996), 301–2.

74. Kendall E. Bailes, "Reflections on Russian Professions," ibid., 50.

75. *RV*, no. 158 (10 July 1913), 2.

76. Ibid., 113 (17 May 1913), 3.

77. F.V. Shlippe, Bakhmeteff Archive ms., Columbia University, 93.

78. Tim McDaniel, *Autocracy, Capitalism, and Revolution in Russia* (Berkeley and Los Angeles, 1988), 50.

79. Korelin, ed., 403.

80. *Trudy Tsentral'nogo statisticheskogo upravleniia*, vol. vii, vyp. 1, *Statisticheskii sbornik za 1913–1917 gg.* (Moscow, 1921), 130–31.

81. Ibid., 198, 207–8, and 211.

82. McKean, 220–21.

83. Of 2,404 strikes in the country in 1913, 56% lasted between a half day and two days, 18% between five to twenty days, and only 5% went longer than thirty days. *Trudy Tsentral'nogo statisticheskogo upravleniia*, 138–39.

84. Ibid., 132–33.

85. Alice K. Pate, "The Liquidationist Controversy: Russian Social Democracy and the Quest for Unity," Mark Melancon and Alice K. Pate, eds., *New Labor History. Worker Identity and Experience in Russia, 1840–1918* (Bloomington, 2002), 119. In 1913 the secret police in Moscow had 11 informants within the Socialist Revolutionary Party and 18 within the Social Democratic organization. From May 1913 to February 1914, Miron Chernomazov, a police informer, edited the Bolshevik newspaper *Pravda* and Roman Malinovskii, one of the Bolshevik deputies in the Fourth Duma, was also a police agent. Jonathan Daly, "The Security Police and Politics in Late Imperial Russia," Anna Geifman, ed., *Russia Under the Last Tsar. Opposition and Subversion* (Oxford, 1999), 233.

86. Pate, 225–26.

87. Hogan, 170–72, 191–92 and 223.

88. *Trudy Tsentral'nogo statisticheskogo upravleniia*, 132–35 and 142–45 and McKean, 251.

89. Korelin, ed., 312–13.

90. McKean, 251.

91. Hogan, 226.

92. Korelin, ed., 401–2.

93. McKean, 42.

94. McDaniel, 253.

95. Pate, 95–97.

96. McDaniel, 253.

97. Leopold Haimson, "Russian Workers' Political and Social Identities: The Role of Social Representations in the Interaction Between Members of the Labor Movement and the Social Democratic Intelligentsia," Reginald E. Zelnik, ed., *Workers and Intelligentsia in Late Imperial Russia. Realities, Representations, Reflections* (Berkeley, 1999), 162.

98. Haimson supports Lenin's view. He argues that the Stolypin land reform displaced many peasants and permanently severed former peasants and workers from the land. As a result new labor recruits from the countryside were forced to assimilate quickly to urban ways and to the values of young urban workers. He goes on, "Here, I think, lies the real explanation for the rapid evolution of and consolidation of the sense of class consciousness and class solidarity that many contemporary observers of the labor scene recorded with such awe."

More established, older workers, he notes, did not join the radical movement. Haimson's argument raises many questions. What Lenin and he mean by class consciousness is unspecified, and how established workers' rejection of radicalism squares with Marx's notion that class consciousness arises from the long experience of workers of capitalist exploitation remains unexplained. Leopold H. Haimson, "The Workers' Movement After Lena. The Dynamics of Labor Unrest in the Wake of the Lena Goldfields Massacre (April 1912–July 1914)," *Russia's Revolutionary Experience. Two Essays, 1905–1917* (New York, 2005), 201–2.

99. Diane Koenker, "Urban Families, Working-Class Youth Groups and the 1917 Revolution in Moscow," David L. Ransel, ed., *The Family in Imperial Russia* (Urbana, 1978), 289–90.

100. E. Anthony Swift, "Workers' Theater and 'Proletarian Culture' in Pre-revolutionary Russia, 1905–17," Zelnik, ed., 260.

101. McKean, 130 and 189; Hogan, 3.

102. For an informed and detailed discussion of agricultural regions, crop conditions, and land values, see George Pavlovsky, *Agricultural Russia on the Eve of the Revolution* (London, 1930).

103. Launcelot Owen argued that 75% of secessions were achieved through coercion. Launcelot Owen, *The Russian Peasant Movement, 1906–1917* (New York, 1963), 82. George Yaney rejects that view and stresses the efforts made by officials to meet peasant concerns. George Yaney, *The Urge to Mobilize. Agrarian Reform in Russia, 1861–1930* (Urbana, Chicago, and London, 1982), 288 and 302.

104. David A.J. Macey, "Government Actions and Peasant Reactions During the Stolypin Reforms," Robert B. McKean, ed., *New Perspectives in Modern Russian History. Selected Papers from the Fourth World Congress for Soviet and East European Studies, Harrogate, 1990* (Basingstoke, 1992), 137.

105. David Kerans, *Mind and Labor on the Farm in Black-Earth Russia, 1861–1914* (Budapest and New York, 2001), 316–18.

106. Macey, 158.

107. Yaney, 286.

108. Judith Pallot, *Land Reform in Russia, 1906–1917. Peasant Responses to Stolypin's Project of Rural Transformation* (Oxford, 1999), 128–29.

109. Ibid., 97.

110. V.A. Kosinskii, "Russkaia agrarnaia reforma," Hoover Institution Archive ms., Stanford University, 69.

111. Ibid., 21–22, 104 and 124.

112. *RV*, no. 201 (31 August 1913), 3.

113. Landless peasants bought 13.4% of the land sold and peasants with fewer than six dessiatinas another 55.7%. V.G. Tiukavkin, *Velikorusskoe krest'ianstvo i Stolypinskaia agrarnaia reforma* (Moscow, 2001), 206, 209, and 213.

114. Lazar Volin erroneously claimed that large-scale farmers constituted the bulk of non-absentee separators and that middle–scale farmers were unaffected. Lazar Volin, *A Century of Russian Agriculture. From Alexander II to Khrushchev* (Cambridge, Mass., 1970), 105.

115. Pallot, 235–39.

116. Ibid., 224.

117. Ibid., 225–29.

118. Tiukavkin, 208.

119. Volin, 109.

120. Pallot, 166–70 and 181–82.

121. Korelin, ed., 415.

122. Yaney, 190.

123. Ibid., 279–80.

124. Pallot, 111.

125. Jane Burbank, *Russian Peasants Go to Court. Legal Culture in the Countryside, 1905–1917* (Bloomington, 2004), 13, 46–47.

126. Ibid., 115–16.

127. Ibid., 76–78, 126.

128. Ibid., 249.

129. Korelin, ed., 415.

130. Jane Burbank, "Legal Culture, Citizenship, and Peasant Jurisprudence: Perspectives from the Early Twentieth Century," Peter H. Solomon, Jr., ed., *Reforming Justice in Russia, 1864–1996* (Armonk, 1997), 95.

131. Pallot, 27.

132. Burbank, *Russian Peasants Go To Court*, xv and 9.

133. For an excellent survey of conscription, see Joshua A. Sanborn, *Drafting the Russian Nation: Military Conscription, Total War, and Mass Politics, 1905–1925* (DeKalb, 2003).

134. Joshua Sanborn, "Military Reform, Moral Reform, and the End of the Old Regime," Eric Lohr and Marshall Poe, eds., *The Military and Society in Russia* (Leiden and Boston, 2002), 507–24.

135. Gregory Vitabaro, "Nationality Policy and the Russian Imperial Officer Corps, 1905–1914," *SR* 66, no. 4 (Winter 2007): 682–701.

136. Yanni Kotsonis, "'Face to Face': The State, the Individual, and the Citizen in Russian Taxation, 1863–1917," *SR* 63, no. 2 (Summer 2004): 221–46.

137. Ibid., "'No Place to Go': Taxation and State Transformation in Late-Imperial and Early-Soviet Russia," *JoMH* (September 2004): 531–77.

138. Burbank, *Russian Peasants Go to Court*, xiv.

CHAPTER 3

1. Robert Fine, "Civil Society Theory, Enlightenment and Critique," Robert Fine and Shirin Rai, eds., *Civil Society: Democratic Perspectives* (London and Portland, Ore., 1997), 9–12. See as well Grazyna Shapika, "Learning to be a Citizen: Cognitive and Ethical Aspects of Post-communist Society Transformation," ibid., 147–49.

2. For a useful discussion of views about civil society and their relevance in imperial Russia, see Joseph Bradley, "Subjects into Citizens: Civil Society and Autocracy in Tsarist Russia," *AHR* 107, no. 4 (October 2002): 1094–1123. Harley Balzer suggests that Russia can best be characterized as a "civic society," in which state and society form a partnership to advance common goals. Harley D. Balzer, "Conclusion: The Missing Middle Class," Harley D. Balzer, ed., *Russia's Missing Middle Class. The Professions in Russian History* (Armonk, 1996), 301.

3. Teodor Shanin, *Russia as a 'Developing Society.' The Roots of Otherness: Russia's Turn of Century*, vol. 1 (London, 1985), 209.

4. Ibid., 203 and 206.

5. See, for example, Joseph Bradley, "Voluntary Associations, Civic Culture and *Obshchestvennost'* in Moscow," Edith W. Clowes, Samuel D. Kassow, and James L. West, eds., *Between Tsar and People: Educated Society and the Quest for Public Identity in Late Imperial Russia* (Princeton, 1991), 131.

6. "Introduction" in Clowes et al., eds., *Between Tsar and People*, 6.

7. Fine, 16–17.

8. Adam B. Seligman, *The Idea of Civil Society* (New York, 1992), 28. Also see John Varty, "Civil or Commercial? Adam Ferguson's Concept of Civil Society," Fine and Rai, eds., 29–48.

9. Seligman, 47–50.

10. Ibid., 54–55.

11. Bradley, "Subjects into Citizens," 1096.

12. Boris Gorshkov has argued along these lines about peasants and civil society in Russia, in "Democratizing Habermas: Peasant Public Sphere in pre-Reform Russia," *RH* 31, no. 4 (Winter 2004): 373–85.

13. Ernest Gellner, *Conditions of Liberty. Civil Society and Its Rivals* (London, 1994), 99–100 and 188.

14. Ibid., 10.

15. For an interesting discussion of Russian liberal hopes for civil society and the obstacles to its realization, see Laura Engelstein, "The Dream of Civil Society in Tsarist Russia: Law, State, and Religion," Nancy Bermeo and Philip Nord, eds., *Civil Society Before Democracy. Lessons from Nineteenth-Century Europe* (Lanham, 2000), 23–41.

16. Seligman, 160–63.

17. Ibid., 104–6.

18. See, for example, the Harley D. Balzer collection, *Russia's Missing Middle Class: The Professions in Russian History,* cited above.

19. Sarah Maza, *The Myth of the French Bourgeoisie. An Essay on the Social Imaginary, 1750–1850* (Cambridge, Mass., 2003), 12.

20. Peter Gay, *Schnitzler's Century. The Making of Middle-Class Culture, 1815–1914* (London, 2001), Chapter 1, passim.

21. David Blackbourn and Geoff Eley, *The Peculiarities of German History. Bourgeois Society and Politics in Nineteenth-Century Germany* (Oxford, 1984), 288.

22. Ibid., 149.

23. Ibid., 144.

24. Leopold Haimson, "The Problem of Social Stability in Urban Russia, 1905–1917, Pt. 1," *SR* 23, no. 4 (December 1964): 624 and 639.

25. Ibid., "'The Problem of Political and Social Stability in Urban Russia on the Eve of War and Revolution' Revisited," *SR* 59, no. 4 (Winter 2000): 849.

26. Susan P. McCaffray, *The Politics of Industrialization in Tsarist Russia. The Association of Southern Coal and Steel Producers, 1874–1914* (DeKalb, 1996), 134.

27. On Marxism as discourse, see Igal Halfin, *From Darkness to Light. Class, Consciousness, and Salvation in Revolutionary Russia* (Pittsburgh, 2000), 12–21.

28. Alexander Herzen, *My Past and Thoughts,* vol. vi, Constance Garnett, trans. (London, 1927), 11–12.

29. E. Anthony Swift, "Workers' Theater and 'Proletarian Culture' in Pre-revolutionary Russia, 1905–1917," Reginald E. Zelnik, ed., *Workers and Intelligentsia in Late Imperial*

Russia. Realities, Representations, Reflections (Berkeley, 1999), 262.

30. Mark Steinberg, "Russia's *fin de siècle*, 1900–1914," Ronald Grigor Suny, ed., *The Cambridge History of Russia*, vol. III, *The Twentieth Century* (Cambridge, 2006), 83.

31. Swift, 278.

32. Ibid., 266.

33. Ibid., 280.

34. Ibid.

35. Mark D. Steinberg, "Proletarian Knowledge of Self: Worker Poets in Fin-de-Siècle Russia," Mark Melancon and Alice K. Pate, eds., *New Labor History. Worker Identity and Experience in Russia, 1840–1918* (Bloomington, 2002), 129–35 and 137.

36. Mark B. Steinberg, "Worker Authors and the Cult of the Person," Stephen P. Frank and Mark D. Steinberg, eds., *Cultures in Flux. Lower-Class Values, Practices, and Resistance in Late Imperial Russia* (Princeton, 1996), 174.

37. Ibid., 157.

38. Mark D. Steinberg, "The Injured and Insurgent Self: The Moral Imagination of Russia's Lower Class Writers," Reginald E. Zelnik, ed., *Workers and Intelligentsia in Late Imperial Russia*, 313 and 320–21.

39. This kind of moralism was particularly apparent in popular literature about rural migrants to cities. See James von Geldern, "Life In-Between: Migration and Popular Culture in Late Imperial Russia," *RR* 55 (July 1996): 365–83.

40. G.R. Swain, "Freedom of Association and the Trade Unions, 1906–14," Olga Crisp and Linda Edmondson, eds., *Civil Rights in Imperial Russia* (Oxford, 1989), 179–80.

41. *RV*, no. 286 (12 December 1913), 5.

42. Alice K. Pate, "St. Petersburg Workers and Implementation of the Social Insurance Law of 1912," Susan P. McCaffray and Michael Melancon, eds., *Russia in the European Context, 1789–1914. A Member of the Family* (New York, 2005), 190–91.

43. A.K. Tsvertkov-Prosveshchenskii, *Mezhdu dvumia revoliutsiiami (1907–1916 gg.)* (Moscow, 1957), 84.

44. *MV*, no. 207 (7 [20] September 1913), 2–3.

45. *Trudy Tsentral'nogo statisticheskogo upravleniia*, vol. vii, *vyp.* 1. *Statisticheskii sbornik za 1913–1917 gg.* (Moscow, 1921), 306.

46. *RV*, no. 154 (5 July 1913), 2.

47. Pate, 194 and 198. For a different view of the relationship between the insurance boards and the Bolsheviks, see the memoir by the Social Democratic worker A.K. Tsvetkov-Prosveshchenskii cited above, 81–86.

48. William Rosenberg, "Representing Workers and the Liberal Narrative of Modernity," Reginald E. Zelnik, ed. *Workers and Intelligentsia in Late Imperial Russia*, 233 and 238–40.

49. Robert B. McKean, *St. Petersburg Between the Revolutions. Workers and Revolutionaries, June 1907–February 1917* (New Haven and London, 1990), 134–35.

50. A.P. Korelin, ed., *Rossiia 1913 god. Statistiko-dokumental'nyi spravochnik* (St. Petersburg, 1995), 370–75.

51. Caspar Ferenczi, "Freedom of the Press under the Old Regime, 1905–1914," Crisp and Edmondson, eds., *Civil Rights in Imperial Russia*, 191–214.

52. Louise McReynolds, *The News Under Russia's Old Regime. The Development of a Mass-Circulation Press* (Princeton, 1991), 162–66.

53. Ibid., 155–59.

54. Ibid., 224–31.

55. Ibid., 239.

56. Page Herrlinger, *Working Souls. Russian Orthodoxy and Factory Labor in St. Petersburg, 1881–1917* (Bloomington, 2007), 92–97.

57. Ibid., 201–2 and 221–25.

58. *RV*, no. 89 (18 April 1913), 4.

59. Herrlinger, 231–34.

60. Mark D. Steinberg, *Proletarian Imagination, Self, Modernity and the Sacred in Russia, 1910–1925* (Ithaca and London, 2002), 225–28.

61. Edward E. Roslof, *Red Priests. Renovationism, Russian Orthodoxy, and Revolution, 1905–1946* (Bloomington, 2002), 5. See also Simon Dixon, "The Church's Social Role in St. Petersburg, 1880–1914," Geoffrey A. Hosking, ed., *Church, Nation, and State in Russia and Ukraine* (Edmonton, 1990), 167–92.

62. Michael Hamm, "Continuity and Change in Late Imperial Kiev," Hamm, ed., *The City in Late Imperial Russia* (Bloomington, 1986), 99.

63. Michael Hamm, "Introduction," Hamm, ed., *The City in Late Imperial Russia* (Bloomington, 1986), 5.

64. Robert W. Thurston, *Liberal City, Conservative State. Moscow and Russia's Urban Crisis, 1906–1914* (Oxford, 1987), 61.

65. *RV*, no. 43 (21 February 1913), 5.

66. Ibid., no. 59 (12 March 1913), 3 and no. 65 (19 March 1913), 4.

67. Ibid., no. 61 (14 March 1913), 6.

68. Ibid., no. 71 (27 March 1913), 3; no. 102 (4 May 1913), 5; no. 103 (5 May 1913), 5; no. 108 (11 May 1913), 7; no. 147 (27 June 1913), 2; no. 171 (25 July 1913), 3; no. 216 (19 September 1913), 4.

69. Ibid., no. 152 (3 July 1913), 3.

70. Thurston, 68 and 75.

71. Blair A. Ruble, *Second Metropolis. Pragmatic Pluralism in Gilded Age Chicago, Silver Age Moscow, and Meiji Osaka* (Cambridge, 2001), 6–21.

72. I.S. Rozental', *Moskva na pereput'e. Vlast' i obshchestvo v 1905–1914 gg.* (Moscow, 2004), 34–37.

73. Thurston, 133–36.

74. Ibid., 163–64.

75. Gary Thurston, "The Impact of Russian Popular Theater, 1886–1915," *JoMH* 55 (June 1983): 238–41 and 267. Also see Murray Frame, *School for Citizens. Theater and Civil Society in Imperial Russia* (New Haven and London, 2006) for a sustained discussion of the role of theater in fostering individual self-consciousness and civic awareness.

76. *RV*, no. 83 (13 April 1913), 3.

77. Rozental', 124–26.

78. Robert Thurston, 122–26.

79. *RV*, no. 210 (11 September 1913), 4.

80. Ibid., No. 217 (20 September 1913), 2.

81. Ibid., no. 220 (25 September 1913), 2–3 and 5.

82. Ibid., no. 224 (29 September 1913), 6.

83. Ibid., no. 234 (11 October 1913), 4.

84. Ruble, 266–67.

85. Robert Thurston, 139–43.

86. Ruble, 267 and 272.

87. Robert Thurston, 159.

88. Ibid., 126–27.

89. Ibid., 8.

90. I.I. Tolstoi, *Dnevniki, 1906–1916* (St. Petersburg, 1997), 452 and 464.

91. Robert Thurston, 158.

92. Frederick W. Skinner, "Odessa and the Problem of Urban Modernization," Michael Hamm, ed., *The City in Late Imperial Russia*, 235–36.

93. Hamm, "Continuity and Change in Late Imperial Kiev," ibid., 100.

94. Haimson, "'The Problem of Political and Social Stability in Urban Russia on the Eve of War and Revolution' Revisited," 852.

95. Evel G. Economakis, *From Peasant to Petersburger* (Basingstoke and New York, 1998), 130.

96. See the study by Susan Morrissey, *Suicide and the Body Politic in Imperial Russia* (Cambridge, 2006).

97. *RV*, no. 74 (30 March 1913), 3 and no. 85 (12 April 1913), 2.

98. Ibid., no. 117 (22 May 1913), 5.

99. Adele Lindenmeyr, "Voluntary Associations and the Russian Autocracy: The Case of Private Charity," The Carl Beck Papers in Russian and East European Studies, no. 807 (Pittsburgh, 1990), 36–40.

100. Adele Lindenmeyr, *Poverty is Not a Vice. Charity, Society and the State in Imperial Russia* (Princeton, 1996), 162–63.

101. Bradley, "Voluntary Associations, Civic Culture and *Obshchestvennost'* in Moscow," 147.

102. Lindenmeyr, "Voluntary Associations and the Russian Autocracy," 42.

103. Bradley, "Voluntary Associations, Civic Culture and *Obshchestvennost'* in Moscow," 147.

104. Lindenmyer, *Poverty is Not a Vice*, 211.

105. *MV*, no. 28 (2 [15] February 1913), 3.

106. Lutz Häfner, "'The Temple of Idleness': Associations and their Public Sphere in Provincial Russia. A Case Study of Saratov, 1800–1917," McCaffray and Melancon, eds., *Russia in the European Context*, 143.

107. A.N. Zorin et al., eds., *Ocherki rodskogo byta dorevoliutsionnogo Povolzh'ia* (Ul'ianovsk, 2000), 423–31.

108. Ibid., 417–20.

109. Ibid., 455–63.

110. Ibid., 44.

111. William Wagner, *Marriage, Property, and Law in Late Imperial Russia* (Oxford, 1994), 14–15 and 62.

112. Laura Engelstein, *Keys to Happiness: Sex and the Search for Modernity in Fin-de-Siècle Russia* (Ithaca and London, 1992), Chapters 1 and 2.

113. Julia Lise Kinnear, "Childhood, Family and Civil Society in Late Imperial Russia: P.F. Kapterev, the St. Petersburg Parents' Circle and Family Education, 1884–1914," Ph.D. dissertation, University of Toronto, 2003.

114. Barbara Engel argues that the ideal of domesticity was weak in Russia, but after 1905 liberal progressives advanced a modern version of the family ideal that stressed the role of the mother in scientifically rearing her children. Her view supports Kinnear's findings. Barbara Alpern Engel, "Women and the State," Suny, ed., *The Cambridge History of Russia*, vol. III, 469.

115. Zorin, 491–500.

116. Ibid., 448–49 and 467.

117. Ibid., 520–21.

118. Häfner, 152.

119. Bradley, "Voluntary Associations, Civic Culture and *Obshchestvennost'* in Moscow," 148.

120. Joseph Bradley, *Voluntary Associations in Tsarist Russia. Science, Patriotism, and Civil Society* (Cambridge, Mass., 2009), 256.

121. Häfner, 144.

122. Lindenmeyr, "Voluntary Associations and the Russian Autocracy," 144–45.

123. Von Geldern, 367.

124. Catriona Kelly, "Popular Culture," Nicholas Rzhevsky, ed., *The Cambridge Companion to Modern Russian Culture* (Cambridge, 1998), 155.

125. Engel, 469.

126. Louise McReynolds, *Russia at Play. Leisure Activities at the End of the Tsarist Era* (Ithaca and London, 2003), 90–94.

127. Ibid., 95–98 and 107–8.

128. Ibid., 237–38.

129. Ibid., 155–67.

130. Ibid., 299.

131. Peter A. Frykholm, "Soccer and Social Identity in Pre-Revolutionary Moscow," *JoSpH* 24, no. 2 (Summer 1997): 144 and 149–50.

132. *RV*, no. 279 (4 [17] December 1913), 3.

133. Stephen Lovell, "Between Arcadia and Suburbia: Dachas in Late Imperial Russia," *SR*, 61, no. 1 (Spring 2002): 66–87 and ibid., *Summerfolk. A History of the Dacha, 1710–2000* (Ithaca and London, 2003), esp. 62–116.

134. Korelin, ed., 357–59.

135. Ibid., 361–64.

136. Charles A. Ruud, "Predprinimatel' I.D. Sytin," L.G. Zakharova, Iu.S. Kukushkin, and T. Emmons, eds., *P.A. Zaionchkovskii 1904–1983 gg. Stat'i, publikatsii i vospominaniia o nem* (Moscow, 1998), 378–79.

137. Jeffrey Brooks, "Popular Philistinism and the Course of Russian Modernism," Gary Saul Morson, ed., *Literature and History. Theoretical Problems and Russian Case Studies* (Stanford, 1986), 97–101.

138. Beth Holmgren, *Rewriting Capitalism. Literature and the Market in Late Tsarist Russia and the Kingdom of Poland* (Pittsburgh, 1998), 119.

139. Ibid., 120–31.

140. Ibid., 98.

141. Ibid., 141.

142. Jeffrey Brooks, *When Russia Learned to Read. Literacy and Popular Literature, 1867–1917* (Princeton, 1985), 293–94.

143. Denise J. Youngblood, *The Magic Mirror. Moviemaking in Russia, 1908–1918* (Madison, 1999), 9–11 and 69; Yurii Tsivian, *Early Cinema in Russia and Its Cultural Reception* (London and New York, 1994), 12 and 34.

144. Tsivian, 25.

145. Ibid., 27.

146. Youngblood, 77–81.

147. Gay, 44.

148. Morrisey, 339.

149. *RV* no. 182 (8 August 1913), 2.

150. Leonid Andreev, "Pis'ma o teatre. Pis'mo pervoe," November 1912. Hoover Institution Archives ms., Stanford University, 1 and 9–10.

151. Tsivian, 23.

152. Jay Leyda, *Kino. A History of the Russian and Soviet Film*, 3rd edition (Princeton, 1983), 61.

153. Tsivian, 150.

154. Ibid., 34 and 150.

155. Youngblood, 66–68.

156. Youngblood, 7–8.

157. Ibid., xiii–xiv.

158. Marc Slonim, *Russian Theatre. From the Empire to the Soviets* (New York, 1962), 244 and Yurii Tsivian, "Russia, 1913: Cinema in the Cultural Landscape," Richard Abel, ed., *Silent Film* (New Brunswick, N.J., 1996), 195.

159. Laurence Senelick, "Theater," Rzhevsky, ed., *The Cambridge Companion to Modern Russian Culture*, 274.

160. Laurence Senelick, "Boris Geyer and Cabaretic Playacting," Robert Russell and Andrew Barratt, eds., *Russian Theatre in the Age of Modernism* (New York, 1990), 35–36.

161. McReynolds, *Russia at Play*, 219.

162. Evgenii Kuznetsov, *Iz proshlogo russkoi estrady. Istoricheskie ocherki* (Moscow, 1958), 273–74.

163. Liudmila Tikhvinskaia, *Povsednevnaia zhizn' teatral'noi bogemy Serebrianogo veka. Kabare i teatry miniatiur v Rossii, 1908–1917* (Moscow, 2005), 225.

164. Slonim, 242.

165. Brooks, "Popular Philistinism," 90–110.

166. Richard Stites, *Russian Popular Culture. Entertainment and Society since 1900* (Cambridge, 1992), 12–14 and 16–21.

CHAPTER 4

1. Christine Ruane, *The Empire's New Clothes. A History of the Russian Fashion Industry, 1700–1917* (New Haven and London, 2009), 102.

2. Ibid., 113.

3. Cynthia H. Whittaker, "The Women's Movement during the Reign of Alexander II: A Case Study in Russian Liberalism," *JoMH* 48, supplement to no. 2 (June 1976): 35–69.

4. Richard Stites, *The Women's Liberation Movement in Russia. Feminism, Nihilism and Bolshevism, 1860–1930* (Princeton, 1978), 169.

5. Jane McDermid and Anna Hillyar, *Women and Work in Russia 1880–1930. A Study in Continuity through Change* (London and New York, 1998), 76.

6. Christine Ruane, *Gender, Class, and the Professionalization of Russian City Teachers, 1906–1914* (Pittsburgh, 1994).

7. *MV.*, no. 112 (16 [29] May 1913), 3.

8. McDermid and Hillyar, 82–83.

9. Laura Engelstein, *The Keys to Happiness. Sex and the Search for Modernity in Fin-de-Siècle Russia* (Ithaca and London, 1992), 282.

10. Marcelline J. Hutton, *Russian and West European Women, 1860–1939. Dreams, Struggles and Nightmares* (Oxford, 2001), 95.

11. Stites, 175.

12. *RV*, no 10 (12 January 1913), 2.

13. Ibid., no. 206 (6 September 1913), 2.

14. Ibid., no. 278 (3 December 1913), 6.

15. Ibid., no. 156 (7 July 1913), 4.

16. Ibid., no. 68 (22 May 1913), 1.

17. A.G. Goikhbarg, *Zakon o rasshirenii prav nasledovaniia po zakonu lits zhenskogo pola i prava zavershchaniia rodovykh imenii* (St. Petersburg, 1913), 13–14, 55.

18. Hutton, 119.

19. *RV*, no. 73 (29 March 1913), 2.

20. O.A. Khasbulatova and N.B. Gafizova, *Zhenskoe dvizhenie v Rossii (Vtoraia polovina xix-nachalo xx veka)* (Ivanovo, 2003), 112–40 passim.

21. Hutton, 117.

22. *RV* no. 35 (14 February 1913), 4.

23. Ibid., no. 41 (19 February 1913), 3.

24. Hutton, 85.

25. Ibid., 117.

26. Barbara Alpern Engel, *Between the Fields and the City. Women, Work and Family in Russia, 1861–1914* (Cambridge and New York, 1994), 79, 102, and 104.

27. McDermid and Hillyar, 59.

28. Jane Burbank, *Russian Peasants Go to Court. Legal Culture in the Countryside, 1905–1917* (Bloomington, 2004), 138–39.

29. Corrine Gaudin, *Ruling Peasants. Village and State in Late Imperial Russia* (DeKalb, 2007), 202–4.

30. *MV*, no. 198 (28 August [10 September] 1913), 3.

31. Ibid., no. 245 (24 October [6 November] 1913), 1.

32. Laura Engelstein documents in fine detail the issues arising from the women's movement in prewar Russia. Engelstein, *Keys to Happiness.*

33. Quoted in McDermid and Hillyar, 133.

34. Denise J. Youngblood, *The Magic Mirror. Moviemaking in Russia, 1908–1918* (Madison, 1999), 136.

35. Herman Bernstein, "Preface," Leonid Andreyev, *Katerina* (New York, 1923), vii.

36. *RV*, no. 65 (19 March 1913), 5 and no. 97 (27 April 1913), 3.

37. Cited in Bernstein, viii. Emphasis in original.

38. Mikhail P. Artzybasheff, "Introduction," *Jealousy; Enemies; The Law of the Savage* (New York, 1923), 26.

39. *RV*, no. 248 (27 October 1913), 6.

40. Ibid., no. 273 (27 November 1913), 5.

41. On literacy, schooling, and modernization, see Daniel P. Resnick, ed., *Literacy in Historical Perspective* (Washington, 1983) and John E. Craig, "The Expansion of Education," *Review of Research in Education*, no. 9 (1981): 151–213.

42. Vera Shevzov, *Russian Orthodoxy on the Eve of Revolution* (Oxford, 2004), 36–41.

43. Chris J. Chulos, *Converging Worlds. Religion and Community in Peasant Russia* (DeKalb, 2003), 84–87 and Shevzov, 5, 8–10.

44. Elise Kimerling Wirtschafter, *Social Identity in Imperial Russia* (DeKalb, 1997), 110–11.

45. Boris B. Gorshkov, "Democratizing Habermas: Peasant Public Sphere in pre-Reform Russia," *RH* 31, no. 4 (Winter 2004): 377.

46. Aaron B. Retish, "Introduction," Retish, *Russia's Peasants in Revolution and Civil War. Citizenship, Identity, and the Creation of the Soviet State, 1914–1922* (Cambridge, 2008).

47. Gorshkov, 377–79.

48. *RV*, no. 6 (8 January 1913), 2.

49. Jeffrey Burds, *Peasant Dreams & Market Politics. Labor Migration and the Russian Village, 1861–1905* (Pittsburgh, 1998), 176–77.

50. Semen Maslov, *Kooperatsiia v krest'ianskom khoziaistve* (Leipzig, 1922), 10–15.

51. Ibid., 171–72.

52. Aleksandr Nikolaevich Naumov, "Iz utselevshchikh vospominanii, 1909–1914 gg.," Hoover Institution Archive ms., Stanford University, 1783–84.

53. Sergei Speranskii, "Mestnoe samoupravlenie," *RV*, no. 1 (1 January 1913), Supplement, 37.

54. Charles Timberlake, "The Zemstvo and the Development of a Russian Middle Class," Edith W. Clowes, Samuel D. Kassow, and James L. West, eds., *Between Tsar and People: Educated Society and The Quest for Public Identity in Late Imperial Russia* (Princeton, 1991), 164 and 168.

55. Burds documents the growth of conspicuous consumption among peasants of the Central Industrial Region of the country after the emancipation. Burds, 145–68.

56. Mikhail Novikov, *Iz perezhitogo* (Moscow, 2004), 243.

57. Engel, 82–83 and 123.

58. Robert A. Rothstein, "Death of the Folk Song?" Stephen P. Frank and Mark D. Steinberg, eds., *Cultures in Flux: Lower-Class Values, Practices, and Resistance in Late Imperial Russia* (Princeton, 1996), 108–20.

59. *RV*, no. 70 (24 March 1913), 4.

60. Neil B. Weissman, "Rural Crime in Tsarist Russia: The Question of Hooliganism, 1905–1914," *SR* 37, no. 2 (June 1978): 229–31.

61. Stephen P. Frank, "Confronting the Domestic Other: Rural Popular Culture and Its Enemies in Fin-de-Siècle Russia," Frank and Steinberg, eds., *Cultures in Flux*, 89.

62. *RV*, no. 110 (14 May 1913), 6.

63. Ibid., no. 43 (21 February 1913), 2.

64. Ibid., no. 7 (9 January 1913), 3.

65. Ibid., no. 184 (10 August 1913), 4–5; no. 202 (1 September 1913), 4; no. 204 (4 September 1913), 6.

66. Stephen Frank argued that the educated saw the countryside as "dangerous" and that fear largely motivated their campaign to reform the peasants. Frank, 103.

67. Yanni Kotsonis, *Making Peasants Backward. Agricultural Cooperatives and the Agrarian Question in Russia, 1861–1914* (London and New York, 1999), 97–98.

68. V.I. Gomilevskii, "Nekotoriia vystavki proiskhodskiia v 1913 godu i imevshiia znachenie dlia sel'skago khoziaistva," *Ezhegodnik Glavnago upravleniia zemleustroistva i zemledeliia po Departamentu zemledeliia za 1913* (Petrograd, 1914), 61.

69. David Kerans, *Mind and Labor on the Farm in Black-Earth Russia, 1861–1914* (Budapest and New York, 2001), 162.

70. The following discussion of the problems of peasant husbandry in Russia is based on Kerans, esp. 45–140. He provides the best-informed account of the farming practices of Russian peasants and the limitations of those practices. His book uses Tambov province as the basis for the study, but the practices and habits of work that he identifies were widespread among peasants in other regions.

71. Ibid., 38–40.

72. Ibid., 398–99.

73. *MV*, no. 272 (26 November [9 December] 1913), 3.

74. Gomilevskii, 61.

75. V.N. Volkov, "Agronomicheskii poezd Moskovsko-Kazanskoi zheleznoi dorogi," *Ezhegodnik Glavnago upravleniia zemleustroistva i zemledeliia po Departamentu zemledeliia, 1914*, 414–21.

76. *Ezhegodnik Glavnago upravleniia zemleustroistva i zemledeliia po Departamentu zemledeliia, 1914*, xiii.

77. R.W. Davies, Mark Harrison, and S.G. Wheatcroft, eds., *The Economic Transformaton of the Soviet Union, 1913-1945* (Cambridge, 1994), 107.

78. Ibid., 109.

79. V.G. Tiukavkin, *Velikorusskoe krest'ianstvo i Stolypinskaia agrarnaia reforma* (Moscow, 2001), 175–76.

80. Some have used such global numbers to diminish the achievements of the reform. B.V. Anan'ich, *Vlast' i reformy. Ot samoderzhavnoi k sovetskoi Rossii* (Moscow, 1996), 595.

81. Peter Toumanoff, "Some Effects of Land Tenure Reform on Russian Agricultural Productivity, 1901-1913," *Economic Development and Cultural Change* 32, no. 4 (July 1984): 865–70.

82. N. Valentinov, "Russkaia derevnia i sel'skoe khoziaistvo za period 1906-1917," Hoover Institution Archive ms., Stanford University, 8.

83. K.A. Krivoshein, *A.V. Krivoshein (1857-1921 g.). Ego znachenie v istorii Rossii nachala xx veka* (Paris, 1973), 107–8.

84. Bernard Pares, *My Russian Memoirs* (London, 1931), 223.

85. Tiukavkin, 198.

86. Retish, esp. Chapter 3.

87. *RV*, no. 170 (24 June 1913), 2.

88. *MV*, no. 191 (20 August [2 September] 1913), 1.

89. George Yaney, *The Urge to Mobilize. Agrarian Reform in Russia, 1861-1930* (Urbana, Chicago, and London, 1982), 263; Lazar Volin, *A Century of Russian Agriculture. From Alexander II to Khrushchev* (Cambridge, Mass., 1970), 104.

90. Kotsonis, 62–69.

91. Ibid., 70–74.

92. Judith Pallot, *Land Reform in Russia, 1906-1917. Peasant Responses to Stolypin's Project of Rural Transformation* (Oxford, 1999), 89–90.

93. Gaudin, 162.

94. Jane Burbank, "Legal Culture, Citizenship, and Penal Jurisprudence: Perspectives from the Early Twentieth Century," Peter H. Solomon, Jr., ed., *Reforming Justice in Russia, 1864-1996. Power, Culture and the Limits of Legal Order* (Armonk, 1997), 87.

95. Gaudin, 171 and 207.

96. *RV*, no. 283 (8 December 1913), 5.

97. Ibid., no. 232 (9 October 1913), 2.

98. Kotsonis, 3, 98, 164.

99. *RV*, no. 28 (2 February 1913), 2.

100. Ibid., no. 152 (3 July 1913), 3.

101. Ibid., no. 19 (23 January 1913), 6.

102. A.D. Bilimovich, *Kooperatsiia v Rossii vo vremeni i posle Bol'shevikov* (Moscow, reprint 2005), 52.

103. *RV*, no 180 (4 August 1913), 2.

104. Ibid., no. 177 (1 August 1913), 2.

105. Nikolai Valentinov, "Rossiia v predvoennyia gody, 1908–1913," Hoover Institution Archive ms., Stanford University, 50.

106. Cathy A. Frierson, *All Russia is Burning. A Cultural History of Fire in Late Imperial Russia* (Seattle and London, 2002), 269–70.

107. Countess N.B. Musin Pushkina, "Tak bylo," Hoover Institution Archives ms., Stanford University, 100.

108. Varvara Dolgorukii, "Gone Forever. Some pages from my life in Russia, 1885–1919," Hoover Institution Archives ms., Stanford University, 70.

109. *RV*, no. 147 (27 June 1913), 4.

110. Ibid., no. 160 (12 July 1913), 3.

111. Ibid., no. 167 (20 July 1913), 3.

112. Ibid., no. 168 (21 July 1913), 2.

113. Ibid., no. 141 (20 June 1913), 5.

114. Ibid., no. 245 (24 October 1913), 6.

115. Ibid., no. 227 (3 October 1913), 6.

116. Ibid., no. 223 (10 October 1913), 6.

117. Gaudin, 210.

118. Retish, 2.

119. Burbank, *Russian Peasants Go To Court*, 266.

120. Frederick Starr, "Tsarist Government: The Imperial Dimension," Jeremy R. Azrael, ed., *Soviet Nationality Policies and Practices* (New York, 1978), 3–38.

121. Charles Steinwedel, "To Make a Difference: The Category of Ethnicity in Late Imperial Russian Politics, 1861–1917," David L. Hoffmann and Yanni Kotsonis, eds., *Russian Modernity. Politics, Knowledge, Practices* (Basingstoke and New York, 2000), 71 and 76–77.

122. Marc Raeff, "Patterns of Russian Imperial Policy Toward the Nationalities," Edward Allworth, ed., *Soviet Nationality Problems* (New York, 1971), 30.

123. Willard Sutherland, "Imperial Space: Territorial Thought and Practice in the Eighteenth Century," Jane Burbank, Mark von Hagen, and Anatolyi Remnev, eds., *Russian Empire. Space, People, Power, 1700–1930* (Bloomington and Indianapolis, 2007), 42–43 and 54.

124. Alexei Miller, "The Empire and the Nation in the Imagination of Russian Nationalism," Alexei Miller and Alfred J. Rieber, eds., *Imperial Rule* (Budapest and New York, 2004), 11–13.

125. Andreas Kappeler, *The Russian Empire* (Harlow, 2001), 283.

126. On russification, see Eli Weinerman, "Russification in Imperial Russia: The Search for Homogeneity in the Multinational State," Ph.D. dissertation, Indiana University, 1995.

127. Alexei Miller, *Imperiia Romanovykh i natsionalizm. Esse po metodologii istoricheskogo issledovaniia* (Moscow, 2006), 92.

128. Jane Burbank and Mark von Hagen, "Coming into the Territory: Uncertainty and Empire," Burbank et al., eds., *Russian Empire*, 8–9.

129. Dominic Lieven, *Empire: The Russian Empire and its Rivals* (London, 2000), 275.

130. Burbank and von Hagen, 9 and 23.

131. Rustem Tsiunchuk, "Peoples, Regions, and Electoral Politics: The State Dumas and the Constitution of New Elites," Burbank et al., eds., *Russian Empire*, 384–85.

132. Ibid., 392.

133. For Il'minskii's method and its uses, see Wayne Dowler, *Classroom and Empire. The Politics of Schooling Russia's Eastern Nationalities, 1860–1917* (Montreal and Kingston, 2001), esp. Chapters 2, 4, and 5.

134. Anan'ich, 570.

135. Dowler, 226.

136. See, for example, *RV*, no. 18 (22 January 1913), 3.

137. Ibid., no. 235 (12 October 1913), 6.

138. Ibid., no. 205 (5 September 1913), 3.

139. Dowler, 228.

140. *RV*, no. 283 (8 December 1913), 5.

141. Dowler, 159–60.

142. Anan'ich, 570.

143. "Postanovleniia chetvertogo vserossiiskii s"ezda Ob"edinennago Russkago Naroda v Moskve," *MV*, no. 101 (3 [16] May 1907), 3.

144. Ben-Cion Pinchuk, *The Octobrists in the Third Duma, 1907–1912* (Seattle and London, 1974), 17–18.

145. "Postanovleniia II-go S"ezda 5–11 ianvaria 1906 g. i Programma," *Vtoroi vserossiiskii s"ezd Konstitutsionno-Demokraticheskoi Partii, 5–11 ianvaria 1906 g.* (White Plains, 1986).

146. *RV*, no. 140 (19 June 1913), 5 and no. 161 (13 July 1913), 3.

147. *MV*, no. 233 (10 [23] October 1913), 1.

148. *RV*, no. 45 (23 February 1913), 4.

149. Ibid., no. 120 (26 May 1913), 6.

150. Ibid., no. 48 (27 February 1913), 4.

151. Ibid., no. 80 (6 April 1913), 4.

152. Ibid., no. 137 (15 June), 3.

153. Anan'ich, 567–68.

154. *RV*, no. 100 (1 May 1913), 2.

155. Ibid., no. 105 (8 May 1913), 2.

156. Ibid., no. 194 (23 August 1913), 1.

157. Ibid., no 195 (24 August 1913), 1.

158. Ibid., no. 102 (4 May 1913), 5.

159. Anan'ich, 575.

160. *RV*, no 52 (3 March 1913), 2.

161. *MV*, no. 151 (2 (15) July 1913), 1.

162. Audrey Altstadt-Mirhadi, "Baku. Transformation of a Muslim Town," Michael Hamm, ed., *The City in Late Imperial Russia* (Bloomington, 1986), 304–9.

163. Anders Henriksson, "Riga. Growth, Conflict, and the Limitations of Good Government," ibid., 179–81 and 194–95.

164. *RV*, no. 19 (23 January 1913), 5.

165. Michael Hamm, "Continuity and Change in Late Imperial Kiev," Hamm, ed., *The City in Late Imperial Russia*, 91–98.

166. *RV*, no. 6 (8 January 1913), 3.

167. Ibid., no. 189 (17 August 1913), 5.

168. Ibid., no. 14 (17 January 1913), 3.

169. Ibid., no 6 (8 January 1913), 3.

170. Ibid., no. 70 (24 March 1913), 5 and no. 85 (12 April 1913), 3.
171. Ibid., no. 194 (23 August 1913), 2.
172. Ibid, no. 256 (13 November 1913), 4.
173. Ibid., no. 294 (21 December 1913), 4.
174. Ibid., no. 275 (29 November 1913), 4.
175. Ibid., no. 89 (18 April 1913), 4.
176. Ibid., no. 154 (5 July 1913), 1 and 3.
177. Ibid., no 120 (26 May 1913), 4 and no. 147 (27 June 1913), 3.
178. Ibid., no. 199 (29 August 1913), 3.
179. Ibid., no. 20 (24 January 1913), 3.
180. Ibid., no. 25 (30 January 1913), 3.
181. Ibid., no. 58 (10 March 1913), 5.
182. *MV*, no. 40 (17 February [2 March] 1913), 3.
183. *RV*, no. 154 (5 July 1913), 4.
184. Ibid., no. 261 (12 November 1913), 5.
185. Ibid., no. 65 (19 March 1913), 4.
186. Ibid., no. 170 (24 July 1913), 4.
187. Ibid., no. 248 (27 October 1913), 8.
188. Ibid., no. 214 (17 September 1913), 4–5 and no. 216 (19 September 1913), 2.
189. On the Beiliss trial, see A.S. Tager, *The Decay of Czarism. The Beiliss Trial* (Philadelphia, 1935); Maurice Samuel, *Blood Accusation* (London, 1966); and Orlando Figes, *A People's Tragedy. The Russian Revolution, 1891–1924* (London, 1997), 242–45.
190. *RV*, no. 220 (25 September 1913), 4.
191. Ibid., no. 217 (20 September 1913), 3.
192. Ibid., no. 224 (29 September 1913), 5.
193. Ibid., no. 262 (13 November 1913), 7.
194. Ibid., no. 269 (21 November 1913), 5.
195. Ibid., no. 266 (17 November 1913), 2.
196. Ernest Gellner, *Conditions of Liberty. Civil Society and Its Rivals* (London, 1994), 104–5.

CHAPTER 5

1. A.A. Kizevetter, *Na rubezhe dvukh stoletii (vospominaniia 1881–1914)* (Prague, 1929, reprint 1974), 522.
2. Leopold Haimson, "The Problem of Social Stability in Urban Russia, 1905–1917," Pt. 2, *SR* 24, no. 1 (March 1965): 2.
3. *RV*, no. 140 (19 July 1913), 2 and no. 143 (22 June 1913), 2.
4. Ibid., no. 63 (16 March 1913), 2; no. 129 (6 June 1913), 1; no. 163 (16 July 1913), 2.
5. For details of the massacre and its subsequent reporting and investigation, see Michael Melancon. *The Lena Goldfields Massacre and the Crisis of the Late Tsarist State* (College Station, Tex., 2006).
6. Leopold H. Haimson, "The Workers' Movement After Lena. The Dynamics of Labor Unrest in the Wake of the Lena Goldfields Massacre (April 1912–July 1914)," *Russia's Revolutionary Experience. Two Essays, 1905–1917* (New York, 2005), 142–45.
7. *MV*, no 136 (14 [27] June 1913), 1.

8. *RV*, no. 14 (17 January 1913), 3; no. 16 (19 January 1913), 1; no. 52 (3 March 1913), 1; no. 131 (8 June 1913), 1.

9. A.P. Korelin, ed., *Rossiia 1913 god. Statistiko-dokumental'nyi spravochnik* (St. Petersburg, 1995), 227–28.

10. V.A. Maklakov, "Vlast' i obshchestvennost' na zakate Staroi Rossii (Vospominaniia)," supplement to *Illiustrirovannaia Rossiia*, n.d., 559.

11. On the quality of some debate in the Duma and the obstruction of bills for ideological or tactical reasons, see A.A. Oznobishin, *Vospominaniia chlena iv-oi gosudarstvennoi dumy* (Paris, 1927), 198–201 and 207.

12. A. Tyrkova-Vil'iams, *Na putiakh k svobode* (New York, 1952), 384.

13. Bernard Pares, *My Russian Memoirs* (London, 1931), 228.

14. Nicholas de Basily, *Memoirs* (Stanford, 1973), 69–71. Also see M.N. Luk'ianov, "V ozhidanii katastrofy: eskhatologicheskie motivy v russkom konservatizme nakanune pervoi mirovoi voiny," *RH* 31, no. 4 (Winter 2004), 435, who argues that rightists saw the Duma as a link between tsar and people and a forum for nationalist ideals.

15. Richard S. Wortman, *Scenarios of Power: Myth and Ceremony in Russian Monarchy*. Vol. 2, *From Alexander II to the Abdication of Nicholas II* (Princeton, 2000), 322.

16. *RV*, no. 77 (3 April 1913), 2.

17. Wortman, 398.

18. D.C.B. Lieven, *Russia and the Origins of the First World War* (London, 1983), 58–60.

19. A.V. Ignat'ev, *Vneshniaia politika Rossii, 1907–1914* (Moscow, 2000), 41.

20. On Russia's foreign policy before World War I, see Ignat'ev and Lieven.

21. Lieven, 45.

22. William C. Fuller, Jr., *Civil-Military Conflict in Imperial Russia, 1881–1914* (Princeton, 1985), 221.

23. Ibid., 199–203 and 227.

24. W.E. Mosse, "Bureaucracy and Nobility in Russia at the End of the Nineteenth Century," *HJ* 3, no. 24 (1981): 605–28.

25. Elise Kimerling Wirtschafter, *Social Identity in Imperial Russia* (DeKalb, 1997), 38–39.

26. Ignat'ev, 32–33.

27. Illarion Sergeevich Vasil'chikov, "Moe naznachenie Gubernskim Predvoditelem Dvorianstva Kovenskoi Gubernii," Bakhmeteff Archive ms., Columbia University. Through various measures the Duma succeeded in raising the budget for the army and navy from 24.8% of state expenditure in 1909 to 28.5% in 1913. Fuller, 227.

28. Fuller, 166 and 195.

29. Ibid., 249–57.

30. See, for example, *RV*, no. 160 (12 July 1913), 1–2.

31. Ibid., no. 300 (31 December 1913), 2–3.

32. Judith Pallot, "The Stolypin Land Reform as 'Administrative Utopia': Images of Peasantry in Nineteenth-Century Russia," Madhavan K. Palat, ed., *Social Identities in Revolutionary Russia* (Basingstoke, 2002), 117–18. Also see George Yaney, *The Urge to Mobilize. Agrarian Reform in Russia, 1861–1930* (Urbana, Chicago, and London, 1982), 358–59.

33. V.S. Diakin, *Burzhuaziia, dvorianstvo i tsarizm v 1911–1914 gg.* (Leningrad, 1988), 115.

34. B.V. Anan'ich, *Vlast' i reformy. Ot samoderzhavnoi k sovetskoi Rossii* (Moscow, 1996), 558.

35. Diakin, 112–13.

36. As of 4 October 1913 the ministries had submitted 443 legislative projects for consideration by the Duma. Of them 366 went before the Duma prior to the summer recess, and the Duma secretariat during the recess approved the remaining 77 for discussion in the second session. *RV*, no. 233 (10 October 1913), 3.

37. Ibid., no. 248 (14 December 1913), 2.

38. Paul Miliukov, *Political Memoirs, 1905–1917* (Ann Arbor, 1967), 268.

39. *RV*, no. 1 (1 January 1914), Supplement, 76.

40. Ibid., no. 236 (13 October 1913), 2.

41. Basily, 69–71.

42. M.M. Kovalevskii, "Vospominaniia M.M. Kovalevskogo," *ISSSR*, no. 5 (1960): 86.

43. Neil B. Weissman, *Reform in Tsarist Russia. The State Bureaucracy and Local Government, 1900–1914* (New Brunswick, N.J., 1981) 203–4; Anan'ich, 600–601.

44. Korelin, ed., 155.

45. John Shelton Curtiss, *Church and State in Russia. The Last Years of the Empire, 1900–1917* (New York, 1940), 296–99.

46. Ibid., 351–53.

47. *RV*, no. 229 (5 October 1913), 1.

48. Anan'ich, 583.

49. Iu.A. Reent, *Obshchaia i politicheskaia politsiia v Rossii (1900–1917 g.)* (Riazan', 2001), 145. On policing in Russia, also see Jonathan W. Daly, *The Watchful State. Security Police and Opposition in Russia, 1906–1917* (DeKalb, 2004), from which this discussion is drawn.

50. *RV*, no. 240 (18 October 1913), 3.

51. Frederick W. Skinner, "Odessa and the Problem of Urban Modernization," Michael Hamm, ed., *The City in Late Imperial Russia* (Bloomington, 1986), 226.

52. Michael F. Hamm, "The Breakdown of Urban Modernization: A Prelude to the Revolutions of 1917." Michael F. Hamm, ed., *The City in Russian History* (Lexington, 1976), 183.

53. *RV*, no. 228 (4 October 1913), 2.

54. F.V. Shlippe, "Memoirs," Bakhmeteff Archive ms., Columbia University, 116–17.

55. *Ezhegodnik Glavnago upravleniia zemleustroistva i zemledeliia po Departamentu zemledeliia za 1913 g.* (Petrograd, 1914), cxxv.

56. *RV*, no. 282 (7 December 1913), 3.

57. V.I. Gomilevskii, "Nekotoriia vystavki proiskhodskiia v 1913 godu i imevshiia znachenie dlia sel'skago khoziaistva," *Ezhegodnik Glavnago upravleniia*, 61.

58. Glavnoe Upravlenie zemleustroistva i zemledeliia, *Obzor deiatel'nosti za 1913 god* (Petrograd, 1915), 107.

59. Ibid., xvii–xviii.

60. Kerans, 421–22.

61. Mary Schaeffer Conroy, "P.A. Stolypin, Marxists, and Liberals versus Owners of Pharmacies and Pharmaceutical Firms in Late Imperial Russia," Mary Schaefer Conroy, ed., *Emerging Democracy in Late Imperial Russia* (Boulder, 1998), 130–33.

62. G.E. Rein, *Iz perezhitogo, 1907–1918*, vol. 2 (Berlin, n.d.), 31–33.

63. Ibid., vol. 1 (Berlin, 1935), 183–85, 193, and 197.

64. Ibid., 187–92.

65. *RV*, no. 128 (5 June 1913), 3.

66. John F. Hutchinson, "Politics and Medical Professionalization after 1905," Harley D. Balzer, ed., *Russia's Missing Middle Class. The Professions in Russian History* (Armonk, 1996), 104.

67. *RV*, no. 97 (27 April 1913), 2.

68. W.E. Butler, "Civil Rights in Russia: Legal Standards in Gestation," Olga Crisp and Linda Edmondson, eds., *Civil Rights in Imperial Russia* (Oxford, 1989), 6–10.

69. Brian L. Levin-Stankevich, "The Transfer of Legal Technology and Culture: Law Professionals in Tsarist Russia," Balzer, ed., *Russia's Missing Middle Class*, 228–30 and 233–37.

70. Fuller, 121–28 and 185.

71. *RV*, no. 195 (24 August 1913), 2; no. 197 (27 August 1913), 2; and no. 209 (10 September 1913), 2.

72. Butler, 3.

73. William G. Wagner, "Civil Law, Individual Rights, and Judicial Activism in Late Imperial Russia," Peter H. Solomon, Jr., ed., *Reforming Justice in Russia, 1864–1996. Power, Culture, and the Limits of Legal Order* (Armonk, 1997), 22–25; ibid., "Ideology, Identity, and the Emergence of a Middle Class," Edith W. Clowes, Samuel D. Kassow, and James L. West, eds., *Between Tsar and People: Educated Society and The Quest for Public Identity in Late Imperial Russia* (Princeton, 1991), 149.

74. Harley D. Balzer, "Introduction," Balzer, ed., *Russia's Missing Middle Class*, 6–8.

75. Hutchinson, 92.

76. Harley Balzer notes, for example, the movement of engineering professionals between private and state activity from the 1860s onward. Harley D. Balzer, "The Engineering Profession in Tsarist Russia," Balzer, ed., *Russia's Missing Middle Class*, 57.

77. Jonathan Coopersmith, *The Electrification of Russia, 1880–1926* (Ithaca and London, 1992), 40, 42, 87–88.

78. Scott W. Palmer, *Dictatorship of the Air. Aviation Culture and the Fate of Modern Russia* (Cambridge, 2006), 54–55.

79. Gregory Vitabaro, "Military Aviation, National Identity, and the Imperatives of Modernity in Late Imperial Russia," Eric Lohr and Marshall Poe, eds., *The Military and Society in Russia* (London and Boston, 2002), 273–83. Some zemstvos were approached by society members to vote public money to the fund. The matter was controversial among zemstvo representatives. *MV*, n. 17 (20 January [2 February] 1913), 3.

80. Palmer, 15.

81. Ibid., 24.

82. Von Hardesty, "Early Flight in Russia," Robin Higham et al., eds., *Russian Aviation and Air Power in the Twentieth Century* (London and Portland, Ore., 1998), 22–25.

83. Ivan Stenbock-Fermor, "Memoirs," Hoover Institution Archives ms., Stanford University, 107.

84. Palmer, 56 and Hardesty, 25.

85. Hardesty, 26.

86. A.A. Bessolytsin, *Stanovlenie predprinimatel'skikh organizatsii v Povol'zhe (konets xix-nachalo xx veka)* (Volgograd, 2004), 255–59.

87. Richard Pipes, *Struve. Liberal on the Right* (Cambridge, Mass., 1980), 182.

88. *R.V.*, no. 241 (19 October 1913), 2 and no. 246 (25 October 1913), 1–2.

89. Ibid., no. 212 (13 September 1913), 4.

90. Joseph Bradley, "Russia's parliament of public opinion: association, assembly,

and the autocracy, 1906–1914," Theodore Taranovski, ed., *Reform in Modern Russian History. Progress or Cycle?* (New York, 1995), 219.

91. *RV*, no. 204 (4 September 1913), 4.

92. Ibid., no. 222 (27 September 1913), 2.

93. Ibid., no. 220 (25 September 1913), 3.

94. Bruce F. Adams, *The Politics of Punishment. Prison Reform in Russia, 1830–1917* (DeKalb, 1996), 170–71.

95. Ibid., 174.

96. *RV*, no. 49 (28 February 1913), 4.

97. E. Anthony Swift, *Popular Theater and Society in Imperial Russia* (Berkeley, Los Angeles, and London, 2002), 69 and 179.

98. Joseph Bradley, *Voluntary Associations in Tsarist Russia. Science, Patriotism and Civil Society* (Cambridge, Mass., 2009), 257. He writes, "As was common on the European continent, especially the German and Scandinavian states, many members of learned societies had a dual identity as scientists and naturalists on the one hand and as civil servants on the other." What linked the two identities was a powerful sense of patriotic public service. Ibid.

99. Julia Lise Kinnear, "Childhood, Family and Civil Society in Late Imperial Russia: P.F. Kapterev, the St. Petersburg Parents' Circle and Family Education, 1884–1914," unpublished Ph.D. dissertation, University of Toronto, 2003, 280.

100. Bradley, *Voluntary Associations*, 257.

101. *RV*, no. 273 (27 November 1913), 3 and no. 299 (31 December 1913), 4.

102. Ibid., no. 31 (7 February 1913), 1.

103. Daly, *Watchful State*, 139–42 and ibid., "The Security Police and Politics in Late Imperial Russia," Anna Geifman, ed., *Russia Under the Last Tsar. Opposition and Subversion* (Oxford, 1999), 232–33.

104. *RV*, no. 44 (22 February 1913), 2.

105. N.A. Roubakine, *Qu'est-ce que la Révolution Russe?* (Geneva and Paris, 1917), 224.

106. *RV*, no. 23 (27 January 1913), 3.

107. Ibid., no. 157 (9 July 1913), 2.

108. Ibid., no. 251 (31 October 1913), 6–7.

109. Ibid., no. 2 (3 January 1913), 5.

110. Ibid., no. 288 (14 December 1913), 2.

111. *MV*, no. 113 (17 [30] May 1913), 1.

112. *Alfavitnyi ukazatel' knigam i broshuram, a takzhe nomeram povremmenykh izdanii arest, na kotorye utverzhden sudebnymi ustanovleniami po 15-e aprel'ia 1914 goda* (Petrograd, 1916).

113. *RV*, no. 267 (19 November 1913), 4.

114. Ibid., no. 181 (6 August 1913), 3.

115. Ibid., no. 271 (24 November 1913), 3.

116. Ibid., no. 262 (13 November 1913), 7.

117. Ibid., no. 242 (20 October 1913), 5.

118. Ibid., no. 255 (5 November 1913), 5.

119. Ibid., no. 248 (27 October 1913), 5; no. 250 (30 October 1913), 4; and no. 256 (6 November 1913), 6.

120. Ibid., no. 261 (12 November 1913), 4.

121. Ibid., no. 251 (31 October 1913), 6.

122. On the regulations governing public events and police practices, see Bradley, "Russia's Parliament," 212–36.

123. *RV*, no. 152 (3 July 1913), 3.

124. Ibid., no. 154 (5 July 1913), 1.

125. Ibid., no. 188 (15 August 1913), 4.

126. Ibid., no. 236 (13 October 1913), 2.

127. Ibid., no. 243 (22 October 1913), 7.

128. Ibid., no. 269 (21 November 1913), 7.

129. Ibid., no. 212 (13 September 1913), 5.

130. Ibid., no. 227 (3 October 1913), 3.

131. I.I. Tolstoi, *Dnevniki, 1906–1916* (St. Petersburg, 1997), 453.

132. *RV*, no. 134 (12 June 1913), 5.

133. Ibid., no. 9 (11 January 1913), 3.

134. Daly, "The Security Police and Politics in Late Imperial Russia," 232–33.

135. *RV*, no. 5 (6 January 1913), 1.

136. Ibid., no. 206 (6 September 1913), 3.

137. A.Ia. Avrekh, *Tsarizm i IV Duma, 1912–1914 gg.* (Moscow, 1981), 123.

Chapter 6

1. *RV*, no. 183 (9 August 1913), 1.

2. Paul Vallière, "Theological Liberalism and Church Reform in Imperial Russia," Gregory A. Hosking, ed., *Church, Nation and State in Russia and Ukraine* (Edmonton, 1990), 108–30.

3. W. Bruce Lincoln, *Between Heaven and Hell. The Story of a Thousand Years of Artistic Life in Russia* (New York, 1998), 267–68.

4. Marshall S. Shatz and Judith Zimmerman, trans. and eds., *Signposts: A Collection of Articles on the Russian Intelligentsia* (Irvine, 1986).

5. Vallière, 125.

6. Bernice Glatzer Rosenthal, *New Myth, New World. From Nietzsche to Stalinism* (University Park, Pa., 2002), 59.

7. Joan Neuberger, "When the Word was the Deed: Workers vs. Employers before the Justices of the Peace," Reginald E. Zelnik, ed., *Workers and Intelligentsia in Late Imperial Russia. Realities, Representations, Reflections* (Berkeley, 1999), 292–308.

8. Marc Raeff, "Codification et Droit en Russie Impériale. Quelques remarques comparatives," *Cahiers du monde russe et soviétique* xx, no. 1 (Jan-Mar 1979): 10–11.

9. Andrzej Walicki, *Legal Philosophies of Russian Liberalism* (Oxford, 1987), 384.

10. Richard S. Wortman, *Scenarios of Power: Myth and Ceremony in Russian Monarchy*, vol. 2. *From Alexander II to the Abdication of Nicholas II* (Princeton, 2000), 444–56.

11. P. Bark, "Memoirs," Bakhmeteff Archive ms., Columbia University, Chapter IV, 26.

12. Wortman, *Scenarios of Power*, 398.

13. *Trekhsotletie tsarstvovaniia doma Romanovykh, 1613–1913* (Moscow, 1913), 128.

14. Cited in Richard Wortman, "The 'Russian Style' in Church Architecture as Imperial Symbol after 1881," James Cracraft and Daniel Rowland, eds., *Architectures of Russian Identity, 1500 to the Present* (Ithaca and London, 2003), 115.

15. Ibid., 116.

16. Peter Durnovo, "Memorandum to Nicholas II," Thomas Riha, ed., *Readings in Russian Civilization*, vol. II (Chicago and London, 1964), 469–70.

17. Nathaniel Knight, "Ethnicity, Nationality and the Masses: Narodnost' and Modernity in Imperial Russia," David Hoffmann and Yanni Kotsonis, eds., *Russian Modernity. Politics, Knowledge, Practices* (London and New York, 2000), 44–66.

18. On the Russian right and the nationalities, see Mikhail Luk'ianov, *Rossiiskii konservatizm i reforma, 1907–1914* (Stuttgart, 2006), Chapter III.

19. Ibid., esp. Chapter II, sections 3 and 4.

20. *MV*, no. 300 (31 December 1913 [13 January 1914]), 1.

21. The following discussion of Russian conservative discourse is largely based on Luk'ianov, Chapter IV.

22. *RV*, no. 109 (12 May 1913), 5.

23. Luk'ianov, 184.

24. *RV*, no. 66 (20 May 1913), 3.

25. I.I. Tolstoi, *Dnevniki, 1906–1916* (St. Petersburg, 1997), 431.

26. *RV*, no. 71 (27 March 1913), 2.

27. Ibid., no. 74 (30 March 1913), 4–5.

28. Ibid., no. 90 (19 April 1913), 2.

29. Sergei Podbolotov, "Monarchists Against Their Monarch: The Rightists' Criticism of Tsar Nicholas II," *RH* 31, nos. 1–2 (Spring–Summer 2004): 107.

30. Luk'ianov, 57.

31. Podbolotov, 118–19.

32. Sarah Maza, *The Myth of the French Bourgeoisie. An Essay on the Social Imaginary, 1750–1850* (Cambridge, Mass., 2003), 5.

33. *RV*, no. 260 (10 November 1913), 2–3.

34. Ibid., no. 278 (3 December 1913), 2.

35. Susan P. McCaffray, *The Politics of Industrialization in Tsarist Russia. The Association of Southern Coal and Steel Producers, 1874–1914* (DeKalb, 1996), 201.

36. *RV*, no. 278 (3 December 1913), 2.

37. Maxim Gorky, *Seven Plays of Maxim Gorky*, Alexander Baksky, trans. (New Haven, 1945), 296–352.

38. *MV*, no. 234 (11 [24] October 1913), 1.

39. See Thomas C. Owen, *Dilemmas of Russian Capitalism. Fedor Chizhov and Corporate Enterprise in the Railroad Age* (Cambridge, Mass., 2005).

40. McCaffray, xviii.

41. Richard Pipes, *Struve. Liberal on the Right* (Cambridge, Mass., 1980), 178.

42. James L. West, "The Riabushinsky Circle. *Burzhuaziia* and *Obshchestvennost'* in Late Imperial Russia," Edith W. Clowes, Samuel D. Kassow, and James L. West, eds., *Between Tsar and People: Educated Society and The Quest for Public Identity in Late Imperial Russia* (Princeton, 1991), 48–49.

43. A. Tyrkova-Vil'iams, *Na putiakh k svobode* (New York, 1952), 383.

44. A.Ia. Avrekh, *Tsarizm i IV Duma, 1912–1914 gg.* (Moscow, 1981), 155–58.

45. Stephen P. Frank, "Confronting the Domestic Other: Rural Popular Culture and Its Enemies in Fin-de-Siècle Russia," Stephen P. Frank and Mark D. Steinberg, eds., *Cultures in Flux: Lower-Class Values, Practices, and Resistance in Late Imperial Russia* (Princeton, 1996), 105.

46. *RV*, no. 107 (10 May 1913), 5.

47. Ibid., no. 152 (3 July 1913), 1.

48. K.D. Kavelin, "Vzgliad na russkuiu sel'skuiu obshchinu," *Sobranie sochenenii K.D. Kavelina*, vol. 2 (St. Petersburg, 1898), col. 183.

49. Susan Heuman, *Kistiakovsky. The Struggle for National and Constitutional Rights in the Last Years of Tsarism* (Cambridge, Mass., 1998), 71 and 89.

50. *RV*, no. 252 (1 November 1913), 1.

51. Ibid., no. 257 (7 November 1913), 2.

52. Richard Wortman, "Property Rights, Populism, and Russian Political Culture," Olga Crisp and Linda Edmondson, eds., *Civil Rights in Imperial Russia* (Oxford, 1989), 29–30.

53. Paul Miliukov, *Political Memoirs, 1905–1917* (Ann Arbor, 1967), 20.

54. Mikhail Novikov, *Iz perezhitogo* (Moscow, 2004), 244.

55. Frank, 74–75, 92, and 103.

56. Ibid., 93–98.

57. Gary Thurston, "The Impact of Russian Popular Theater, 1886–1915," *JoMH* 55 (June 1983): 238, 243, 253–54, and 260–67.

58. Evgenii Kuznetsov, *Iz proshlogo russkoi estrady. Istoricheskie ocherki* (Moscow, 1958), 272.

59. Mark D. Steinberg, "Melancholy and modernity: emotional and social life in Russia between the revolutions," *JoSH* 41, no. 4 (Summer 2008): 813–29.

60. Ibid., 819.

61. V.I. Lenin, "The Development of Capitalism in Russia," *Collected Works*, vol. 3 (Moscow, 1960), 545.

62. Ibid., 545–46.

63. Leopold H. Haimson, "Lenin, Martov and the Issue of Power," *Russia's Revolutionary Experience, 1905–1917. Two Essays* (New York, 2005), 15–16.

64. Leon Trotsky, *1905* (New York, 1971), 50.

65. Ibid., 322.

66. V.I. Lenin, "On the Slogan for a United States of Europe," Robert C. Tucker, ed., *The Lenin Anthology* (New York, 1975), 203.

67. Boris I. Kolonitskii, "Antibourgeois Propaganda and Anti-'Burzhui' Consciousness in 1917," *RR* 53, no. 2 (April 1994), 183–96.

68. John Bowlt, *The Silver Age: Russian Art of the Early Twentieth Century and the "World of Art" Group* (Newtonville, 1979), 85. The World of Art (*Mir Iskusstva*) formed at the very end of the nineteenth century. It grew out of an arts and craft movement inspired by Princess Tenisheva's center for fabric and furniture design at her Talashkino estate and Savva Mamontov's arts and crafts studios at his Abramtsevo estate. The World of Art movement combined a fascination with Russian arts and crafts, folklore, and history with openness to new Western influences. Above all it sought to unite the arts into a grand synthesis. The *World of Art* magazine, which for years received a subsidy from the imperial family, celebrated Russian primitivism while at the same time bringing European Art Nouveau and post-Impressionism to a Russian audience.

69. Rosenthal, 3.

70. Fedor Sologub, "O simvolizme Sologuba," Fedor Sologub, *Sobranie sochinenii v shesti tomakh*, vol. 6 (Moscow, 2002), 402 and 404.

71. Jeffrey Brooks, *When Russia Learned to Read. Literacy and Popular Culture, 1861–1917* (Princeton, 1985), Chapter IX.

72. Daniel R. Brown, "The Penny Press and its Readers," Frank and Steinberg, eds., *Cultures in Flux*, 166.

73. Charles Baudelaire, "Le Peinture de la vie moderne," *Oeuvres Complètes*, II (Paris, 1976), 695.

74. Modris Eksteins, *Rites of Spring. The Great War and the Birth of the Modern Age* (Toronto, 1989), xvi.

75. Nina Gur'ianova, *Ol'ga Rozanova i rannii russkii avangard* (Moscow, 2002), 44–45.

76. This brief summary is based on the excellent discussion of Nietzsche's influence on Russian modernism in Rosenthal, 3–12.

77. Ibid., 16.

78. Quoted in L.A. Kolobaeva, *Russkii simvolizm* (Moscow, 2000), 6.

79. Sologub, 407.

80. Georgii Chulkov, "Simvolizm kak mirootnoshenie," Sologub, *Sobranie sochinenii v shesti tomakh*, vol. 6, 561–62.

81. Betty F. Moeller-Sally, "The Theater as Will and Representation: Artist and Audience in Russian Modernist Theater, 1904–1909," *SR* 57, no. 2 (Summer 1998): 357 and 370.

82. *RV*, no. 265 (16 November 1913), 5.

83. John E. Bowlt, "Art," Rzhevsky, ed., *The Cambridge Companion to Modern Russian Culture*, 214–15.

84. Andrey Biely, *St. Petersburg*, John Cournos, trans. (New York, 1959), 72.

85. Camilla Gray, *The Russian Experiment in Art, 1863–1922* (London, 1986), 137–38.

86. Lincoln, 289–90.

87. Jane A. Sharp, "Beyond Orientalism. Russian and Soviet Modernism on the Periphery of Empire," Rosalind P. Blakesley and Susan E. Reid, eds., *Russian Art and the West. A Century of Dialogue in Painting, Architecture, and the Decorative Arts* (DeKalb, 2007), 120.

88. Ann M. Lane, "Bal'mont and Scriabin: The Artist as Superman," Bernice Glatzer Rosenthal, ed., *Nietzsche in Russia* (Princeton, 1986), 209 and 213.

89. Rosenthal, 45.

90. *RV*, no. 265 (16 November 1913), 5.

91. Rosenthal, 44–47.

92. Moeller-Sally, 359–60.

93. Rosenthal, 46.

94. Lincoln, 273.

95. Lane, 209 and 213.

96. Fedor Sologub, "Zalozhniki zhizni," Sologub, *Sobranie p'es*, vol. 2 (St. Petersburg, 2001), 188.

97. Ibid., 199.

98. Ibid.

99. Jenifer Presto, "Unbearable Burdens: Aleksandr Blok and the Modernist Resistance to Progeny and Domesticity," *SR* 63, no. 1 (Spring 2004): 6–25.

100. Gur'ianova, 45.

101. Lincoln, 297.

102. Rosenthal, 39 and 96.

103. Geneviève Cloutier, "Elena Guro: art, spiritualité et cognition," *CSP* xlix, nos.

3–4 (September–December 2007): 260–61.
    104. Joan Neuberger, "Culture Besieged: Hooliganism and Futurism," Frank and Steinberg, eds., *Cultures in Flux*, 190–91.
    105. K. Tomashevsky, "From 'Vladimir Mayakovsky.'" *The Drama Review* 15, no. 4 (Fall 1971): 99–100.
    106. Ewa Bartos and Victoria Nes Kirby, trans. and eds., "Victory over the Sun," ibid., 117.
    107. Ibid., 104.
    108. Ibid., 109.
    109. Bartos and Kirby, trans., 119.
    110. Lincoln, 291–92.
    111. Bartos and Kirby, trans., 110.
    112. Ibid., 115.
    113. Ibid., 121.
    114. Mikhail Matyushin, "Futurism in St. Petersburg," *The Drama Review* 15, no. 4 (Fall 1971): 102.
    115. Tomashevsky, 100.
    116. Moeller-Sally, 364–68.
    117. Chulkov, 562.
    118. Michael Green, "Boris Pronin, Meyerhold and Cabaret: Some Connections and Reflections," Robert Russell and Andrew Barratt, eds., *Russian Theatre in the Age of Modernism* (New York, 1990), 79–81.
    119. George Santayana, *Dominations and Powers: Reflections on Liberty, Society and Government* (New York, 1951), 212.

CONCLUSION

    1. *Trudy Tsentral'nogo statisticheskogo upravleniia* VII, vyp. 1. *Statisticheskii sbornik za 1913—1917 gg.* (Moscow, 1921), 142–45.
    2. For a balanced discussion of the July 1914 strike and the potential for revolution, see Robert B. McKean, *St. Petersburg Between the Revolutions. Workers and Revolutionaries, June 1907–February 1917* (New Haven and London, 1990), 298–317.
    3. Leopold H. Haimson, "The Workers' Movement After Lena. The Dynamics of Labor Unrest in the Wake of the Lena Goldfields Massacre (April 1912–July 1914)," *Russia's Revolutionary Experience. Two Essays, 1905-1917* (New York, 2005), 207 and 229. In his earlier work he argued that in 1914 the polarization between workers and the educated was matched by the divide between educated society and the tsarist regime. Leopold Haimson, "The Problem of Social Stability in Urban Russia, 1905–1917," *SR* 24, no. 1 (March 1965), 2.
    4. Nikolai Valentinov, "Rossiia v predvoennyia gody, 1908–1913," Hoover Institution Archives ms., Stanford University, 11–13.

Bibliography

Archival Sources

Bakhmeteff Archive, Columbia University

Andreevskii, Vladimir M.
Bark, Peter
Shlippe, F.V.
Vasil'chikov, Illarion Sergeevich

Hoover Institution Archives, Stanford University

Andreev, Leonid
Gronskii, P.P.
Kosinskii, V.A.
Musin Pushkina, Countess N.B.
Naumov, A.N.
Stenbock-Fermor, Count Ivan
Tatishchev, Boris Alekseevich
Valentinov, Nikolai [N. Volskii]
Wassiltchikoff, Princess Lydia

Newspapers

Moskovskie vedomosti
Russkie vedomosti

Diaries, Documents, Memoirs, Plays

Alfavitnyi ukazatel' knigam i broshuram, a takzhe nomeram povremmenykh izdanii arest, na ko-torye utverzhden sudebnymi ustanovleniami po 15-e aprel'ia 1914 goda. Petrograd, 1916.
Artzybasheff, Mikhail P. *Jealousy; Enemies; The Law of the Savage.* New York, 1923.
Bartos, Ewa, and Victoria Nes Kirby, trans. and eds. "Victory over the Sun." *The Drama Review* 15, no. 4 (Fall 1971): 107–24.
Basily, Nicholas de. *Memoirs.* Stanford, 1973.
Baudelaire, Charles. "Le Peinture de la vie moderne." *Oeuvres Complètes*, II. Paris, 1976.
Biely, Andrey. *St. Petersburg.* John Cournos, trans. New York, 1959.

Chulkov, Georgii. "Simvolizm kak mirootnoshenie." Fedor Sologub, *Sobranie sochinenii v shesti tomakh*, vol. 6. Moscow, 2002.

Dobroliubov, N.A. "Temnoe tsarstvo." *Izbrannoe*. Moscow, 1970.

Durnovo, Peter. "Memorandum to Nicholas II," Thomas Riha, ed. *Readings in Russian Civilization*, vol. II. Chicago and London, 1964.

Ezhegodnik Glavnago upravleniia zemleustroistva i zemledeliia po Departamentu zemledeliia za 1913 g. Petrograd, 1914.

Ezhegodnik Glavnago upravleniia zemleustroistva i zemledeliia po Departamentu zemledeliia, 1914. Petrograd, 1915.

Glavnoe Upravelenie zemleustroistva i zemledeliia. *Obzor deiatel'nosti za 1913 god.* St. Petersburg, 1915.

Golovina, O.N. "Iubelei Doma Romanovykh, 1613–1913." *Vestnik Khrama—Pamiatnika*, nos. 145–46.

Goikhbarg, A.G. *Zakon o rasshirenii prav nasledovaniia po zakonu lits zhenskogo pola i prava zavershchaniia rodovykh imenii.* St. Petersburg, 1913.

Gomilevskii, V.I. "Nekotoriia vystavki proiskhodskiia v 1913 godu i imevshiia znachenie dlia sel'skago khoziaistva."

Gorky, Maxim. *Seven Plays of Maxim Gorky.* Alexander Baksky, trans. New Haven, 1945.

Herzen, Alexander. *My Past and Thoughts*, vol. vi. Constance Garnett, trans. London, 1927.

Kavelin, K.D. "Vzgliad na russkuiu sel'skuiu obshchinu." *Sobranie sochenenii K.D. Kavelina*, vol. 2. St. Petersburg, 1898.

Kizevetter, A.A. *Na rubezhe dvukh stoletii (vospominaniia 1881–1914).* Prague, 1929, reprint 1974.

Kokovtsov, V.N. *Out of My Past. The Memoirs of Count Kokovtsov.* Stanford, 1935.

Korelin, A.P., ed. *Rossiia 1913 god. Statistiko-dokumental'nyi spravochnik.* St. Petersburg, 1995.

Kovalevskii, M.M. "Vospominaniia M.M. Kovalevskogo." *ISSSR*, no. 5 (1960): 76–100.

Krivoshein, K.A. *A.V. Krivoshein (1857–1921 g.). Ego znachenie v istorii Rossii nachala xx veka.* Paris, 1973.

Kryzhanovskii, S.E. *Vospominaniia.* Berlin, nd.

Lenin, V.I. "The Development of Capitalism in Russia." *Collected Works*, vol. 3. Moscow, 1960.

———. "On the Slogan for a United States of Europe." Robert C. Tucker ed. *The Lenin Anthology.* New York, 1975.

Maklakov, V.A. "Vlast' i obshchestvennost' na zakate Staroi Rossii (Vospominaniia)." Supplement to *Illiustrirovannaia Rossiia*, n.d.

Matyushin, Mikhail. "Futurism in St. Petersburg." *The Drama Review* 15, no. 4 (Fall 1971): 101–5.

Miliukov, Paul. *Political Memoirs, 1905–1917.* Ann Arbor, 1967.

Novikov, Mikhail. *Iz perezhitogo.* Moscow, 2004.

Oznobishin, A.A. *Vospominaniia chlena iv-oi gosudarstvennoi dumy.* Paris, 1927.

Pares, Bernard. *My Russian Memoirs.* London, 1931.

"Postanovleniia II-go s"ezda 5–11 ianvaria 1906 g. i Programma." *Vtoroi vserossiiskii s"ezd Konstitutsionno-Demokraticheskoi Partii, 5–11 ianvaria 1906 g.* White Plains, 1986.

Rein, G.E. *Iz perezhitogo, 1907–1918*, vol. 2. Berlin, n.d.

Rodzianko, M.V. "Krushenie imperii (Zapiski predsedatelia Russkoi Gosudarstvennoi Dumy)." *Arkhiv russkoi revoliutsii* xvii. Berlin, 1926, reprint The Hague, 1970.

Sologub, Fedor. "O simvolizme Sologuba." Fedor Sologub, *Sobranie sochinenii v shesti tomakh*, vol. 6. Moscow, 2002.

———. *Sobranie sochinenii v shesti tomakh*, vol. 6. Moscow, 2002.

———. "Zalozhniki zhizni." *Sobranie p'es*, vol 2. St. Petersburg, 2001.

Tolstoi, I.I. *Dnevniki, 1906–1916*. St. Petersburg, 1997.

Tomashevsky, K. "From 'Vladimir Mayakovsky.'" *The Drama Review* 15, no. 4 (Fall 1971): 93–101.

Trekhsotletie tsarstvovaniia doma Romanovykh, 1613–1913. Moscow, 1913.

Trotsky, Leon. *1905*. New York, 1971.

Trudy Tsentral'nogo statisticheskogo upravleniia, vol. vii, vyp. 1, *Statisticheskii sbornik za 1913–1917*. Moscow, 1921.

Trufanoff, Sergius M. (Iliodor). *Mad Monk of Russia*. New York, 1918.

Tsvetkov-Prosveshchenskii, A.K. *Mezhdu dvumia revoliutsiiami (1907–1916 gg.)*. Moscow, 1957.

Tucker, Robert C., ed. *The Lenin Anthology*. New York, 1975.

Tyrkova-Vil'iams, A. *Na putiakh k svobode*. New York, 1952.

Volkov, V.N. "Agronomicheskii poezd Moskovsko-Kazanskoi zheleznoi dorogi." *Ezhegodnik Glavnago upravleniia zemleustroistva i zemledeliia po Departamentu zemledeliia za 1913*. Petrograd, 1914.

Zaks, B. "Neskol'ko dannykh po statistike russkogo bibliotechnogo dela. (Eksponaty Obshchestva Bibliotekovedeniia na Leipzigoi vystavke 1914 g.)." *Bibliotekar'*, vyp. 3 (1914).

BOOKS AND ARTICLES

Abel, Richard, ed. *Silent Film*. New Brunswick, 1996.

Acton, Edward. *Rethinking the Russian Revolution*. London, 1990.

Adams, Bruce F. *The Politics of Punishment. Prison Reform in Russia, 1830–1917*. DeKalb, 1996.

Aksenov, A.I. *Genealogiia Moskovskogo kupechestva xviii v. Iz istorii formirovaniia russkoi burzhuazii*. Moscow, 1988.

Altstadt-Mirhadi, Audrey. "Baku. Transformation of a Muslim Town," Michael Hamm, ed. *The City in Late Imperial Russia*. Bloomington, 1986.

Anan'ich, B.V. *Vlast' i reformy. Ot samoderzhavnoi k sovetskoi Rossii*. Moscow, 1996.

Atkinson, Dorothy. *The End of the Russian Land Commune, 1905–1930*. Stanford, 1983.

Atkinson, Dorothy, Alexander Dallin, and Gail Warshofsky Lapidus, eds. *Women in Russia*, Stanford, 1977.

Avrekh, A.Ia. *Tsarizm i IV Duma, 1912–1914 gg.* Moscow, 1981.

Bailes, Kendall. "Reflections on Russian Professions." Harley D. Balzer, ed. *Russia's Missing Middle Class. The Professions in Russian History*. Armonk, 1996, 39–54.

Balzer, Harley D. "Conclusion. Russia's Missing Middle Class." Harley D. Balzer, ed. *Russia's Missing Middle Class. The Professions in Russian History*. Armonk, 1996.

———. "The Engineering Profession in Tsarist Russia." Harley D. Balzer, ed. *Russia's Missing Middle Class. The Professions in Russian History*. Armonk, 1996, 55–88.

———. "Introduction." Harley D. Balzer, ed. *Russia's Missing Middle Class. The Professions in Russian History*. Armonk, 1996.

Balzer, Harley D., ed. *Russia's Missing Middle Class. The Professions in Russian History*. Armonk, 1996.

Bater, James, "Between Old and New. St. Petersburg in the Late Imperial Era." Michael Hamm, ed. *The City in Late Imperial Russia*. Bloomington, 1986.

Becker, Seymour. *Nobility and Privilege in Late Imperial Russia*. DeKalb, 1985.

Bernstein, Herman. "Preface." Leonid Andreyev. *Katerina*. New York, 1923.

Bessolitsyn, A.A. *Stanovlenie predprinimatel'skikh organizatsii v Povol'zhe (konets xix-nachalo xx veka)*. Volgograd, 2004.

Bhat, Girish N. "The Consensual Dimension of Late Imperial Russian Criminal Procedure: The Example of Trial by Jury." Peter H. Solomon, ed. *Reforming Justice in Russia*. Armonk, 1997.

Bilimovich, A.D. *Kooperatsiia v Rossii vo vremeni i posle Bol'shevikov*. Moscow, 2005 reprint.

Blackbourn, David, and Geoff Eley. *The Peculiarities of German History. Bourgeois Society and Politics in Nineteenth-Century Germany*. Oxford, 1984.

Blakesley, Rosalind P., and Susan E. Reid, eds. *Russian Art and the West. A Century of Dialogue in Painting, Architecture, and the Decorative Arts*. DeKalb, 2007.

Bokhavov, Aleksandr. "Hopeless Symbiosis: Power and Right-Wing Radicalism at the Beginning of the Twentieth Century." Anna Geifman, ed. *Russia Under the Last Tsar. Opposition and Subversion, 1894–1917*. Oxford, 1999, 199–213.

Bonnell, Victoria E. *Roots of Rebellion: Workers' Politics and Organizations in St. Petersburg and Moscow, 1900–1914*. Berkeley, 1983.

Bovykin, B.V. "Predislovie." Iu.A. Petrov. *Kommercheskie banki Moskvy. Konets xix v.— 1914 gg*. Moscow, 1995.

Bowlt, John. "Art." Nicholas Rzhevsky, ed. *The Cambridge Companion to Modern Russian Culture*. Cambridge, 1998.

———. *The Silver Age, Russian Art of the Early Twentieth Century and the "World of Art" Group*. Newtonville, 1979.

Bradley, Joseph. "Moscow. From Village to Metropolis." Michael F. Hamm, ed. *The City in Late Imperial Russia*. Bloomington, 1986.

———. *Muzhik and Muscovite: Urbanization in Late Imperial Russia*. Berkeley, 1985.

———. "Russia's Parliament of Public Opinion: Association, Assembly, and the Autocracy, 1906–1914." Theodore Taranovski, ed. *Reform in Modern Russian History. Progress or Cycle?* New York, 1995, 212–36.

———. "Subjects into Citizens: Civil Society and Autocracy in Tsarist Russia." *AHR* 107, no. 4 (October 2002): 1094–1123.

———. "Voluntary Associations, Civic Culture and *Obshchestvennost'* in Moscow." Edith W. Clowes, Samuel D. Kassow, and James L. West, eds. *Between Tsar and People. Educated Society and the Quest for Public Identity in Late Imperial Russia*. Princeton, 1991, 131–48.

———. *Voluntary Associations in Tsarist Russia. Science, Patriotism, and Civil Society*. Cambridge, Mass., 2009.

Brooks, Jeffrey. "Popular Philistinism and the Course of Russian Modernism." Gary Saul Morson, ed. *Literature and History. Theoretical Problems and Russian Case Studies*. Stanford, 1986, 90–110.

———. *When Russia Learned to Read. Literacy and Popular Literature, 1861–1917*. Princeton, 1985.

Brower, Daniel R. "Urban Revolution in the Late Russian Empire." Michael Hamm, ed. *The City in Late Imperial Russia*. Bloomington, 1986, 319–53.

———. "Urban Russia on the Eve of World War One. A Social Profile." *JoSH* 13, no. 3 (Spring 1979): 424–36.

Brown, Daniel R. "The Penny Press and Its Readers." Stephen P. Frank and Mark D. Steinberg, eds. *Cultures in Flux. Lower-Class Values, Practices, and Resistance in Late Imperial Russia.* Princeton, 1996, 145–67.

Brown, Julie V. "Professionalization and Radicalization: Russian Psychiatrists Respond to 1905." Harley D. Balzer, ed. *Russia's Missing Middle Class. The Professions in Russian History.* Armonk, 1996, 143–67.

Burbank, Jane. "Legal Culture, Citizenship, and Penal Jurisprudence: Perspectives from the Early Twentieth Century." Peter H. Solomon, Jr., ed. *Reforming Justice in Russia, 1864–1996. Power, Culture, and the Limits of Legal Order.* Armonk, 1997, 82–106.

———. *Russian Peasants Go to Court. Legal Culture in the Countryside, 1905–1917.* Bloomington, 2004.

Burbank, Jane and Mark von Hagen. "Coming into the Territory: Uncertainty and Empire." Jane Burbank, Mark von Hagen, and Anatolyi Remnev, eds. *Russian Empire. Space, People, Power, 1700–1930.* Bloomington and Indianapolis, 2007.

Burbank, Jane, Mark von Hagen, and Anatolyi Remnev, eds. *Russian Empire. Space, People, Power, 1700–1930.* Bloomington and Indianapolis, 2007.

Burds, Jeffrey. *Peasant Dreams & Market Politcs. Labor Migration and the Russian Village, 1861–1905.* Pittsburgh, 1998.

Butler, W.E. "Civil Rights in Russia: Legal Standards in Gestation." Olga Crisp and Linda Edmondson, eds. *Civil Rights in Imperial Russia.* Oxford, 1989.

Caporaso, James A., ed. *The Elusive State. International and Comparative Perspectives.* Newbury Park, London, New Delhi, 1989.

Carstensen, Fred V. "Foreign Participation in Russian Economic Life: Notes on British Enterprise, 1865–1914." Gregory Guroff and Fred V. Carstensen, eds. *Entrepreneurship in Imperial Russia and the Soviet Union.* Princeton, 1983.

Chermenskii, E.D. *IV gosudarstvennaia duma i sverzhenie tsarizma v Rossii.* Moscow, 1976.

Chulos, Chris J. *Converging Worlds. Religion and Community in Peasant Russia, 1861–1917.* DeKalb, 2003.

Cloutier, Geneviève. "Elena Guro: art, spiritualité et cognition." *CSP* xlix, nos. 3–4 (September–December 2007): 255–72.

Clowes, Edith W., Samuel D. Kassow, and James L. West, eds. *Between Tsar and People: Educated Society and The Quest for Public Identity in Late Imperial Russia.* Princeton, 1991.

Conroy, Mary Schaeffer. "P.A. Stolypin, Marxists, and Liberals versus Owners of Pharmacies and Pharmaceutical Firms in Late Imperial Russia." Mary Schaeffer Conroy, ed. *Emerging Democracy in Late Imperial Russia.* Boulder, 1998, 112–42.

Conroy, Mary Schaeffer, ed. *Emerging Democracy in Late Imperial Russia.* Boulder, 1998.

Coopersmith, Jonathan. *The Electrification of Russia, 1880–1926.* Ithaca and London, 1992.

Cracraft, James. *The Church Reform of Peter the Great.* London, 1971.

Cracraft, James, and Daniel Rowland, eds. *Architectures of Russian Identity: 1550 to the Present.* Ithaca and London, 2003.

Craig, John E. "The Expansion of Education." *Review of Research in Education*, no. 9 (1981): 151–213.

Crisp, Olga, and Linda Edmondson, eds. *Civil Rights in Imperial Russia.* Oxford, 1989.

Curtiss, John Shelton. *Church and State in Russia.* New York, 1940.

Daly, Jonathan W. "The Security Police and Politics in Late Imperial Russia." Anna Geifman, ed. *Russia Under the Last Tsar: Opposition and Subversion, 1894–1917.* Oxford, 1999, 217–40.

———. *The Watchful State. Security Police and Opposition in Russia, 1906–1917.* DeKalb, 2004.

Davies, R.W., Mark Harrison, and S.G. Wheatcroft, eds. *The Economic Transformation of the Soviet Union, 1913–1945.* Cambridge, 1994.

Demin, V.A. *Gosudarstvennaia Duma Rossii (1907–1917): Mekhanizm funktsionirovaniia.* Moscow, 1996.

Diakin, V.S. *Burzhuaziia, dvorianstvo i tsarizm v 1911–1914 gg.* Leningrad, 1988.

———. *Germanskie kapitaly v Rossii. Elektroindustriia i elektricheskii transport.* Leningrad, 1971.

Dixon, Simon. "The Church's Social Role in St. Petersburg, 1880–1914." Geoffrey A. Hosking, ed. *Church, Nation, and State in Russia and Ukraine.* Edmonton, 1990, 167–92.

Dowler, Wayne. *Classroom and Empire. The Politics of Schooling Russia's Eastern Nationalities, 1860–1917.* Montreal and Kingston, 2001.

Dukes, Paul, *Catherine the Great and the Russian Nobility.* Cambridge, 1967.

Edelman, Robert. *Gentry Politics on the Eve of the Russian Revolution. The Nationalist Party, 1907–1917.* New Brunswick, N.J., 1980.

Edmondson, Linda. "Was there a Movement for Civil Rights in Russia in 1905?" Olga Crisp and Linda Edmondson, eds. *Civil Rights in Imperial Russia.* Oxford, 1989.

Egorov, B.G. "Kooperativnoe dvizhenie v dorevoliutsionnoi Rossii (novyi vzgliad)." *Voprosy istorii,* no. 6 (2005): 3–18.

Eksteins, Modris. *Rites of Spring. The Great War and the Birth of the Modern Age.* Toronto, 1989.

Engel, Barbara Alpern. *Between the Fields and the City. Women, Work and Family in Russia, 1861–1914.* Cambridge and New York, 1994.

———. "Women and the State." Ronald Grigor Suny, ed. *The Cambridge History of Russia,* vol. III, *The Twentieth Century.* Cambridge, 2006.

Engelstein, Laura. "The Dream of Civil Society in Tsarist Russia: Law, State, and Religion." Nancy Bermeo and Philip Nord, eds. *Civil Society before Democracy: Lessons from Nineteenth-Century Europe.* Lanham, 2000, 23–41.

———. *Keys to Happiness: Sex and the Search for Modernity in Fin-de-Siècle Russia.* Ithaca and London, 1992.

Erlich, Victor. *Modernism and Revolution: Russian Literature in Transition.* Cambridge, Mass., 1994.

Evtuhov, Catherine, et al. *A History of Russia. Peoples, Legends, Events, Forces.* Boston and New York, 2004.

Falkus, Malcolm. "Aspects of Foreign Investment in Tsarist Russia." *The Journal of European Economic History* 8, no. 1 (Spring 1979): 5–36.

Ferenczi, Caspar. "Freedom of the Press under the Old Regime, 1905–1914." Olga Crisp and Linda Edmondson, eds. *Civil Rights in Imperial Russia.* Oxford, 1989, 191–214.

Figes, Orlando, *A People's Tragedy. The Russian Revolution 1891–1924.* London, 1997.

Fine, Robert. "Civil Society Theory, Enlightenment and Critique." Robert Fine and Shirin Rai, eds. *Civil Society. Democratic Perspectives.* London and Portland, Ore., 1997, 7–28.

Fine, Robert, and Shirin Rai, eds. *Civil Society. Democratic Perspectives.* London and Portland, Ore., 1997.

Frame, Murray. *School for Citizens. Theater and Civil Society in Imperial Russia.* New Haven and London, 2006.

Frank, Stephen P. "Confronting the Domestic Other: Rural Popular Culture and Its Enemies in Fin-de-Siècle Russia." Stephen P. Frank and Mark D. Steinberg, eds. *Cultures in Flux. Lower-Class Values, Practices, and Resistance in Late Imperial Russia.* Princeton, 1996, 74–107.

Frank, Stephen P., and Mark D. Steinberg, eds. *Cultures in Flux. Lower-Class Values, Practices, and Resistance in Late Imperial Russia.* Princeton, 1996.

Freeze, Gregory L. "Church and Politics in Late Imperial Russia: Crisis and Radicalization of the Clergy." Anna Geifman, ed. *Russia Under the Last Tsar. Opposition and Subversion, 1894–1917.* Oxford, 1999, 269–97.

———. *The Parish Clergy in Nineteenth-Century Russia: Crisis, Reform, Counter-reform.* Princeton, 1983.

———. "The Soslovie (Estate) Paradigm and Russian Social History." *AHR* 91, no. 1 (1986): 11–36.

Frierson, Cathy A. *All Russia is Burning! A Cultural History of Fire in Late Imperial Russia.* Seattle and London, 2002.

———. "Of Red Roosters, Revenge and the Search for Justice: Rural Arson in European Russia in the Late Imperial Era." Peter H. Solomon, Jr., ed. *Reforming Justice in Russia, 1864–1996. Power, Culture and the Limits of Legal Order.* Armonk, 1997, 109–30.

———. *Peasant Icons: Representations of Rural People in Late Nineteenth Century Russia.* New York, 1993.

Frykholm, Peter A. "Soccer and Social Identity in Pre-Revolutionary Moscow." *JoSpH* 24, no. 2 (Summer 1997): 143–54.

Fuller, William C., Jr. *Civil-Military Conflict in Imperial Russia, 1881–1914.* Princeton, 1985.

———. *The Foe Within. Fantasies of Treason and the End of Imperial Russia.* Ithaca and London, 2006.

Gatrell, Peter. *Government, Industry and Rearmament in Russia, 1900–1914. The Last Argument of Tsarism.* Cambridge, 1994.

———. *The Tsarist Economy, 1850–1917.* London, 1986.

Gaudin, Corinne. "'No Place to Lay My Head': Modernization and the Right to Land During the Stolypin Reforms." *SR* 57, no. 4 (Winter 1998): 747–73.

———. *Ruling Peasants. Village and State in Late Imperial Russia.* DeKalb, 2007.

Gay, Peter. *Schnitzler's Century. The Making of Middle-Class Culture, 1815–1914.* London, 2001.

Geifman, Anna, ed. *Russia Under the Last Tsar. Opposition and Subversion, 1894–1917.* Oxford, 1999.

Gellner, Ernest. *Conditions of Liberty. Civil Society and Its Rivals.* London, 1994.

Gerschenkron, Alexander. "Agrarian Policies and Industrialization in Russia, 1861–1917." M.M. Postan, ed. *Cambridge Economic History of Europe*, vol. 6, pt. 2. Cambridge, 1965.

———. *Economic Backwardness in Historical Perspective: A Book of Essays.* Cambridge, Mass., 1962.

Girault, René. *Emprunts russes et investissements français en Russie, 1887–1914.* Paris, 1994.

Glickman, Rose. "The Russian Factory Woman, 1880–1914." Dorothy Atkinson, Alexander Dallin, and Gail Warshofsky Lapidus, eds. *Women in Russia.* Stanford, 1977.

Golub, Spencer. "The Silver Age, 1905–1917." Robert Leach and Victor Borovsky, eds. *A History of Russian Theatre.* Cambridge, 1999.

Gorshkov, Boris B. "Democratizing Habermas: Peasant Public Sphere in pre-Reform Russia." *RH* 31, no. 4 (Winter 2004): 373–85.

———. "Factory Children: An Overview of Child Industrial Labor and Laws in Imperial Russia, 1840–1914." Michael Melancon and Alice K. Pate, eds. *New Labor History. Worker Identity and Experience in Russia, 1840–1918.* Bloomington, 2002.

———. "Toward a Comprehensive Law: Tsarist Factory Labor Legislation in European Context, 1830–1914." Susan P. McCaffray and Michael Melancon, eds. *Russia in the European Context, 1789–1914. A Member of the Family.* New York, 2005.

Gorsuch, Anne. *Youth in Revolutionary Russia. Enthusiasts, Bohemians, Delinquents.* Bloomington and Indianapolis, 2000.

Gray, Camilla. *The Russian Experiment in Art, 1863–1922.* London, 1986.

Green, Michael. "Boris Pronin, Meyerhold and Cabaret: Some Connections and Reflections." Robert Russell and Andrew Barratt, eds. *Russian Theatre in the Age of Modernism.* New York, 1990.

Gregory, Paul R. *Before Command. An Economic History of Russia from Emancipation to the First Five-Year Plan.* Princeton, 1994.

———. "Russian Industrialization and Economic Growth. Results and Perspectives of Western Research." *JfGOE* 25, no. 2 (1977): 200–18.

———. *Russian National Income, 1885–1913.* Cambridge, 1982.

Gur'ianova, Nina. *Ol'ga Rozanova i rannii russkii avangard.* Moscow, 2002.

Häfner, Lutz. "'The Temple of Idleness': Associations and the Public Sphere in Provincial Russia. A Case Study of Saratov, 1800–1917." Susan P. McCaffray and Michael Melancon, eds. *Russia in the European Context, 1789–1914. A Member of the Family.* New York, 2005, 141–60.

Haimson, Leopold H. "Lenin, Martov and the Issue of Power." *Russia's Revolutionary Experience, 1905–1917. Two Essays.* New York, 2005.

———. "'The Problem of Political and Social Stability in Urban Russia on the Eve of War and Revolution' Revisited." *SR* 59, no. 4 (Winter 2000): 848–75.

———. "The Problem of Social Stability in Urban Russia, 1905–1917," *SR* 23, no. 4 (December 1964): 619–42, and 24, no. 1 (March 1965): 1–22.

———. "Russian Workers' Political and Social Identities: The Role of Social Representations in the Interaction between Members of the Labor Movement and the Social Democratic Intelligentsia." Reginald E. Zelnik, ed. *Workers and Intelligentsia in Late Imperial Russia. Realities, Representations, Reflections.* Berkeley, 1999.

———. "The Workers' Movement After Lena. The Dynamics of Labor Unrest in the Wake of the Lena Goldfields Massacre (April 1912–July 1914)." *Russia's Revolutionary Experience. Two Essays, 1905–1917.* New York, 2005.

Halfin, Igal. *From Darkness to Light. Class, Consciousness, and Salvation in Revolutionary Russia.* Pittsburgh, 2000.

Hamburg, G.M. *Politics of the Russian Nobility, 1881–1905.* New Brunswick, N.J., 1985.

———. "The Russian Nobility on the Eve of the 1905 Revolution." *RR* 38, no. 3 (July 1979): 323–38.

Hamm, Michael. "The Breakdown of Urban Modernization: A Prelude to the Revolutions of 1917." Michael Hamm, ed. *The City in Russian History.* Lexington, 1976, 182–200.

———. "Continuity and Change in Late Imperial Kiev." Michael Hamm, ed. *The City in Late Imperial Russia.* Bloomington, 1986.

———, ed. *The City in Late Imperial Russia.* Bloomington, 1986.

———, ed. *The City in Russian History.* Lexington, 1976.

Hardesty, Von. "Early Flight in Russia." Robin Higham et al., eds. *Russian Aviation and Air Power in the Twentieth Century.* London and Portland, Ore., 1998.

Healey, Dan. *Homosexual Desire in Revolutionary Russia. The Regulation of Sexual and Gender Dissent.* Chicago and London, 2001.

Henriksson, Anders. "Riga. Growth, Conflict, and the Limitations of Good Government." Michael Hamm, ed. *The City in Late Imperial Russia.* Bloomington, 1986.

Herrlinger, Page. *Working Souls. Russian Orthodoxy and Factory Labor in St. Petersburg, 1881–1917.* Bloomington, 2007.

Heuman, Susan Eva. *Kistiakovsky. The Struggle for National and Constitutional Rights in the Last Years of Tsarism.* Cambridge, Mass., 1998.

Higham, Robin, et al., eds. *Russian Aviation and Air Power in the Twentieth Century.* London and Portland, 1998.

Hittle, J.M. *The Service City. State and Townsmen in Russia, 1600–1800.* Cambridge, Mass., and London, 1979.

Hoffmann, David L., and Yanni Kotsonis, eds. *Russian Modernity. Politics, Knowledge, Practices.* London and New York, 2000.

Hogan, Heather. *Forging Revolution. Metalworkers, Managers, and the State in St. Petersburg, 1890–1914.* Bloomington and Indianapolis, 1993.

Holmgren, Beth. *Rewriting Capitalism. Literature and the Market in Late Tsarist Russia and the Kingdom of Poland.* Pittsburgh, 1998.

Hosking, Geoffrey A., ed. *Church, Nation, and State in Russia and Ukraine.* Edmonton, 1990.

Hosking, Geoffrey A., and Roberta Thompson Manning. *The Russian Constitutional Experiment. Government and Duma, 1907–1914.* Cambridge, 1973.

———. "What Was the United Nobility?" Leopold H. Haimson, ed. *The Politics of Rural Russia, 1905–1914.* Bloomington and London, 1979.

Hutchinson, John F. *Late Imperial Russia 1890–1917.* London and New York, 1999.

———. "Politics and Medical Professionalization after 1905." Harley D. Balzer, ed. *Russia's Missing Middle Class. The Professions in Russian History.* Armonk, 1996, 89–116.

Hutton, Marcelline J. *Russian and West European Women, 1860–1939. Dreams, Struggles and Nightmares.* Oxford, 2001.

Ignat'ev, A.V. *Vneshniaia politika Rossii, 1907–1914.* Moscow, 2000.

Ioannidore, Anastasia. "The Politics of the Division of Labour: Smith and Hegel on Civil Society." Robert Fine and Shirin Rai, eds. *Civil Society. Democratic Perspectives.* London and Portland, Ore., 1997, 49–62.

Ivanova, N.A. *Promyshlennyi tsentr Rossii, 1907–1914.* Moscow, 1995.

Johnson, Robert E. *Peasant and Proletarian. The Working Class of Moscow in the late Nineteenth Century.* New Brunswick, N.J., 1979.

Kalmykov, Sergei V. "Commercial Education and the Cultural Crisis of the Moscow Merchant Elite." James L. West and Iurii Petrov, eds. *Merchant Moscow. Images of Russia's Vanished Bourgeoisie.* Princeton, 1998, 104–16.

Kappeler, Andreas. *The Russian Empire.* Alfred Clayton, trans. Harlow, 2001.

Kassow, Samuel D. "Professionalism Among University Professors." Harley D. Balzer, ed. *Russia's Missing Middle Class. The Professions in Russian History.* Armonk, 1996, 197–221.

———. "Russia's Unrealized Civil Society." Edith W. Clowes, Samuel D. Kassow, and James L. West, eds. *Between Tsar and People: Educated Society and The Quest for Public Identity in Late Imperial Russia.* Princeton, 1991, 367–71.

Kelly, Catriona. "Popular Culture." Nicholas Rzhevsky, ed. *The Cambridge Companion to Modern Russian Culture*. Cambridge, 1998.

Kerans, David. *Mind and Labor on the Farm in Black-Earth Russia, 1861–1914*. Budapest and New York, 2001.

Khasbulatova, O.A., and N.B. Gafizova. *Zhenskoe dvizhenie v Rossii (Vtoraia polovina xix-nachalo xx veka)*. Ivanovo, 2003.

Kinnear, Julia Lise. "Childhood, Family and Civil Society in Late Imperial Russia: P.F. Kapterev, the St Petersburg Parents' Circle and Family Education, 1884–1914." Unpublished Ph.D. dissertation. University of Toronto, 2003.

Knight, Nathaniel. "Ethnicity, Nationality and the Masses: Narodnost' and Modernity in Imperial Russia." David L. Hoffmann and Yanni Kotsonis, eds. *Russian Modernity. Politics, Knowledge, Practices*. London and New York, 2000, 41–66.

Koenker, Diane. *Moscow Workers and the 1917 Revolution*. Princeton, 1981.

———. "Urban Families, Working-Class Youth Groups and the 1917 Revolution in Moscow." David L. Ransel, ed. *The Family in Imperial Russia*. Urbana, 1978.

Kolobaeva, L.A. *Russkii simvolizm*. Moscow, 2000.

Kolonitskii, Boris I. "Antibourgeois Propaganda and Anti-'Burzhui' Consciousness in 1917." *RR* 53, no. 2 (April 1994): 183–96.

Korelin, Avenir P. "The Social Problem in Russia, 1906–1914: Stolypin's Agrarian Reform." Theodore Taranovski, ed. *Reform in Modern Russian History. Progress or Cycle?* New York, 1995.

Kotsonis, Yanni. "'Face to Face': The State, the Individual, and the Citizen in Russian Taxation, 1863–1917." *SR* 63, no. 2 (Summer 2004): 221–46.

———. "How Peasants Became Backward: Agrarian Policy and Cooperatives in Russia, 1905–1914." Judith Pallot, ed. *Transforming Peasants: Society, State and the Peasantry, 1861–1930*. London and New York, 1998, 15–36.

———. *Making Peasants Backward. Agricultural Cooperatives and the Agrarian Question in Russia, 1861–1914*. London and New York, 1999.

———. "'No Place to Go': Taxation and State Transformation in Late-Imperial and Early-Soviet Russia." *JoMH* (September 2004): 531–77.

Krawchenko, Bohdan. "Agrarian Unrest and the Shaping of a National Identity in Ukraine at the Turn of the Twentieth Century." Madhavan K. Palat, ed., *Social Identities in Revolutionary Russia*. Basingstoke, 2000, 18–33.

Kusova, N.G. *Riazanskoe kupechestvo. Ocherki istorii xvi-nachala xx veka*. Riazan', 1996.

Kuznetsov, Evgenii. *Iz proshlogo russkoi estrady. Istoricheskie ocherki*. Moscow, 1958.

Lane, Ann M. "Bal'mont and Scriabin: The Artist as Superman." Bernice Glatzer Rosenthal, ed. *Nietzsche in Russia*. Princeton, 1986.

Lary, Nikita. "Film." Nicholas Rzhevsky, ed. *The Cambridge Companion to Modern Russian Culture*. Cambridge, 1998.

Leach, Robert, and Victor Borovsky, eds. *A History of Russian Theatre*. Cambridge, 1999.

Levin-Stankevich, Brian L. "The Transfer of Legal Technology and Culture: Law Professionals in Tsarist Russia." Harley D. Balzer, ed. *Russia's Missing Middle Class. The Professions in Russian History*. Armonk, 1996, 223–49.

Leyda, Jay. *Kino. A History of the Russian and Soviet Film*, 3rd edition. Princeton, 1983.

Lieven, D.C.B. *Russia and the Origins of the First World War*. London, 1983.

———. *Empire: The Russian Empire and its Rivals*. London, 2000.

———. "The Security Police, Civil Rights, and the Fate of the Russian Empire, 1855–1917."

Olga Crisp and Linda Edmondson, eds. *Civil Rights in Imperial Russia.* Oxford, 1989.

Lilla, Mark. *The Reckless Mind. Intellectuals in Politics.* New York, 2001.

Lincoln, W. Bruce. *Between Heaven and Hell. The Story of a Thousand Years of Artistic Life in Russia.* New York, 1998.

Lindenmeyr, Adele. *Poverty is Not a Vice. Charity, Society, and the State in Imperial Russia.* Princeton, 1996.

———. "Voluntary Associations and the Russian Autocracy: The Case of Private Charity." The Carl Beck Papers in Russian and East European Studies, no. 807. Pittsburgh, 1990.

Lohr, Eric, and Marshall Poe, eds. *The Military and Society in Russia.* Leiden and Boston, 2002.

Lovell, Stephen. "Between Arcadia and Suburbia: Dachas in Late Imperial Russia." *SR* 61, no. 1 (Spring 2002): 66–87.

———. *Summerfolk: A History of the Dacha, 1700–2000.* Ithaca and London, 2003.

Löwe, Heinz-Dietrich. "Russian Nationalism and Tsarist Nationalities Policies in Semi-Constitutional Russia, 1905–1914." Robert B. McKean, ed. *New Perspectives in Modern Russian History. Selected Papers from the Fourth World Congress for Soviet and East European Studies. Harrogate, 1990.* Basingstoke, 1992, 250–77.

Luk'ianov, Mikhail. *Rossiiskii konservatizm i reforma, 1907–1914.* Stuttgart, 2006.

———. "V ozhidanii katastrofy: eskhatologicheskie motivy v russkom konservatizme nakanune pervoi mirovoi voiny." *RH* 31, no. 4 (Winter 2004), 419–46.

Macey, David A.J. "Agricultural Reform and Political Change: The case of Stolypin." Theodore Taranovski, ed. *Reform in Modern Russian History. Progress or Cycle?* New York, 1995, 163–89.

———. "Government Actions and Peasant Reactions During the Stolypin Reforms." Robert B. McKean, ed. *New Perspectives in Modern Russian History. Selected Papers from the Fourth World Congress for Soviet and East European Studies. Harrogate, 1990.* Basingstoke, 1992, 133–73.

MacNaughton, Ruth Delia, and Roberta Thompson Manning. "The Crisis of the Third of June System and Political Trends in the Zemstvos, 1907–1914." Leopold H. Haimson, ed. *The Politics of Rural Russia, 1905–1914.* Bloomington and London, 1979, 228–59.

Markov, Vladimir. *Russian Futurism; A History.* Berkeley and Los Angeles, 1968.

Maslov, Semen. *Kooperatsiia v krest'ianskom khoziaistve.* Leipzig, 1922.

Maslov, S.L. *Zemstvo i ego ekonomicheskaia deiatel'nost' za 50 let sushchestvovaniia, 1864–1914.* Moscow, 1914.

Maza, Sarah. *The Myth of the French Bourgeoisie. An Essay on the Social Imaginary, 1750–1850.* Cambridge, Mass., 2003.

McCaffray, Susan P. *The Politics of Industrialization in Tsarist Russia. The Association of Southern Coal and Steel Producers, 1874–1914.* DeKalb, 1996.

McCaffray, Susan P., and Michael Melancon, eds. *Russia in the European Context, 1789–1914. A Member of the Family.* New York, 2005.

McDaniel, Tim. *Autocracy, Capitalism, and Revolution in Russia.* Berkeley and Los Angeles, 1988.

McDermid, Jane, and Anna Hillyar. *Women and Work in Russia 1880–1930. A Study in Continuity through Change.* London and New York, 1998.

McDonald, David M. "United Government and the Crisis of Autocracy, 1905–1914." Theodore Taranovski, ed. *Reform in Modern Russian History. Progress or Cycle?* New York,

1995, 190–211.

McKay, John P. *Pioneers for Profit. Foreign Entrepreneurship and Russian Industrialization, 1885–1913.* Chicago and London, 1970.

McKean, Robert B. "The Bureaucracy and the Labour Problem, June 1907–February 1917." Robert B. McKean, ed. *New Perspectives in Modern Russian History. Selected Papers from the Fourth World Congress for Soviet and East European Studies. Harrogate, 1990.* Basingstoke, 1992, 222–49.

———. *St. Petersburg Between the Revolutions. Workers and Revolutionaries, June 1907–February 1917.* New Haven and London, 1990.

McKean, Robert B., ed. *New Perspectives in Modern Russian History. Selected Papers from the Fourth World Congress for Soviet and East European Studies. Harrogate, 1990.* Basingstoke, 1992.

McReynolds, Louise. *The News Under Russia's Old Regime. The Development of a Mass-Circulation Press.* Princeton. 1991.

———. *Russia at Play. Leisure Activities at the End of the Tsarist Era.* Ithaca and London, 2003.

———. "V.M. Doroshevich: The Newspaper Journalist and the Development of Public Opinion in Civil Society." Edith W. Clowes, Samuel D. Kassow, and James L. West, eds. *Between Tsar and People: Educated Society and The Quest for Public Identity in Late Imperial Russia.* Princeton, 1991, 233–47.

Melancon, Michael. *The Lena Goldfields Massacre and the Crisis of the Late Tsarist State.* College Station, Tex., 2006.

Melancon, Michael, and Alice K. Pate, eds. *New Labor History. Worker Identity and Experience in Russia, 1840–1918.* Bloomington, 2002.

Mikhailov, Nikolai V. "The Collective Psychology of Russian Workers and Workplace Self-Organization in the Early Twentieth Century." Michael Melancon and Alice K. Pate, eds. *New Labor History. Worker Identity and Experience in Russia, 1840–1918.* Bloomington, 2002, 77–94.

Miller, Alexei. *Imperiia Romanovykh i natsionalizm. Esse po metodologii istoricheskogo issledovaniia.* Moscow, 2006.

Miller, Margaret. *The Economic Development of Russia, 1905–1914,* 2nd edition. London, 1967.

Miller, Martin. *Freud and the Bolsheviks. Psychoanalysis in Imperial Russia and the Soviet Union.* New Haven and London, 1998.

Mironov, Boris, with Ben Eklof. "Peasant Popular Culture and the Origins of Soviet Authoritarianism." Stephen P. Frank and Mark D. Steinberg, eds., *Cultures in Flux. Lower-Class Values, Practices, and Resistance in Late Imperial Russia.* Princeton, 1996, 54–73.

———. *The Social History of Imperial Russia, 1700–1917.* Boulder, 2000.

Moeller-Sally, Betsy F. "The Theater as Will and Representation: Artist and Audience in Russian Modernist Theater, 1904–1909." *SR* 57, no. 2 (Summer 1998): 350–71.

Moon, David. *The Russian Peasantry, 1600–1930. The World the Peasants Made.* London and New York, 1999.

Morrissey, Susan. "Suicide and Civilization in Late Imperial Russia." *JfGOE* 43, no. 2 (1995): 201–17.

———. *Suicide and the Body Politic in Imperial Russia.* Cambridge, 2006.

Morson, Gary Saul, ed. *Literature and History. Theoretical Problems and Russian Case Studies.* Stanford, 1986.

Mosse, W.E. "Bureaucracy and Nobility in Russia at the End of the Nineteenth Century." *HJ* 3, no. 24 (1981): 605–28.

Neuberger, Joan. "Culture Besieged: Hooliganism and Futurism." Stephen P. Frank and Mark D. Steinberg, eds. *Cultures in Flux. Lower-Class Values, Practices, and Resistance in Late Imperial Russia*. Princeton, 1996, 185–203.

———. "When the Word was the Deed: Workers vs. Employers before the Justices of the Peace." Reginald E. Zelnik, ed. *Workers and Intelligentsia in Late Imperial Russia. Realities, Representations, Reflections*. Berkeley, 1999, 292–308.

Nichols, R.L., and T.G. Stavrou, eds. *Russian Orthodoxy Under the Old Regime*. Minneapolis, 1978.

Orlovsky, Daniel T. "Professionalism in the Ministerial Bureaucracy on the Eve of the February Revolution of 1917." Harley D. Balzer, ed. *Russia's Missing Middle Class. The Professions in Russian History*. Armonk, 1996, 267–92.

Owen, Launcelot. *The Russian Peasant Movement, 1906–1917*. New York, 1963.

Owen, Thomas C. *Capitalism and Politics in Russia. A Social History of the Moscow Merchants*. Cambridge, 1981.

———. *The Corporation Under Russian Law, 1800–1917*. Cambridge and New York, 1991.

———. *Dilemmas of Russian Capitalism. Fedor Chizhov and Corporate Enterprise in the Railroad Age*. Cambridge, Mass., 2005.

———. "Doing Business in Merchant Moscow." James L. West and Iurii Petrov, eds. *Merchant Moscow. Images of Russia's Vanished Bourgeoisie*. Princeton, 1998, 29–36.

Pallot, Judith. "Did the Stolypin Land Reform Destroy the Peasant Commune?" Robert B. McKean, ed. *New Perspectives in Modern Russian History. Selected Papers from the Fourth World Congress for Soviet and East European Studies. Harrogate, 1990*. Basingstoke, 2002, 117–32.

———. *Land Reform in Russia, 1906–1917. Peasant Responses to Stolypin's Project of Rural Transformation*. Oxford, 1999.

———. "The Stolypin Land Reform as 'Administrative Utopia': Images of Peasantry in Nineteenth-Century Russia." Madhavan K. Palat, ed. *Social Identities in Revolutionary Russia*. Basingstoke, 2002, 113–33.

Pallot, Judith, ed. *Transforming Peasants: Society, State and the Peasantry, 1861–1930*. London and New York, 1998.

Palmer, Scott W. *Dictatorship of the Air. Aviation Culture and the Fate of Modern Russia*. Cambridge, 2006.

Pate, Alice K. "The Liquidationist Controversy: Russian Social Democracy and the Quest for Unity." Michael Melancon and Alice K. Pate, eds. *New Labor History. Worker Identity and Experience in Russia, 1840–1918*. Bloomington, 2002, 95–122.

———. "St. Petersburg Workers and Implementation of the Social Insurance Law of 1912." Susan P. McCaffray and Michael Melancon, eds. *Russia in the European Context, 1789–1914. A Member of the Family*. New York, 2005, 189–201.

Pavlovsky, George. *Agricultural Russia on the Eve of the Revolution*. London, 1930.

Petrov, Iu.A. *Kommercheskie banki Moskvy. Konets xix v.-1914 gg.* Moscow, 1995.

Pinchuk, Ben-Cion. *The Octobrists in the Third Duma, 1907–1912*. Seattle and London, 1974.

Pipes, Richard. *Struve, Liberal on the Right, 1905–1944*. Cambridge, Mass., 1980.

Podbolotov, Sergei. "Monarchists Against Their Monarch: The Rightists' Criticism of Tsar Nicholas II." *RH* 31, nos.1–2 (Spring–Summer 2004): 105–20.

Porter, Thomas. *The Zemstvo and the Emergence of Civil Society in Late Imperial Russia.* San Francisco, 1991.

Porter, Thomas, and William Gleason. "The Zemstvo and the Transformation of Russian Society." Mary Schaeffer Conroy, ed. *Emerging Democracy in Late Imperial Russia.* Boulder, 1998, 60–87.

Potkina, Irina V. "Moscow's Commercial Mosaic." James L. West and Iurii Petrov, eds. *Merchant Moscow. Images of Russia's Vanished Bourgeoisie.* Princeton, 1998, 39–44.

Pravilova, Ekaterina. *Finansy imperii. Den'gi i vlast' v politike Rossii na natsional'nykh okrainakh, 1801–1917.* Moscow, 2006.

Presto, Jenifer. "Unbearable Burdens: Aleksandr Blok and the Modernist Resistance to Progeny and Domesticity." *SR* 63, no. 1 (Spring 2004): 6–25.

Raeff, Marc. "The Bureaucratic Phenomena of Imperial Russia, 1700–1905." *AHR* 84, no. 2 (April 1979): 399–411.

———. "Codification et Droit en Russie Impérial. Quelques remarques comparatives." *Cahiers du monde russe et soviétique* xx, no. 1 (January–March 1979): 5–13.

———. "Patterns of Russian Imperial Policy Toward the Nationalities." Edward Allworth, ed. *Soviet Nationality Problems.* New York, 1971.

Ransel, David L., ed. *The Family in Imperial Russia.* Urbana, 1978.

Read, Christopher. *Religion, Revolution and the Russian Intelligentsia, 1900–1912. The Vekhi Debate and Its Intellectual Background.* London and Basingstoke, 1979.

Reent, Iu.A. *Obshchaia i politicheskaia politsiia v Rossii (1900–1917 g.).* Riazan', 2001.

Resnick, Daniel P., ed. *Literacy in Historical Perspective.* Washington, 1983.

Retish, Aaron B. *Russia's Peasants in Revolution and Civil War. Citizenship, Identity, and the Creation of the Soviet State, 1914–1922.* Cambridge, 2008.

Riha, Thomas. *A Russian European. Paul Miliukov in Russian Politics.* South Bend and London, 1969.

Robinson, Harlow. "Music." Nicholas Rzhevsky, ed. *The Cambridge Companion to Modern Russian Culture.* Cambridge, 1998.

Rogger, Hans. "Afterthoughts." Eugen Weber and Hans Rogger, eds. *The European Right: A Historical Profile.* Los Angeles, 1965.

———. "Russia." Eugen Weber and Hans Rogger, eds. *The European Right: A Historical Profile.* Los Angeles, 1965, 443–500.

———. "Was There a Russian Fascism? The Union of the Russian People." *JoMH* xxxvi, no. 4 (December 1964): 398–415.

Roosa, Ruth AmEnde. *Russian Industrialists in an Era of Revolution. The Association of Industry and Trade, 1906–1917.* Armonk and London, 1997.

Rosenberg, William G. "Representing Workers and the Liberal Narrative of Modernity." Reginald E. Zelnik, ed. *Workers and Intelligentsia in Late Imperial Russia. Realities, Representations, Reflections.* Berkeley, 1999, 228–59.

Rosenthal, Bernice Glatzer. *New Myth, New World. From Nietzsche to Stalinism.* University Park, Pa., 2002.

Rosenthal, Bernice Glatzer, ed. *Nietzsche in Russia.* Princeton, 1986.

Roslof, Edward E. *Red Priests. Renovationism, Russian Orthodoxy, and Revolution, 1905–1946.* Bloomington, 2002.

Rothstein, Robert A. "Death of the Folk Song?" Stephen P. Frank and Mark D. Steinberg, eds. *Cultures in Flux. Lower-Class Values, Practices, and Resistance in Late Imperial Russia.* Princeton, 1996, 108–20.

Roubakine, N.A. *Qu'est-ce que la Révolution Russe?* Geneva and Paris, 1917.

Rozental', I.S. *Moskva na pereput'e. Vlast' i obshchestvo v 1905–1914 gg.* Moscow, 2004.

Ruane, Christine. *The Empire's New Clothes. A History of the Russian Fashion Industry, 1700–1917.* New Haven and London, 2009.

———. *Gender, Class, and the Professionalization of Russian City Teachers, 1860-1914.* Pittsburgh, 1994.

Ruble, Blair A. *Second Metropolis. Pragmatic Pluralism in Gilded Age Chicago, Silver Age Moscow, and Meiji Osaka.* Cambridge, 2001.

Russell, Robert, and Andrew Barratt, eds. *Russian Theatre in the Age of Modernism.* New York, 1990.

Ruud, Charles A. "Predprinimatel' I.D. Sytin." L.G. Zakharova, Iu.S. Kukushkin, and T. Emmons, eds. *P.A. Zaionchkovskii 1904–1983 gg. Stat'i, publikatsii i vospominaniia o nem.* Moscow, 1998.

Samuel, Maurice. *Blood Accusation.* London, 1966.

Sanborn, Joshua. "Military Reform, Moral Reform, and the End of the Old Regime." Eric Lohr and Marshall Poe, eds. *The Military and Society in Russia.* Leiden and Boston, 2002.

Sanborn, Joshua A. *Drafting the Russian Nation: Military Conscription, Total War, and Mass Politics, 1905–1925.* DeKalb, 2003.

Santayana, George. *Dominations and Powers: Reflections on Liberty, Society and Government.* New York, 1951.

Seligman, Adam B. *The Idea of Civil Society.* New York, 1992.

Senelick, Laurence. "Boris Geyer and Cabaretic Playwriting." Robert Russell and Andrew Barratt, eds. *Russian Theatre in the Age of Modernism.* New York, 1990.

———. "Theater." Nicholas Rzhevsky, ed. *The Cambridge Companion to Modern Russian Culture.* Cambridge, 1998.

Shanin, Teodor, *Russia as a 'Developing Society.' The Roots of Otherness: Russia's Turn of Century,* vol. 1. London, 1985.

Shapika, Grazyna. "Learning to be a Citizen: Cognitive and Ethical Aspects of Postcommunist Society Transformation." Robert Fine and Shirin Rai, eds. *Civil Society: Democratic Perspectives.* London and Portland, Ore., 1997.

Sharp, Jane A. "Beyond Orientalism. Russian and Soviet Modernism on the Periphery of Empire." Rosalind P. Blakesley and Susan E. Reid, eds. *Russian Art and the West. A Century of Dialogue in Painting, Architecture, and the Decorative Arts.* DeKalb, 2007.

Shatz, Marshall S., and Judith Zimmerman, trans. and eds. *Signposts: A Collection of Articles on the Russian Intelligentsia.* Irvine, 1986.

Shepelev, L.E. *Aktsionernye kompanii v Rossii.* Leningrad, 1973.

———. *Tsarizm i burzhuaziia v 1904–1914 gg.* Leningrad, 1987.

Shevzov, Vera. *Russian Orthodoxy on the Eve of Revolution.* Oxford, 2004.

Skinner, Frederick W. "Odessa and the Problem of Urban Modernization." Michael Hamm, ed. *The City in Late Imperial Russia.* Bloomington, 1986.

Slocum, John W. "Who and When were the *Inorodtsy*: The Evolution of the Category of 'Aliens' in Imperial Russia." *RR* 57 (April 1998): 173–90.

Slonim, Marc. *Russian Theater. From the Empire to the Soviets.* New York, 1962.

Smith, S.A. "Workers and Civil Rights in Tsarist Russia, 1899–1917." Olga Crisp and Linda Edmondson, eds. *Civil Rights in Imperial Russia.* Oxford, 1989.

Solomon, Peter H., Jr., ed. *Reforming Justice in Russia, 1864–1996. Power, Culture and the*

Limits of Legal Order. Armonk, 1997.

Solov'ev, Iu.B. *Samoderzhavie i dvorianstvo v 1907–1914 gg.* Leningrad, 1990.

Starr, Frederick. "Tsarist Government: The Imperial Dimension." Jeremy R. Azrael, ed. *Soviet Nationality Policies and Practices.* New York, 1978.

Steinberg, Mark D. "The Injured and Insurgent Self: The Moral Imagination of Russia's Lower Class Writers." Reginald E. Zelnik, ed. *Workers and Intelligentsia in Late Imperial Russia. Realities, Representations, Reflections.* Berkeley, 1999, 309–29.

———. "Melancholy and modernity: emotions and social life in Russia between the revolutions." *JoSH* 41, no. 4 (Summer 2008): 813–29.

———. *Proletarian Imagination. Self, Modernity, and the Sacred in Russia, 1910–1925.* Ithaca and London, 2002.

———. "Proletarian Knowledge of Self: Worker Poets in Fin-de-Siècle Russia." Mark Melancon and Alice K. Pate, eds. *New Labor History. Worker Identity and Experience in Russia, 1840–1918.* Bloomington, 2002.

———. "Russia's *fin de siècle*, 1900–1914." Ronald Grigor Suny, ed. *The Cambridge History of Russia,* vol. III, *The Twentieth Century.* Cambridge, 2006.

———. "Worker Authors and the Cult of the Person." Stephen P. Frank and Mark D. Steinberg, eds. *Cultures in Flux. Lower-Class Values, Practices, and Resistance in Late Imperial Russia.* Princeton, 1996.

Steinwedel, Charles. "To Make a Difference: The Category of Ethnicity in Late Imperial Russian Politics, 1861–1917." David L. Hoffmann and Yanni Kotsonis, eds. *Russian Modernity. Politics, Knowledge, Practices.* London and New York, 2000, 67–86.

Stites, Richard. *Russian Popular Culture. Entertainment and Society since 1900.* Cambridge, 1992.

———. *The Women's Liberation Movement in Russia. Feminism, Nihilism and Bolshevism, 1860–1930.* Princeton, 1978.

Stockdale, Melissa Kirschke. *Paul Miliukov and the Quest for a Liberal Russia, 1880–1918.* Ithaca and London, 1996.

Suny, Ronald Grigor, ed. *The Cambridge History of Russia,* vol. III, *The Twentieth Century.* Cambridge, 2006.

Sutherland, Willard. "Imperial Space: Territorial Thought and Practice in the Eighteenth Century." Jane Burbank, Mark von Hagen, and Anatolyi Remnev, eds. *Russian Empire. Space, People, Power, 1700–1930.* Bloomington and Indianapolis, 2007.

Swain, G.R. "Freedom of Association and the Trade Unions, 1906–14." Olga Crisp and Linda Edmondson, eds. *Civil Rights in Imperial Russia.* Oxford, 1989.

Swift, E. Anthony. *Popular Theater and Society in Imperial Russia.* Berkeley, Los Angeles, and London, 2002.

———. "Workers' Theatre and 'Proletarian Culture' in Pre-revolutionary Russia, 1905–1917." Reginald E. Zelnik, ed. *Workers and Intelligentsia in Late Imperial Russia. Realities, Representations, Reflections.* Berkeley, 1999.

Tager, A.S. *The Decay of Czarism. The Beiliss Trial.* Philadelphia, 1935.

Taranovski, Theodore, ed. *Reform in Modern Russian History. Progress or Cycle?* New York, 1995.

Thurston, Gary. "The Impact of Russian Popular Theater, 1886–1915." *JoMH* 55 (June 1983): 237–67.

Thurston, Robert W. *Liberal City, Conservative State. Moscow and Russia's Urban Crisis, 1906–1914.* Oxford, 1987.

Tikhvinskaia, Liudmila. *Povsednevnaia zhizn' teatral'noi bogemy Serebrianogo veka. Kabare i teatry miniatiur v Rossii, 1908–1917.* Moscow, 2005.

Timberlake, Charles. "The Tsarist Government's Preoccupation with the Liberal Party in Tver' Province, 1890–1905." Mary Schaeffer Conroy, ed. *Emerging Democracy in Late Imperial Russia.* Boulder, 1998, 30–59.

———. "The Zemstvo and the Development of a Russian Middle Class." Edith W. Clowes, Samuel D. Kassow, and James L. West, eds. *Between Tsar and People: Educated Society and the Quest for Public Identity in Late Imperial Russia.* Princeton, 1991, 164–79.

Tiukavkin, V.G. *Velikorusskoe krest'ianstvo i Stolypinskaia agrarnaia reforma.* Moscow, 2001.

Toumanoff, Peter. "Some Effects of Land Tenure Reform on Russian Agricultural Productivity, 1901–1913." *Economic Development and Cultural Change* 32, no. 4 (July 1984): 861–72.

Tsiunchuk, Rustem. "Peoples, Regions, and Electoral Politics: The State Dumas and the Constitution of New Elites." Jane Burbank, Mark von Hagen, and Anatolyi Remnev, eds. *Russian Empire. Space, People, Power, 1700–1930.* Bloomington and Indianapolis, 2007.

Tsivian, Yuri. *Early Cinema in Russia and Its Cultural Reception.* London and New York, 1994.

———. "Russia, 1913: Cinema in the Cultural Landscape." Richard Abel, ed. *Silent Film.* New Brunswick, 1996, 194–214.

Tsvertkov-Prosveshchenskii, A.K. *Mezhdu dvumia revoliutsiiami (1907–1916 gg.).* Moscow, 1957.

Vallière, Paul. "Theological Liberalism and Church Reform in Imperial Russia." Geoffrey A. Hosking, ed. *Church, Nation, and State in Russia and Ukraine.* Edmonton, 1990, 108–30.

Varty, John. "Civil or Commercial? Adam Ferguson's Concept of Civil Society." Robert Fine and Shirin Rai, eds. *Civil Society. Democratic Perspectives.* London and Portland, Ore., 1997.

Verner, Andrew. "Discursive Strategies in the 1905 Revolution: Peasant Petitions from Vladimir Province." *RR* 54, no. 1 (January 1995): 65–90.

Vinogradoff, Eugene D. "The Russian Peasantry and the Elections to the Fourth State Duma." Leopold H. Haimson, ed. *The Politics of Rural Russia, 1905–1914.* Bloomington and London, 1979, 219–60.

Vitabaro, Gregory, "Military Aviation, National Identity, and the Imperatives of Modernity in Late Imperial Russia." Eric Lohr and Marshall Poe, eds. *The Military and Society in Russia.* Leiden and Boston, 2002.

———. "Nationality Policy and the Russian Imperial Officer Corps, 1905–1914." *SR* 66, no. 4 (Winter 2007): 682–701.

Volin, Lazar. *A Century of Russian Agriculture. From Alexander II to Khrushchev.* Cambridge, Mass., 1970.

Von Geldern, James. "Life In-Between: Migration and Popular Culture in Late Imperial Russia." *RR* 55 (July 1996): 365–83.

Vucinich, Wayne S., ed. *The Peasant in Nineteenth-Century Russia.* Stanford, 1968.

Wagner, William G. "Civil Law, Individual Rights, and Judicial Activism in Late Imperial Russia." Peter H. Solomon, Jr., ed. *Reforming Justice in Russia, 1864–1996. Power, Culture, and the Limits of Legal Order.* Armonk, 1997, 21–43.

———. "Ideology, Identity, and the Emergence of a Middle Class." Edith W. Clowes, Samuel D. Kassow, and James L. West, eds. *Between Tsar and People: Educated Society and the Quest for Public Identity in Late Imperial Russia*. Princeton, 1991, 149–63.

———. *Marriage, Property, and Law in Late Imperial Russia*. Oxford, 1994.

Waldron, Peter. *Between Two Revolutions. Stolypin and the Politics of Renewal in Russia*. Salisbury and New York, 1998.

Walicki, Andrzej. Legal Philosophies of Russian Liberalism. Oxford, 1987.

Weber, Eugen, and Hans Rogger, eds. *The European Right: A Historical Profile*. Los Angeles, 1965.

Weeks, Theodore R. "Defending Our Own: Government and the Russian Minority in the Kingdom of Poland, 1905-1914." *RR* 54, no. 4 (October 1995): 539–51.

Weinerman, Eli. "Russification in Imperial Russia: The Search for Homogeneity in the Multinational State," Ph.D. dissertation. Indiana University, 1995.

Weissman, Neil B. *Reform in Tsarist Russia. The State Bureaucracy and Local Government, 1900-1914*. New Brunswick, N.J., 1981.

———. "Rural Crime in Tsarist Russia: The Question of Hooliganism, 1905-1914." *SR* 37, no. 2 (June 1978): 228–40.

Werth, Paul W. "Schism Once Removed: Sects, State Authority, and Meanings of Religious Toleration in Imperial Russia." Alexei Miller and Alfred Rieber, eds. *Imperial Rule*. Budapest and New York, 2004.

West, James L. "The Riabushinsky Circle: *Burzhuaziia* and *Obshchestvennost'* in Late Imperial Russia." Edith W. Clowes, Samuel D. Kassow, and James L. West, eds. *Between Tsar and People: Educated Society and The Quest for Public Identity in Late Imperial Russia*. Princeton, 1991, 41–56.

West, James L., and Iurii Petrov, eds. *Merchant Moscow. Images of Russia's Vanished Bourgeoisie*. Princeton, 1998.

Whittaker, Cynthia H. "The Women's Movement during the Reign of Alexander II: A Case Study in Russian Liberalism." *JoMH* 48, supplement to no. 2 (June 1976): 35–69.

Wirtschafter, Elise Kimerling. *Social Identity in Imperial Russia*. DeKalb, 1997.

———. *Structures of Society. Imperial Russia's "People of Various Ranks."* DeKalb, 1994.

Wortman, Richard. "Property Rights, Populism, and Russian Political Culture." Olga Crisp and Linda Edmondson, eds. *Civil Rights in Imperial Russia*. Oxford, 1989.

———. "The 'Russian Style' in Church Architecture as Imperial Symbol after 1881." James Cracraft and Daniel Rowland, eds. *Architectures of Russian Identity, 1500 to the Present*. Ithaca and London, 2003.

———. *Scenarios of Power: Myth and Ceremony in Russian Monarchy*, vol. 2. *From Alexander II to the Abdication of Nicholas II*. Princeton, 2000.

Wynn, Charters. *Workers, Strikes, and Pogroms. The Donbass-Dnepr Bend in Late Imperial Russia, 1870-1905*. Princeton, 1992.

Yaney, George. *The Urge to Mobilize. Agrarian Reform in Russia, 1861-1930*. Urbana, Chicago, and London, 1982.

Youngblood, Denise J. *The Magic Mirror. Moviemaking in Russia, 1908-1918*. Madison, 1999.

Zaionchkovskii, P.A. *Pravitel'stvennyi apparat samoderzhavnoi Rossii v xix v.* Moscow, 1978.

Zelnik, Reginald E., ed. *Workers and Intelligentsia in Late Imperial Russia. Realities, Representations, Reflections*. Berkeley, 1999.

Zorin, A.N. et al., eds. *Ocherki rodskogo byta dorevoliutsionnogo Povolzh'ia*. Ul'ianovsk, 2000.

Index

agricultural assistance, 73, 163–64, 242; agronomists and, 276; state and, 210; zemstvos and, 38, 70, 84, 158–59, 161, 210–11

agricultural trains, 161

agriculture, 19, 29–31, 38; development of compared to western states, 29; German attitude toward, 162; in Central Industrial and Black Earth regions, 30–31; industrial crops, 162

agronomists, 158–59, 160–61, 163, 188, 210, 276

Alexander Academy of Military Justice, 216

All-Russian Agricultural Congress, 230

All-Russian Artisans' Exhibition, 67, 211

All-Russian Congress of Clerks, 184

All-Russian Congress of Dentists, 184

All-Russian Congress of Factory Panel Doctors, 109, 110

All-Russian Congress of Stock Market Committees, 64

All-Russian Congress of the Representatives of Meshchane Societies, 67

All-Russian Congress on the Question of Public Education, 175

All-Russian Stock Market Congress, 184

All-Russian Union of Organizations, Societies, and Activists in Public and Private Relief, 125

All-Russian Women's Congress, 109

amnesty, 224–25

Andreev, Leonid, 146, 147, 148, 226, 303; *Ekaterina Ivanovna*, 149–50

anticapitalism, 16, 62, 241

anti-Polonism, 181

anti-Semitism, 5, 54, 63–64, 181–83, 184, 186, 241

antiwesternism, 16, 62, 234–36, 241, 243, 244, 247, 253, 262

Armand, I.F., 146

Armenia, 60, 173, 181

Armenian Church, 180

army, 177, 179, 225; estate structure and, 86–87; internal repression and, 201, 216; literacy and, 23; modern warfare and, 86; Nicholas II and, 199; State Duma and, 199–200

arson, 84–85, 157

art, 257, 267, 268; commerce and, 263; modernism and, 256–57, 258, 260–61, 262–63; Nietzsche on, 258–59; science and, 265–66

artisan production, 3, 22, 25, 36, 38, 67, 98, 111, 126, 181, 211, 242, 254

Artsybashev, Mikhail, 150

Association of Industry and Trade, 61–63; civic responsibility and, 66; *laissez-faire* and, 65; on trade unions, 202

Association of Southern Coal and Steel Producers, 63, 66, 97; on universal social services, 65, 247

Austro-Hungarian Empire, 21, 26, 27, 28, 38, 154, 176, 198

aviation, 218–19, 277; civic consciousness and, 220

Bailes, Kendall, 71

Baku, 63, 74, 137, 181, 272

Balkan wars, 18, 154, 197–98; conservative support for, 243–44

Ballets Russes, 261

Baltic Germans, 54, 57, 60, 174, 181
Baltic states, 23, 37, 81, 173
banking, 18, 30, 36, 41, 43, 54, 155, 201;
  foreign investment in, 40, 43–44;
  private, 41–42; State Bank, 41–42, 54
Baptists, 115
Basily, Nicholas, 195; on reactionary
  ministers, 204
Baudelaire, Charles, 257
Beiliss, Mendel, 182, 185; trial of, 186–87,
  227, 237
Belorussia, 20, 174, 177, 282
Bely, Andrei, 137, 265; on music, 263; *St.
  Petersburg,* 262
Berdiaev, Nikolai, 235
Bergson, Henri, 259, 266
Birth of Tragedy from the Spirit of Music,
  258
birth rate, 20, 22
Black Sea, 61, 81, 198
Blaue Reiter, 261
Blériot, Louis, 218, 220
Blok, Aleksandr, 135, 137; on family, 265
Bloody Sunday, 74
Bogatyr Society for Physical Education, 131
Bogdanov, Aleksandr, 78
Bolsheviks, 163, 255, 272; health insurance
  and, 112; workers and, 78
book publishing, 15, 20, 156, 175, 221, 226;
  middle-class values and, 134–35
Bosnia-Herzegovina, 198
bourgeoisie, 14, 16, 59, 128, 136, 273;
  civil society and, 60; coherence of, 66,
  96–97, 119; conservatives on, 242–43;
  Herzen on, 107, 235; historiography on,
  64; intelligentsia on, 233, 245–46, 269;
  Marxists on, 107, 255; middle-class
  identity and, 245; Nietzsche on, 259;
  peasants and, 189; workers and, 125,
  139. *See also* middle class
Bradley, Joseph, 129, 223, 224
brattsy, 116, 281
Breshko-Breshkovskaia, Ekaterina, 224
Brianskii, V.D., 121
Brooks, Jeffrey, 135, 257
budget, 24, 26
Bulgaria, 28, 198, 243

Bunin, Ivan, 138
buntarstvo, 78, 281
Burbank, Jane, 86, 88, 171
Burds, Jeffrey, 154
bureaucracy, 59, 91, 128, 195, 202, 209,
  239, 273; civil society and, 129,
  190–91, 224; composition of, 56–57,
  172, 209–10, 223–24; conflict within,
  191–93, 199–200, 231; conservatives
  on, 240–41; law and, 196; nationalism
  and, 178, 189; nobility and, 209; public
  and, 190, 222–23, 231
Burliuk, David, 136

cabaret. *See* theater
capitalism, 22, 182, 247, 270; civil society
  and, 93, 96, 98; conservatives and,
  182, 241–43; cooperatives and, 171;
  intelligentsia and, 91, 233, 248; Lenin
  on, 254–55; liberals and, 250–51, 278;
  popular culture and, 130; populists and,
  253–54; workers' attitudes toward, 74,
  79, 149
Caspian Sea, 61
Catherine the Great. *See* Romanova
Catholic Church, 177
Caucasus, 54, 56, 173, 174, 175, 180–81
censorship, 113, 222; of books, 203, 226; of
  library holdings, 178, 227
census: of 1897, 22, 51; plans for new,
  19–20
Central Statistical Bureau, 20
Chaliapin, Fedor, 261
charities, 124–26, 130, 188, 222–23, 274
chastushka, 156, 281
China, 180; Russian foreign policy and,
  198; trade with, 5, 28
Chukovskii, Kornei, 257, 263
Chulkov, Georgii, 260, 269
Chulkov, Vasilii, 263
Church of England, 186
Churikov, Ioann, 116
cities, 20–21, 26; bourgeois revolution
  and, 106–7, 117; civil society and,
  116–17, 140, 171; education and,
  23–24; elections in, 117–18, 181, 229;
  electorate, 117; social estates in, 21,

52, 58, 66, 117, 153, 156; state and, 116–17, 209–10, 212–13, 227, 231; civil society, 11, 12, 14–16, 50, 62, 89, 90–94, 119, 141, 154, 168, 183, 188, 234, 253, 269, 270; bourgeoisie and, 60, 95–96, 97, 247; cities and, 116–17, 140, 171; education and, 92, 95, 97, 125, 140, 273; in historiography, 92, 95; integralism and, 235; law and, 236; nation-state and, 15, 178, 187, 189; *obshchestven-nost'* and, 91–92; obstacles to, 94–95, 140 participation of bureaucrats in 129, 190–91, 224; peasants and, 151, 168, 170; voluntary associations and, 126–30; women and, 150, 151; workers and, 107, 109–12, 116

classes, 13–14, 53, 59, 70, 90, 94–95, 108, 117, 130, 188, 221, 251, 254, 273; integration of, 119, 122, 125–26, 135–37, 168, 273–74; Marx on, 98

Clerks' Mutual Aid Society [of Kazan'], 126, 128–29

clubs, 14, 64, 77, 131; civil society and, 129, 274; flying, 219; football, 132, 274; in Kazan', 127–29; Ukrainian, 178

Code of Religious Consistories, 206

commercial employees, 14, 68; legislation in State Duma on, 69

Committee for Strengthening the Fleet through Voluntary Contributions, 218

commune, 31–33, 55, 84, 157, 165, 202, 292; conservatives on, 242; Herzen on, 235, 253–54; intelligentsia and, 249–51; liberals on, 250–51; Marxists on, 254–55; populists on, 253–54; repartition and, 34, 79–80, 162, 163, 277; separators and, 35, 83, 163, 248–49; Slavophiles on, 234; Stolypin land reform and, 34–35, 45, 79–83, 157, 163–65, 202, 242, 248–49, 282; yields on, 162–63, 276–77

companies, 131, 218; foreign, 40, 42, 54, 241; Jews and, 63, 182; management of, 42–43; peasant, 36; Russian, 12, 39, 40–41, 43, 47, 50; syndicates and, 39, 66

Congress of Cooperative Societies, 109, 222

Congress of the Representatives from

Societies of People's Universities, 109

Congress of the Representatives of Municipal Government, 222

Congress of Vegetarians, 116

Congress on Public Education, 110

Congress on Women's Education, 230

congresses, 72, 157, 214, 215; business, 220–21; Jews and, 183–84; peasants and, 166–67; state and, 221–22, 274–75; workers and, 109–10

conscription, 33, 86–87, 154

conservatism, 123, 232, 234–35, 241, 278; bureaucratic, 239–40; capitalism and, 241–42; foreigners and, 241; Jews and, 241–42; monarchy and, 236, 240, 244; parliamentary government and, 240; women and, 144–45; zemstvo reform and, 56

Constantinople, 198

Constitutional Democratic Party, 57, 190, 194, 248, 282; anticapitalism and, 248; hooliganism and, 157; on peasant property, 250–51; school language policy and, 177; women's suffrage and, 146

constitutionalism, 191, 196, 231

consumerism, 106–7, 131, 133, 188; attitudes toward, 114, 139, 256; books and, 134–35, 274; film and, 137, 274; peasant, 155–56, 171

consumption, 30, 36, 38, 45, 47, 62, 282; of culture, 114, 131–32, 134–35, 137, 139, 155, 188, 274

cooperatives, 3, 15, 36–38, 68, 77, 95, 116, 171, 211, 221, 242; boards of, 166–67, 286; intelligentsia and, 166, 167–68; peasant mentality and, 158, 166, 168, 188–89; peasant participation in, 166–67, 169

corporate law, 12, 43

cottage industry, 36, 37, 211, 221. *See also* artisan production

Council of Ministers, 6, 56, 63, 64, 145, 179, 183, 192, 203, 213, 216, 226, 240, 243; divisions within, 196–97, 200–2, 205, 218; labor mediation courts and, 202; on strikes, 75–76; parish reform and, 206; police reform and, 207–8; press law and, 203, 225–26

credit, 15, 18, 41–42, 47, 48, 67, 112, 148, 167, 208, 222, 228, 248, 275; cooperatives and, 12, 15, 36, 42, 116, 158, 211

Crimea, 621, 83, 182

culture, 15; consumption of, 114, 130, 131–32, 134–35, 137, 139, 155, 188, 274; *dacha,* 132–33, 155, 281; intelligentsia on, 266–67. *See also* popular culture

D'Annunzio, Gabrielle, 261

defense spending, 46–47

demography, 19–22; economy and, 27–28

Department of Railways, 143

Diaghelev, Sergei, 261

discourse, 14, 16–17, 62, 65, 98, 108–9, 233–34; conservative, 239–44; dynastic, 236–39; integralist, 234–36; liberal, 244–51; modernist, 256–70; radical, 253–56

Dobroliubov, N.A., 59, 245

Dolgorukaia, Varvara Princess, 169

Drama in the Futurists' Cabaret 13, 137

duma, 55, 59, 110, 117, 125, 175, 184, 222, 224, 291; budget, 209; education and, 118; elections, 117–18, 181, 229; electorate, 117; Moscow, 119–21; state and, 116–17, 209–10, 212–13, 227, 231; St. Petersburg, 121–23

Dubrovin, A.I., 185

Durnovo, P.N., 239

dvoeverie, 153, 281

Dzhunkovskii, V.F., 230

Economic Dialogues, 220

economy, 11–12; dependency and, 43–44; education and, 19, 26–27, 63; historiography and, 11, 44–45; imperial integration and, 48; markets and, 12, 50; population growth and, 27–28; state role in, 44–47

education, 22–26, 56, 67, 70, 76, 95, 127, 128, 157, 191, 224, 277; agricultural, 19, 70, 84, 171, 202, 210–11, 276; budgets for, 24–26, 117; civil society and, 92,

95, 97, 125, 140, 273; dumas and, 26, 117–18, 122–23; economy and, 19, 26–27, 63; family, 128, 223–24; intelligentsia and, 70; Jews and, 182; non-Russian, 174–77; peasants and, 151–52, 165–66, 167, 169, 170, 249; physical, 131; schools for, 23–24; social mobility and, 135; women and, 15, 142–43, 145, 146, 150, 230; workers and, 78, 107, 110, 120, 188, 274; zemstvos and, 25–26, 65, 70, 209

Ekaterina Ivanovna, 149–50

Eksteins, Modris, 258

electrification, 218

Emancipation reforms, 4, 13, 17, 30, 32–33, 54, 79, 142, 155, 167

employers' societies, 15, 220–21

Engelstein, Laura, 128

engineers, 42–43, 63, 127–28, 218–19; female, 143; positivism and, 71–72; Taylorism and, 39

Entente, 198

estrada. See theater

Eurasianism, 262

Evangelicals, 115–16

Evreinov, Nikolai, 148, 263, 268

exceptionalism, 16–17, 234–35, 244, 246, 278

exile system, 224–25

fairs, 139, 153, 155; at Nizhnii-Novgorod, 58–59, 60, 133, 184

family, 92, 96, 115, 127, 139, 141, 144, 145, 169; bourgeois, 127–28, 140, 156, 188, 224, 273, 278; businesses, 43; imperial, 6–8, 10, 79, 195, 219, 228, 244; merchant, 59; modernism and, 264–65; noble, 57; peasant, 31, 33, 35, 38, 79–80, 81, 148, 151, 153, 162, 164, 171, 189, 251; worker, 124

Family Club [of Kazan'], 127

federalism, 174, 187

fel'dshers, 72, 144, 153, 163, 183, 185, 213, 281

Fifth International Congress on the Treatment of the Mentally Ill, 72

Filosofova, A.P., 146

film, 8, 15, 16, 135–36; intelligentsia on,

136–37; middle-class values and, 112, 135–36, 274; women and, 149
Finland, 6, 20, 48, 173, 177, 179, 187
fire brigades, 168, 189, 222, 276
fire insurance, 168, 189, 221
First All-Russian Congress on the Struggle against Alcohol, 109–10
fistfighting, 4, 252
football (soccer), 16, 131–32, 274; dacha culture and, 132
foreign policy, 196–97, 198, 201, 243, 247
Fourth All-Russian Congress of Commercial Office Workers, 68, 184
France, 21, 27, 28, 38, 39, 41, 42, 44, 46, 47, 48, 71, 72, 73, 96, 126, 135, 198, 206, 218, 220, 245; defense loan and, 197–98
Frank, Stephen, 249
Frierson, Cathy, 168
fuel shortage, 29, 40, 49, 65, 112, 246
Fundamental Laws, 12, 174, 196, 205, 237, 240; nationalism and, 171; rights and, 51, 193, 215, 236
Futurism, 146–47, 265–69; hooliganism and, 266; Italian, 261–62; *Victory over the Sun*, 266, 268; *zaum* and, 268, 283

Gakhel, Joseph, 219
Gastrol' Rychalov, 138
Gatrell, Peter, 49
Gaudin, Corinne, 170
Gaugin, Paul, 261
Gay, Peter, 96, 127, 136
Gazeta kopeika, 114
Gendarme Corps, 207, 230
Georgia, 173, 180
Georgian Church, 180
Germans, 34, 54, 128, 200, 244
Germany, 20, 21, 27, 28, 43, 46, 48, 73, 96–97, 117, 126, 129, 168, 176, 200, 206, 239, 258; attitude to land reform of, 162; Ottoman Empire and, 198; Russian trade with, 28
Gerschenkron, Alexander, 11, 44–45
Gippius, Ginaida, 136
Glinka, Mikhail, 7
gold standard, 45
Goncharova, Natalia, 136, 150, 261, 267; on Russian art, 262
Goremykin, I.L., 196
Gorkii, Maxim, 138, 246; *The Zykovs,* 246
governors, 6, 56, 117, 125, 163, 172, 196, 203, 208, 213, 222, 225; reinforced security and, 216
gradonachal'nik. See prefect
gradonachal'stvo, 117, 281
Great Britain, 27, 28, 39, 44, 46, 126, 192, 195, 198
Gregory, Paul, 27, 29, 50
Grigor'ev, Dmitrii, 115
Grigorovich, D.P., 219
Guardianship of Popular Temperance, 223
Guchkov, A.I., 222, 231
Guerrier courses, 142
Guro, Elena, 265

health insurance fund, 69, 73, 110–11, 112, 182, 201–02, 274; Bolshevik and Menshevik views of, 112; women and, 147, 151, 188
Hegel, G.W.F. von, 92–93, 94, 141, 154
Herzen, A.I., 4, 235, 242, 259; on peasant commune, 253–54; on workers, 107
Higher Courses for Women, 25, 142–43
historiography 12, 13, 60, 279, 286n27; land shortages and, 30–31; late Imperial Russia and, 17, 44–45; Marxist-Leninist, 60; on civil society, 92, 95; on empire, 172–73; on obshchestvo, 13, 78–79; on Russian merchants, 60; on state and society, 190; on the economy, 11, 45; on workers, 78, 97, 273
history, 23, 26, 45, 101, 93, 119, 142, 146, 172, 258, 278, 279; Marxism and, 98; Russian exceptionalism and, 234; Symbolism and, 137
hockey, 16, 132, 274
Hogan, Heather, 78
Holmgren, Beth, 134
Holy Synod, 153, 156, 175, 182, 205–6, 277, 288
hooliganism, 77, 156–58, 206, 249; Futurism and, 266; zemstvo attitudes towards, 157–58, 276
Hostages to Life, 264–65

ideology, 247; civil society and, 94; intelligentsia and, 264
Il'ia Muromets, 219
Il'minskii, N.I., 174–75
Imperial All-Russian Aero Club, 219
industrial crops, 162
industrialization, 38–40, 47; state role in, 44–47
industry, 9, 14, 18, 22, 29, 38–41, 44–45, 47; anticapitalism and, 16, 62, 241; antiwesternism and, 62, 235; banks and, 42, 44; cottage, 37–38; state and, 44–47, 48–49; syndicates in, 39–40, 62, 65–66, 220
inheritance, 35, 216; female, 145, 188; peasant, 164, 275
inorodtsy, 6, 52, 281
Insurance Council, 110
intelligentsia, 36, 67, 77, 114, 136, 148–49, 153, 158, 222, 260, 263, 264–65, 281; as a middle class, 5, 70–72, 89, 119, 233, 244–45, 247; creative, 130–31, 133, 136, 256–57, 271; dacha culture and, 133; integralism and, 235; law and, 236; narod and, 239, 261, 278; obschestvo and, 13, 91, 97; peasants and, 165, 166, 167–68, 248, 254; state and, 190, 217; workers and, 77, 97, 108, 112–13, 256, 272; Ukrainian, 181
integralism, 16, 244–46, 256
International Congress of Criminologists, 207
International Women's Council, 146
International Women's Day, 147
International Women's Socialist Secretariat, 146
International Women's Suffrage Alliance, 146
investment, 12, 26, 40, 45, 46, 57, 61, 155; agricultural, 19, 40; foreign, 40–43, 44–45, 50, 62, 65; portfolio, 43, 44; Russian, 41, 43, 44, 50, 63
Italy, 21, 206, 261
Iushinskii, Andrei, 185
Ivanov, Viacheslav, 262, 268
Ivitsk Agricultural Society, 148

jadid school, 176, 282
Jealousy, 150
Jews, 5, 60, 72, 128, 181, 182, 199, 215; anti-Semitism, 54, 182, 185–86, 241; expulsions from educational institutions of, 183; in the Pale, 64, 182–83, 184; laws on resettlement to the Pale of, 183; public defense of, 63–64, 184
joint stock corporations, 40–41, 43
Judaism, 186
judicial reform, 187
Judicial Statute of 1864, 214
justice of the peace, 214–15, 236
juvenile courts, 221, 223, 254

Kadets. *See* Constitutional Democratic Party
Kandinskii, Vasilii, 261
Kappeler, Andreas, 172
kassy, 78. *See also* health insurance fund
Kavelin, K.D., 250
Kazan', 127, 142, 144, 167, 174, 274; voluntary associations in, 126–29
Kazan' Cathedral, 16–17, 19
Kelly, Catriona, 131
Keys to Happiness, 135
Kharkov Medical Society, 186, 227
Khlebnikov, Velemir, 266
khutor, 34, 35, 84, 157, 160, 162, 164, 249, 276–77, 282; intelligentsia on, 248–49
Kiev, 22, 35, 64, 69, 117, 123, 137, 142, 177–78, 181, 183, 214, 219, 221, 222, 230, 248
Kiev Commercial Institute, 64, 183–84
Kievlianin, 186
Kine-Zhurnal, 136
Kinnear, Julia, 128
Kirgiz, 180
Kistiakovskii, Bogdan, 250
Kizevetter, A.A., 190
Kobzar, 178
Koenker, Diane, 78
Kogan, N.S., 3
Kokovtsov, Vladimir, 6, 9, 47, 58, 59, 196, 200, 203
Kollontai, A.M., 146

Koloskov, Ivan, 115
Konovalov, A.I., 64
Kostroma, 8, 10, 191, 229
Kovalevskii, M.M., 205
Kovno, 35, 81, 185
Krivoshein, A.V., 80
Kruchenykh, Aleksei, 266–68
Krupskaia, N.K., 146
kulaks, 168, 248
Kuprin, Aleksandr, 147–48
kustar'. See cottage industry

labor mediation courts, 202
land captain, 10, 55, 151; role in land
   reform of, 80
land reorganization, 34–35, 37, 54, 80, 165,
   202, 210, 242; results of, 83, 162, 163
land settlement commissions, 163, 170
land shortages, 30–31
land tenure, 7, 15, 19, 38, 202, 276; communal, 31–33; household, 35
land use practices, 33, 38, 40, 79–80, 82,
   84, 159–61, 210, 276
language policy, 174–78
Larionov, Igor, 136
Larionov, Mikhail, 261–62, 267; on
   Russian art, 262
Latvia, 175, 181, 183
law, 48, 129, 144, 179, 182, 192, 194, 195,
   227–29, 234, 236, 247, 268–69, 278;
   corporate, 12, 43; electoral, 55, 146,
   174, 194 ; family 127–28; inheritance,
   145, 188, 226; insurance, 120–21, 201;
   Jews and, 182, 183, 185; marital separation, 145, 216–17, 277; Nicholas II and,
   196, 237, 240; peasants and, 15, 85, 88,
   170; press, 54, 203, 226; property, 63,
   165, 275; state and, 140, 206, 214–16,
   230, 236; tax, 87, 170; women and, 141,
   144, 145, 146, 147, 148
League for Women's Equality, 156
leisure, 4, 15–16, 130–31, 132–33; middle-
   class attitudes to, 125, 127, 140; sport
   and, 16, 131–32, 252, 274
Lena goldfields massacre, 73–74, 97, 201;
   Manukhin report on, 192–93
Lenin, V.I., 78, 136, 238; on capitalism,

254–55; on praktiki, 77
liberalism, 107, 235, 268, 271, 278;
   bourgeoisie and, 247, 254; in the
   Church, 116, 248–51; non-Russian
   nationalities and, 176–77; Stolypin
   reform and, 250–51
libraries, 26, 119, 127, 129, 152, 166, 178;
   struggle for control of, 226–27
Lindenmeyr, Adele, 135
liquor monopoly, 46, 88, 228
literacy, 22–23, 26, 125; modernization
   and, 151–52; peasants and, 153, 168,
   275; workers and, 107, 122
Literary Herald, 134
Lithuania, 183
lubki, 134, 282
Lykoshin commission, 156–57

Maiakovskii, Vladimir, 136, 266, 269
Main Administration for Land Reorganiza-
   tion and Agriculture, 7, 80, 149, 200,
   276; education and, 25; Ministry of the
   Interior and, 202; peasant mortgages
   and, 164; zemstvos and, 210–11
Main Administration for State Health
   Protection, 212
Main Administration of Military Justice,
   216
Makarov, A.A., 192
Maklakov, N.A., 202, 214, 216; confirmation of mayors and, 204, 229; State
   Duma and, 203
Maklakov, V.A., 194
Malevich, Kazimir, 261, 262, 266–67
Manchuria, 180
Manukhin, S.S., 192–93
Marinetti, Filippo Tommaso, 261
market: civil society and, 95, 97, 140, 141;
   culture and, 15, 124, 130–31, 133–34;
   peasants and, 38, 148, 151, 154, 161,
   162, 171, 175
Markov, N.E., 241
marriage, 20, 128, 143, 150; modernists
   and, 264–65; peasants and, 151, 156,
   249; separation law, 216–17, 223, 277;
   workers and, 115, 123–24
marshals of the nobility, 6, 55, 57, 151

Marx, Karl, 93, 98

Marxism, 60, 116, 243; as salvationism, 98; integralism and, 270; in Russia, 233, 254–55; proletarian consciousness and, 107, 109, 112, 256

Maslov, Semen, 154

Matiushin, Mikhail, 266, 268

mayor, 6, 58, 72, 117–18, 121, 123, 204, 229, 243, 281

McCaffray, Susan, 66, 97

McDaniel, Tim, 73

McKean, Robert, 78

medical-sanitary administration, 212–13

Mediterranean Sea, 198

Meierhold, Vsevolod, 261

Mensheviks, 78, 107, 112

Merchant Club [of Kazan'], 128–29

merchants, 5, 6, 9, 10, 26, 42, 58–60, 64, 126, 128, 183, 219, 246–47; at Nizhnii Novgorod Fair, 58–59, 184; conservatives on, 241, 243, 246; in historiography, 60; intelligentsia and, 59, 62, 89, 137, 245; nobility and, 57–58, 59

Merezhkovskii, Dmitrii, 253

meshchane, 66–67

meshchanstvo, 22

Meshcherskii, V.P., 186

Metallist', 149

middle class, 14, 16, 53, 57, 59–60, 67, 88–89, 94, 95–97, 125, 127, 131–32, 135–37, 140, 142, 181, 188, 248, 270, 273–74, 279; in historiography, 44, 95–97; identity, 245–46, 251; intelligentsia and, 133, 233, 244–45, 247, 265, 269; press and, 113–15, 277–78; rural, 155, 245, 276; women, 142–46, 150, 188; workers and, 90, 107–9, 112–13, 122, 126, 139, 146. *See also* bourgeoisie

military courts, 216

Military-Medical-Surgical Academy, 34, 143, 192

Miliukov, P.N., 197, 204, 250

ministerial boycott, 203–4

Ministry of Education, 24–26, 152, 206, 226–27, 229, 230, 234; school language policy and, 175

Ministry of Finance, 87, 200, 223

Ministry of Foreign Affairs, 197

Ministry of the Interior, 48, 55, 69, 123, 147, 157, 184, 191, 200–201, 205, 208, 222, 224, 239, 277; health insurance and, 211–12; labor policy and, 201–2; land reform and, 202; press reform law and, 225–26; police reform and, 207–8; school language policy and, 175

Ministry of the Navy, 27

Ministry of Transport and Communications, 218, 226

Ministry of Trade and Industry, 4, 24, 43, 183; education and, 24; labor policy and, 69, 201–2; women and, 144

Ministry of War, 27, 87, 192, 224; internal repression and, 201; State Duma and, 200

Minsk, 35, 117, 184

Modernism, 257–58; art and, 263–64; bourgeoisie and, 269–70; in Russia, 260–63; democracy and, 268–69

modernity, 13, 283, 257, 282; melancholy and, 251–53; pluralism and, 90, 139

modernization, 13, 29, 33, 51, 75, 86, 119, 172, 203, 218, 220, 231, 238, 241–42, 277; literacy and, 151–52

Monarchists' Union, 7, 185

Mongolia, 198, 262

Morozova, V.A., 120

mortality, 21, 212

mortgages, 174–75

Moskovskie vedomosti, 5, 6, 148, 180, 226, 241, 246

Moscow, 3, 8, 10, 20–21, 22, 52, 67–68, 111, 122, 135, 137, 243; city duma, 117–19, 123, 209; education and, 25–26, 120, 123, 131, 142–43, 170; Jews and, 183–85; merchants of, 59–60, 245, 246–47, 262; sports in, 141–42; tram drivers' strike in, 120–21

Moscow Artisans' Mutual Aid Society, 67

Moscow Conservatory, 143

Moscow Criminal Investigation Section, 207

Moscow District Union of Consumer Societies, 68

Moscow Higher Technical Institute, 219

Moscow Merchants' Society, 42, 58, 59
Moscow Meshchane Society, 67
Moscow Monarchist League, 7
Moscow Mutual Aid Society for Merchant
    Employees, 77
Moscow Society of Aeronautics, 219
Moscow Society of Factory and Mill
    Owners, 5, 48; health insurance and,
    63; on trade unions, 120, 122
Moscow Society of Metalworkers, 228
Moscow Society of People's Universities,
    120
Moscow Society of Workers in the Printing
    Arts, 110
municipal elections of 1912–1913, 117–19
Municipal Statute of 1892, 117, 213, 222
Musin Pushkina, N.B. Countess, 168
Muslim Club [of Kazan'], 127
Muslims, 67, 128, 174, 176, 181
mutual aid societies, 14, 67–68, 77, 126–27,
    129, 242; civil society and, 274
Mutual Aid Society of Moscow Typogra-
    phers, 67
Mutual Aid Society of Notaries, 227

narod, 13, 91, 235, 237, 278, 282
nationalism, 20, 42, 62, 172–73, 175, 180,
    187, 189, 238, 241, 247; Balkan wars and,
    197–98, 243–44; civil society and, 15,
    178, 187, 189; conservatism and, 176,
    239–40; in State Duma, 178–79, 197;
    state bureaucracy and, 178, 189, 239
Nationalist Party, 57, 176, 179, 181
Naumov, A.N., 155
Neuberger, Joan, 266
New Club [of Kazan'], 127–28, 129
newspapers, 8, 15, 69, 111, 117, 124,
    127, 149, 175, 178, 179, 225–26, 228,
    248, 275; middle-class values and, 66,
    113–15, 154, 246, 274, 277–78; State
    Duma and, 195, 204. *See also* press
Nicholas II. *See* Romanov
Nietzsche, Friedrich, 3, 259, 263, 264,
    269; *Birth of Tragedy from the Spirit of
    Music,* 258; modernists and, 258, 263,
    266–67; on art, 258; Santayana on, 269
Nikol'skii, B.V., 244

Nizhnii Novgorod, 58, 60, 133, 157, 184,
    209
nobility, 9, 54, 70, 87, 125, 161, 164–65,
    205; in professions, 56; in state service,
    53; on electoral reform, 55–56; political
    affiliations of, 56–57; zemstvo and,
    54–55, 151
Nobles Club [of Kazan'], 128
Novikov, Mikhail, 155–56, 251
Novoe vremia, 113, 222, 243

obshchestvennost', 91, 93, 282
obshchestvo, 91–92, 191, 292; civil society
    and, 93; in historical discourse, 190; in
    historiography, 13–14, 97; masses and,
    92, 97
obshchina. See commune
otrub, 34, 35, 84, 160, 162, 164, 276–77,
    282
October Manifesto, 12, 58–59, 187, 193,
    222, 231, 278
Octobrists, 57, 177, 179, 247, 248
Odessa, 5, 118, 123, 137, 181, 183–84, 219,
    220
Odessa Aero-Club, 219
Odessa Medical Society, 5
Odessa Society of Dentists, 184
officer corps, 86–87, 199, 201, 207, 216,
    225
official nationality, 240
Ogarev, N.P., 4
Okhrana, 207, 218
Old Believers, 67
Orthodox Church, 6–7, 176, 182, 205,
    241; Beiliss trial and, 186; divorce and,
    217; parish reform and, 152–53, 206;
    peasant critics of, 165–66, 206, 275;
    State Duma and, 205–6; workers and,
    115–16
Orthodoxy, 6, 205, 240; integralism and,
    235; peasants and, 153; Slavophiles on,
    234, 260
Ottoman Empire, 28, 176, 180, 198
Owen, Thomas, 60

Pale, 64, 182, 184, 262
Pan-Islamism, 176, 189

Pan-Turkism, 176, 189
parent committees, 229–39
Pares, Bernard, 60, 162, 195
pastoralism, 251–53
Pate, Alice, 110, 112
patriarchy, 76, 85, 128, 142, 147, 149, 156, 164, 188, 254
patronage societies, 222–23, 282
patronaty. See patronage societies
Peasant Land Bank, 32, 35–36
peasants, 4, 8, 30–31, 32, 34, 37, 39, 55, 88, 133, 144, 163; agronomists and, 158–59, 160–61, 163, 188, 277; civil society and, 15, 151, 168, 170; consumption by, 30, 155, 274; cooperatives and, 166–68, 276; economic self-sufficiency and, 153–54; fashion and, 155–56; fire brigades and, 168, 189, 222, 276; harvesting and sowing practices of, 159–60; heterogeneity of, 79–80, 279; hooliganism and, 156–58; in cities, 21, 52, 58, 153, 156; inheritance and, 164, 275; innovation and, 4, 31, 33, 81, 82–83, 159–60, 161–62; land purchases and, 32, 34, 35–36; land reform and, 80–84, 158, 163, 275; land use practices of, 33, 38, 40, 79–80, 82, 84, 159–61, 210, 276; law and, 42, 55, 84, 85–86, 88, 165, 236, 171; literacy and, 16, 153, 168, 275–76; market economy and, 38, 154, 171, 175; parish reform and, 152–53, 166, 275; property and, 164–65, 273; religion and, 152–53; resistance to land reorganization of, 84; savings of, 30, 41–42, 167; separators and, 32; the tsar and, 7, 10, 236–37; zemstvos and, 163, 166, 168, 210–11, 276; zemstvo elections and, 164, 169–70, 275
Pedagogical Museum of Military Educational Institutions, 223
People's Houses, 15, 139
Persia, 28, 180, 198
Petersburg Higher Women's (Bestuzhev) Courses, 142–43
Peter the Great. *See* Romanov
pharmacies, 211–12

Picasso, Pablo, 261
Pirogov Society of Russian Doctors, 124, 213
pluralism, 90, 139
pogroms, 181–82, 186
Poland, 8, 48, 81, 177, 179, 183, 187
Poles, 8, 20, 52, 54, 60, 128, 173, 174, 176, 181–82, 184, 185
Polish language, 173, 177, 178, 179
police, 3, 5, 72, 80, 120, 146, 178, 183–84, 185, 200–201, 202, 213, 243, 266; criminal investigation and, 207; film and, 136; reform of, 157, 206–8; workers and, 74, 76–77, 78, 111, 147, 272, 274
police monitor, 3, 222, 228
Polivanov, A.A., 199
Polytechnical Museum, 3, 261
popular culture, 15–16, 108–9, 116, 131, 139, 140, 171, 251, 256, 289; civil society and, 171, 270, 274; commercialization of, 90; consumption and, 16, 130; elite attitudes toward, 131, 251, 256–57; workers and, 109, 116
population, 11, 19–22, 51, 181, 253, 278; economy and, 27–28; literacy and, 22–23; rural, 29–30, 33, 141, 156; urban, 20–21, 52, 274
populism, 235, 241, 253–54; modernism and, 262–63, 268
Populism, 253–54
positivism, 71, 150, 256
Potkina, Irina V., 60
praktiki, 77, 282
Pravda, 107, 111
Pravilova, Ekaterina, 48
Prechistenskie courses, 120
prefect, 117, 121–22, 213
press, 140, 175, 186, 191, 192–93, 197, 199, 200, 205, 215, 216, 219, 224, 230, 233, 245, 246, 247, 253, 268, 274, 277; censorship of, 224, 232; civil society and, 66, 113–15, 154, 246, 274, 277–78; reform of press law, 203, 235–36. *See also* newspapers
professions, 14, 21, 57, 59, 72, 89, 111, 123, 125, 128–29, 199, 213, 248, 261, 273;

state and, 70–71, 212, 217, 223; women and, 142–44; zemstvo and, 72, 155, 276

Progressive Party, 113, 221, 247–48, 278

property, 12, 55, 132, 145, 152, 182, 215, 242, 263; civil society and, 92–93; law and, 63, 165, 216, 275; liberalism and, 248, 250; peasants and, 34, 36, 88, 164–65, 168, 170, 273, 275; women and, 148, 150

Prosvite, 227

public, 13–14, 26, 53, 56, 62, 69, 95, 121, 129–30, 133–34, 136, 190; civil society and, 140–41; press and, 113–14; state and, 12, 87, 90–93, 122, 190–91, 193, 208, 216–19, 221, 228, 231, 241–42

Raeff, Marc, 236

railways, 44, 46, 48, 119, 131, 143, 213; Trans-Siberian, 58

Rasputin, Grigorii, 9, 244

Rech', 225, 250

Rechtsstaat, 250

redemption payments, 30, 33, 87, 165

Rein, G.E., 212–13

reinforced security, 216

religion, 23, 86, 172, 176, 205, 215, 225, 235, 265; peasants and, 152–53; workers and, 115–16

Repin, Il'ia, 138

resettlement, 37, 83–84, 165, 213; indigenous populations and, 180

revolution of 1905, 27, 29–30, 33, 45, 54, 70, 86, 115, 124, 143, 170, 181, 182, 188, 193, 201, 217, 222, 273, 279

Riabushinskii, Dmitrii, 219

Riabushinskii, P.P., 247

Riazan', 4, 157, 170, 186, 229; merchants of, 58–59

Riga, 22, 175, 181, 209

roads, 48, 207–8

Rodina club, 178

Rodzianko,M.V., 9, 204

Romanov, Emperor Alexander III, 216, 238

Romanov, Emperor Nicholas I, 240

Romanov, Emperor Nicholas II, 6–8, 10, 138, 191, 206, 205, 212, 239, 273; anti-Semitism and, 182, 237; bureaucracy and, 9, 172, 195–96; civic nation and, 11, 203, 236–37, 238–39; conservatives and, 244; foreign policy and, 196–97; Great Russian culture and, 238, 277; industrial development and, 238; legal accountability and, 195–96, 240; narod and, 10, 237; officer corps and, 199, 237–38; State Duma and, 9, 179, 193–94, 203

Romanov, Emperor Peter I, 6, 53, 205, 238

Romanov, Grand Duke Aleksandr Mikhailovich, 218

Romanov, Tsar Mikhail, 8, 236–37

Romanov tercentenary, 5–11, 57, 58, 184, 191–92, 203, 214, 237, 238; amnesty and, 224–25

Romanov, Tsarevich Alexei, 7, 10

Romanova, Dowager Empress Maria Feodorova, 9

Romanova, Empress Alexandra, 7, 9–10, 244

Romanova, Empress Catherine II, 6, 183

rossiiskii, 172, 238, 282

Ruble, Blair, 118

Russian Assembly, 7

Russian empire, 6, 11, 20, 26, 27, 95, 112, 134, 177, 194, 233; civil society and, 188–89, 190, 214, 274, 277; economic integration of, 48; in historiography, 172–73

Russian Football Union, 132

Russian Social Democratic Party, 77, 111, 147, 255, 272–73

Russian Tourist Society, 131

Russian Warrior, 219

Russian Women's Mutual Philanthropic Society, 145

russification, 173

Russkoe znamia, 185

russkii, 172, 238, 282

Russo-Baltic Carriage Works, 219

Russo-Japanese War, 27

Ruud, Charles, 133

Russkie vedomosti, 37, 66, 113, 154, 166, 168, 180, 183, 228, 245–46, 249, 250, 278

Rybnikov, A., 37

Sabler, V.K., 206
Saint-Simon, Henri Comte de, 71
Salazkin, A.S., 58, 59, 60
samosud, 85, 282
Santayana, George, 269
Sazonov, Pavel, 108
Sazonov, S.D., 197
Schelling, Friedrich von, 259
schools, 22–25, 59, 64, 68, 123, 124, 127,
    144, 180, 191, 215, 230; agronomic, 158,
    210; Baltic German, 181; church-parish,
    205–6; jadid, 176; Jews and, 183–84;
    libraries in, 226–27; non-Russian, 172,
    174–77; parents' committees in, 229;
    rural, 152, 155, 165–66
Schopenhauer, Arthur, 259
Schumpeter, Joseph, 133
Second All-Russian Artisans' Exhibition,
    211
Second All-Russian Congress of Factory
    Panel Doctors, 109–10
Section to Aid in the Establishment of
    Rural, Factory, and School Theater, 120
Senate, 6, 9, 32, 182, 183, 214, 227;
    Military-Medical-Surgical Academy
    and, 192–93; on confirmation of
    appointments, 229
separators, 35, 80, 83, 84, 163; intelligentsia
    on, 258–59
Shabanova, A.I., 146
Shaniavskii People's University, 72, 119
Sharapov, S.F., 243
Shestov, Lev, 260
Shevchenko, T.G., 178, 226
Shcheglovitov, I.G., 204
Shidlovskii, M.V., 219
Shtiurmer, B.V., 204
Siberia, 20, 37, 48, 56, 61, 69, 82, 111, 117,
    161, 167, 202, 228; resettlement to,
    83–84,
Sikorskii, Igor, 219
Silovskii, P.P., 191–92, 193, 196
Simferopol, 182
Skriabin, Aleksandr, 263
Slavophilism, 234, 236, 240, 246, 260–263;
    capitalism and, 247–48
Smirnova, V.K., 3

Smolensk, 81, 117, 169, 170, 185
sobornost', 137, 234, 236, 282
social estates, 8, 14, 51–53, 70, 88–89, 90,
    94, 118, 126, 128–29, 171–73, 187, 241,
    273, 275, 278; conscription and, 86–87;
    elections and, 54–55, 208–9; merchant,
    9, 58–61, 66, 245; *meshchane,* 66–67,
    88; noble, 9, 53–57, 70, 87, 125, 161,
    164–65, 205; peasant, 79–80, 88, 151
Socialist Revolutionary Party, 254
society. *See obshchestvo*
Society for Electricity in Russia, 41
Society for the Dissemination of Technical
    Knowledge, 126
Society for the Empowerment of Private
    Clerks, 68
Society for the Patronage of Juveniles, 223
Society of Commercial Employees [of
    Kazan'], 126, 129
Society of Employees in Administrative
    and Social Institutions [of Kazan'], 127
Society of Merchants Employees, 228
Society of Office Workers and Accoun-
    tants, 68
Society of Professional Shop Assistants, 68
Society of the Archangel Michael, 7
Society of Women Doctors [of Kazan'], 127
Sologub, Fedor, 257, 260, 261, 263;
    Hostages to Life, 264–65
Solov'ev, V.S., 234–35, 256, 260, 265
soslovie. See social estates
Soviet Union, 17, 139
Special Office on Urban Affairs, 213–14
Special Section of the Department of
    Police, 207
starosta, 6–7, 282
state, 190–93; as monolith, 12, 190,
    195; differences within, 195–208;
    industrialization and, 46–47, 48–49;
    local self-government and, 70, 72–73,
    116÷17, 188, 208–11, 213–14, 221,
    231; professionals and, 71–72, 217–21;
    public and, 10, 12–13, 26, 56, 70, 87,
    91, 122, 190–93, 199, 208, 209, 216–17,
    221–24, 231–32, 241–42
State Council, 6, 9, 34, 178, 193–94, 203,
    204, 212, 221; female lawyers and, 144;

reactionary politics of, 56, 145, 178–79, 195, 205–6, 273, 277; Russian nationalism and, 178; women's suffrage and, 146
State Duma, 6, 9, 10, 34, 87, 145, 147, 157, 183, 192, 193–94, 203, 205, 212, 219, 221, 239, 247, 281; army and, 199–200; church and, 205–6; commercial classes and, 64, 69; effectiveness of, 194–95, 231, 240; elections to, 55–56, 112, 174; employers' societies and, 220; foreign policy and, 197; franchise for, 174, 194, 204, 239; ministerial boycott of, 213–14; Nicholas II and, 203, 237, 240; peasant faction in, 152, 165–66, 176; police reform and, 207–8; press reform and, 226; representation in, 56–57; Russian nationalism and, 178–79, 197; women's suffrage and, 142, 146, 204; workers' curia and, 78
Stenka Razin, 145
stock exchange committees, 4, 59, 144, 220, 241
Stolypin land reform, 15, 19, 35, 276; achievements of, 35–36; commune and, 34–35, 45, 157, 163–65, 202, 242, 248–49, 282; credit and, 42; household tenure, 35; legislation, 34; peasant reception of, 80–83, 85, 275; productivity and, 162–63; resistance to, 83–84, 254
Stolypin, P.A., 12, 34, 244
Straits, 198
Stravinsky, Igor, 263
strikes, 74–75, 120, 192, 201–2; Council of Ministers on causes of, 75–76; metalworkers and, 272; of Moscow tram drivers, 130–31; St. Petersburg, 76–77
St. Petersburg, 6, 20, 22, 47, 61, 121, 243, 252; duma, 115–16, 119, 122–23; strikes in, 74–75, 76–78, 97, 201, 272
St. Petersburg Parents' Circle, 223
St. Petersburg Society of Factory and Mill Owners, 63, 122; on trade unions, 76
St. Petersburg Women's Technical Institute, 143
suicide, 124, 136, 249, 253
Sukhomlinov, V.A., 199–200

Supreme Military Court, 216
Susanin, Ivan, 8
Symbolism, 136–37, 268; art and, 259, 261, 265; family and, 265; integralism and, 256–57; transformation and, 265
syndicates. *See* industry
Sytin, I.D., 133–34

Table of Ranks, 53
tariffs, 44–45, 50, 56, 96, 179
Tatars, 60, 182, 262
Tatlin, Vladimir, 261
taxation, 30, 123, 170, 209, 277; citizenship and, 87–88
Taylorism, 39, 74
teachers, 34, 72, 120, 122, 124, 126, 127, 131, 177, 234, 276; female, 143, 144, 149; in non-Russian schools, 175–76; of agronomy, 158, 163
technology, 25, 50, 71, 218; Futurists and, 267; Russian dependence on, 38–39, 44
telegraph, 46, 48, 69
telephone, 3, 48, 69, 135, 155
theater, 15, 137–40, 178, 223, 228, 261; cabaret, 131, 137, 138, 269; estrada, 139, 281; intelligentsia on, 136; miniature, 137–38; modernism and, 263–64, 266; movie, 135–36, 138; rural, 15, 120, 252; women and, 149–50; workers and, 108, 120, 138, 252
theosophy, 259, 263
textbooks, 11, 234
Third Women's Club, 227
Thurston, Gary, 252
Tikhomirov, Lev, 226, 241, 246
Timashev, S.I., 63, 192
third element, 155, 276
Tolstoi, I.I., 123, 229, 243
Tolstoi, L.N, 68, 134, 137, 226, 230
Toumanoff, Peter, 162
trade, 5, 15, 22, 28, 47, 48, 61, 64, 67, 95, 179, 180, 220; Association of Industry and Trade on, 61–62, 63; balance, 28–29, 44; exports, 28, 31, 44–45, 49, 62, 198; imports, 28, 44, 45, 62; Jews and, 54, 181, 183; peasants and, 58, 79, 153, 165, 167, 248

trade unions, 74, 77–78, 115, 120; women in, 147
Tragedy of Vladimir Maiakovskii, 266
Trotskii, Leon, 255
Trubetskoi, Evgenii, 235
Trudovik Party, 255
Tyrkova-Vil'iams, Ariadne, 195

Ukraine, 20, 35, 39, 61, 81, 183, 237, 261
Ukrainian Art Society, 178
Ukrainian Club, 178
Ukrainian Literary-Dramatic Society, 178
Ukrainians, 20, 174, 177–78, 181, 182, 236
Union of the Russian People, 5, 7, 181, 226; on non-Russian education, 176
Union of Workers in Tailoring, 69
United Nobility, 54, 56, 57, 89, 273
United States, 20, 27, 39, 48, 161, 261
Utro Rossii, 113, 278

Valentinov, Nikolai, 273
Vasilchikova, Lidiia, 59
vegetarianism, 113, 116, 221
Vekhi, 235, 250
Verbitskaia, Anastasia, 135
Vial'tseva, Anastasia, 131
Victory over the Sun, 266, 268
village society, 32, 84, 147, 163, 189; assembly of, 32–33, 34, 35; peasant commune and, 32–33
Vilno, 81, 182, 185, 227
vodka, 46; state monopoly on, 26, 223, 237
Vol'f Bookstore News, 145
Vol'f, M.O., 144
Volga River, 8, 10, 61, 67, 126, 173, 174, 237
volost', 10, 32, 143, 155, 163, 165, 293; reform of, 55, 56, 146, 164, 203, 205, 230
volost' court, 55–56, 84–86, 88, 148, 236, 275; hooliganism and, 157; women and, 85–86, 148
voluntary associations, 14, 124–30; bureaucrats in, 191; civil society and, 92, 130, 140, 274; in Kazan', 126–29; peasants and, 170; regulations for, 69, 124; state and, 222–24; state repressions of, 14, 227–28

von Geldern, James, 130
Vtorov stores, 69

Wagner, William, 127, 217
War Industries Committee, 221
Warsaw University, 184
Western Europe, 59, 94, 96, 120; comparisons with Russia, 16, 18, 21–22, 29, 38, 43, 140, 142, 209, 275; Slavophiles on, 234–35
Winter Palace, 7
Witte, S.Iu., 44–45, 48
women, 3, 5, 21, 87, 96, 114, 125, 126, 135, 141, 145, 146, 227, 254; as consumers, 142, 155; as legal persons, 87, 145, 188, 275; as local activists, 3, 148–49; as professionals, 142–43, 149, 188; civil society and, 131, 141–42, 150–51; courts of law and, 86, 148, 275; divorce and, 216–17; education and, 5, 24–25, 59, 142–44, 183, 230; factory mechanization and, 75; health insurance funds and, 147; in drama, 149–50; in film, 149; inheritance and, 145, 164; in legal profession; in medicine, 149; peasant, 79, 147–49, 151, 156, 188–89; resistance to land reorganization of, 84; stock exchange committees and, 144; suffrage and, 145–46; trade unions and, 147; workers, 115, 146–47, 149, 151, 188; zemstvos and, 143
Women's Medical Institute, 25, 143
Women's Progressive Party, 146
workers, 16, 22, 39, 52, 63, 67, 69–70, 73–74, 76–77, 78, 79, 88, 89, 112, 119, 122–23, 136, 181, 228, 236, 250, 256, 274, 278–279; capitalism and, 74–75; civil society and, 14–15, 90, 107–8, 109–10, 138, 188; demands of, 75–76, 111–12; female, 146–47; health insurance legislation and, 69, 110–11, 182, 201; Herzen on, 107; in historiography, 97–98; Lena, 192–93; Lenin on, 77–78; marriage and, 115, 123–24; on party factionalism, 111; on women in work place, 149; philanthropy and, 125–26;

poetry and, 109; *praktiki,* 77–78; press and, 113–15; religion and, 115–16; society and, 126; strikes of, 73–74, 130–31, 272–73; theater and, 108–9, 120, 138–39, 252; tsarism and, 74

World of Art, 256, 266

Yaney, George, 84, 290
Youngblood, Denise, 149

zaum, 268, 282
Zdanevich, Il'ia, 262
Zemshchina, 113
zemskii sobor, 8, 237, 283
zemstvo, 3–4, 6, 48, 65, 70, 110, 125, 143, 157, 169, 176, 188, 208–9, 212, 228, 230, 264, 293; agricultural assistance and, 38, 70, 84, 158–59, 161, 276; civil society and, 15, 155, commercial classes and, 59, 64–65; cooperation with state of, 70, 73, 188, 209, 210–11, 214, 221; education and, 25, 70, 151; elections, 169–70, 209–10, 229, 275; hooliganism and, 157–58; libraries and, 226–27; noble representation in, 54–55, 151; peasants and, 163, 164, 166, 168, 169–70, 275; petty credit and, 158, 208, 211; reform of, 55–56, 59, 67, 164–65, 179; Rein Commission and, 212–13